Quality

Quality: A Critical Introduction, fourth edition, continues to provide a complete knowledge platform for all those wishing to study the development of the theory and practice of quality management.

Exploring the basics of management theory and the work of the quality gurus, who have formed the foundation of current practice, this new edition builds upon the previous editions' unique critical perspective of quality. A number of key management practices are considered including the new ISO 9001:2015 standards, EFQM, systems thinking, systems practice, business process re-engineering, Six Sigma, organisational learning, intelligent organisation, skills based quality management and service quality management. An extended, in-depth case study completes the text, exploring organisational performance transformation through the use of key methodologies, such as: soft systems; viable systems modelling; process analysis, job design and statistical methods.

Replete with examples, vignettes and diagrams, this comprehensive textbook is ideal for those new to the field of quality management and for students on undergraduate and postgraduate courses in Operations Management where quality management is taught.

John Beckford is an independent consultant and Visiting Professor in the Department of Science, Technology, Engineering and Public Policy at University College London and in the Centre for Information Management at Loughborough University, UK.

An authoritative overview of Quality both in theory and in practice. Essential reading not just for Quality students but practitioners, managers and anyone interested in doing this better.

Mark Chadwick, *Director of Business Services, Fusion 21*

Compelling and thought provoking. *Quality* gives an important systemic and triple bottom line perspective (economy, environment, social) on the imperative of Quality. Specifically, highlighting that quality is to a large degree dependent on customer perceptions, and the importance of aligning organisational purpose and performance evaluation with enabling/delivering the type and quality of outcomes customers expect/demand. Significantly, Quality requires more than a focus purely on the efficiency of internal processes.

Dr Tom Dolan, *Research Associate and Centre Co-ordinator,*
International Centre for Infrastructure Futures (ICIF)

Quality
A Critical Introduction

Fourth edition

John Beckford

LONDON AND NEW YORK

Fourth edition published 2017
by Routledge
2 Park Square, Milton Park, Abingdon, Oxon OX14 4RN

and by Routledge
711 Third Avenue, New York, NY 10017

Routledge is an imprint of the Taylor & Francis Group, an informa business

First edition published by Routledge 1998
Second edition published by Routledge 2002
Third edition published by Routledge 2010

British Library Cataloguing in Publication Data
A catalogue record for this book is available from the British Library

Library of Congress Cataloging in Publication Data
A catalog record for this book has been requested

ISBN: 978-1-138-18609-5 (hbk)
ISBN: 978-1-138-18612-5 (pbk)
ISBN: 978-1-315-64402-8 (ebk)

Typeset in Bembo
by Sunrise Setting Ltd., Brixham, UK

Printed and bound in Great Britain by
TJ International Ltd, Padstow, Cornwall

Quality:

n. the essential attribute of anything

Collins, *New English Dictionary*, 1968

Contents

Illustrations

Figures

Table

Boxes

Vignettes

Preface to the fourth edition

Introduction

As I prepare this fourth edition of *Quality: A Critical Introduction* it is 2016, some 20 years since I prepared the first, in which much has changed and much remained the same.

A key part of my preparation has been to explore recent texts and talk to experts in the field: writers, teachers, practitioners and some who, like me, are all three. It was inevitable, I suppose, that opinions on the third edition (Beckford, 2010) would form a standard distribution curve. A small proportion are fully pro, a similarly small proportion are fully anti, most are distributed equally either side of a general opinion that the essential core of the book remains sound, but it needs updating.

Fair enough, 20 years is a long time. So, throughout the text I have updated the material to reflect the changes in my own thinking and understanding and to ensure that the interpretation I present has relevance to the needs and challenges of organisations in the 21st century. As with the previous revisions, small changes have been made for the sake of clarity and substantial changes introduced to reflect developments in knowledge and thinking since the last edition was written.

This book then continues to be primarily an exploration of how we can interpret 'quality' through different ways of thinking and what that can mean for quality practice, rather than a practitioner's guide on 'how to do' quality. It is quite clear for me that the pursuit of quality is one dimension of the pursuit of organisational effectiveness. The literature within the discipline offers a number of useful and unique insights, and the practise of the discipline has undoubtedly brought benefits to many thousands of organisations. Quality, however, is not an end in itself but rather one of many means of achieving the goal of organisational survival.

Building on the third edition, I have increased the emphasis on Lean Thinking (in chapter 11, Taiichi Ohno) and included a dedicated chapter (14) covering ISO Standards and EFQM. Six Sigma is covered in chapter 17. Similarly, with the astounding growth in the capability and availability of information technologies and the rapid emergence of internet-based businesses, it feels right to revisit the notions of quality management for the service sector – an area still neglected in both theory and practice, so touched on in several chapters.

I have retained the material on systemic quality management and, despite protests from some reviewers as to its relevance, have retained and reinforced the material around systems thinking and, in particular, management cybernetics. As the world of work and management becomes ever more reliant on information itself, on connectivity, information systems, information technology and the emergence of the 'internet of things' (Greengard, 2015) to go with the internet of data, it becomes equally important that we adopt and exploit thinking that is capable of dealing with it. For me, as I explore in depth in *The Intelligent Organisation*

(Beckford, 2016), management cybernetics rooted in a systemic appreciation of the world offers the most useful approach and tools for addressing contemporary management challenges. I suggest, perhaps a little contentiously, that those who have not yet comprehended the systemic mindset need to do so. The fragmentation of processes and partiality of behaviours driven, perhaps demanded, by the reductionist approach are, for me, significant inhibitors of organisational effectiveness and viability. It is notable that Ohno's 'Toyota Production System', now widely called 'Lean', Senge's 'Learning Organisation', Business Process Reengineering and ISO 9001:2015 ALL call for the organisation to be dealt with as a system. It would be perverse for me not to treat quality as a systemic challenge and offer thinking accordingly.

In this edition I have further connected the specific quality literature to the broader management literature. This reflects, and is indeed intended to encourage, the broadening of thinking in the quality field. As it is in many disciplines, so it is in the quality field, that those who become expert in the field rapidly find that the constraints in which that expertise rests are too narrowly drawn, too confining, for them to address the challenges they encounter. Hence, under the banner of quality, they encroach on other areas as others encroach on theirs. Many battles ensue about respective positioning of each party's tanks . . . the organisation is struggling!

So, rather than attempt to reinforce boundaries, I have chosen to trample all over them. This book, ostensibly about 'quality', celebrates the insights that it offers to other disciplines and that those disciplines offer to it, and it does so at three interacting levels of consideration:

Philosophy: Why are we doing this?
Strategy: What options and choices do we have?
Operations: How should we do this?

Much of the traditional literature is stuck in the 'how'; perhaps it is time to revisit the why and the what?

Who should use this book?

Quality provides a complete and coherent knowledge platform for all those (whether students or managers) wishing to fully understand the theory and practice of quality. It does NOT offer the latest quality focused 'miracle' cure for all organisational ills. Instead the book brings together in a single text the plethora of ideas, approaches and methods espoused in the pursuit of quality in recent years. It draws on the published writings of many quality experts and incorporates the practical experience of the author and his associates in using these ideas throughout the world.

It features:

- a complete introduction to quality in the context of management thinking;
- in-depth reviews of the contributions of the 'Quality Gurus' and contemporary management authors to quality theory and practice;
- international case studies drawing on the public and private sectors;
- particular emphasis on the neglected service sector, as well as manufacturing industry.

Structure

I have resisted the temptation to restructure the whole book; if I were to do that, then it would not be the fourth edition of this book but a wholly new one.

Part one provides a foundation for the book by considering the arguments surrounding the pursuit of quality, the role of quality in the organisation, barriers to its implementation and the developments in management thinking which appear to underpin the quality movement.

Part two provides a critical review of the works of those writers who have made a distinct and valuable contribution to the achievement of quality. These are Philip Crosby, W. Edwards Deming, Armand Feigenbaum, Kaoru Ishikawa, Joseph Juran, John Oakland, Shigeo Shingo and Genichi Taguchi.

Part three commences with a review of relevant ISO standards and EFQM which offer a practical synthesis of the gurus' work, then moves beyond these traditionally based approaches to consider the value to be derived from contemporary management thinking. This part relates to the quality theme ideas ranging from the emergence of contingency theory to the more radical notions of critical systems thinking, re-engineering and organisational learning. Here I connect the work explicitly to the ideas of *The Intelligent Organisation* (Beckford, 2016).

Part four maintains the approach of the third edition by embedding the theory in the 'Practice of Quality' in the form of an extensive case study through which the theory and application of quality methods, tools and techniques is demonstrated.

How to use this book

Quality, as with all textbooks, provides a simplified perspective of its topic and of the daily realities of pursuing quality in organisations. The information is presented in what seems to me a logical, systematic order, teasing apart topics which are necessarily closely inter-related.

The clue to successful reading is to recognise that connections exist between the various parts and topics (these connections are regularly made within the text). The chapters then, while presented in one particular order, need not be read in that order. Equally, the chapters can be read in the traditional number order although each is able to stand alone, offering a perspective on a particular topic. Hence, some chapters are short, some long.

Each part of the book commences with a user guide to the content and makes suggestions about how to maximise learning from it. These introductions each summarise the major points made in the contained chapters.

Practical illustrations and short vignettes will be found in each chapter. These will help consolidate your learning as well as being informative and entertaining, and you will find that remembering the story helps you to remember the key points of the associated chapter. These illustrations arise from my own knowledge and practice, or have been contributed by friends and colleagues drawing on their working experience.

Each chapter concludes with a question which might be used as a formal assignment or a discussion topic for classroom or study group work. Attempting to answer these questions will help to reinforce and consolidate learning. If you cannot adequately answer the question, you should revisit the chapter to enhance your knowledge. Working through the book in this way will help you to develop your knowledge in a systematic and critical way.

The author

John Beckford is a Visiting Professor in the Department of Science, Technology, Engineering and Public Policy at University College London and in the Centre for Information Management in the School of Business and Economics at Loughborough University. He holds a PhD in Organisational Cybernetics from the University of Hull, is a Fellow of the Cybernetics Society, a Member of the Institute of Management Services, a Fellow of the Royal Society for the Arts and a Fellow of the Institute of Engineering and Technology. He is the author of *The Intelligent Organisation* (2016) and has published numerous refereed journal and conference papers and regularly delivers seminars and workshops to organisations internationally in both the public and private sectors.

John has run his consulting practice, Beckford Consulting, since 1990, after a first career in banking. He has worked in the UK, USA, Middle and Far East, Southern Africa and Australasia in a variety of sectors, including infrastructure, water, software, finance, steel, public and private healthcare, public education, food, property, retail, manufacturing, rail and transport. These organisations include SAP, Northern Rail, GNER, The Congregation of the Sisters of Nazareth, Fusion21, the BBC, Arena Group, Network Rail, ARUP, AbbVie, Northumbrian Water and City FM.

More can be found at *www.beckfordconsulting.com* and on the site dedicated to this book: *www.beckfordonquality.com*.

Acknowledgements

I am extremely grateful to all those who have helped in the development and production of this book. First to the many managers and students who have debated quality ideas with me and contributed ideas to the book – especially Dr. Bill Moore, Simon Brissenden, Mark Chadwick and Keith Elford. Their contributions have altered and shaped my views. Second is Dr. Peter Dudley with whom I have enjoyed many robust discussions and who developed with me the Service Quality Management System.

Third are the reviewers of the third edition who have supported the work of preparing this edition and guided my thinking. I have attempted to address the issues they have raised but I remain responsible for any errors, oversights or omissions. Fourth are the many organisations who have allowed the sharing of their quality experiences, and Amy Laurens and Nicola Cupit at Routledge for encouraging this new edition. Special thanks are due to Sara who, as well as reading, reviewing and editing the draft text, continues, along with Paul and Matthew, to show amazing tolerance, support and friendship.

Part one

Introducing quality

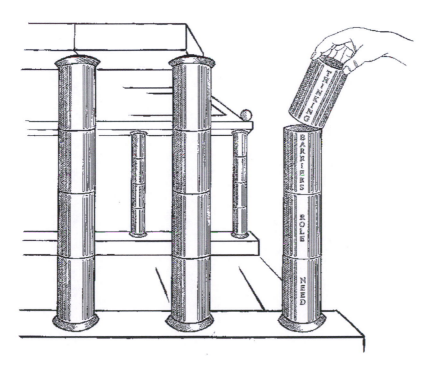

User guide

Part one introduces the whole quality debate. Chapter 1, which has been substantially revised from the previous editions, examines the arguments for and against the pursuit of quality considering both the needs and the opportunities. It examines the economic, social, environmental and governance imperatives. It includes the requirements of Corporate Social Responsibility and Corporate Governance and how they relate to quality issues. Chapter 2 considers the role of quality in the organisation considering the strategic and operational aspects of quality and the debate as to its fit to the organisation. Chapter 3 focuses on barriers to the pursuit of quality, highlighting how the established cultures, systems and processes of organisations continue to inhibit quality initiatives. In chapter 4 the 'classical' and 'human relations' schools of management thinking are introduced and their apparent influence on the thinking of the quality gurus elaborated.

This part of the book provides the necessary foundation for a study of quality by examining the four key dimensions:

- the opportunity and need for quality;
- the role of quality;
- the barriers to its achievement;
- the thinking which underpins the dominant approaches to management.

1 The quality imperative

'Integrate the three pillars of social well-being, economic prosperity and environmental protection.'

Gisbert Glaser, International Geosphere–Biosphere Programme, cited by James Lovelock, 2006

Introduction

Quality has emerged and remained as a dominant concern of management and in management thinking for over 60 years and there continues to be a need to sustain product quality in manufacturing. A new focus began to emerge in the 1980s on quality in services, especially for the post-industrial and information-based economies. While there has been some progress in this regard, it seems that most organisations are still rooted in a manufacturing model of quality and consider achieving service quality to be about process and technique rather than about people and behaviour. Hence true quality of service continues to be elusive for many. For me quality, especially in a service context, should be about the outcome for the customer, not the standardisation of the service output.

The initial ideas in the quality movement arose from American theorists and practitioners, while early commercial applications were predominantly amongst Japanese companies. The need for enhanced quality was perhaps ignored or rejected as unnecessary in the West where demand was growing faster than supply. Since the mid 1980s, when the success of Japanese companies began to impinge seriously on Western markets, commercial organisations throughout the world have embraced, at least in part, the theories and practices of the quality movement. In 2016, many national governments continue to pursue quality initiatives, although these are often driven more by cost reduction desires than the genuine pursuit of service improvement.

Governments are under increasing pressure to achieve service levels equivalent to those of private organisations and have sought to modernise and enhance public offerings through the application of quality methods – sometimes in conjunction with private finance, privatisation or the creation of non-Governmental Executive Agencies. European governments continue to engage in 'Best Practice' and 'Best Value' programmes and active support of the Business Excellence Model as a framework for service quality improvement.

This chapter is concerned with 'why' quality has achieved this apparent pre-eminence amongst the concerns of so many managers. It presents three arguments for the pursuit of quality (the economic, the social and the environmental) before considering the specific challenge for service organisations. Finally the chapter considers the problems generated in organisations by the use of the word 'quality' itself. Each of these is pursued through a systemic perspective on management and achievement of quality.

1.1   The economic imperative

During the post World War Two years consumer demand grew to such an extent that the manufacturing focus in the Western world was on productivity – increases in volume of products and the efficiency of both the production equipment and the labour force. Effectively, growing markets were starved of products, and with rapidly increasing economic prosperity, everything that could be produced could be sold. Unfulfilled demand meant that organisations were under no pressure to focus on the quality of product and perhaps perceived that they had already achieved the ultimate standards. Coupled to this, consumer expectations of product longevity and reliability, especially for novel technologies, were relatively low compared with today, as was the technology of both the products and the manufacturing processes.

As markets matured and growth consequently stabilised, organisations faced with increasing costs of production, particularly the cost of labour, waste and, in the early 1970s, the dramatic increase in the cost of energy, began to challenge their established ways of working. Some organisations further increased the pressure on workers for productivity gains while pursuing cost reductions in their supply chain and through research and development. Others relied on the emerging technologies of automation, robotics and electronic data processing. Most adopted a mix of these approaches. Where technologically and financially feasible, other organisations followed the more traditional approach of exporting jobs to lower cost manufacturing centres, especially in South East Asia. This practice is still ongoing with continuing growth of manufacturing in China and the sub-continent of India, notwithstanding a slow down in 2015 and the re-onshoring of some jobs as the cost-benefit profiles have changed. Rather than reducing costs through improving their processes, many organisations relocated manufacturing plants to take advantage of lower-cost labour. Organisations began exporting service-based jobs through the creation of overseas contact centres and 'shared-service' centres. Increasingly jobs based on knowledge (such as software development) are following the same route, capitalising in the Indian sub-continent on high levels of education. What is interesting today is to see the extent to which jobs in both manufacturing and service sectors are returning to their country of origin.

This phenomenon of industrial organisations chasing cheap labour can be traced from the late 19th century, when manufacturing emerged in America with its ready supply of cheap land and labour and a highly entrepreneurial culture. At that time European organisations began to establish overseas operations. From the mid 1960s Western organisations developed operations in Asia. The first of these to emerge, Singapore, Hong Kong and Taiwan, are now mature economies (GDP per capita is at or beyond Western levels) and they in turn have been losing jobs to their newly emergent and lower-cost neighbours such as Cambodia, Indonesia, Korea and Vietnam.

Change in the European economy over recent years has delivered a partial reversal of this trend. Many Asia-based companies have relocated some manufacturing operations to Europe, as labour is relatively cheaper than before, the workforce has the skills required for high-quality manufacturing operations and the cost of transporting finished goods is substantially reduced. Local manufacturing also helps to overcome import tariffs and other trade defence actions. Notable organisations following this trend include Sony, Nissan, Toyota and Honda from Japan and Lucky Goldstar from Korea. The most productive car plant in the UK is owned and operated by Nissan in Sunderland, UK (although Nissan itself is now in a well established partnership with Renault–France). One Asian airline relocated much of its paper processing and accounting work to Australia from Hong Kong, and a UK airline operates its customer call–centre from the Middle East. The number of emergent, relatively low cost economies has also increased substantially in recent years, not just with the Far East countries but also those of Eastern Europe. Each of these new producers and economies adds to the level of competition in the established markets.

It seems relatively clear that where technology and total costs enable it, employment opportunities are drawn to cheap labour. The economic consequences for the originating economies are currently uncertain. While it was easy to observe relative growth in the wealth of emerging economies and decline in those which were mature, the overall impact now seems to be one of equalisation supported by free movement of capital but also, significantly, propelled by exploitation of weaknesses in tax regimes. Much of what is now happening appears to be driven by the cost of funding and financing and the opportunities for tax minimisation, all acting to drive behaviour in the global market. There may be profits for the 'home' economy to repatriate (after tax!) but the jobs and much of the wealth remain in the host manufacturing economy, as that is where the workers spend their wages. The shift of economic effort from production to not just service-based activity but financing-based activity since around 2000 has been significant, with much capital flowing into financial services products which might once have been directly invested in plant and machinery. This shift introduces a layer of complexity but also a layer of cost to the more traditional sectors, together with a shift in risk profiling. When the demand for return on capital increases and a greater proportion of the capital employed is borrowed (in one way or another), then it is to be expected that users of that capital will seek to derisk their businesses. They will do so by refining that which they already do, reducing research and development activity. So, they may seek ways to reduce the cost of producing established goods and services but may, in some sectors at least, be unwilling or unable to invest in new products. It is notable that the leading technology companies are investing huge sums in absolute terms but tiny sums relative to their total income in new products and services, but even then much of what they are working on is a slightly better version of an existing product, rather than something fundamentally new.

It still seems to be the case that work continues to follow low total costs – of which today direct production cost is only one. If the observed cycle continues, it is apparent that, at best, long-term rebalancing of the relative power of economies is inevitable. Mature economies may well decline as emergent economies develop the knowledge, skills and abilities to absorb a greater proportion of both manufacturing and service sector jobs.

In parallel with this phenomenon and notwithstanding the substantial apparent progress in products, services and information technology in recent years, it also appears that for many products, with the exception of certain emerging products and services such as computer games and leisure facilities, demand is, in effect, satisfied. Consumers are operating in a replacement cycle for a large proportion of established products (for example cars, domestic appliances, home entertainment equipment, even personal computers), albeit new features and functionality ensure a degree of obsolescence in some products. In this replacement phase of the product life cycle, consumers are demanding greater reliability and longevity from their purchases, and these characteristics are significant in their decision making. It also appears that for many products, diversity and choice are expanding, with competitive products from emergent economies challenging those of the established players. Here it is worth noting the work of Stewart (2009) in which he suggests that some organisations may be using their market power to hold back innovation and protect their competitive position.

Consider outcome not just process

I discovered this story on a social media site, and it makes the point about outcome focused quality better than a supposed 'case study' ever could.

> We took the kids for dinner at Pizza Express. There was a very friendly lady dining alone at the next table who clearly had special needs. When the time came for her to pay the bill, her bank card was declined. The waitress told her, in a very kind way, that there was a problem but she would call her manager for help.
>
> Jeremy immediately leapt up and told the waiting staff that we would pay for the lady's meal. However, when the manager arrived he explained to the lady that she couldn't use her bank card to pay, but not to worry; Pizza Express authorises the restaurant to give away two free meals per month and that, on this occasion, they would like to provide her with a free meal. She was extremely grateful and apologetic that she had been unable to pay. We were relieved that the lady had been treated in such a dignified way and that she was not placed in a difficult position.
>
> Then, the Manager approached our table. He said that, as we had shown such generosity, he would like to donate the second free meal that the restaurant was able to offer to us. We were absolutely dumbfounded! I have never heard of any chain restaurant behaving in such a generous way. We were quite overcome. I made sure that the lady was able to get home OK, then we thanked the staff and left ourselves.
>
> I think Pizza Express, and in particular the manager of the Surbiton branch, deserve a massive pat on the back. I told the manager that my younger son has special needs and I was really impressed.

This case demonstrates true quality of service leading to a terrific outcome – the enhanced reputation of the restaurant chain which will surely be good for business!

So much for private industry, but what of the public sector – does the same economic imperative apply? The pursuit of quality is equally important to this sector of every economy. From their behaviour and actions throughout the world, governments can be observed to be dissatisfied with the cost and effectiveness of many public services. For some years there has been a trend towards privatisation, commercialisation or agency status of many public sector bodies, imposing on them many of the same constraints faced by private sector, profit oriented institutions. The share of GDP absorbed by governments is unacceptable to many voters and potentially damaging to economies. Since 2010 the UK government has pursued an apparent policy of 'austerity', an approach reflected in the actions of many governments under various labels. One part of this is a political drive to reduce the size of government and is accompanied by privatisation of some activities and localisation of others. I make no claim as to whether these actions are good or bad, but what they do is change the situation and circumstances under which public services must achieve what they think of as service quality. What government appears to be clinging to is the right to measure and hold the provider to account for service provision whilst allowing them to conduct the activity, although it is concerned with the output (was it done?), not the outcome (did it work?). This will present a significant challenge to the achievement of consistent service quality, since reducing costs will either be achieved through narrowing the scope of a service, redesigning its delivery or perhaps failing to provide it – as has been seen in some services.

At the same time in those relatively wealthy established economies such as the UK, there has been a drift of public service consumers away from the public offerings towards private service, perhaps in conjunction with the emergence of Executive Agencies and the privatisation of public services such as railways. 'Trusts' are now well established in the NHS and Clinical Commissioning Groups established with the primary health care providers to procure provision of medical services, some of which are being purchased from non-NHS organisations in both the private and not-for-profit sectors. These organisations are at 'arms-length' from government, finding and managing their own finances while remaining dependent on the State for the bulk of their income. These changes occur where the public service is perceived by government to be failing to meet the needs of its service users, where they believe costs are high (or out of control) or where industrial relations challenges are likely to damage the standing of the party in government. Perhaps the longest established example of this in the UK is the franchising of rail services and the placing into a not-for-profit status (albeit owned by the government) of the rail infrastructure network provider (although at the time of writing the government is understood to be considering a third, new model for this, as the first two have clearly not worked well).

It is fair to suggest that if public services do not address the problems which their users observe, then they must eventually fall into disrepair, either collapsing altogether through lack of public support or offering a lower standard of service to the less well off members of the society which supports them and increasing the unit cost of such provision. The pursuit of quality in their products and services offers these institutions the opportunity to provide comparable services to those available in the private sector. I argue that there is nothing inherently 'better' about a privately owned and offered service than a public one. It is merely that the economic imperative for survival has traditionally been greater in the private sector.

The economic imperative for quality is essentially quite simple – survival for the individual organisation and industries and ultimately the local, national and global economies. The 'gurus' promise that achieving quality will reduce costs and improve productivity, and certainly many of the tools can lead to those things. As consumers become more selective in their choices, quality can no longer be considered an optional extra but is essential for any organisation in a saturated market-place. Only the strongest will survive – and will do so by scavenging customers from lesser organisations. This phenomenon can be observed in the motor industry, where the premium manufacturers are stretching their product down into the mid-market and the mass-market are stretching their product up – very soon there will be no mid-market!

From the perspective of the total economy of a nation, it is more cost effective to cure quality problems than it is to export jobs or lose them to alternative or overseas suppliers. At the same time in economies increasingly focused on service provision, not product provision, long-term success and survival will go to those organisations that enable their customers to achieve the outcomes they desire.

1.2   The social imperative

In parallel with the developments in technology over the last 50 years or so has been massive development in our understanding of human-kind. Through the works of management writers and practitioners such as Barnard's Executive Functions (1938), psychology with Mayo (1949), Herzberg et al (1959) and McGregor (1960), Beer's organisational cybernetics (1959, 1979, 1981, 1985), the soft systems approaches of Ackoff (1981) and Checkland (1981), management theorists and scientists have become aware of many alternative ways of designing and managing jobs and organisations. Again, reference to Stewart (2009) is worthwhile here; he suggests that the work of these 'experts' does not have the predictive power that good science would suggest is necessary – so tinge your thinking with caution. However, with the homespun philosophical and short-term arrogance of 'If it ain't broke, don't fix it', coupled to a level of complacency and/or fear of change – 'We've always done it like that' – managers and academics have collectively failed to embrace the many possibilities that these developments in thinking make available to us. Many academics (though by no means all) at universities and colleges continue to teach classical methods because either it is all they know or because they reject the 'new' ideas. Expansion of Higher Education opportunities coupled to significant changes in recent years in the funding mechanisms, as well as the evaluation of and reward for research outputs, has led to a situation where not all academics can be active researchers in the disciplines which they teach. With increasing teaching loads and continued growth in information availability powered by the internet, it is probably not possible to keep fully up to date with emerging ideas. Those who are active researchers tend to be engaged in those relatively few institutions which are well established and well funded, a situation that some argue is self-reinforcing. Practically for managers, it is often easier in the short term to keep things as they are – particularly when the focus is forced onto the short-term financial performance measures by higher management and external demands.

Managers in organisations predominantly pursue a short-term, incremental improvement methodology rooted in the established norms of their situation, rather than, admittedly somewhat more ambitiously, pursuing the true potential of their organisation. Commonly, managers know only the 'budget' for their function and are unaware of what *could* be achieved if constraining norms were overthrown and they truly realised the potential of the resources (human, mechanical and informational) they have at their disposal.

To bring about change in the established order of anything always involves the expenditure of energy: to overcome the initial resistance, to persist with the change programme through the 'painful' times and to provide the changed infrastructure to support the new order. As Machiavelli suggested in *The Prince* (1513):

> It must be considered that there is nothing more difficult to carry out, nor more doubtful of success, nor more dangerous to handle, than to initiate a new order of things. For the reformer has enemies in all those who profit by the old order, and only lukewarm defenders in all those who would profit by the new order, this lukewarmness arising partly from fear of their adversaries, who have the laws in their favour; and partly from the incredulity of mankind, who do not truly believe in anything new until they have had the actual experience of it.

> (Machiavelli, *The Prince*, trans. Bull, 1961)

Similarly the impact of any change programme, at least in the short term, may reduce the ability of the organisation to acquire fresh supplies of energy. This energy, for most organisations, is expressed in the form of money. Where the money is not made available, for example in the public sector or in low-margin industries (commodity manufacturing and distribution) or where the demand for high investment returns restricts the available cash, then the change programmes will often fail.

An equivalent energy is required from the most senior management in terms of their commitment to supporting the change. Whilst most frequently expressed in financial terms, the failure of support very often rests in the very human desire of managers to work with what they believe they understand; to deliver what has worked in the past and seek to preserve their power and position within the organisation. It is a rare manager who will voluntarily relinquish his or her own position for the good of the organisation. Observing change programmes is a little like watching a corrupt game of musical chairs at the senior level – when the music stops everybody is sitting in a different place – but the total number of chairs has often not changed! Consequently, the ways in which we run organisations and manage people are often extremely wasteful of the human capabilities and talent of the majority. In *The Intelligent Organisation* (2016) I challenge this, suggesting that the capability for change needs to be embedded in every role so that far from running change programmes, the organisation has power embedded to change itself.

The social imperative for achieving quality is further enhanced by the continuing emergence and importance of the idea of 'Corporate Social Responsibility' (CSR). This is challenging managers in new ways. CSR is concerned with the wider impact of the organisation on its stakeholders. CSR is defined in a wide variety of ways with no universal agreement. However, Crane, Matten and Spence (2008) have explained it as follows:

> The [six] core characteristics of CSR are the essential features that tend to be reproduced in some way in academic or practitioner definitions.

Their six core characteristics are shown in Table 1.1.

Ohno, founder of the Toyota Manufacturing method (Ohno, 1988) takes as his theme the elimination of waste, 'muda', as the basis of effectiveness in organisations. This systematic approach, discussed at length in chapter 11, recognises that waste can encompass people,

Table 1.1 Characteristics of corporate social responsibility

Voluntary	acceptance of responsibility for actions that goes beyond that prescribed by law;
Internalising/Managing externalities	recognising impacts beyond the organisation and accepting them as belonging to it;
Stakeholders	recognising responsibility beyond shareholders and customers to embrace the wider society;
Alignment	the understanding that there is no necessary conflict between CSR and profitability. Addressing the alignment of corporate and social interests;
Practices and values	this is not simply about the adoption of 'good' practices as avoiding a negative, but about an internal belief system that recognises CSR as a good thing in its own right;
Beyond philanthropy	an assumption that CSR is a mainstream way of doing business, not an addition that keeps society happy.

systems, production machines and society, and it is this societal dimension that is dealt with here. From origination to consumption to ultimately disposal or recycling, every action by an organisation and its human actors imparts both positive and negative impacts to society. CSR argues that managers have a responsibility to minimise the negative impacts – and follows this into practical activities, whether they be enhanced company driver training to reduce accidents and improve economy, support for community activities such as sponsoring clubs or involvement of local communities directly in the development of long-term plans. Each of these, and a myriad of other actions, are intended to reduce any negative impact of the organisation on its social environment and encourage it to 'behave' as a good 'corporate citizen'. This might be the point of Taguchi's 'Quadratic Loss Function' (1987) which attempts to calculate the 'loss imparted to society from the time the product is shipped'.

Both CSR and the Toyota method exploit the understanding that many of the people affected by inefficient, ineffective systems know both that the system is ineffective and, importantly, how to fix it. Ineffective systems are not only wasteful but demoralising and destructive to the talents of their members and users. It is staggering how often those responsible for a job can identify a 'short cut' which enables the job to be completed on time and within specification, whereas the organisation of the system itself would drive towards at least one and often both of these important parameters being missed.

One effect of the failure of organisations to fully exploit the talents they employ is that they lose them! Recent years have seen a huge rise in the number of new, small professional service organisations whose proprietors and directors, disenchanted with the limitations of life in large organisations, have the confidence and ability to build their own, independent organisations. The joke on the large organisations is that they then, very often, hire back at much greater expense the very set of talents and skills which they previously failed to exploit! The large organisation loses in two ways – it has to actively compete to obtain the particular skills it needs at higher cost, and the career model provided to young employees features the organisation as victim rather than predator. The underlying message to talented young staff is that they will not be able to exploit their talents within the organisation.

At the operational level, many organisations have failed to respond to improvements in our understanding of human behaviour and in levels of education. They continue to manage their staff through a Taylorist (1911) mental model, imposing bureaucracy and regulation and insisting on mindless adherence to 'the procedure'. Whilst there are many circumstances in which adherence to the procedure is essential for safety or consistency, there are similarly many circumstances where 'the procedure' inhibits rather than enhances quality. This particularly applies to the service sector and will be explored in section 1.4, 'The Service Challenge'. However, even in manufacturing, the regulatory and policing burden imposed by a heavily proceduralised organisation could be substantially reduced by a higher initial investment in training and development which could release the talents of those employed. Similarly, contemporary information systems have the inherent capability to release individuals from the drudgery of data capture and reporting. However, many such systems are poorly designed and executed, often replacing manual bureaucracy with its electronic equivalent and allowing the same mistakes to be made faster and at greater cost. The benefit to be obtained from enhanced people development and effective Information Systems investment would dramatically outweigh the cost of providing it. A well developed member of staff who understands WHY something should be done in a particular way will do so willingly, reducing the cost of supervision. Perhaps more importantly they will be able to appreciate when the procedure has become inappropriate and, if not free to change it, will at least be able to bring it to the attention of those who have that authority. 'I was only following orders' is not a guarantee of success in manufacturing any more than in any other walk of life. Relatively well educated staff in a relatively wealthy, high-employment economy have choices. If they are not treated appropriately they will exercise them! As Drucker (1969) noted, 'with every pair of hands you hire you get a free brain', so why not use it?

If individuals have the capacity to perform more complex tasks to higher standards or in greater volume than the system permits, then managers are wasting resources. This is in itself sufficient evidence of the need for change quite apart from the potential benefit to human spirit. From the perspective of social cohesion, it must be the responsibility of every manager to maximise the opportunity for development for each of his or her fellow workers. This will surely lead to a more satisfied workforce, a commitment to the organisation and a society more at ease with itself.

The negative risk of minimising apparent waste of human resources is that if quality is achieved, and markets do not grow to absorb increased higher volume outputs, there may be a substantial increase in levels of unemployment. This will arise because organisations will find it unnecessary (and costly – since there are indirect additional costs involved in employing extra staff) to retain current numbers of employees. This led in the 1980s to the fashion for 'down-sizing' in organisations, reducing staff numbers to the minimum level.

As has been seen in many conurbations, high levels of unemployment tend to create conditions of social isolation, a sense of hopelessness and unease, often leading to unrest and anti-social behaviour such as drug and alcohol abuse or increasing crime rates. Examples of this were riots in Liverpool, Birmingham and other UK cities, the increase in drug abuse reported in crime statistics, increased levels of shoplifting and the rise in illegitimate births particularly amongst teenagers. It cannot be regarded as acceptable that by achieving quality we also achieve social destruction. Neither can it be regarded as sustainable to produce poor quality outputs in order to maintain employment in the short term – above all else, consumer markets will not allow this.

While neither universally welcomed nor universally successful, one of the remarkable phenomena to emerge since the 2008 financial crisis has been a substantial further rise in the number of micro-businesses. These have covered all sectors and all parts of the market and have shown how individuals will, when the need or the opportunity arises, address the unemployment challenge by finding different and new ways in which to add value to their fellow man. Much of this growth has been enabled by information technologies and the many opportunities for new goods and services that have emerged in the beginning of 'The Second Machine Age' (Brynjolfsson & McAfee, 2014).

Further work is required to address this issue. It may be argued that by succeeding in the pursuit of quality, any particular country will act as an attractor of industries leading to economic success for that country. Inevitably this would have international consequences which are beyond the capacity of any individual or normal organisation to address. In the meanwhile the markets will not wait, and action must be taken to preserve, maintain and develop all industries.

The second imperative for quality then stems from the responsibility of all managers to minimise waste of costly human resources and maximise satisfaction through work for their colleagues in order to support social cohesion within their own sphere of influence.

1.3   The environmental imperative

The third imperative for quality is environmental. Driven by the experiments and per-spectives of writers such as Lovelock (1979, 1988, 1991, 2001, 2006, 2009) and the emergence of the environmental movement, it is now widely recognised that the world has finite natural resources, particularly fossil fuels, and that the use of these appears damaging to the total ecology of the planet (IPCC, 2014). Renewable energy sources, such as solar power, wind energy or wave energy, are increasingly available and have improved dramatically in both cost and performance over recent years. While Lovelock in *Homage to Gaia* (2001) has presented an argument for the adoption of nuclear power as an available alternative to fossil fuels, this is unlikely to prove any more acceptable to the established power groups than his arguments against fossil fuels were in the 1970s. In the UK in particular there is a move, yet to be actioned, towards the building of new nuclear power generation facilities, whilst in Germany they are being progressively closed.

In this early part of the 21st century, concern about damage to the environment has been elevated to a primary concern of governments of all nations. Governments of the most mature economies are making substantial commitments (e.g. the UN Paris Agreement, 2016), some legally binding, some not, to reduction in carbon dioxide emissions, which are widely seen as a contributory factor to global warming. Although there is not universal agreement on the impact of such emissions, there is substantial agreement that they should be reduced.

Other international accords are being actively pursued to reduce fossil fuel emissions, and the 'Kyoto Agreement', which demands substantial reductions in harmful emissions, led to the establishment of a not always successful market in which the right to produce emissions can be bought and sold. This provides an economic incentive for organisations to pursue the environmental imperative.

ISO 14000, revised in 2015, is the Environmental Management Standard and is becoming more widely accepted and adopted in the major economies and, like the early versions of ISO 9000, is becoming seen as the minimum acceptable standard with which companies should seek to conform.

While it might be argued that a narrow focus on environmental sustainability detracts from the broader arguments about the overall sustainability of organisations, recent international accords on environmental protection and emissions reductions shows that organisations can no longer afford to pay only lip service to this subject. The European Union has developed legislation designed to substantially and rapidly reduce emissions from new motor cars (from inception to destruction) with lower acceptable levels of pollution being set for every manufacturer, standards being increased and enforced for the recycling of the components of vehicles and individual governments setting tax incentives for consumers to drive less polluting vehicles. Sadly in 2015 it was determined that at least one manufacturer had engaged in activity on a massive scale which appears to cheat the legislation. Meanwhile numerous cities have introduced or are introducing low emissions zones and some, as soon as 2020, will have introduced zero emissions zones. Legislation will force the hands of manufacturers and suppliers if they do not address this themselves. Experience suggests that an innovation designed by a manufacturer will be cheaper and more effective than one which is legislated into existence.

Operating our organisations without a sharp focus on quality is to be wasteful of limited resources. Quality products, processes, systems and services minimise the use of the factors of production (human, material, land and money), maximise the reliability and longevity of products and thereby minimise lifetime damage to the environment. For example, a process which achieves Crosby's 'Zero Defects' (1979), Shingo's 'Poka-Yoke' (1987) or Ohno's 'muda' standard (1988) involves no rework or rectification. Processes such as these then make minimum use of money, materials and labour in achieving output and consequently minimise damage to the environment compared with a process producing any number of defective outputs.

Clearly it is too much to expect any one individual or organisation to 'save the world'. Each individual or organisation can however be expected to make a contribution to this at the appropriate level – that is their own level and the ones above and below. The levels could be thought of as the individual, the organisation, the stakeholders, the local community, the national community and the international community.

Each of us perhaps has responsibility to minimise use of resources in the completion of our duties. The execution of that duty must be supported by organisations creating conditions which enable work to be carried out with minimum waste. This might simply mean ensuring that tools are properly functional (sharp, accurate), that sufficient time is permitted for the task to be carried out with appropriate care and that the individual worker holds the necessary skill set to complete competently the given task.

Management have the additional responsibility of considering the total effectiveness of the organisation in terms of its use of all resources and the environmental implications of their actions. This may mean making investments to reduce environmental damage, and that must of course be supported by the other stakeholders in the enterprise. The shareholders must accept responsibility for the actions of the organisation and be prepared to accept the returns generated by an organisation which fully accepts its responsibilities, even if they are less in the short term than competing investments. This thinking links back to the notion of Corporate Social Responsibility outlined in section 1.2.

A substantial conflict may arise for some companies when it comes to additional investment. In the chemicals industry, economic reality is that simply to keep pace with their competitors, organisations must reduce costs, year on year, by around 3%. In an industry dominated by high-volume manufacturers of predominately low margin, commodity products, this is a challenging target, especially for smaller companies. When coupled to increases in the regulatory governance of the organisation and the testing, storage and use of its products, the target becomes harder. To achieve sustainable improvements in quality (however that may be defined in the circumstances), to enhance the skill set of the employees and to ensure the long-term viability of the organisation against this background of, in effect, falling margins is harder still. It may well be that the only truly sustainable business strategy (as far as the capital held by the organisation is concerned) is to leave the industry! The ultimate challenge is not simply to improve quality and reduce costs to remain competitive but to achieve a position which satisfies competing ethical demands – the imperatives to preserve jobs for society, to improve quality of product, to minimise damage to the environment, not to imperil the local (or wider) community and to satisfy shareholder demands.

The community in which any organisation exists must hold and impose expectations on its behaviour as regards environmental matters whilst at the same time accepting its own responsibilities. For example, if it wishes to continue purchasing the relevant product, the community must impose expectations as regards the processing or recycling of waste, but must also provide an appropriate mechanism for that process. To achieve necessary economic scale, some facilities may need to be provided at the community level, for example incinerators and recycling plants. It is the responsibility of the community, through local government, to ensure that these are available.

At a national level, the same considerations apply. The nation has a responsibility to itself, its citizens and the international community. This responsibility includes setting, maintaining and enforcing environmental standards and expectations and creating conditions (perhaps through the use of taxes and duties) which reinforce those expectations.

At the international level, the responsibilities are much the same. Creation and enforcement of environmental standards must be undertaken by the international community. While other aspects of organisational life may be very different, for example wage rates, organisational culture and so on, the international community must demand common environmental standards from all those wishing to be part of that community.

At every level there is a need and a responsibility to educate and inform on environmental matters and to understand the needs from a total, rather than partial, perspective. Thus the third imperative for quality is to address the rising desire for reductions in environmental damage, helping to ensure the survival of all species. A responsibility which pertains at every level of the world community.

1.4   The service challenge

The origins of the quality movement and the philosophies, tools and techniques rest in the manufacturing sector which formed the greater part of the economy of most nations when the movement began. It was manufacturing that addressed the contemporary issue of quality and it might be argued has, at least at one level, 'solved' the specific problem of manufacturing quality. The organisational and economic world has, however, changed. During the greater part of the 20th century, manufacturing was the dominant economic force in every advanced economy; the service sector was relatively small, employing small numbers of highly qualified professionals. In the 'post-industrial' or 'knowledge' economy, manufacturing is generally high-volume, highly automated, highly specialised, highly important, as already stated, but represents a much smaller proportion of total economic activity and employs a similarly small proportion of the workforce. The service sector is now the dominant employer and generator of economic growth. For example, in Hong Kong, since the 1960s a strong manufacturing economy, around 70% (depending on the basis of measurement) of economic activity is derived from the service sector. Similar proportions pertain in the Western economies.

The challenge for the service sector is to develop ways of addressing the 'quality problem' which are appropriate to the needs of a sector whose principal asset is people and where the application of the skills and knowledge of those people it employs is the key differentiator between 'good' and 'bad' service. To date, the signs are not encouraging. I wrote in 2010 that:

> Many organisations are simply adapting the manufacturing models of quality to the service sector to no great effect.

Sadly not much has changed. Many organisations are still trying to deliver service quality through a focus on process rather than people.

Manufacturing models of quality continue to rely on an outmoded understanding of quality, organisation, people and consumers. They tend to be incremental in their impact and create bureaucracy, ultimately falling into disrepute and disuse. The focus of manufacturing-based quality systems has often been on doing that which is required to secure the necessary 'badge', not on delivering quality. Applied to the provision of services, these models are mechanistic and alienating, lead to de-skilling of the workforce and devalue the notion of professionalism. They generate situations where the words used – 'Have a nice day' – are considered more important than the emotion conveyed. Words without meaning, without sincerity, without commitment will not suffice for quality in a service organisation – particularly one where, however long the procedure chart, it never quite reaches the specific needs of the individual consumer (Beckford & Dudley, 1998a; Dudley, 2000). Where the words are insincere, and the customer's problem or need does not fit the organisation's procedures, the relationship has no future. The desired output may be achieved; the desired outcome is not.

Whereas addressing quality in manufacturing rested on the resolution of tangible, visible, persistent issues, quality in services is totally different. Service quality is only directly measurable in relation to the tangible aspects of the transaction – did the teller cash the cheque and pass over the right amount of money? This is measurable, verifiable, auditable. Did the teller handle this customer in the way that she or he wanted to be handled? Opinions might vary. The teller may well have used the 'right' words, but did they employ the 'right' manner? The teller may think so, the customer may not – neither can irrefutably prove their viewpoint.

Service quality is then intangible and instantaneous. It perishes with the completion of the transaction and cannot subsequently be verified or audited. It depends not on what actually happened but on how the parties to the transaction feel about what happened. The manufacturing models of quality cannot deal with the problem of service quality because they focus on the tangible, not the intangible, and because the means by which they verify and audit quality are post-hoc. Service quality cannot be verified after the event; it must be assured beforehand and verified after the event by discovering whether customer and organisation attained their desired outcomes.

The key to quality in service provision is not standardisation and verification but skills, knowledge and education. Organisations that are successful at delivering service quality recognise that it has at least three dimensions:

- What is done – the process
- How it is done – the skills
- Why it is done – the behaviours

Service quality arises when the individuals providing the service follow a good process, have the technical skills (competences) to do it right and understand why the customer matters – so they engage in an authentic, genuine relationship.

I am the lucky possessor of two cars, a Jaguar and an Alfa Romeo. Technically they are competent, well assembled and functionally suitable. They achieve the output of journey completion with great reliability – just like their competitors – so, why those cars and not others? Subjectively, and what matters to me as a discriminating customer, is that the supplying dealerships demonstrate through every engagement that they really care about me, and THAT is what wins the deal.

Organisations providing services, if they are to succeed, must move beyond process control to develop authentic relationships with their clients, and they will only do that by engaging in authentic relationships with their staff!

1.5 A problem with 'quality'

Inevitably there is more than one 'problem with quality'. The first problem, a precursor to the second, is the way in which organisations pursue quality programmes, very often adopting a neo-Taylorist (1911) or neo-managerialist philosophy (Taylor's work is briefly explored in chapter 4) and driving quality through the traditional models espoused by the gurus (part two). The second problem is the understanding of precisely what is meant by quality and its role in generating effective organisations.

Section two explored the social imperative for quality. It is this imperative which must be recognised in order for organisations to address the first problem of quality. Simply the traditional, industrial model of quality focuses on control, conformance and standardisation. This approach treats the human actors in the situation as expensive, unreliable, unthinking parts and in many cases is actively distrustful of them. This leads to expensive, and often ineffective, inspection and audit routines and on occasion to the generation of products and services which the organisation wishes to make rather more than the consumer wishes to buy. In the manufacturing context consumers simply purchase elsewhere; in the service context it leads to disuse of the service by the consumers or revolt. It has been observed, for example, that the methodology adopted by certain government agencies in the UK rests on this industrial model, and there has, in more than one instance, been vociferous protest from the affected professionals – the nearest they will get to revolution – although potential breakaway groups have emerged in some sections.

In general, those working within such organisations will not give their best work to the organisation because the organisation does not want it. It simply requires them to follow the laid down procedure. They will act to produce those aspects of performance which the organisation measures (normally productivity and some narrow measure of quality such as reject rate) and do the job with the minimum of positive engagement. Given the opportunity, they will seek work elsewhere. The organisation, in adopting this model, will simply drive away over time those staff most capable of genuinely adding value to its functioning.

The problem rests in a fundamental misunderstanding of the role and responsibility of managers, leading to a massive schism between the managers and the managed. The first core assumption underpinning the neo-Taylorist approach is that the managers know best. More often than not, this is simply not the case (Townsend, 1970). The second core assumption is that when things go wrong, as they will in any organisation from time to time, it is somebody's fault – and that somebody is not a manager (or at least not a manager at the level of the person identifying the fault!). Thus we create organisations in which the managers instruct the workers in what to do and then blame them when it does not work. The key change required is the acceptance of real responsibility and accountability by those who give the instructions. A new generation of organisations is needed where genuine communication occurs between the managers and the managed and there is real collaboration between these participants to solve the problems of the organisation.

The first problem is driven by the second problem, which is the understanding of what quality really means in the context of creating an effective organisation. Typically the focus of quality action has been very narrow, looking only at that part of the organisation which makes a physical product or, in the service sector, directly interacts with the customer. The balance of the organisation – very often the greater part of it – is uninvolved.

The narrow focus of quality programmes and initiatives followed the early development of the quality movement, which was focused on standardisation and improving manufac-turing performance. Such a focus can no longer be considered acceptable when what it often means is that the organisation focuses on doing the wrong thing better rather than on doing the right thing! Quality improvement in a product no longer suited to its market, for whatever reason, will not solve the problems of the organisation; it is futile. The organisation will simply lose money at a slightly lower rate. Quality in this interpretation means doing the right thing right! By implication the organisation must have a shared understanding of its present and future market or environment, it must have products positioned to meet the known and anticipated expectations of its customers or users and it must have strategies in place to enable it to respond at an appropriate rate to the changes as they occur. For many managers this means that their own ego must be subordinated to the organisational interest. Nobody can win unless the organisation wins!

An effective organisation is capable both of dealing with its current market or environment and of anticipating and responding to emergent changes in that market to ensure its own survival. Quality, thought of in that way, is not an operational, single function issue but an organisation wide, systemic issue. In such an organisation the impact, either direct or indirect, on every other part is explicitly recognised. Quality will then be embedded in every part and every level of the organisation, rather than isolated and handed over to the production or customer service director who cannot possibly deliver it in isolation.

Summary

This chapter has identified and elaborated three imperatives for the contemporary pursuit of quality – economic, social and environmental – and then moved to examine the difficulties and challenges faced by the service sector. From these different perspectives, brief arguments have been developed which not only justify but collectively demand that the idea of quality be pursued in every aspect of every organisation.

KEY LEARNING POINTS

Five arguments about quality: Economic, Social, Environmental, Service challenge, Problem of quality

Economic:
mature markets, saturation coverage; work follows (relatively) cheap labour; manufacturing drives services income – economies must be balanced; the public sector must deliver better services at the same or lower cost to meet public expectations; ultimate demand is economic survival.

Social:
non-quality goods and services are wasteful of human capabilities and talent; working in a non-quality environment is ultimately demoralising for the individual; the imperative is to minimise waste of talent and maximise satisfaction; corporate social responsibility is simply defined as the requirement (legal and social) for the organisation to be a good citizen.

Environmental:
the world has finite material resources; we have a responsibility to minimise waste and environmental damage.

Service challenge:
Services represent 70% of post-industrial economies; industrial quality control models do not work in the service context; key to quality in services is skilled people.

Problem of quality:
two problems – neo-Taylorist management approach, isolation of quality to the productive part of the organisation; resolution through systemic approach to quality based on doing the right things right in every part and level of the organisation.

Question

How can an organisation survive if it does not respond to the imperatives outlined in this chapter?

2 Quality: A strategic decision?

'It's them that take advantage that get advantage i' this world'

George Eliot, 1859

Introduction

The successful pursuit of a quality programme requires the dedication of substantial organisational resources, and it is vital to understand whether and how this generates value for the organisation. As long ago as 1996, Jiang Zemin, then President of the PRC, called on the Chinese to 'focus on quality, not quantity' – this in the world's largest emerging economy, treating quality not just as an organisational priority but as a national one. Evidence of its success can be seen in the massive and continuing economic growth of China since that exhortation and its emergence as a significant manufacturer of a wide range of consumer goods – from electronics to cars. In 2008, China relaunched the MG brand in the UK having re-established final assembly of sports cars at the old Rover plant in Longbridge, the same year as it launched the brand in China itself. While Chinese companies such as Geely now own Western brands like Volvo, and Chinese companies are making investment in UK energy production, Western companies, working with local partners, are now well established manufacturing in China. All organisations and countries seeking to achieve economic success must take quality seriously.

This chapter explores the role and implications of quality in the organisation through consideration of the conventionally recognised different levels of management decision making (operations, administration and strategy). The idea of 'normative' decision making (Beer, 1979), that is decisions based on identity (values, beliefs, soul), are introduced to enhance understanding. The implications for an organisation of pursuing a strategy for quality will be assessed starting with operational management.

2.1 Operations management

Operations management is concerned with the day to day activities which ensure that the organisation fulfils its present purposes and objectives. These may include short run profitability, achievement of particular levels of output, yield or productivity. Operational decisions are generally more or less immediate in their impact on the organisation, affecting what happens during a particular day, shift or even part shift where there are product changes during the course of a shift. Flexible production systems make this an increasing factor in modern manufacturing. Jaguar, for example, make multiple vehicles on the same production line. In the service sector, immediate operational decisions are often about the short-term allocation of staff resources to meet continuously varying customer volumes.

The objective of operations management is to deliver today's products and services into today's market but faster, cheaper and with less negative environmental impact than ever before. Operational management is not focused on the long term but on creating an ever better version of 'now'.

The chapters in part four of this book will show how the dominant tools and approaches of the quality experts are focused on this operational level. They are intended to assist the manager and staff in the production of quality goods and services on a daily basis, focusing on prevention of error and minimisation of rework or rectification, aiming to minimise inspection and to achieve continuous improvement. These things are often achieved through the use of measurement system outputs at the 'shop-floor' level to inform organisational devices such as quality circles and work-improvement teams. These attempt to engage people in reflection on the difficulties and problems experienced in creating a product or delivering a service and, through their joint efforts, seek to reduce them.

In terms of the needs of the organisation, an analogy can be suggested with Herzberg et al's (1959) ideas (Figure 2.1) on motivation theory. Herzberg suggested that working conditions affecting motivation fall into two broad bands, hygiene factors and motivating factors. Hygiene factors are those characteristics of the working environment which, if absent, will lead to dissatisfaction. Their presence will not motivate workers but will create conditions in which motivation becomes possible. Motivating factors are those characteristics of the work which will inspire those involved to greater efforts.

For the purposes of this analogy we can equate the hygiene factors to the need for operational quality. The absence of an operational quality focus will mean higher levels of error and failure. Its presence will not guarantee greater quality, since so many aspects are driven by other parts of the organisation such as planning, design and marketing.

The role of operational management is to deliver the current quality expectations of the organisation – but this can only be done within the constraints imposed by higher order decision making. Clearly, if product or service quality is not an inherent part of the thinking and decision making at higher levels in the organisation, it will be impossible to achieve at the operational level.

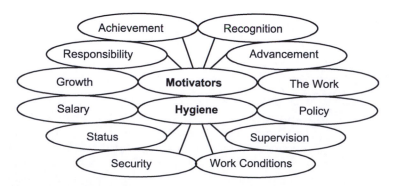

Figure 2.1 Herzberg's two factor theory of motivation.

2.2   Administrative management

Administrative management is concerned with the allocation, use and control of the current operational resources of an organisation to achieve its present purposes and objectives. It is the control function for operational management. Administrative managers acting within the constraints imposed on them from higher management seek to optimise the use of resources in the pursuit of organisational goals.

At this level of the organisation, reliance is placed more on data and information than on the physical artefacts themselves or the attributes of a service. Decisions are based on the recorded outcomes and achievements. Here, organisations have missed something of great importance. Whilst they have often automated production and service delivery quite extensively, they have, in many instances, left a massive amount of work to be done to capture performance data, collate it, turn it into information for decisions and report it – promptly, accurately and usefully. Organisations could substantially benefit from re-considering how THIS management loop on their processes could benefit from significantly more effective use of information technologies. There have been major advances in information technologies over the last 20 years, yet most organisations have failed to fully capitalise on them (Beckford, 2016).

Administrative management allows the first serious constraint upon the achievement of quality to come into focus. The administrative manager, for example a factory or production manager, may find her or himself in a position of conflict between meeting the customer expectations in terms of volume of product delivered and meeting those customers' expectations on quality of product or service. At this point, the priorities imposed upon this manager from above, perhaps a reflection of the true values of the organisation, will determine the outcome of any conflict. The question is simply:

'Which does the organisation regard as more important to deliver, volume or quality?'

In addition to observing the behaviour of the manager, clues can be found in review of the performance measurement system of the organisation. If this emphasises volume, then delivery of volume will prevail at the expense of quality and vice versa. Remember that very often it is what gets rewarded that gets done – whatever the form of the reward!

A quality management system (whether or not certified to ISO 9001:2015 or other standard systems) should form one significant element of the performance management system employed by the administrative manager. However, if quality is not perceived as a priority within the overall management system, then it will probably not be perceived as a priority at this level.

It is also important to realise that the pursuit of quality does not apply solely to the outward facing, operational aspects of the organisation but also to the support and administrative processes which enable its functioning. For example, an HR recruiting system should be thought of as a productive process (delivering staff to the operational system, its customer, who meet the technical, attitudinal and behavioural criteria necessary to perform the tasks required). If it fails to do this, then it is unreasonable to expect the operational processes to function to appropriate quality standards. The same thinking applies to training, to reward systems, to equipment and materials procurement and so on.

The administrative manager then has a dual responsibility for the delivery of quality, neither of which is more important than the other; they are equally necessary. One is to create the operational conditions which make it possible for the product or service to meet customer expectations. The other is to ensure that his or her own systems and processes deliver outputs to the operational 'customers' which meet their needs and expectations.

2.3   Strategic management

Strategic management is concerned with the scope of an organisation's activities, its markets, products or services and market position. It addresses questions of how the organisation should develop and adapt itself for the future. Any strategic process necessarily leads to outcomes with a degree of uncertainty. Strategic decisions are best thought of in terms of desired results and probable outcomes rather than the relative absolutes which may be associated with operational or administrative decisions. Despite or rather, perhaps, because of this, and as with administrative management, quality must be inherent in the strategic process itself to maximise the probability of success and reduce the chances of failure. The classic, often quoted example of such a failure is that of IBM, which determined for itself that the future of computing rested in mainframe systems. A decision which led to the organisation falling behind competitors in the development of personal computers with associated failure, at least initially, to gain market share. IBM is hugely successful globally, so one reverse did not kill it; strategic failures in other organisations have not been so benign.

The process of strategy formulation must be subjected to the same rigorous approach to quality as the operational processes. However, it must be considered whether the decision to pursue a quality programme or become a quality organisation is itself strategic.

While, according to Stewart (2009), Porter's work is explanatory rather than predictive of success and hence we should treat it with some caution, Porter (1996) suggests that:

> operational effectiveness and strategy are both essential to superior performance

but also makes the point in relation to organisational effectiveness that:

> many companies have been frustrated by their inability to translate those gains into sustainable profitability.

He suggests that practices such as benchmarking and technology transfers between organisations create conditions where performance gains achieved by one organisation are rapidly replicated in others, potentially leading to a sustained stalemate – no long-term winners and no long-term losers – with an increasing homogeneity of product and service characteristics. It appears increasingly true, particularly for information technology products such as smartphones and tablets, that rapid competitor replication of functionality is relatively easy. Product differentiation rests in appearance and design. In other markets, banking, for example, the lack of meaningful product differentiation appears to lead to an absence of meaningful competition. In this case, the common regulation drives down process and product difference, meaning that the true differentiator is quality of service, but as the products are increasingly delivered on line with minimal (or no) human interaction, even that difference is lost and the service becomes increasingly a utility. A service purchased through necessity, not desire.

If strategic management is about creating and sustaining competitive advantage for an organisation, then perhaps the pursuit of quality, particularly in a collaborative environment, may be the very opposite of strategic. If it acts to reduce competitive advantage rather than increase it, and to increase similarities between organisations, there is potential for all to pursue the same quality goal – which may not represent the true potential of the product or service. However, that is not to say that the pursuit of quality has no strategic implications. Porter's work implies that every organisation in a particular market will seek to emulate the behaviour of the 'best'. This is inevitably not the case. Some organisations will not willingly collaborate. They may regard process knowledge (one key to organisational effectiveness) in the same proprietary manner as they regard a particular brand or item of intellectual property. For example, in the petro-chemical industry, the aphorism 'the product is the process' is used. In the USA it is not unknown for a process to be subject to patent.

Equally, because of differences in organisational environment, a working practice which delivers benefits for one organisation in a particular cultural or social setting will not necessarily deliver the same benefits for another in a different one. Developing quality and performance programmes internationally has highlighted the extent to which the success of any change or innovation and the business benefit it delivers is not simply a function of its relevance to the process but, to a very great extent, the knowledge, skills, attitudes and behaviours of both the management and the workforce involved. An innovation which works in London or New York may not work well in Tokyo or Hong Kong and vice versa. Even where cultures are more closely aligned, such as in South East Asia, what works in Singapore will not necessarily work in Hong Kong. Hofstede (1980) has examined this aspect in some depth. Apparent loss (or gain) of competitive advantage will not spread uniformly and universally across any industry, particularly where advantage can be gained through differentials in labour costs and/or the return on investment in technology.

Meanwhile, the leading organisations, that is the ones against which others benchmark, seek to avoid complacency and further improve their products and processes to sustain their perceived advantage. For any industry there will be leaders and followers with some lag between innovation by the leader and its dissemination to others within the industry – either through benchmarking or creative imitation. This lag will serve to sustain competition within the industry and hence support either price or cost advantage for the leading organisations. It is improbable that any innovation will bring benefits to an entire industry at the same instant, except where it is externally driven, such as by governmental or regulatory authority involvement, or where the structure of the industry demands it. Innovation in the banking system, such as a new inter-bank clearing system, would necessarily have to be adopted by all members at the same time. An improvement in operational effectiveness will then, in most circumstances, generate a gain for the innovating organisation until that improvement is emulated by others. A focus on constant innovation and improvement fits quite neatly into Porter's (1980) strategy of 'differentiation', the creation of a market perception of value advantage.

The strategic implications go much further than this. If we look outward at the strategic environment, the effect of improved quality on customer behaviour can be examined. For perishable or consumption goods, there is perceived to be little impact. Improvement in the quality of a loaf of bread or a mushroom may affect customer choice but, if anything, is likely to lead to advantage for one player against others and a slight overall increase in volume, assuming a relatively mature market. It is when we examine consumer durables that the full impact becomes clear.

Any established consumer durable will be subject to constraints of growth in volume. There is only a finite market for items like cars, washing machines, microwaves or dishwashers. Buying activity is largely determined by the need to replace, or possibly upgrade, existing equipment. The quality of these items, in the consumer's mind, is perhaps determined by a number of factors. Inevitably these will include reliability and longevity as well as other factors, such as price, appearance, noise level in operation and brand. If a manufacturer of consumer durables focuses on improving reliability and longevity, then that will stretch the replacement cycle (the period of time between purchases) with a direct impact on apparent market size. Thus improved quality will act to reduce the overall volume of sales of a particular item and, if the market is mature, then the growth opportunity for any one supplier is determined by the number of consumers who can be acquired from competitors. In addition, the implications feedback into the organisation to affect the volume of output necessary for the manufacturer to meet demand. This directly affects every strategic decision made by the organisation, because those strategic decisions imply the commitment of substantial resources towards a desired outcome. Thinking in the pattern:

> improving quality means increased sales
> increased sales need increased manufacturing capacity

may be fundamentally flawed. First, quality improvement will lead to greater volume output from existing facilities. Second, improvements in quality should substantially extend the replacement cycle, leading to a loss of total market volume. The motor industry exemplifies this potential with an additional twist – changes in legislation regarding safety and environmental impact, coupled to the massive growth in car technology, have increased the capital cost of cars, which has led to a change in the manufacturers' business models. They are now focused on hiring out vehicles (under various leasing and contract hire schemes) rather than outright sales and making additional profits, at least in some cases, through interest rate arbitrage rather than through the sales of the vehicles. In essence, the lessor pays a fee which is sufficient to cover the depreciation on the vehicle over the life of the contract, paying interest at one rate; the manufacturer borrows money in the markets and/or from government to fund the capital but at a lower cost, generating income from the difference. When the vehicle is eventually sold (some two or three years later) the capital is repaid. This sort of business model appears to be gaining ground.

It can be concluded, then, that the pursuit of quality must be considered as strategic. First, the process for formulating strategy must exhibit quality characteristics – that is, the process itself must be correctly designed and implemented. Second, the impact of the choice to pursue quality fits with the generic strategy of differentiation. Third, the pursuit of quality has an impact on strategic decisions, because it may generate changes in consumer behaviour. This in turn may obviate the need to establish additional facilities or new distribution channels.

2.4   Normative decisions

The conventionally recognised levels of decision making in organisations have been considered. However, the changing nature of the world of organisations and the increasing concern with ethical issues such as morality, environmentalism and so on demands that we go further. Normative management decisions, whether explicit or not, define the nature and identity of the organisation itself, the values, expectations and beliefs lived by its members. The norms so derived should ensure that the organisation makes a good ethical fit with all of its stakeholders and with society in general – that is Corporate Social Responsibility.

Although all the component parts (people, factories, brands, products, services) of an organisation may change, its identity can remain the same. The essential attributes that define it as itself and nothing else are sustained. These attributes, exhibited in the behaviours of its directors and employees, reflect its character, its image (Morgan, 1986). It might be honest, courageous and ethical or be cowardly, abusive in its relations and lacking in integrity. Regardless of the specific products or services, such attributes come through in every engagement between the organisation and its stakeholders, define how it is treated in its market-place and determine its success.

An organisation which does not generate a good 'fit', a shared sense of identity with its stakeholders, will either lose customers, because it does not reflect their expectations, or fall into disregard. Similarly, an organisation which does 'fit' is much more likely to be forgiven for an occasional lapse or transgression. While customer loyalty to organisations and particularly brands does exist to the extent that some brands become synonymous with the product – the Hoover, Sellotape, Post-it notes – and is encouraged through various loyalty schemes, these will not retain customers who are genuinely unhappy with products or services.

Political parties are particularly prone to failure of fit when they do not listen to an electorate that holds them in power. When the norms of a particular political grouping no longer reflect the wishes of their society, they will be deposed, either through democratic process or by revolution. Similar observations can be made of commercial organisations. When the characteristics of the products or services do not meet the expectations of consumers, or the behaviour of the organisation is considered unacceptable, the customers will 'vote with their feet' and buy elsewhere – and other stakeholders will follow. When sales and profit targets are not met, the shareholders in the organisation, increasingly the large financial institutions, will depose the Chief Executive and appoint a new one in an attempt to correct the situation. Thus it is imperative for organisational survival (and the self-preservation of the powerful) that they listen to the demands of customers and formulate organisational norms which will meet them.

The pursuit of quality by so many organisations in recent years is precisely this kind of response. Consumers in mature markets are seeking the reassurance of reliable, high-quality goods and services (as defined by themselves), with the number and variety of choices available to them. Organisations which do not respond will fail.

The gurus of quality, as will be seen in part two, all stress the need for senior management commitment to the idea of quality in order to ensure its achievement. Normative management is where this commitment arises. The feedback of consumer expectations to senior management closes the loop for the organisation in determining behaviour. This loop explains why senior management must hold and believe in this commitment.

Normative decisions determine what questions and decisions are acceptable to the organisation at the strategic level. They therefore pre-control (Espejo & Schwaninger, 1993) strategic decision making. Strategic decisions create potential new value for the organisation, how profits will be made tomorrow. This, in turn, pre-controls the potential decisions at the administrative and operational levels, today's profits. At this point, and notwithstanding the potential for marketing activity to influence consumer behaviour, the organisation largely loses control to the market. If the normative decisions are incorrect, the consumers will not buy.

In many organisations the normative decisions are expressed through devices such as mission statements or publicised 'visions' which attempt to express the values for which the organisation stands. The values so expressed need to be enacted in the behaviour of the senior management and reflected in the performance measurement and reward systems of the organisation, or the junior management and operational staff will not respond to them. It is vital, as Handy (1985) so eloquently puts it, that the Senior Management 'walk the talk'.

Summary

This chapter has reviewed the role and positioning of quality in the context of the four levels of management decision making – operational, administrative, strategic and norm–ative. It has made clear that quality must be inherent throughout the organisation in order for it to survive. While the principal traditional tools of quality focus on the operational and administrative aspects, this chapter has shown that it must extend well beyond this. If the senior management are not absolutely committed to quality in everything that they say and do, then the organisation will not 'care' about quality. If this caring is absent, then it is impossible to build a quality organisation.

KEY LEARNING POINTS

Four levels of management decision: Operational, Administrative, Strategic, Normative

Operations:
immediate impacts, day to day activity.

Administrative:
allocation of resources to achieve objectives.

Strategic:
activity scope, development directions.

Normative:
the nature of the organisation, values, beliefs and expectations.
Quality must be inherent at every level.

Question

How closely aligned are the proclaimed 'norms' and values of your organisation with the actual behaviour of the management?

3   Barriers to quality

'What gets measured gets done'

Tom Peters, 2016

Introduction

This chapter aims to introduce readers to some barriers which prevent the achievement of quality. It will identify what those barriers are, how they arise and how they can be identified or recognised. The barriers have been grouped under four main headings:

- Systems and procedures;
- Culture;
- Organisation design;
- Management perspectives.

These headings encompass a variety of other factors which are symptoms rather than fundamental issues. The final part of the chapter will look at identifying the costs of quality, that is, the costs incurred by the organisation in making errors.

3.1   Systems and procedures

Organisations of all sizes, and especially in the highly regulated business environments now existing, operate through a more or less bureaucratic process. They are organised through a hierarchical system of offices or 'bureaux' (Weber, 1924) and maintain that organisation through formal reports, documents and record keeping – both internal and external. This is not in itself a bad thing, indeed it is essential to the delivery of a standardised product – particularly in service organisations or those operating through distributed delivery networks such as retail chains, fast food operators or banks. Without a standardised approach, the customer may easily be confused and the organisation itself spiral out of control – standardisation of every process is 'the' key ingredient of commercial success for fast food chains.

However, problems can arise with such systems. First, systems and procedures can become fixed; that is, they become 'frozen' into the organisation and its information systems such that pressure for change and adaptation meets with high resistance. In this instance, when change is necessary to meet a new level of customer expectations, it can be difficult to achieve. This is a barrier to the achievement of quality. It can be recognised when staff use expressions such as 'We've always done it like that'. This approach of using precedent as the basis of current decisions is common in many aspects of life, in particular in the practice of law, which relies heavily on past cases, and in civil administration. Readers may recall *Yes Minister* (Lynn & Jay, 1982) when Sir Humphrey and the Minister James Hacker were discussing the Honours system:

> I told him not to be silly. This infuriated him even more.
> 'There is *no reason*', he said, stabbing the air with his finger, 'to change a system which has worked well in the past.'
> 'But it hasn't,' I said.

In the contemporary organisational climate, the reliance on precedent must be open to question if emergent threats are to be neutralised and advantage taken of opportunities, even if such precedents were at one time reliable. Organisations and individuals rapidly become comfortable with a learned pattern of response – the process – and lose sight of its effectiveness (or otherwise) in the pursuit of consistency and efficiency. 'Doing the wrong thing right' is often easier for an established organisation than learning to do the right thing.

A particular problem arises from the use of procedures in service organisations. Whilst procedures help to ensure standardisation and repeatability, they can, as suggested in chapter 1, miss the customer! Every service transaction is unique. While following a common pattern – each successive customer at the supermarket checkout goes through an identical process – the human interaction taking place is specific to the particular customer being dealt with – not the one before, nor the one after. If the customer, as they often do, has a problem or issue which does not fit the procedure, then the transaction may 'fail', not in the process itself (though that is possible) but in the human interaction. The customer may walk away dissatisfied with the service. The output is delivered, but not the outcome. The problem of maintaining the 'sense' of service is challenged even more with the move to self-service tills and other forms of customer self-service. If I don't speak to a member of staff, then where is the 'service'?

It is often neither practical nor reasonable in a service transaction to attempt to create a procedure which covers every conceivable circumstance. It is the attempt to do so which leads to the bureaucratic management systems which, so often, fall into disuse and disrepute. Public and personal safety demand that before an aircraft departs, the cockpit crew work through extremely rigorous pre-flight checklists. These are designed to test and verify the functioning of every control and safety system to ensure that the aircraft is fit for the flight and that it will not endanger its crew, passengers or the public at large. This routine is essential and possible. The aircraft, a machine, has a defined and limited number of systems, each of which has two essential conditions, working or not-working. Failure or uncertainty in relation to any control or safety critical system means that the aircraft cannot depart.

Compare this with a visit to the dentist. While there is a set of procedural or process steps through which the dentist and patient must pass, neither the dentist nor the patient is a machine. The number of variables in the transaction is incalculable: the mental and physical condition of the dentist, the mental and physical condition of the patient, the moods of both, their past experiences of each other (and of other patients and other dentists), the extent to which the patient is currently suffering pain, the events they experienced on the way to the clinic. Each and every one of these factors will influence the transaction. Now, try to write the procedure chart for this! During the course of a quality project, a dentist was asked to do this. He had written seven pages before he got the patient's mouth open!

Variety, the number of possible states of the system (Beer, 1981), proliferates enormously in service transactions. Every possible question or requirement from a customer demands a specific response and a route for getting to that response. In a financial services organisation it was calculated that, for only six 'core' transactions with clients, variety had proliferated such that they had nearly 3,000 individual procedures, each an adaptation or derivation from another and each designed to meet the specific requirement of a customer or small group of customers. Even with this number of possibilities there were numerous individual customers who fell through the gaps between the procedures. This has a number of drawbacks. Quite apart from continuing to fail in meeting customer expectations, the cost of maintaining, policing and auditing such a system far outweighs its benefit – to either business or customer. A better solution, especially given the highly qualified, professional staff employed, would have been to focus on the six core processes, and then develop and rely on the skills, knowledge and experience of the staff and allow them to exercise judgement in closing the gap between the high–order process outcome and the specific requirements of the individual customer. Human beings make excellent variety managers.

The second challenge, the perception of what is important, is probably as great a barrier to quality, particularly in the context of a Crosby (1979) style quality programme. Such a programme relies heavily on an exhortative, evangelical approach. In most cases, managers and staff focus on achieving those aspects of performance which are explicitly measured. The systems and procedures of the organisation, especially those involving performance measurement, tend to determine which characteristics of the organisation receive the most attention. Beckford reported (1993) a cake factory where the performance of the production department was monitored against two simple measures – volume throughput and labour utilisation. The production managers sought to maximise these two characteristics in their daily work with considerable success. Complaints about quality, arising from either the internal Quality Control function or from the customers, were acknowledged but ignored in pursuit of productivity. A business issue arising from this case was that the production managers were manufacturing for reject. The demand to increase throughput and labour utilisation was not capped by the simple expression – 'to the extent of customer orders'. In order to keep throughput high, the production managers were generating volumes significantly higher than customer demand. The excess production was sold off (at materials cost only) to a local secondary market trader. While outside the direct scope of the consulting assignment, it was necessary for the subject organisation to redesign its measurement system before any sustainable improvement could be achieved.

The barrier to quality revealed here is that of workforce perception of what is important. Staff in an organisation will seek to achieve the targets which are established through reported measurement – those things which the organisation instructs them through its measurement system to regard as important. Discovering such a barrier in an organisation is easy – simply look at the way in which performance is measured; this tells you what the organisation regards as important. Even where quality performance is formally measured, and it often is not, its importance can be judged against the priority it is given when compared to productivity or other measures.

Overcoming these barriers will be dealt with in later chapters of this book. For now, it is sufficient to say that systems and procedures must be (re)designed to support the achievement of quality with particular attention paid to the selection of performance criteria. If quality is a desired characteristic of the outputs of the organisation, it will somehow and to some degree need to be measured and must take account of the expectations of customers – whether internal or external.

3.2   Culture

The development of a quality culture is a critical area of the achievement of quality, but what is culture? Clutterbuck & Crainer (1990: 195) describe it as:

> a set of behavioural and attitudinal norms, to which most or all members of an organisation subscribe, either consciously or unconsciously, and which exert a strong influence on the way people resolve problems, make decisions and carry out their everyday tasks.

Schein (1988), cited by Clutterbuck & Crainer (1990: 196), suggests that culture describes the 'artefacts, values and underlying assumptions' that govern behaviour within the organisation. For the purposes of this book it is 'values' and 'beliefs' that are the key cultural drivers, although these may be expressed in a variety of ways. They often emerge from the measurement systems and procedures which are seen to communicate to staff and workers what senior management consider important about performance. Eventually, such aspects become culturally embedded; that is, they become a part of the value system of the organisation.

Beliefs and values are also often expressed through the rituals, stories and myths of the organisation. These are exchanged through both formal and informal processes and may be seen as guiding new entrants towards particular forms of behaviour and attitudes. Those who do not conform may be seen as radicals and remain outside the 'cultural web' (Johnson & Scholes, 1993: 60) of the organisation.

Entrenched norms of behaviour are some of the most difficult aspects of an organisation to change. Where achievement of quality has previously been considered relatively unimportant, it requires considerable determination and effort to change the established values. Again, a case history can perhaps explain the point. Many companies are currently abandoning the formal dress codes, even enjoying 'Dress-down Friday' when smart casual clothes are expected.

Relative informality in office dress has become normal, taking a generation to pervade the workplace. Meanwhile, notwithstanding those companies that merely insist that 'employees will wear clothes', there is a much more individual approach emerging in Western organisations while in some Asian companies, all employees – up to and including the Chief Executive – wear common corporate workwear. The argument for this, like the 'office clothes' argument above, is that it helps to reduce or even eradicate differences between grades, enhances communication and improves the bond between employees. Relative to changing attitudes to quality, changing the dress code can be considered easy.

Politics in the organisational context does not usually refer to overt competition between groups with differing ideologies, although this is possible. Normally, it is experienced as covert competition for power, position and influence between sub-groups in the organisation; that is, for positions of influence and authority from which they can manage the organisation to reflect their own preferences. These groupings may have their roots in a particular technical or functional ability, for example marketing, finance or production, or in common backgrounds, such as groups who joined the organisation at the same time and whose careers developed together, or who share some educational or sporting history. Working as a sub-cultural group within the organisation's total culture, such groups often exercise immense, frequently tacit influence. When such groupings are strong they may, even unwittingly, place the interests of the group before those of the organisation itself. This presents another barrier to quality. From the perspective of such sub-groups, achievement of quality must come to be seen as a meta-cultural requirement. The interests of the particular group must become aligned with, or subordinated to, the interest of the organisation in pursuing quality.

Linking with the issues of measurement and politics, do the employees of the organisation care about the work, and in particular about the quality of the product or service? If they do not, for whatever reason, then quality will probably not be achieved. Such attitudes are often driven by management through the priorities that they set and the results through which they manage the organisation. For example, if those who are rewarded well by the organisation are those who produce most, regardless of quality, then productivity (output) will be the focus of everyone's attention. If, on the other hand, quality is rewarded in preference to volume, then quality will be dominant.

Achievement of quality, particularly in the 'kaizen' (continuous improvement) sense, depends upon an appropriate level of innovation. Creativity (the origination and implementation of new ideas or innovations) is often suppressed in organisations in pursuit of the status quo. This is revealed through the use of such expressions as 'Don't rock the boat' or 'Yes, you're right, but in the interests of your career/overtime/colleagues . . . .'.

A lack of creativity in the organisation is more often a sign that it is stifled by the context than that the people themselves are not creative.

Hi tec demands high conformance

It is interesting to note the cultures that emerge in the unconventional world of the hi-tec companies. They often proclaim determination to throw over the norms and conventions of traditional organisations and reject the traditional notions of hierarchical structures, adherence to processes and normal working patterns. They abolish offices and, in some cases, install ball pits, football tables, plastic grass, pool tables, 'white spaces' for meetings and various other apparent innovations.

Sadly, the truth is that hierarchy will emerge in any society or form of organisation and that rather than existing in an organisation operating under Weberian rational-legal authority (the system of offices), they adopt an approach based on charismatic authority, i.e. one which depends upon the personal qualities of the leader(s). Hence we associate many of the successful hi-tec companies (Amazon, Apple, Microsoft, Facebook, Paypal) with individuals (Jeff Bezos, Steve Jobs, Bill Gates, Mark Zuckerberg, Elon Musk).

In order for an individual to survive and thrive in such an environment, he or she must adhere to the cultural norms. The binding, conforming effect of culture is often far stronger than that of rules and procedures. Heretics, non-believers, are no longer burned at the stake, but they will not survive.

Interestingly, as such organisations grow and mature, and particularly if they go through a financially challenging period, they will rapidly adopt the more conventional, rational-legal forms of organisation and the processes of all types that go with them.

It is always possible to run a skunk-works on a charismatic basis, but, as Pugh and Hickson (1989), citing Weber, point out:

> A bureaucratic organization is the most efficient form of organization possible. 'Precision, speed, unambiguity, reduction of friction and of material and personal costs – these are raised to the optimum in the strictly bureaucratic administration.'

Many of those characteristics reflect the aspirations of a quality management system and are, in a competitive market, the key to survival.

Large or successful organisations often emit a *hum* of satisfaction. They have an air of smugness, complacency and contentment with the way things are which can be almost tangible. This 'hum' comes through in their advertising, their websites and, often, in the patronising air of their customer service staff. Such a situation imposes an immense barrier to quality since there is no apparent compulsion or impetus for change. Frequently such satisfaction is present in organisations which have a short-term focus – perhaps a lack of foresight. They assume that if all is (or appears!) right in this period, then everything will surely be alright in the next. Disasters and near disasters frequently overtake such organisations.

Perhaps the best illustration of lack of foresight is given by Handy (1990: 7–8):

> I like the story of the Peruvian Indians who,
> seeing the sails of their Spanish invaders on
> the horizon put it down to a freak of the
> weather and went on about their business,
> having no concept of sailing ships in
> their limited experience. Assuming continuity,
> they screened out what did not fit and let
> disaster in. I like less the story that a frog if
> put in cold water will not bestir itself if
> that water is heated up slowly and gradually
> and will in the end let itself be boiled
> alive, too comfortable with continuity to
> realize that continuous change at some
> point becomes discontinuous and demands
> a change in behaviour.

In the prevailing turbulent business environment, an assumption of continuity is highly dangerous; there are global political shifts, new and emerging technologies, substantial challenges with regard to environmental protection and massively changing demographics. While pursuing quality with its implications of continuous improvement, standardisation and regularity, it is equally vital to be alert to the potential for discontinuous change, especially since strategic advantage may rest in such discontinuities.

The last barrier to quality which will be briefly explored under the general heading of culture is that of accountability. Achievement of quality requires that errors be acknowledged, rectified, and their sources tracked down and future error prevented.

In many organisations this process is inhibited by a sub-culture which adopts a penal attitude. The realisation of error is followed by a process of detection, prosecution – sometimes persecution – and punishment. This book is not the place for a debate on the societal value of such an approach, but it can be suggested that it is likely to be essentially negative in its effects. This may in turn lead to a situation where, as Deming (1982: 107) suggests, 'fear grips everyone'. In such a situation, errors may be suppressed or hidden. Where this is not possible, for example in manufacturing organisations, there will be a tendency to avoid punishment by blaming others and by a refusal to accept responsibility.

This barrier can be overcome by recognising that errors are normally opportunities for learning – the basis for modifying a process, system, skill or behaviour to inhibit or prevent future occurrences. Naturally there must be a limiting case, when the error is consciously or deliberately provoked, when those responsible must be found and an appropriate response generated. However, in most organisations, and in many circumstances, the cause of error can be traced to some failure in the design or execution of a process, in the training of the employee or in the equipment provided for the completion of the task. These aspects should be the first focus of attention and, in a quality organisation, will inhibit the use of disciplinary action. In many cases, though, they are the last. Managers often prefer to find someone to blame, perhaps because it is easier to do that than to accept responsibility for their own failure – from this approach arises the blame culture. For example, one organisation employed a group of administrative staff to operate a post office and administration system, servicing the needs of an off-site sales force. The salesmen rarely visited the office and relied heavily on the administrators to maintain diaries and timetable customer visits. An activity-based reward system meant that the sales force were absolutely reliant on the administrative system to ensure that they were paid the correct amount for the work done. Time lags in the system caused regular delays in payment. Work done was not paid for, and adventurous salesmen submitted claims for work which was incomplete, relying on the time lags to beat the system. Inevitably, problems arose in this operation. Members of the sales force began to fall behind with commitments; others received no pay at the end of certain months. After some delay, an administrator and two of the sales force left the organisation; their temporary contracts were not renewed due to poor performance. Today, no member of the workforce will take any action without at least one management signature. This ensures that they have to take no responsibility. The system, the driver of the problems, is unchanged.

3.3   Organisation design

When discussing organisation design, it is not simply the organisation structure – the classic pyramidal hierarchy, or more recently the very flat organisation chart – which is to be considered. It must also incorporate the interactions between units, the information and management systems and their total inter-relatedness. As Beer (1985: i) suggests, the organisation chart may be seen as 'frozen out of history', revealing who to blame when things go wrong but not showing how the organisation actually works. A number of barriers to achievement of quality can be found in this area.

The first, and most frequent, error is institutionalised conflict. This occurs when an organisation (or its performance management system) has been designed in such a way that conflict between quality and some other characteristic, such as productivity, is inherent. This is commonly found where the Quality Control or Assurance Manager reports to the Production Manager. In such a case, the need to meet customer orders will often override the need to achieve quality standards. In effect, the Quality Manager is redundant since no value is added to the operation of the organisation by his or her presence. Flood (1993: 210–221) reports how when production fell short of customer orders at Tarty Bakeries, the production manager would pass as acceptable output which had already been rejected by the quality inspectors.

This situation, replicated in many organisations, presents a major barrier to quality. A structure must be created in which the quality function is independent of the production function and, as shall be seen, where quality is inherent in the product, the process and, importantly, the culture. This leads to a situation where rather than rejects and errors being 'inspected out', quality can be 'baked in' to the product.

The second barrier to quality in this context is the design of the organisation's information systems. This does not simply mean the computerised management or executive information system, but the whole of the data generation and capture, data processing and information reporting activity of the organisation, both formal and informal. These activities must generate the right information, in the right format, at the right time and deliver it to the right decision maker(s) if it is to be of any benefit. Vitally, the information itself must be presented in a way that informs the decisions that managers need to make. Most frequently, users of information spend much time analysing and discussing historical errors whilst paying little attention to the current situation and none to the future. While they may be criticised for this, it is as much a function of the design of the information system as a matter of managerial desire. Hindsight is always 20-20, and a common requirement in organisations is for managers to explain what went wrong, to justify mistakes and failures. Such organisations are attempting to manage their past and not their future, perhaps because they find this easier to do – a little like driving a car by looking in the rear view mirror to see where you have been!

The informal system refers to communication through devices such as Unions and other staff bodies, and the grapevine. Beer (1985: 58–59) encourages this informal communication between functions, which may be concerned with immediate operational matters such as the timing of the next batch of a product, or with longer-term issues such as competition for capital. However he specifically sees this communication as supplementary to and not in the place of the formal systems. Beckford (1993: 300–323) shows how the Union and the grapevine were perceived by both management and staff as the most reliable information sources in an organisation. It is worth making the point at this stage that managers cannot stop communication within an organisation. Data will find a means of transmission whatever barriers are placed in the way, but the organisation will only be effective if the communication channels are properly designed.

Another aspect of this information system is performance measurement. Briefly recapping on section 3.1, performance measurement tends to determine which aspects of the organisation will be perceived as important. Those characteristics or outputs which are measured will be the focus of the workforce; those which are not measured will likely be ignored. Thus the design of the measurement system, its prime content and the way its outputs are responded to by managers, may be expected to drive the performance of the organisation.

Similarly, many organisations operate with no formal measurement system at all; everything is done by 'gut feel' and rule of thumb. In these circumstances, quality simply cannot be known to have been achieved since, even if it has been defined, it is not being measured. As the conversation goes in Alice in Wonderland (Carroll, 1866):

ALICE 'Would you tell me, please, which way I ought to walk from here?'
CHESHIRE CAT 'That depends a good deal on where you want to get to,'
ALICE 'I don't much care where,'
CHESHIRE CAT 'Then it doesn't matter which way you walk,'
ALICE 'So long as I get *somewhere*,'

An appropriate form and degree of measurement is vital. That is enough to know what is happening but not so much that the 'measured' feel burdened or oppressed by the system, since in such a case they may seek to pervert the results. Perhaps, as Beer (1985: 102) proposes in the context of autonomy, we should have as much measurement 'as guarantees cohesion. . .'.

The next barrier to quality is one of the understanding and articulation of roles in the organisation. This is particularly so amongst the staff involved in the control and development functions, such as general management, marketing, human resource management, accounting, strategic planning and so on. There is a tendency amongst many such staff to delve down into the operations of the organisation, perhaps taking direct control when errors occur or the unexpected happens. While doing so they will be neglecting their own roles within the organisation. This 'fire-fighting' or 'crisis' style of management is seen in many organisations as heroic, with plaudits and awards handed to those who perform in this way. However, as the apocryphal saying goes:

> when you are up to your armpits in alligators, it's easy to forget that the original objective was to drain the swamp.

Solving today's crisis is extremely important, but, as suggested by Senge (1990: 15), that is to deal with 'symptoms not underlying causes'. A low level intervention by senior management will rarely address the root, or fundamental cause, of the problem, and *that* is their proper role, not to deal with operational matters. The operational managers must be allowed the freedom and given the support to solve their own problems. If senior management continually intervene in a junior manager's daily problem solving activity, two things will occur. First, the junior manager will never learn to solve his or her own problems, thus reducing organisational effectiveness and increasing costs. Second, the senior manager's work will never get done and consequently the organisation will hurtle out of control into the nearest obstacle because nobody is watching where it is going.

The final barrier which we will explore in this section is that of irrelevant, or inappropriate, activities. This section is titled 'Organisation design'. Frequently the truth is that an organisation has not been designed; it has grown and undergone metamorphoses almost of its own accord. Many features of an established organisation – whether they be structural, such as department or units; organisational, that is activities and procedures; or cultural and attitudinal – have not been not intentionally and deliberately created. Often they just grow. They arise, perhaps to support some long forgotten or superseded purpose of the organisation and are simply never stopped. Cases are common where procedures have become institutionalised and carried on for years. In one example a Manager once requested a particular report which had to be produced by hand. That the Manager had long since moved on (and retired) and no further request had ever been received for the report was not seen as a reason for stopping, 'after all, you never know'! Equally, that a computerised version of the same report was available had not been noticed and 'anyway, the technology is unreliable'.

A similar process occurs with what, in Business Process Re-engineering (Hammer & Champy, 1993), are known as cowpaths. These are the routes through an organisation which develop naturally without the purposeful intervention of the staff. A procedure in use may never have been the subject of deliberate design; it may have simply developed and its users become accustomed to it, complete with all its unique peculiarities and foibles. Such processes, often developed around the talents and skills of individuals, become the 'norm' but are often inefficient, sometimes ineffective; everybody complains about them, but they are seen as nobody's responsibility.

These cowpaths and inappropriate processes may well present barriers to the achievement of quality, since they are an 'unconscious' part of the organisation and their quality inhibiting properties may not be recognised.

3.4 Management perspectives

Management perspective does not simply refer to the attitude to quality, but to the whole management ethos of the organisation as it impacts on quality – a subject which was touched upon in the previous chapter. The issue of corporate politics has already been raised in section 3.1 so will not be covered again here.

In order for an appropriate attitude to be developed to quality, then quality must be recognised as an issue. This means that the current status of a product or service must be openly acknowledged. Frequently, companies adopt an ostrich like attitude to quality – they find it easier to blame poor performance on a host of other reasons. For example, when a previously successful sales performance declines, a common reaction is to focus on market changes, the sales team or activity by competitors rather than on the product or service itself. Issues such as pricing and margins are often raised, perhaps leading to a focus on manufacturing performance in terms of productivity. Rarely is quality of product or service considered as a potentially primary issue at the outset.

It is essential that quality be treated as a potential part of the problem and be considered as a possible cause of decline. Even where a company is performing well, a positive attitude to quality needs to be developed and maintained. A product which is considered 'good enough' probably is not in today's competitive markets. There is no room for such complacency. The motor industry has over the last 40 years fully embraced this idea with every successive generation of vehicles being 'better' in all respects than its predecessor and where a manufacturer gets this wrong – as they will from time to time – the market punishes them by not buying the product.

A further barrier to achievement of quality is a focus on short-term results; that is the result in a particular shift, day, week, quarter or even year. Often salary or wage packages and performance bonuses are related directly to short-term performance. Therefore currently acceptable performance parameters are used as a reason (or excuse) for not addressing the issue of quality. While not necessarily so, it is often the case that a focus on quality, or any other major change programme, will lead to a short-term decline in performance (particularly of productivity) whilst staff and management adjust to changes – this is known as a 'hockey stick' effect. This may be related to a complete change of emphasis, where achieving quality of output needs to override, perhaps for the first time, achieving quantity of output. The change required in management attitudes is fundamental, away from pure productivity to productivity with quality. After all, output which is rejected, either internally or by the customer, cannot really be considered as output at all – it is waste.

Thus a major barrier to achieving quality may be built in to the reward system of the organisation. This can only be overcome by changing that system – it cannot be overcome through exhortations, evangelism, penal action or statistical measurement. Effective change may mean negotiating fresh terms with a variety of stakeholders in the enterprise, from the workforce and their bonus system, to the shareholders or providers of equity and loan capital whose short-term interests may be affected and will need to be addressed.

Management often focuses on 'output today at all costs'. No real concern with or interest in quality is evident. In order to boost performance, a focus is maintained exclusively on current output. In the event of an apparent or expected shortfall in output, the rate of production is increased in an attempt to compensate. Such increases are usually doomed to failure unless the system of production itself is addressed.

A food factory case study highlights the problem. The production lines had an established level of throughput for each of their various product lines, an optimal rate at which the equipment and operators could cope, and a 'satisfactory compromise' was reached between productivity and quality. The established or recorded reject rate, with which the management were quite content, was 10%.

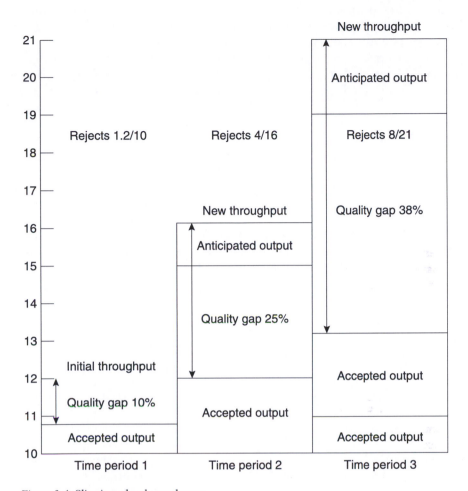

Figure 3.1 Slipping clutch syndrome.

In the event that production was likely to fall short of customer orders, the throughput rate across the product range would be increased from an average of twelve units per minute to an average of sixteen units per minute. It was assumed by the factory management that this would give a net increase of around 33% in output over the running time compared to optimal rate running. In practice, an increase of only about 10% was achieved, the balance of additional throughput being rejected for failing to achieve the required quality standard. Naturally, the management's reaction was to speed up the process even further, seeking to gain the elusive extra output. Figure 3.1 shows the effect of *slipping clutch syndrome* diagrammatically.

While portrayed for the sake of simplicity as a step change, in practice, the quality gap widened on a progressive basis with every small increase in output. The greater the throughput, the greater the reject rate, every increase in running speed generating an ever reducing increase in acceptable output. One other major factor in this case was that the necessary work rate of the individual members of staff had to increase in line with the speed of the production belt – something which would not generally be sustainable regardless of the quality issue. The major solution applied in this particular case was to reduce throughput and thereby reduce the quality gap, ensuring that operators had sufficient time with each unit to reach the appropriate quality standard. A series of other measures were also taken – simply changing production rates was not the entire solution to the subject company's quality problems.

Each of the barriers highlighted in this section reflects a common mindset on the part of management. That mindset is called reductionism, the belief that anything can be understood by continually breaking it down into parts, breaking the parts down into further parts – and so on – this is often called an analytical approach. The reductionist mindset seeks individual causes for individual effects and reflects the mechanistic thinking which has dominated Western science.

Contemporary thinking suggests that a holistic approach to problem solving is more effective. That is one which deals with systems as wholes, which recognises the inter-relationships and inter-dependencies between parts of a system, which acknowledges that fixing one part of a system will not necessarily improve the whole and might even make it worse! Such an approach broadens the attack on a problem by widening the scope of enquiry to study also those factors which influence it – its inputs – as well as considering the consequences of any changes – the effect on outputs. For example, simply replacing the tyres on a motor car, whilst potentially improving grip, will do little or nothing to improve the overall performance of the car.

3.5   Costs of quality

The last issue to be briefly explored in this chapter is the costs of quality. This means the direct and invisible costs unnecessarily incurred by any organisation which does not have an effective quality system in place – what Ohno calls 'muda' or 'waste'. Direct costs means those costs arising as a result of the non-achievement of quality and visibly attributable to that fact. Invisible costs means those costs arising in the organisation as a result of not achieving quality but not visibly attributable to that fact – those where the relationship between non-quality and the cost may not have been discerned by the organisation.

Any production system for a product or service which is not designed to achieve the quality standard 'first time, every time' will incur rework and rectification costs. These are the costs of putting right errors, performing again a particular task or disassembling and reassembling (or scrapping) a product. Traditionally such costs have been treated by organisations as part of the overall cost of production, and a percentage is included in the price of every item sold for the ones that go wrong. Thus acceptance of error is institutionalised, carefully hidden but properly accounted for – surely this makes everybody happy!

In the era of quality, with lean production systems and just-in-time delivery, with very fine margins being eroded in highly competitive markets, these costs need to be uncovered and reduced if not eradicated. They must be challenged, not accepted. All processes receive inputs in the form of either materials or information from prior steps in the chain. That is to say that each process is the customer of either an internal or external supplier. If the inputs received are defective, then costs may be incurred in a number of ways.

The first way, and potentially the most damaging, is that entire consignments have to be returned, holding up or stopping production and leading to unfilled orders and lost revenue. A common answer to this is to increase holding stocks (ensuring that there is sufficient to cover a break in supply). Such an approach simply increases stocking costs, reducing the supply of working capital available to the organisation and inhibiting its overall performance – it does nothing to solve the quality problem.

The second way is that costs are incurred validating the quality of goods or information received before it is processed. Inspecting out supplier failures is simply to absorb part of the supplier's operating cost. Why would you do that? Costs can also be incurred by not inspecting goods received, leading to the use of defective parts or information at the next stage of production. This ensures that the final product will also fail, leading back to rework and rectification.

A third way is that goods received are inspected and defective parts rectified before use. This again generates cost which should have been incurred by the supplier. I recently heard of a major premium motor manufacturer receiving completed, painted body panels from a supplier which it was scrapping because the paint finish was defective. To 'solve' this, they had engaged another supplier to rectify the paintwork. This neither solves the problem (which needs to be addressed by the original supplier) nor reduces the costs!

Inspection, as an auditing activity, can never be completely eradicated. Reports generated by inspection provide higher level management with information necessary for them to control and develop the operation. However, inspection is most commonly used as the quality mechanism, the one procedure which attempts to ensure that products and services are being provided at the agreed level. For such an approach to quality to work, it requires at least a statistically valid sampling approach, and 100% confidence requires 100% inspection, an impossible task in nearly all industries. Although frequently attempted, this is rarely successful and always inordinately expensive. It is often impractical. Beckford (1993: 308) refers to an inspection system with a notional target of 100% – in practice 5% was supposedly achieved. The target figure was not practical given throughput, and was in any case irrelevant, since the product to be inspected was sealed into a plastic bag, inside a cardboard box – the only inspection was of the box, provided by an independent external supplier, not the product!

The level of inspection can be significantly reduced where quality is inherent in both the product and the process. Effective auditing can be substituted. This has a direct impact on both the cost of the activity and its utility.

Invisible costs are much harder to identify and specify, but are nonetheless incurred when quality has not been addressed properly. They may include:

- Dissatisfied customers who fulfil future needs with an alternative supplier;
- Customer site service and maintenance costs, often operated as a separate business division. The costs of customer service are very often driven by the inadequacies and failures of the design and manufacturing process;
- In-process rework costs (costs incurred by remaking unfinished products within a process). Beckford (1993: 300–323) reports a case where the reported reject figure of 10% ignored in-process rectification which amounted to a further 25% of throughput;
- High staff turnover leading to increased recruitment and training costs as a result of dissatisfied staff leaving;
- Capital costs for equipment and warehousing to provide for rectification of defective parts and storage of additional materials;
- Reduced availability of internal working capital, leading to unnecessary reliance on loan/overdraft capital (i.e. increased gearing).

Such costs are rarely attributed directly to the quality issue. However, they are in an interdependent relationship with all the other factors of the business and so to a large extent they are related to and driven by quality.

Summary

This chapter has reviewed a number of the barriers to quality, looking particularly at the issues of systems and procedures, culture, organisation design and management approach. The chapter concluded with a brief look at some of the costs of quality.

KEY LEARNING POINTS

Four principal barriers to quality: Systems & procedures, Culture, Organisation design, Management perspectives

Systems & procedures:
supporting or inhibiting the pursuit of quality?

Culture:
attitudes, values & beliefs. Is the culture supportive of quality?

Organisation design:
does the organisation design support or inhibit quality achievement?

Management perspectives:
is quality recognised as a problem? Is the focus right for achieving quality? Is the mindset holistic or reductionist?

Two categories of quality cost:
Direct, Invisible

Direct costs:
Rework, Rectification, Defective inputs, Inspection.

Invisible costs include:
Lost customers, in-process errors, high staff turnover, unnecessary capital costs, reduced availability of working capital.

Question

Identify barriers to quality in your own organisation; consider what might be done to overcome them.

4 The emergence of management

'Management is the art of getting things done through others'

Mary Parker Follett (attrib), 2016

Introduction

This chapter introduces the principal models that still appear to govern much management activity. The formal study of management has only emerged as a discipline in its own right over the last hundred or so years – indeed it is still considered by many (particularly practising managers) as being at least as much 'black art' as science. Theoretical and practical development of the discipline have more or less paralleled the emergence of the major corporations – though it is evident that many are still managed according to a Taylorist-Weberian model, i.e. scientistic and bureaucratic. Prior to the emergence of the joint-stock company and the industrial revolution, permanent large scale organisations (other than states, which were often extremely volatile) were limited to the various churches and the standing armies and navies of the wealthier nations. The majority of the workforce were either agricultural labourers living at not much better than a subsistence standard of living, land-owning farmers, tradesmen and craftsmen or professionals such as doctors and lawyers.

Following the industrial revolution, agricultural workers were drawn from the country to the towns and cities to improve their standard of living, often becoming factory workers. The increasing size of such organisations (and the increasing wealth and desire to pursue other interests of the factory owners) created the opportunity for the emergence of the professional manager – those whose job it is to oversee and supervise the activities of the workers on behalf of owners. The need to manage these large scale organisations and the drive for additional profitability can be interpreted as having given impetus to the study of management. The development of early management theories is the topic of the next sections.

The principal early models in organisation (or management) theory are the 'Classical', also known as the Traditional or Rational, and the 'Human Relations'. These two approaches have their own particular strengths and weaknesses, and these will be explored. These theories are considered to some extent as the causes of many quality problems and as being reflected in the dominant quality models which will be considered in the next part of the book.

4.1 Classical theory

The classical or 'machine' (Morgan, 1986: 20) model of organisation reflects the supposed scientific management approach developed by Frederick Taylor (1911), the classical theory of Henri Fayol (1916) and Max Weber's Bureaucracy Theory (1924). These collectively still dominate mainstream management thinking. Each seems to regard the design of organisations as a technical exercise only and depends upon the reduction (fragmentation or dissection) of an organisation into its component parts for analysis and redesign for efficient operation.

The 'machine' approaches to organisation arose in the late 19th and early 20th centuries and may be considered as logical extensions of the advances then being made in machine technology. Machines are, in general, designed to perform specified tasks at known input/output rates and within specified tolerances; these management approaches assume that organisations can be similarly designed.

Frederick Taylor's Scientific Management (Taylor, 1911) is based on four key principles (see Box 4.1) of scientific task design, scientific selection, management–worker co-operation and equal division of work.

Huczynski and Buchanan (2013) see Taylor's objectives as being first, to improve efficiency by increasing output and reducing 'underworking', what Taylor described as 'natural soldiering' and 'systematic soldiering'. Second, Taylor sought to achieve 'standardisation of job performance, by dividing tasks up into small and closely specified sub tasks'. Finally, to instil discipline, 'by establishing hierarchical authority and introducing a system whereby all management's policy decisions could be implemented'.

Whilst Taylor recognised that the worker in a given situation had a 'mass of rule of thumb or traditional knowledge', which constituted his 'principal asset or possession', he had a poor view of the capabilities and intelligence of the worker. For example, he believed that:

> the science of handling pig iron is so great and amounts to so much that it is impossible for the man who is best suited to this type of work to understand the principles of this science, or even to work in accordance with these principles without the aid of a man better educated than he is.

Taylor interpreted the organisation as a machine, capable of being specified, designed and controlled by management to achieve a given purpose. The workmen were viewed as selectable to become standardised machine parts, interchangeable with every other of like design and to be used at the sole discretion of management. Users of 'competency frameworks' for selection and development of staff may at this point want to reflect on

---

Box 4.1   Principles of scientific management

Frederick Taylor:

'. . . develop a science for each element of a man's work, which replaces the old rule of thumb method'.

'. . . scientifically select and then train, teach and develop the workman, whereas in the past he chose his own work and trained himself as best he could'.

'. . . heartily co-operate with the men so as to insure all of the work being done in accordance with the principles of the science which has been developed'.

ensure that '. . . There is an almost equal division of the work and the responsibility between the management and the workmen. The management take over all the work for which they are better fitted than the workmen, while in the past almost all of the work and the greater part of the responsibility were thrown upon the men'.

the similarities to scientific management. His approach was later followed by Gilbreth and Gantt who both attempted to humanise Scientific Management, recognising the need for rest (Gilbreth) and human needs and dignity (Gantt). Taylor's key assumption that the worker was principally motivated by money was retained, and this assumption still underpins management thinking in many organisations.

Henri Fayol (1916) used the 'machine' metaphor in writing that:

> The body corporate of a concern is often compared with a machine or plant or animal. The expressions, 'administrative machine', 'administrative gearing', suggest an organism obeying the drive of its head and having all of its effectively interrelated parts move in unison towards the same end, and that is excellent.

This perception of the excellence of the 'machine' view is evident in his proposals for organising and managing. He proposed that 'to organise a business is to provide it with everything useful to its functioning: raw materials, tools, capital, personnel' and saw six sets of activities as producing the organisation: Technical, Commercial, Financial, Security, Accounting and Managerial. Fayol's proposed duties of managers reinforce this view; these are given in Box 4.2.

Box 4.2   Duties of managers

Henri Fayol:

To ensure that the plan is judiciously prepared and strictly carried out.

See that the human and material organisation is consistent with the objectives, resources and requirements of the concern.

Set up a single, competent, energetic guiding authority.

Harmonise activities and co-ordinate efforts.

Formulate clear, distinct, precise decisions.

Arrange for efficient selection – each department must be headed by a competent, energetic man, each employee must be in that place where he can render greatest service.

Define duties clearly.

Encourage a liking for initiative and responsibility.

Have fair and suitable recompense for services rendered.

Make use of sanctions against faults and errors.

See to the maintenance of discipline.

Ensure that individual interests are subordinated to the general interest.

Pay special attention to unity of command.

Supervise both human and material order.

Have everything under control.

Fight against excess of regulation, red tape and paper control.

Box 4.3   Principles of management

Henri Fayol:

Division of work (specialisation)

Authority

Discipline

Unity of Command

Unity of Direction

Subordination (the interest of the organisation is more important than that of the individual)

Remuneration

Centralisation (a question of continuously varying proportion)

Scalar chain

Order

Equity

Stability of tenure

Initiative

Esprit de corps

The managerial duties reflect Fayol's fourteen principles of management shown in Box 4.3.

Some of these managerial duties and principles of management appear to conflict with the machine view and with each other. For example, 'Define duties clearly' and 'Encourage a liking for initiative and responsibility', or 'specialisation' and 'initiative', the first of which in each case would appear to preclude or at least make the second more difficult.

The admonition to managers to 'fight against excess of regulation, red tape and paper control' stands in sharp contrast to his view that the work should be 'clearly divided, judiciously planned and strictly carried out', aspects which carry with them an implication of machine like precision and heavy reliance on record keeping.

The overall impression remains that Fayol, like Taylor, viewed the organisation as a machine. The management were responsible for forecasting, planning, organising, commanding, co-ordinating and controlling whilst the 'workers', distinguished by 'technical ability characteristic of the business', were component parts to be fitted into the machine at the most appropriate place with 'a place for everyone and everyone in his place'.

Max Weber's 'Bureaucracy Theory' (1924) developed from his views of three types of legitimate authority in organisations: rational, traditional and charismatic. Traditional authority rests on established acceptance of a natural order of society – the rulers and the ruled, perhaps reflecting the idea of monarchy. Charismatic authority rests on the personal devotion of individuals to a particular leader. Both of these styles of management exist in organisations today. For example, traditional authority is found in many of the patriarchal family owned businesses of Asia, while charismatic authority may be considered as the style of organisations such as Google, Amazon, Apple and some religious organisations. Rational authority, control through a bureaucracy system of offices, has come to dominate most organisations.

Rational authority was seen by Weber (cited in Pugh, 1990: 3–13) as representing legal authority, with 'obedience owed to the legally established impersonal order'. He considered that the 'purest type of exercise of legal authority is that which employs a bureaucratic

Box 4.4   Principles of bureaucracy

Max Weber:

Specialisation:	Each office (or 'bureau') has a defined area of expertise;
Hierarchy:	Supervision and control of lower offices by higher ones;
Rules:	Exhaustive, stable rules, learned by all;
Impersonality:	Equality of treatment for all according to the rules;
Appointment:	Selection according to competence not election;
Full-time:	Occupation of office as the primary task of the individual;
Career:	Promotion, tenure and seniority within the system;
Segregation:	The official activity is distinct from the private individual.

administrative staff', and that bureaucracy was not simply desirable but indispensable to cope with the complexities of organisations at that time. He considered that the increasing general technical knowledge had as a consequence a need for an increase in the particular technical knowledge of individuals, in order for them to effectively administer an organisation.

A bureaucracy was seen by Weber as being composed of a hierarchical organisation of 'offices' (or bureaux), each acting according to the rules and norms of the organisation within a specified area of competence. Individuals within this structure were appointed on rational grounds to perform a specified function, without gaining rights to that appointment or having ownership of the organisation. All decisions, rules and acts were to be recorded in writing in order, together with the 'continuous organisation of official functions', to 'constitute the office'. Weber saw a clear choice in organisations between 'bureaucracy and dilettantism' and proposed that bureaucracy was an inevitable requirement to support large organisations.

The machine view is evident again in this case, Weber proposing that every function and every act of every office is capable of being specified to an exact degree. People were clearly viewed as functionaries within the bureaucracy, bringing no human element to the conduct of the affairs of the organisation.

4.2   Critical review

Several assumptions about the world and organisational life seem to underlie these three rational views of organisation. These need to be stated before considering their strengths and weaknesses.

The first assumption is that an organisation can be regarded as isolated from the influence of and interaction with its environment. While this may have been an acceptable view in a fast growing, producer–led economy, it clearly cannot be considered appropriate in con-sumer–led, low–growth and highly competitive markets. Despite the observations of Galbraith (1974) concerning producer dominance, organisations must respond to the needs and demands of external stakeholders if they are to survive. In the mature, post–industrial economies, enabled by instant communications and ready access to global sources of information, the informed consumer genuinely does have the potential to determine the fate of organisations. Any organisation which does not respond to changes in its environment, whether that be the market, economic, political or technological changes, will soon fail. Intelligent organisations co–evolve with their environments, each influencing the other. An internally focused organisation does not have the capability to respond in this way. In *The*

Intelligent Organisation (2016) Beckford talks of the almost symbiotic relationship between the organisation and its environment; the 'machine' view clashes with that.

The second assumption is that an improvement in the performance of a part of the organisation will necessarily improve the performance of the whole. There appears to be some merit in this idea at the purely mechanical level – the repair or replacement of a defective part will possibly generate some restoration of the intended performance level – but that is not an improvement. However the approach ignores inter-dependence within the organisation. This means that the whole will only perform at the level of the weakest or slowest part. Similarly, the idea of 'emergent properties' is ignored – the conception that the whole may be more than the sum of the parts and that it may exhibit characteristics as a whole that do not exist in any of the parts. These characteristics cannot be addressed except by considering the capacity for interaction. The ideas of systemic thinking will be pursued explicitly in parts three and four. It was suggested in chapter 1 that quality is not an issue which can be isolated but must be pursued systemically, organisation wide; the classical model of organisation cannot cope with this need.

The third assumption is that the organisation must be studied only from the perspective of the goals of management. Later studies have shown that true organisational effectiveness depends on the co-operation of many parties to the organisation. Commonly called 'stakeholders', these parties include owners, employees, customers, suppliers and those outside the organisation who are affected by its activities and behaviour. The contemporary concept of 'good corporate citizenship', expressed through the emergent literature on Corporate Social Responsibility, recognises the need for organisations to take account of the wishes of the community in which they exist. This assumption is further challenged by continuing changes in the ISO standard(s), which now sees the customer as the focus of organisational performance and, as mentioned above, the behaviour of sophisticated, informed consumers.

The final assumption is that an organisation can be designed and understood in 'machine' terms. It can be created to perform a given task and once designed need not be adapted. Operating in a global economy which is best characterised as turbulent and dynamic and subject to rapid changes in technology and customer expectations, any organisation which cannot adapt reasonably readily cannot expect to survive.

Each of these assumptions has been challenged through developments in thinking about organisations and in ideas about human well-being since the 1920s. Practical experience of using the model in organisations has also shown that the assumptions are flawed.

4.3   Reiteration

Flood & Jackson (1991: 8–9) provide a useful summary of the 'machine' view. They consider that it is useful in practice when the organisation operates in a stable environment, performing a straightforward task, such as repetitive production of a single product and when the 'human parts' are prepared to follow 'machine-like' commands. They suggest that its usefulness is limited since it reduces the adaptability of organisations, and the 'mindless contribution' is difficult to maintain with 'mindful parts', leading to dehumanisation or conflict.

The strengths of the model are:

- systematic, methodical analysis of specific tasks;
- assistance in establishing order in organisations;
- a useful guide to creating organisations where demands on individuals need to be precise or exact, for example in the nuclear industry or multiple-outlet operations such as banks.

Its weaknesses are thought of as:

- its failure to recognise environmental interaction;
- failure to acknowledge the interdependence of parts;
- no inherent capacity for adaptation;
- the model is static not dynamic;
- people are 'dehumanised';
- goals are inherent in the design;
- the focus on control may encourage inefficiency;
- it cannot help with informal or virtual organisations such as network arrangements, which are increasingly common;
- it is diagnostic but not prescriptive.

It can be seen then that whilst the machine view offers some assistance, its weaknesses are such that it must be considered an inadequate approach for managers today. The impact of this thinking on quality will be considered in section 4.7.

4.4   Human relations theory

Whilst benefits could and may still be obtained from the rational approaches, their lack of humanity is demonstrated by the difficulties which emerge during their application with the people involved. The human relations model of organisation emerged as a means of addressing these difficulties and was the first significant challenge to the 'machine' view.

The 'organic' or 'organism' (Morgan, 1986: 39–76) analogy stems from the origins of modern systems thinking in the biological sciences and attempts to deal with attainment of survival of the system or organisation rather than achievement of particular goals. While survival may be seen as a legitimate goal, it may not sufficiently represent the purpose of the organisation. This organic view first found expression in organisations through what has become known as the Human Relations Model. This considers that attention must be paid to the human aspects of organisation and gives primacy to the roles, needs and expectations of the human participants. Particular emphasis is given to issues of motivation, management style and participation as critical success factors.

The 'Hawthorne' studies of Roethlisberger and Dickson with Mayo (Mayo, 1949) may be interpreted as an early systems approach to management (Flood & Carson, 1988). Although they were originally focused on the application of scientific management principles, the findings led away from this perspective. They later recognised the need to capture and understand the relatedness of all the parts involved. Later work in this field by Maslow (1970) and Herzberg et al (1959) did not adopt the systemic perspective. These later developments still adopt a reductionist and 'closed system' view of the organisation, concentrating on improving the performance of parts not the whole and emphasising internal rather than external influences on the organisation.

Mayo (op. cit.) argued that:

> In modern large-scale industry the three persistent problems of management are:-
> - The application of science and technical skill to some material good or product;
> - The systematic ordering of operations;
> - The organisation of teamwork – that is, of sustained co-operation.

Following Chester Barnard (1938), Mayo reported findings suggesting that the first two of these would operate to make an industry effective, the third to make it efficient. He considered that the application of science and technical skill and the systematic ordering of operations were attended to, the first by continuous experiment, the second being already well developed in practice. He saw the third element as neglected but necessary if the organisation as a whole was to be successful.

Mayo became involved in the Hawthorne studies after they had examined the effects on workers of changes in the physical environment. Experiments had shown that social and psychological factors were present, and the studies became focused on these human issues. Records were kept of every aspect of changes made and their impact to establish a 'systemic' view. Further experiments were conducted and followed by formal interviews which revealed that many of the particular organisation's difficulties related to emotional rather than rational conditions. Further experiment showed that informal group pressures had more influence on output and performance than the economic pressures of the formal organisation.

While a later review of Mayo's work by Stewart (2009) has cast doubt upon the veracity of the Hawthorne studies, they are generally credited with having discovered the importance of groups in organisations, the influence of the observer on the observed and the need to ensure that the goals and objectives of staff are not in conflict with those of the organisation. Notwithstanding subsequent criticisms of the research methodology and interpretation of the findings, the studies are generally seen as the foundations of the human relations approach.

Maslow (1970), whilst seeing that the 'individual is an integrated, organised whole', proposed a hierarchy of human needs. These needs were: physiological (food and health), safety (security), belongingness and love (the need to belong to a group), esteem (the need to be valued by oneself and others) and self-actualisation (the need to be all that one can be). He suggested that the needs were all contained within each other such that 'if one need is satisfied then another emerges', although the satisfied need remains present.

Maslow's 'Hierarchy of Needs' is usually presented as in Figure 4.1.

Frederick Herzberg et al (1959), in his studies of motivation in the industrial and commercial context, built upon the foundation laid by Maslow. Through a series of observations and interviews with samples of people at work, he found that two sets of

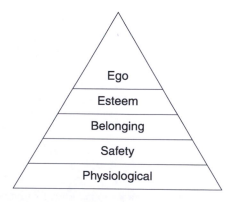

Figure 4.1 Maslow's hierarchy of needs.

factors influenced the level of motivation. These were the 'hygiene' and 'motivating' factors discussed in chapter 2. Briefly, 'hygiene' factors concerned the maintenance of conditions that were conducive to satisfaction. If satisfactory conditions did not pertain, then the worker would be dissatisfied with his job position; conversely, achievement of a satisfactory standard would not positively motivate. Positive motivation would be derived from 'motivators', factors which were seen as actively encouraging an increased contribution, and these tend to be unique to each individual. These factors were summarised in chapter 2, Figure 2.1.

Herzberg concluded that in order for organisations to achieve improved levels of performance, they must address both types of factor. He considered that 'good hygiene will prevent many of the negative results of low morale', but this on its own was not enough, suggesting: 'our emphasis should be on the strengthening of motivators'. This he saw as being achieved by restructuring jobs, providing workers with some degree of control over their achievement, meaningful job rotation, selection of staff to match the needs of the task, effective supervision through planning, organising and support (a link with Taylor's work) and appropriate participation.

Finally, Herzberg recognised that 'there are large segments of our society to which these prescriptions cannot possibly apply'. He considered that these people could obtain a good life from 'fruitful hobbies and improved lives outside the job', and that 'the greatest fulfilment of man is to be found in activities related to his own needs as well as those of society'.

4.5   Critical review

Again, several assumptions about the world and people seem to underpin the Human Relations approaches to organisation, some of which represent a major shift in thinking from the machine view. From the organisation design perspective, the influence of the environment is still largely neglected, and there continues to be a focus on improving the performance of parts rather than the whole.

The first major shift, and perhaps the most significant, is the assumption that people may be motivated by rewards from work other than money. This assumption is of great significance in mature economies, where ever rising salaries and wages are not a realistic prospect. If motivation is to be maintained in such circumstances, it is vital that managers recognise this assumption and discover which characteristics of the work and its environment are likely to stimulate staff.

The second assumption is concerned with the abilities of people. Whereas the machine view largely suggests limited ability and finite competence, the human relations view acknowledges much greater, albeit variable, competence and encourages a greater degree of autonomy and flexibility. It stresses delegation of decision making and enrichment of jobs, in direct contrast to the simplification associated with classical theory.

4.6   Reiteration

The Human Relations model gives primacy to the role of the people in the organisation and suggests ways of increasing their satisfaction. However, it does nothing for the achievement of the objectives of the organisation and says little about how the complex tasks of the organisation could be structured.

Flood & Jackson (1991: 10) consider that the 'organic' view is of practical value when there is an open relationship with the environment, when survival or adaptation needs are predominant and when the environment is complex. They believe that the Human Relations view fails. First, because it does not recognise that organisations are socially constructed phenomena which, it can be argued, need to be understood from the perspective of the participants. Second, because the emphasis is on harmonious relations, whereas conflict and coercion are often present. Third, because change is often environmentally driven, rather than driven by the organisation itself.

The principal strength of the 'organic' model is the emphasis that it places on the human element of organisations, recognising that people are not 'machine' parts but individuals who have needs and desires.

There are, though, a number of weaknesses in this approach that make it inadequate for the needs of contemporary managers. Firstly, notwithstanding the warning from Herzberg that human needs could be and, for some people, need to be met outside the workplace, the assumption underlying many applications of the Human Relations approach is that these needs must be met at work. A corollary to this in the 21st century is that technology is enabling continuous connectivity of the individual to the workplace such that, for some, they are never 'not at work'. This shift may have profound implications for individuals and organisations.

Secondly, the Human Relations model does not allow for the supremacy of organisational goals and objectives, its needs driven by technology, or the operating environment, over human goals and needs. Such supremacy may be necessary to ensure the survival of the organisation. Finally, the model does not assist with the specifics of designing and structuring organisations to cope with the complex tasks faced by contemporary managers nor with the interface of the organisation with its environment.

This 'organic' view, whilst offering some significant advantages over the 'machine' view, still appears inadequate.

4.7   Relevance to quality

The Classical and Human Relations theories of management have relevance to quality for a number of reasons. First they remain the dominant approaches to management in many cultures and contexts. They retain this dominance because they do have considerable value and appear to offer simple, fast solutions to management problems while serving to support the currently powerful groups in organisations. Second many management schools and training organisations do not teach the more contemporary and arguably radical ideas, rejecting them in favour of the traditional approaches. It must be acknowledged that in a newly developing country where the workforce are perhaps unfamiliar with the concept of having a job, the highly disciplined and somewhat autocratic styles which fit with the traditional view of organisation may offer advantages in the short term. In more sophisticated contexts, this is unlikely to be the case and may indeed be directly damaging to the organisation.

The football match – Reductio ad absurdum

Imagine for a moment a football match played according to the method of Classical management theory. Each move, by each player, would need to be specified in advance, each response to each move would need to be similarly specified, oh, and we would need to agree the intended result before the game started. Any variation from the design would need to be referred by the Captain to the Manager.

Fortunately, some Human Relations theory could kick in here. While Classical management would allow us to select people with the skills for the job and organise them in a systematic arrangement of offices (positions) and so on, Human Relations theory would encourage the players to realise their own goals whilst management would motivate, empower and encourage them.

Now, imagine if one team (The Factory XI) were playing according to the rules of Scientific Management while the other (The Head Office Helpers) were playing according to Human Relations theory.

Yes, some organisations do that!

Furthermore, there is the loss of skill and status associated with the introduction of modern, highly productive and factory-based methods of working. For example, when agricultural or craft workers left the land or traditional occupations to work in factories, their accumulated store of knowledge became redundant. The progressive de-skilling of the workforce, particularly associated with increased specialisation and mechanisation in factories, has served to reinforce this situation. Previously a worker would have exercised a large share of his or her skill, knowledge and abilities in the completion of a task. However, the factory style operation requires much less of this, and for this reason much of the pride of the worker in the job has been lost. This may reasonably be considered to be a primary driver of quality problems in organisations. Trist & Bamforth (1966; in Pugh, 1990: 393–416) make this point in relation to the sociological idea of 'responsible autonomy' in a three man coal getting team.

While the 'Human Relations' approach, which emerged in response to the problems associated with the classical school, may appear to offer the solution, this is not the case. The 'HR' view gives priority to the needs of the individuals over the organisation. In this case, the potential exists for the needs of the customers to be completely ignored in the pursuit of employee satisfaction. Thus it may be considered more important to go home on time, or take a tea break, than to meet a customer's expectations. Similarly, the organisation may develop products and services which exercise the skills, knowledge and aspirations of its workers rather than fulfilling a customer's needs.

Clearly, both of these schools of thought offer advantages to the organisation. All too often these advantages are pursued internally (because they are internally focused) and the needs of the customer are neglected.

Part two of the book considers the work of the 'Quality Gurus'. The influence of the 'Classical' and 'Human Relations' schools of management thinking on these writers will be apparent. While all stress the importance of the customer, perhaps in response to the internally focused approaches just outlined, they also place emphasis on tools and techniques which seem to sit most comfortably with the traditional approaches, and suffer from many of the same problems in the contemporary context.

Summary

Through a critical review this chapter has shown the inadequacy of the dominant Classical and Human Relations theories used by managers to deal with the complexity of contemporary organisations. In the final section, a comment was offered on the relevance of these theories to quality.

KEY LEARNING POINTS

Study of managing has emerged in parallel with emergence of large organisations

Principal dominant models of organisation:
Classical – 'machine' model
Human Relations – 'organic' model

Classical management theorists:
Frederick Taylor – Scientific Management;
Henri Fayol – Administrative Management;
Max Weber – Bureaucracy Theory.

Human Relations theorists:
Elton Mayo – The Hawthorne studies;
Abraham Maslow – The hierarchy of human needs;
Frederick Herzberg – Two factor theory of motivation.

Each model is considered responsible for some aspects of contemporary quality problems.

Question

Which model of management is applied in YOUR organisation?

Part two

The quality gurus

User guide

Part two provides a comprehensive introduction to writers and practitioners whose ideas continue to dominate the quality movement. It concludes with a review of quality management systems and some of the quality prizes and awards.

In every significant field of human endeavour there is continual change and development. Many ideas and approaches to addressing specific issues are considered and tried, but very few withstand the rigours of testing to become established in the mainstream of theory and practice and to become the conventional wisdom in the field. Those writers and practitioners whose ideas come to form this body of accepted knowledge, who lead and advise a movement, become known as 'gurus'. It is notable that although quality systems and approaches continue to develop, the new work is primarily derivative and enhancing of the established, rather than fundamentally innovative. It might be thought in consequence that the issue of quality has been resolved as knowledge in the field has matured, but as will be seen in this section, the thinking is incomplete and there is not a single authoritative source.

This part of the book focuses on the theory and practice espoused by nine writers and practitioners of quality management. They are those whose philosophies, methods and tools have survived and become best practice; collectively I call them 'The Quality Gurus'.

The aim is to enable readers to develop a critical understanding of the contributions to quality of Philip Crosby, W. Edwards Deming, Armand V. Feigenbaum, Kaoru Ishikawa, Joseph Juran, John Oakland, Taiichi Ohno, Shigeo Shingo and Genichi Taguchi. These writers have made the most significant and enduring contributions to quality management, and I have drawn on what I consider to be their most significant and useful outputs. The work of each is explored through a five point critical framework:

- Philosophy;
- Assumptions;
- Methods;
- Successes and failures;
- Critical review.

Through this approach the reader should develop a platform for understanding the strengths, weaknesses and different perspective of each writer. While each of those featured has much in common with the others, there are significant differences in their interpretations of the quality problem and their solutions. Although the work of some may be more widely applied than others, none of the views can be deemed absolutely 'right' or 'wrong'; they are simply different, evolved from the differing backgrounds, knowledge and experiences of the various writers. Each is based on the particular guru's view of the world and is valid from his theoretical and practical perspective. While being critical of these perspectives in our own contemporary contexts, it is important to respect the contexts in which the approaches were developed.

5   Philip B. Crosby

'What costs money are the unquality things – all the actions that involve not doing jobs right the first time'

Philip Crosby, 1979

Introduction

Philip Crosby (1926–2001) graduated from Western Reserve University and had a professional career in quality management. Following military service, he went into quality control in manufacturing where he worked his way from Line Inspector to Quality Director and Corporate Vice-President of ITT. Based on many years of practical experience, his first book became a best seller and led him to establish the consulting organisation Philip Crosby Associates Incorporated and the Quality College based in Florida. He is described by Bendell (1989) as 'particularly well marketed and charismatic', by the *Financial Times* (26th November 1986) as having 'the look of a sunbelt Senator rather than a man from the quality department' and by Bank (1992) as exhorting his message with 'almost religious fervour'. Clearly a man who acted as he spoke or 'walked the talk'. His approach has been well received; over 60,000 managers were trained at the Quality College and his quality books, particularly *Quality Is Free* and *Quality without Tears*, continue to sell well.

5.1   Philosophy

Crosby's philosophy is seen by many, for example Gilbert (1992), to be encapsulated in his five 'Absolutes of Quality Management' (Box 5.1). Each of these absolutes will be examined in turn to consider its meaning.

Box 5.1   Five absolutes of quality management

Philip Crosby:
- Quality is defined as conformance to requirements, not as 'goodness' nor 'elegance';
- There is no such thing as a quality problem;
- It is always cheaper to do it right first time;
- The only performance measurement is the cost of quality;
- The only performance standard is zero defects.

First is Crosby's definition of quality. It suggests that when he talks about a quality product or service he is referring to one which meets the requirements of the customer or user. Dale et al (2007) see this as:

> quality is not comparative, there is no such thing as high quality or low quality, or quality in terms of goodness, feel, excellence and luxury. A product or service either conforms to requirements or it does not.

This means in turn that those requirements must be pre-defined and that 'measures must be taken continually to determine conformance' (Flood, 1993: 22). The requirements may, of course, include both quantitative and qualitative aspects although, as we shall see, Crosby's target emphasis is towards the quantitative, that is 'Zero Defects'. The first fundamental belief then is that quality is a measurable aspect of a product or service and that quality is achieved when expectations or requirements are met.

Crosby's second absolute is that 'There is no such thing as a quality problem'. He is implying that poor management creates the quality problems – they do not create themselves or exist as matters separate from the management process. Simply, a product and its quality do not exist in a vacuum; they are a result of the management process, and if that process has inherent quality then a quality product will emerge. The second belief then is that management must lead the workers towards a quality output.

Third, 'It is always cheaper to do it right first time'. Logothetis (1992) suggests that 'A company which relies on mass inspection of the final output to improve quality is doomed to stagnation'. It is possible to go further than this and suggest that a company focused on inspection will be achieving more than it deserves if it stagnates. It is more likely, in the long run, to fail altogether. Here, Crosby is making clear his belief that inspection is a cost and that quality needs to be *designed into* a product, not that flaws should be *inspected out*. This is taken as a belief in the potential to achieve conformance to requirements by developing a quality process and product from the outset with no expectation of failure. Prevention of error is better than rectification.

Fourth, 'The only performance measurement is the cost of quality'. Crosby clearly believes that the cost of quality is always a measurable item, for example rework, warranty costs, rejects, and that this is the only basis on which to measure performance. It is, as suggested by Logothetis (1992: 85) the 'price of non conformance'. As a practical measurement of quality this might generally be considered to be useful, although it cannot be seen as the only measure, but rather as a direct monetary measure of quality within the overall performance of the organisation. Crosby's belief in a quantitative approach is evident.

Finally, 'The only performance standard is zero defects'. The idea here is that perfection is the standard to aim for through sound initial process and product design, continuous improvement, and underpinning that, zero defects is an achievable and measurable objective. Here again Crosby's fundamental belief in the quantitative approach to quality is made clear with perfection, that is Zero Defects, proposed as the target. This however perhaps reflects Crosby's background in the manufacturing sector and a narrow definition of the 'service' product in terms of process. In services it is entirely possible to deliver a quality output (the service transaction is completed) but still fail to achieve a quality outcome (the customer is not happy).

Summarising Crosby's perspective on quality, there appear to be three essential strands:

- a belief in quantification;
- leadership by management;
- prevention rather than cure.

Quality is suggested by Crosby to be an inherent characteristic of the product, not an added extra. He believes, for example, that 20% of manufacturing cost relates to failure, while for service companies this is around 35%. He considers that the workers must not be blamed for error, but rather, that management should take the lead and that the workers will then follow. Crosby suggests that 85% of quality problems are within the control of management.

5.2   Assumptions

The first assumption is that Crosby focuses attention on the management process as the key driver of quality. That is to say that if the management process is not designed and operated to achieve quality, then a quality product or service cannot arise. If a causal chain view of the development of a product or service is adopted, then it is easy to see value in this assumption. For example, with quality defined as 'conformance to requirements' then it is absolutely essential that requirements are defined and communicated amongst all stakeholders. If this first step is not taken, for example the company manufactures what it can rather than what the consumers demand, then there will be an eternal quality problem, since customer requirements can never be met. This constraint, to define conformance requirements, must be met for every aspect of the product – design, function, colour, delivery, price and so on. In the service context it may be very difficult to operationally define some aspects of requirements and to deliver them consistently, since they depend on human behaviour and emotions, some of which sit outside the control of the provider.

The second assumption is that 'Zero Defects' is an achievable objective. The implication here is that any product can reliably be made, in relevant volumes, entirely free of defects. This raises the question of exactly what constitutes a defect. Working in this respect from Crosby's quality definition – conformance to requirements – any product which conforms to requirements is defect free. This again highlights the importance of the product specification in determining what constitutes quality.

The third assumption is that it is possible to establish a company that 'does not start out expecting mistakes', where errors are not expected or inevitable. While this is an admirable ideal, it must be considered exceedingly difficult to achieve in practice. Culture, staff, levels of training and skill, aptitude for the particular task are all aspects that move over time. For example, in any large manufacturing facility, routine absences for holidays and training will run at around 10% while labour turnover is also likely to run at a level of 5–10% simply from natural causes such as ill-health and retirement. To achieve and maintain a consistency of expectation of zero defects in these circumstances may be seen as unreasonable – unless the management is sufficiently determined in its resolve to achieve quality that it will invest the necessary funds in training and development. Operationally, and particularly where some qualitative or subjective judgement element applies to a product, managers are often faced with a dilemma between delivering volume and achieving conformance to requirements.

This problem was frequently met by management at Tarty Bakeries (Flood, 1993: 209–221) making hand-decorated cakes, where the Production Manager could fulfil one or the other requirement exactly. More often he would make a subjective decision that cakes rejected at inspection actually conformed to requirements! This again leads back to the basic issue of 'requirements' – what are they, how are they defined, who decides them, how can conformance be audited?

Crosby is not particularly illuminating on this issue which, as can be seen, has critical impact. In the context of a physically hard and readily definable product, specifying requirements is essentially straightforward. In the context of services or natural products such as foods, whether processed or not, and services, certain characteristics of the product are less tangible, or even intangible, except at the point of consumption. Consequently it is very difficult to specify requirements and even more difficult to know whether these have been met. Since you cannot have your cake and eat it, it is difficult to know if it matched the requirements unless these requirements are so loosely specified as to be almost meaningless.

Natural products

The adoption of just-in-time supply chains and the consequent need for standardisation of product is, relatively, easy to attain for manufactured products. This is much harder where the product is natural, as in the case of agricultural output.

In agriculture, while the input specification can be managed (seed materials, fertilisers or other growth stimulants), there are a number of factors that either fall outside the scope of the farmer to manage (the amounts of sunshine and rain) OR in order for them to be managed they require artificial conditions (growing in an environmentally controlled building or in a non-native location where the weather is more predictable). Either of these solutions incurs additional cost (the capital cost of the building, the operating cost of heating or cooling) or 'food miles' transporting the product from the non-native growing location. Neither of these solutions solves the problem that a natural product can be encouraged to grow in conformance to a shape, size or weight, but ultimately cannot be forced. If the requirement is very precise (and conformance to it is insisted upon) then THAT will require excess production in order that all the non-conformant product can be thrown away.

An intelligent and thoughtful approach to understanding the TRUE requirements of the end consumer is important.

5.3   Methods

Crosby's principal method is his fourteen-step programme for quality improvement. It is essentially very straightforward and relies on a combination of both quantitative and qualitative aspects.

The first two steps may be seen as addressing cultural aspects of the organisation. The first is about management commitment, the management accepting responsibility for and the obligation to achieving quality. Such a commitment constrains management to consistently behave in a quality achievement oriented manner. This may proscribe or inhibit many of the traditional ways in which they have managed – however effective or ineffective.

When linked to the second step – the formation of quality improvement teams – a further traditional boundary is broken. Organisations are still structured predominantly on functional lines. Crosby specifically requires multi-disciplinary teams. This means that managers

Box 5.2 Fourteen step quality programme

Philip Crosby:

Step 1) Establish management commitment – it is seen as vital that the whole management team participates in the programme; a half hearted effort will fail.

Step 2) Form quality improvement teams – the emphasis here is on multi-disciplinary team effort. An initiative from the quality department will not be successful. It is considered essential to build team working across arbitrary, and often artificial, organisational boundaries.

Step 3) Establish quality measurements – these must apply to every activity throughout the company. A way must be found to capture every aspect, design, manufacturing, delivery and so on. These measurements provide a platform for the next step.

Step 4) Evaluate the cost of quality – this evaluation must highlight, using the measures established in the previous step, where quality improvement will be profitable.

Step 5) Raise quality awareness – this is normally undertaken through the training of managers and supervisors, through communications such as videos and books, and by displays of posters, etc.

Step 6) Take action to correct problems – this involves encouraging staff to identify and rectify defects, or pass them on to higher supervisory levels where they can be addressed.

Step 7) Zero defects planning – establish a committee or working group to develop ways to initiate and implement a Zero Defects programme.

Step 8) Train supervisors & managers – this step is focused on achieving understanding by all managers and supervisors of the steps in the Quality Improvement Programme in order that they can explain it in turn.

Step 9) Hold a 'Zero Defects' day to establish the attitude and expectation within the company. Crosby sees this as being achieved in a celebratory atmosphere accompanied by badges, buttons and balloons.

Step 10) Encourage the setting of goals for improvement. Goals are of course of no value unless they are related to appropriate time-scales for their achievement.

Step 11) Obstacle reporting – this is encouragement to employees to advise management of the factors which prevent them achieving error free work. This might cover defective or inadequate equipment, poor quality components, etc.

Step 12) Recognition for contributors – Crosby considers that those who contribute to the programme should be rewarded through a formal, although non-monetary, reward scheme. Readers may be aware of the 'Gold Banana' award given by Foxboro for scientific achievement (Peters & Waterman, 1982).

Step 13) Establish Quality Councils – these are essentially forums composed of quality professionals and team leaders, allowing them to communicate and determine action plans for further quality improvement.

Step 14) Do it all over again – the message here is very simple. Achievement of quality is an ongoing process. However far you have got, there is always further to go!

and other staff must break out of their 'comfort zones' and, inevitably, relinquish some of the 'expert' and 'position' power (Handy, 1985: 124–126) that goes with the functional organisation. A whole hearted embrace by management of these two steps alone may be considered a major achievement!

The third and fourth steps are quantitative and directly linked again – the fourth is simply not possible without the third. Measurement is a necessary precursor to evaluation.

These steps in turn provide a platform for the fifth step – raising quality awareness, a more qualitative issue. To make the quality training relevant for supervisors and managers, it needs to be set firmly in the context of the quality status of the firm as evidenced by the measurements. This step also may be seen to act as re-affirmation of the first two steps – gaining commitment and the multi-functional approach. Through measurement and evaluation, the interrelatedness of quality issues across internal boundaries can be highlighted.

Step six is take action. The other steps are worthless unless they lead to preventative and corrective action. At this point staff really must 'walk the talk'. It has both qualitative and quantitative aspects. If the numbers generated through the measurement system are simply used as clubs to beat the heads of the staff, they are unlikely to prove very helpful. The numbers must be used to provide guidance and support to the action taken, and the actions taken must be in harmony with the words spoken!

Once this step has commenced, the organisation can be seen to have established a sound platform for quality improvement – staff and management are committed, and action is being taken. It could be argued at this stage that provided the momentum of improvement is maintained, quality will continuously improve. Crosby's process, however, sees this as insufficient; with the process firmly established he proposes an increased effort and impetus towards 'Zero Defects' (ZD). This is the thrust of step seven – Zero Defects Planning – which strives to establish a ZD programme, an essentially quantitative target but achieved through both soft and hard approaches. Step eight involves training of supervisors and managers so that they can pass on the programme to their subordinates. This tactic of 'train the trainer' is a powerful mechanism for culturally embedding the behaviour changes that are required – provided always that the more senior managers similarly embrace the changes.

Step nine, Zero Defects day, may be seen as both a celebration of achievements to date and a new beginning to the quality improvement programme. This takes Zero Defects as a very precise, quantifiable and achievable objective; following the previous steps it has to be accepted as possible and necessary by the whole organisation. Step ten is a natural consequence of step nine and requires commitment to achieving goals for improvement tied to defined and relatively short-term time scales. Again it is quantitative in nature, the results being directly measurable.

Step eleven – obstacle reporting – is a communication device which recognises that failure to achieve quality in one area may be related to failure in another, or to local factors which inhibit quality achievement. This process enables those facing problems to report them, and importantly, it places obligations on management to address those issues. Time frames for response and action are built into this step which requires both a change in culture – the acceptance by management of criticism from the workers – and a change in the nature of managers' roles. It will be insufficient for managers to concentrate on their own direct areas of responsibility, particularly for problems which cross functional boundaries. They will have to work with managers of other areas to achieve the targets.

Step twelve requires acknowledgement of the contribution of staff to the process – a direct reward for the efforts made. Crosby is very specific that these rewards should be formal but non-monetary. This step is largely cultural in its impact. Recognising and rewarding the contributors to the programme is a device for reinforcing amongst the whole staff a particular kind of behaviour, further embedding a quality culture.

The establishment of Quality Councils at step thirteen is seen as 'institutionalising' the quality programme – making it a part of the embedded culture. It becomes at this stage an integral part of the way in which the company is managed and controlled. Mainly qualitative in nature, it will affect many aspects of the way in which the staff of the company behave in the future.

The final step – 'Do it all over again' – is Crosby's reminder that quality improvement never stops. Any change programme will, over time, lose energy simply because the original, perhaps revolutionary, leaders will achieve the objectives which they set themselves. They may find it difficult to maintain the initial enthusiasm and drive. In order to sustain and develop the programme it will be necessary to pump new energy into it by the appointment of fresh people and the establishment of new objectives.

Crosby's 'Quality Vaccine' (Logothetis, 1992: 82–83) is an essential part of his process. It is based on three principal ingredients:

- Integrity;
- Dedication to communication and customer satisfaction;
- Company wide policies and operations which support the quality thrust.

Logothetis (op. cit.) proposes a triangle (Figure 5.1) of interaction between these three ingredients which must be supported by Crosby's belief in how the vaccine is administered. This again has three strands:

- Determination – awareness that management must lead;
- Education – for management and staff;
- Implementation – creating an organisational environment where achievement of quality is regarded as the norm, not the exception.

This chapter is not intended to provide an exhaustive account of methods, tools and techniques; those are introduced later. Aspects of Crosby's approach will be returned to in more detail, dealing with 'How' rather than 'What' in the appropriate chapters. This section has, however, provided an introduction to the principal strands of Crosby's method which

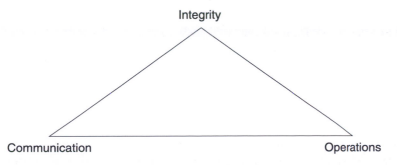

Figure 5.1 Philip Crosby's triangle of interactions.

can be seen as based largely in quantitative outcomes and to rely heavily on an evangelical attitude, amongst both the management and the staff.

5.4   Successes and failures

Quality gurus, like doctors, are prone to advertising their successes and burying their failures. Companies act similarly – a successful quality programme will be advertised in order to attract customers – a failure will be swept under the carpet, with executives pretending that it never happened. It thus becomes impossible to find reported empirical evidence of failure.

Success, on the other hand, is shared. The guru proclaims the success of his method, while the company proclaim the success of their strategy and acknowledge the contribution made by their interpretation of the particular guru's approach. Chrysler's Lee Iacocca, for example, cited by Bank (1992: 75), says:

> we established our own Chrysler Quality Institute in Michigan, modelled after his [Crosby's] operation – our company's put about twenty thousand of our people through it . . . and I admit they do return with QUALITY stamped on their foreheads.

It can be explicitly seen here that Crosby's contribution has been acknowledged but that Chrysler have used this work as a model. What we cannot see is how closely the model follows the original!

With his consulting company, Quality College and overseas operations firmly established, Crosby must be acknowledged as having been successful. It is also the case that sufficient client organisations must have found the approach useful to have sustained the development and growth of that organisation over a lengthy period of time. It must be concluded that there is some real value to be found in his approach.

Flood (1993: 27–28) acknowledges this in identifying five strengths to Crosby's work. Summarising, he sees these as:

- Clarity;
- Recognition of worker participation;
- Rejection of a tangible quality problem, acceptance of the idea of solutions;
- Crosby's metaphors – 'vaccine' and 'maturity';
- Crosby's motivational style.

Flood also criticises perceived weaknesses. He sees:

- Danger of misdirected effort from 'blaming' workers;
- Emphasis on marketing more than recognition of barriers;
- The management and goal orientation of the fourteen-step programme as failing to 'free workers from externally generated goals';
- Potential for 'Zero Defects' to be interpreted as zero risk;
- Ineffectiveness in coercive power structures.

Looking at the strengths, it could be argued that clarity and simplicity of approach are not necessarily beneficial in dealing with increasingly complex problems. The adequacy of any problem solving tool must be measured in terms of its suitability for the problem being addressed; the sophistication of the process and tools used must, at least, match that of the problem. So, yes it needs to be comprehensible, but that is not necessarily the same as simple.

The value of worker participation cannot be denied. First, the people who do the work may be the only people who can recognise the roots of a particular problem. Second, their involvement implies easier acceptance of ownership of the programme and the solutions.

The conception that all quality issues can be resolved is very useful in provoking ideal goal seeking behaviour amongst the participants in the situation. Bank (1992: 23) compares this to the ice-skaters Torville and Dean aiming for perfect scores even though they may not be attainable. He cites Thomas J. Watson, founder of IBM, as saying, 'It's better to aim at perfection and miss than it is to aim at imperfection and hit it'. Acceptance that certain problems cannot be solved could be seen as reinforcing behaviour and attitudes which ensure that they never will be.

Creativity and leadership must be seen as essential strands in quality improvement. However, while some writers see great strength in Crosby's approach to this, there is also, perhaps, inherent danger. The 'charismatic' or 'evangelical' style adopted by Crosby has also been criticised by Juran. Crosby, cited by Bank (op. cit.: 76) says, 'Dr. Juran seems to think I am a charlatan and hasn't missed many opportunities to say that over the years'. The founding charge here seems really to be one of a lack of substantial underpinning to Crosby's approach, perhaps reflecting other comments about promotion 'through slogans and too often full of platitudes'.

There can be no doubt that many of the most sustained management theories and approaches through the years have been well marketed, yet when examined by others are demonstrated to have theoretical or methodological weaknesses. This is almost inevitably true. Theories validated within one paradigm can probably always be disputed from within another. Similarly, it is often said that there is no such thing as bad publicity, and to quote Oscar Wilde (1890) in *The Portrait of Dorian Gray*, 'There is only one thing in the world worse than being talked about, and that is not being talked about'. That Crosby was an effective self-publicist cannot be denied, however, this does not necessarily detract from the value of what was being said.

Turning to the weaknesses, it is arguable whether the interpretation of Crosby as 'blaming the workers' is reasonable. Bendell (1989), for example, states that Crosby 'does not believe that workers should take prime responsibility for poor quality; the reality, he says, is that you have to get management straight first'. Bendell further suggests that in Crosby's approach, 'management sets the tone on quality and workers follow . . . the initiative comes from the top'. Thus it could be argued that rather than creating a 'blame the workers' culture, the Crosby approach is a form of empowerment, led by the management. The difficulty rests in how the messages are translated by the managers in the middle – and that to a large extent depends upon how they receive them and their competence in conveying them.

The issue of platitudes and lack of substance has already been largely addressed, and goal orientation comes into focus. It is clear that Crosby only considers one goal for the organisation and that is 'Zero Defects'. Flood's criticism here is much better founded. The external setting of goals by the management is far from empowering or emancipatory and neglects to address workers' perception of their own values and needs. It must be recognised, however, that the requirement for quality is being driven from the environment of the organisation. If survival of the organisation is to be achieved, then quality products which 'conform to requirements' are an essential feature.

Misinterpretation of 'Zero Defects' as meaning the avoidance of risk is another reasonable point. There will always be an element of risk involved in a change of behaviour or process. To overcome the danger of risk aversion, management must develop a cultural environment where risks can be calculated and minimised and where learning from mistakes is encouraged, perhaps incorporating ideas of the Learning Organisation (Senge, 1990).

Flood's strongest criticism is of the assumption that people will work in an open and conciliatory manner. He makes it clear that in a political or coercive context this will not apply. Many management writers agree that an element of politics and coercion is present in most organisations, whether or not this is explicit. There will always be a dominant group or sub-group, and it is suggested that the fully open and conciliatory atmosphere is an ideal rather than an easily achievable objective.

5.5   Critical review

Overall, the foundation of Crosby's approach can be seen in two elements. First, his extensive professional background in quality will have provided the quantitative bias to his method and, second, his reportedly charismatic personality will have provided the qualitative aspects.

The general value of measurement in establishing standards and objectives for quality is readily recognisable, while the principles are transferable between organisations and people. The value of the qualitative issues are much harder to evaluate and transfer. The majority of managers would not perhaps consider themselves to be 'charismatic' (Weber, 1924) leaders, an epithet more readily used in respect of others than oneself. A whole hearted commitment to quality achievement throughout the organisation is undoubtedly required; what is questionable is whether the exhortative, inspirational slogans and platitudes will work in all circumstances and for all managers.

The process and quantitative aspects of Crosby's programme – a word which in itself implies a discrete activity rather than ongoing management behaviour – may be readily transferable. However, the management style adopted will have to reflect the needs, values and personalities of those involved in the programme.

Similar comments can be applied to other aspects of the approach. For example, while encouraging reward, Crosby suggests that these should not be monetary. The reward, to be truly meaningful to the recipient, should reflect his or her needs and aspirations. For an individual whose focus is professional achievement, then public recognition of his or her contribution may be all the reward that is required. For an individual on low wages, perhaps seeking to reduce personal indebtedness or, in an extreme case, to pay for life preserving medical treatment, a monetary reward may be precisely right.

Reflection is also necessary on the suitability of the approach for different industries. With his manufacturing background Crosby has developed an approach which reflects that. It is essentially possible, in the manufacturing environment, to know when a defect free output is achieved. This is far more difficult in the service sector where definitions of the product are harder to generate and delivery is almost impossible to control.

Certain aspects of service are relatively straightforward to quantify, for example how many times the telephone rings before it is answered, or precisely what words of greeting are used – although there have been cases reported where the telephone was being answered too promptly, frightening the customers! Other aspects are less susceptible to measurement and control, for example tone of voice. The nature of many of these transactions is that the service is provided and consumed instantly. While they can, to some extent, be designed and planned, their production is uncontrollable. They also depend on factors which are perhaps outside the ability of the organisation to effectively influence. These factors include the expectations of the customer, his or her mood, the sort of day they have already experienced and the level of service they have received before. These factors cannot be known until after service has commenced.

Therefore Crosby's approach has to be marked with some cautions about its general applicability across a range of industries and cultures. What works very well for Philip Crosby at ITT, or for Lee Iacocca at Chrysler, may not work in a bank in Hong Kong, or on a North Sea oil production platform.

Summary

This chapter has presented the work of Philip Crosby through a five point critical framework. It has described his philosophy and its underpinning assumptions, outlined his principal methods, examined the successes and failures of the approach and summarised this in a brief critical review. Readers may refer to Crosby's own works, particularly *Quality Is Free* (1979), to enhance and develop their own knowledge and understanding.

KEY LEARNING POINTS

Philip B. Crosby

Definition of quality:
conformance to requirements.

Five absolutes of quality management:

- Quality as conformance;
- No such thing as a Quality Problem;
- Always cheaper first time;
- Only measurement of performance is the cost of quality;
- Zero defects.

Three key beliefs:
Quantification; Management leadership; Prevention.

Principal methods:
Fourteen step quality programme; the 'Quality Vaccine'

Question

Consider the management processes in your organisation. How do they support or inhibit quality goods and services?

6   W. Edwards Deming

'The basic cause of sickness in American industry . . . is failure of top management to manage'

W. Edwards Deming, 1986

Introduction

W. Edwards Deming, who died in 1993, is considered by many as the founding father of the quality movement. Perhaps the most widely known of the gurus both within and outside the quality field, Deming held a Doctorate in Physics from Yale and was a keen statistician, working in the U.S. Government for many years in the Department of Agriculture and the Bureau of Census. According to Bendell (1989: 4) Deming rose to prominence in Japan where he was closely involved in the post-war development of quality for which Bendell suggests 'he is considered largely responsible'. Heller (1989) sees Deming as having a 'passionate belief in man's ability to improve on the poor and the mediocre, and even on the good', a belief which shall be seen is evident in both his theory and his practice. Logothetis (1992: xii) sees Deming as advocating 'widespread use of statistical ideas, with management taking a strong initiative in building quality in'. Summers (2009) describes Deming's 'mission to teach optimal management strategies for effective organisations' while Bank (1992: 62), cites Hutchins's belief that a major contribution made by Deming to the Japanese quality movement was in helping them to:

> cut through the academic theory, to present the ideas in a simple way which could be meaningful right down to production worker levels.

Summarising, Deming's approach can be seen as founded in the traditional scientific method (arising from his physics and statistics background) whilst he was also a very capable communicator. Although as Bendell (1989: 5) suggests, it is 'difficult to delimit his [Deming's] concepts' due to the constant refinement and improvement of his ideas, his successful and widely read book *Out of the Crisis* (1986) presents his approach to both management and quality in its most succinct, coherent form.

6.1   Philosophy

Deming's initial approach, reputedly rejected by American industry at the outset, was based on his background in statistical methods. His quantitative method provided a 'systematic, rigorous approach to quality' (Bendell, 1989: 4). Drawing on the work of the statistician Walter Shewhart – his tutor – Deming urged a management focus on causes of variability in manufacturing processes.

Deming's first belief can be seen here; that there are 'common' and 'special' causes of quality problems. 'Special' causes are those relating to particular operators or machines and requiring attention to the individual cause. 'Common' causes are those which arise from the operation of the system itself and are the responsibility of management.

Deming believed in the use of Statistical Process Control (SPC) charts as the key method for identifying special and common causes and enabling diagnosis of quality problems. His aim was to remove 'outliers', that is quality problems relating to the special causes of failure. This was achieved through training, improved machinery and equipment and so on. SPC enabled the production process to be brought 'under control'. Remaining quality problems were considered to be related to common causes, problems inherent in the 'design' of the production process, not its operation. Eradication of special causes enabled a shift in focus to common causes to further improve quality.

Deming's second belief is apparent here; a quantitative basis for identifying and solving problems. It is suggested by Bendell (1989: 4) that this statistically based approach brought its own problems. He reports lack of technical standards and limitations of data and, perhaps more importantly, 'human difficulties in the form of employee resistance and management lack of understanding as to their roles in quality improvement', particularly in the American applications. Bendell considers that perhaps 'too much emphasis was being given towards the statistical aspects'. This suggests that Deming's approach strongly reflects the 'machine' view of organisations outlined in chapter 4. It is also fair to make two further observations. First, most students do not learn statistics beyond secondary education level. Their grasp of the subject is usually tenuous and consequently many find it hard to fully comprehend the results. Second, given contemporary information technology, the results which Deming's methods reveal could be presented more meaningfully. As with other experts in their fields, the value of Deming's work could be obscured by our ability to interpret it.

Notwithstanding these problems, Deming became a national hero in Japan, and his methods were widely taken up. In 1951 the 'Deming Prize' for contributions to quality and dependability was launched, and in 1960 he was awarded the 'Second Order of the Sacred Treasure', Japan's premier Imperial honour.

A third strand to Deming's work was the formulation of his systematic approach to problem solving; an approach which is now commonplace and frequently reinterpreted in other methodologies – for example the EPDCA cycle in Oakland's work – and is central to the application of the ISO 9001:2015 standard. This has become known as the Deming, Shewhart or PDCA cycle – Plan, Do, Check, Action, illustrated in Figure 6.1.

The cycle is continuous. Once it has been systematically completed, it recommences without ceasing. This is in agreement with Crosby's admonition, already considered, to 'Do it all over again'. The approach is seen as re-emphasising the responsibility of management to be actively involved in the organisation's quality programme, while Logothetis (1992: 55) considers that it provides the basis for a 'self-sustaining quality programme' and it reflects the adaptive notion of intelligent organisation (Beckford, 2016).

Two further beliefs can be derived here. First is in a systematic, methodical approach contrasting sharply with the ad hoc and random behaviour of many quality initiatives. The second is in the need for continuous quality improvement action. This contrasts sharply with the overtones in Crosby's approach, which suggest a discrete set of activities.

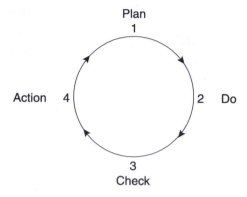

Figure 6.1 The Plan-Do-Check-Action cycle.

Deming's later work focused on Western, and particularly American, management, and he elaborated seven fundamental beliefs (the 'Seven Deadly Sins' – Box 6.1) about bad management practices which he considered must be eliminated before Western styles of management could support a successful quality initiative.

Sin 1, 'lack of constancy' is seen by Logothetis (1992: 46) as urging 'an absolute and constant commitment on the part of senior management to quality, productivity and innovation'. Inherent in this is a continuing drive towards better quality and reliability of product in order to drive down costs, protect investment and employment, create and enlarge markets and hence generate more jobs. This provides a positive, achievement orientation for the organisation. Deming (1986: 98) criticises management for being 'run on the quarterly dividend', a situation which has only been exacerbated over the last 30 years.

Sin 2, 'short-term profit focus', is seen as challenging and potentially defeating the 'constancy of purpose' previously urged. Deming (1986: 99) suggests that:

> Anyone can boost the dividend at the end of the quarter. Ship everything on hand, regardless of quality: mark it shipped, and show it all as accounts receivable. Defer till next quarter, so far as possible, orders for material and equipment. Cut down on research, education, training.

Box 6.1   The Seven Deadly Sins

W. Edwards Deming:

Sin 1)   Lack of constancy;
Sin 2)   Short-term profit focus;
Sin 3)   Performance appraisals;
Sin 4)   Job-hopping;
Sin 5)   Use of visible figures only;
Sin 6)   Excessive medical costs;
Sin 7)   Excessive costs of liability.

Here, Deming is making clear his belief in a management approach with a long-term orientation. Deming gives explicit recognition to the need to satisfy shareholder expectations, but points out that they must go beyond the immediate return on capital to consider the long-term future of the organisation.

Much criticism has been levied in recent years at what is now known as 'short-termism' in the City of London, on Wall Street, in Exchange Square or Raffles Place. Readers may wish to consider whether issues such as the increasing ownership of shares by financial institutions and the difficulties of making money by making products in a harsh business environment are influential here. Pension and investment companies are frequently the largest stockholders in public companies; their requirements and the reward packages of their employees are often tied to short-term performance. Similarly, investment bankers and traders in 'derivative' financial products are further dissociating the underlying value of products and companies from the valuation of the business itself.

Sin 3, performance appraisal, is considered by Deming (1986: 102) to 'nourish short-term performance' and 'leave people bitter, crushed, bruised, battered, desolate, despondent, dejected, feeling inferior'. Logothetis (1992: 47) sees appraisal as encouraging 'rivalry and isolation' and demolishing teamwork, again leading back to a focus on individual and short-term results, noting that 'people who attempt to change the system (for the better) have no chance of recognition'.

While acknowledging Deming's belief in the potential damage that a poor appraisal system can cause, this is perhaps more to do with system design than a necessary outcome of performance review. Most of us need and enjoy recognition of our achievements and can benefit from the guidance delivered through a constructive and effective appraisal system. This perhaps partly reflects the esteem element in Maslow's hierarchy of needs.

Job-hopping, regular movement of management between jobs either within or between organisations, is the fourth sin. Originally seen as a particular attribute of Western management, this is now endemic, reflecting changes in employment practices and career paths. Job-hopping is considered to lead to instability and further reinforce the short-term orientation of the organisation. Logothetis (1992: 39) suggests that it destroys teamwork and commitment and ensures that many decisions are taken in whole or partial ignorance of the circumstances surrounding them. The argument is for commitment of management and staff to the long-term future of the organisation.

Sin 5 is the 'use of visible figures only'. Here Deming criticises failure to recognise and evaluate intangible aspects of the organisation, for example the additional sales generated through satisfied customers, the benefits to productivity and quality derived from people feeling part of a success story, the negative impact of performance appraisal and barriers to achieving quality. Deming (1986: 123) considers that managers who believe that everything can be measured are deluding themselves and suggests that they should know before they start that they will be able to quantify only 'a trivial part of the gain'. This is a belief in intangible, invisible benefits arising from good management practice. It does, however, conflict with his espousal of statistical methods, since the reliable measurement of intangibles is notoriously difficult. That said, the measurement of performance across the business processes rather than simply in the vertical silos is both achievable and beneficial. Lessons could perhaps be drawn from organisational psychology which can help to measure some of the aspects that Deming considered intangible and by re-examining the organisational and financial structure of the organisation, which often obscures where the true profits and costs arise.

The sixth and seventh sins, while revealed by Deming, are given little attention by other writers on his work. His points are simply made. The sixth sin, medical costs, both in direct lost labour costs and indirect in the sense of medical insurance premiums, are met largely by the employer. Thus they are an additional cost to be recovered in the price of the product. Deming (1986: 98) refers to William Hoglund of the Pontiac Motor Division, informing him that the direct cost of medical care to the company exceeded the amount spent on steel for every vehicle produced! This cost, along with pensions, continues to be a major issue for organisations and has been cited as significant in the future of the UK Steel Industry.

The cost of insurance is driven by claims experience and actuarial expectation, and it is arguable whether Deming is making a fair point. Medical costs are currently covered in every developed nation. If they are not supported by private insurance schemes such as prevail in the USA, France, Singapore and many other nations, they may be met by a national scheme such as the NHS in the UK. Either way, the company bears the cost, through direct contribution, or by increased basic wages which enable the employees to meet the cost themselves. It is doubtful whether there is any real difference in the cost related to this between employers in the USA or the UK and other developed nations.

The seventh and final sin is one that is now considered to be gaining further ground, 'liability costs'. The world appears increasingly litigious, and while many potential liability issues are insurable, many others are not. The costs of these must be borne by the organisation, a factor that threatens the future of the Volkswagen Group after the emissions revelations of 2015.

Summarising Deming's philosophy, we can identify a number of clear strands. There are evident beliefs in:

- quantitative, statistically valid, control systems;
- clear definition of those aspects under the direct control of staff, i.e. the 'special causes' and those which are the responsibility of management, 'the common causes'. Deming suggests that these are as high as 94%;
- a systematic, methodical approach;
- continuous improvement;
- constancy and determination;

which taken together cover the first five of his 'Deadly Sins', the other two being highly arguable.

Along with Crosby, Deming (1986: ix) considers that quality should be designed in to both the product and the process. He believes that 'transformation of the style of American (sic) management' is necessary, requiring a 'whole new structure, from foundation upward'.

6.2   Assumptions

First, while initially focusing attention on existing processes to derive immediate improvement – the eradication of 'special causes' of failure – it is rapidly refocused to the management process and attitudes. Deming seems to believe that these must be, in his own words, 'transformed' in order for sustained improvement to be achieved. The management is seen to be responsible and, significantly, to be capable of undertaking the proposed transformation. He does not suggest, in organisation design or psychological terms, how this should be achieved.

Second is the assumption that statistical methods, properly used, will provide quantitative evidence to support changes. At the same time he recognises that some aspects cannot be easily measured and suggests that managements frequently fail to take seriously those aspects which they consider unmeasurable.

The third key assumption is that continuous improvement is both possible and desirable. Taking his definition of quality as 'meeting the needs of the customer, both present and future' (1986: 5), this has to be questioned. If the needs of the customer are fully understood and fully met, where is the benefit in further improvement?

The next assumption is that continuous improvement supported by a long-term orientation will enable the organisation to meet customers' 'future needs'. If, however, the contemporary world is characterised as Handy (1990) suggests by 'discontinuous change' or subject, as Taleb (2010) suggests, to 'Black Swan' events, then a long-term view and continuous improvement may no longer be enough. Perhaps organisations must be built which can anticipate and prepare for sudden, maybe catastrophic, change. Continuous improvement and incremental change may not be sound recipes in a discontinuous world. The 'boom and bust' of the dotcom businesses is another example, as is the financial catastrophe which faced the world in 2008 and from which in 2016 some economies are still feeling the effects. While many businesses were undoubtedly built on weak foundations, many others should have been capable of survival. The inevitable collapse of the weak (and the strong which became weak through unmanaged risk-taking) brought down many of the strong.

Deming's final assumption, as with Crosby, is about the service sector. Simply, he sees that the prime role of the service sector, in the context of a national economy, rests in enabling manufacturing to do its job. He suggests (1986: 188) for example that:

> A better plan for freight carriers would be to improve service and thus to decrease costs. These cost savings, passed on to manufacturers and to other service industries, would help American industry to improve the market for American products, and would in time bring new business to carriers of freight.

While offering specific advice about quality improvement in the service sector, Deming, unlike Crosby, does explicitly recognise the difficulty of measuring certain aspects of it. He seems also to assume an initially altruistic effort which contrasts sharply with his accusations of short-termism. To some extent he is possibly correct – cost-savings can be passed back down the supply chain and in a truly competitive market would occur.

The implications of his assumption about the role of services should also be considered. Few local communities thrive when their manufacturing base is lost. The ship building, coal mining and steel making communities in the UK continue to suffer slower economic growth, social fragmentation and significant unemployment. Many service sector jobs can now be clearly seen to depend upon local manufacturers through purchase of services by the major organisations and spending of wages by the employees. Wealth generated by an employer is in large part expended in the same community. As the manufacturing sector has declined, so too has the service sector in those communities.

Those sectors where services have thrived are in areas of specialist technical expertise such as banking, insurance, finance and other knowledge based industries. These industries have a less dependent relationship on the manufacturing sector than say, retailing and real estate. Notwithstanding these particular aspects, there is perhaps a warning at a national and multi-national level. If individual communities cannot be adequately sustained when manufacturing is lost to them, then is there any future for nations if the manufacturing base as a whole is lost?

6.3   Methods

Deming has four principal methods:

- The PDCA cycle;
- Statistical Process Control;
- The Fourteen Principles for Transformation;
- The Seven Point Action Plan.

The first of these has been introduced and will not be dealt with further here. The second, Statistical Process Control, will be explored in part four. The Fourteen Principles for Transformation and Seven Point Action Plan will provide the major content of this section.

Statistical Process Control is a quantitative approach based on measurement of process performance. Essentially a process is considered to be under control, i.e. stable, when inevitable random variations in output fall within determined upper and lower limits. That is seen by Deming as the process having achieved a position where the special causes of failure have been eradicated.

A control chart, a sample of which is provided at Figure 6.2, is used to record the values associated with an event in a process. Statistical analysis of the values recorded reveals the mean value and the normal distribution. Normal variation from this mean value for the particular process in its established state is conventionally taken as any value within +/− three standard deviations of the mean. Events which fall outside that normal variation are 'special' and should prove tractable to individual diagnosis and treatment. Events falling within the norms have 'common' causes; they are a product of the organisation of the system and require treatment at the system level. Here we can refer directly to Deming (1986: 315) and re-emphasise the role of management in the development of quality:

> I should estimate that in my experience most troubles and most possibilities for improvement add up to proportions something like this:
>
> 94% belong to the system (responsibility of management) 6% special.

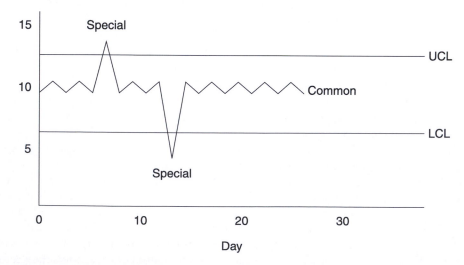

Figure 6.2 Sample control chart.

It has to be acknowledged here that Deming's split of special and common causes, and consequently his allocation of responsibility for error, relates directly to the product of SPC. At $+/-$ three standard deviations in a stable system it is inevitable that 95% of errors will belong to the system – 95% being two standard deviations in a normal distribution. Three standard deviations (99.7% approximately of results) are recognised through SPC as representing stability, a system under control. The standard ($+/-$ three sigma) was originally devised by Shewhart to minimise net economic loss from rectifying mistakes, the objective of Taguchi's 'quadratic loss function' to be elaborated in chapter 12.

We can now turn to the first main focus of this section, Deming's Fourteen Principles for Transformation. These, like Crosby's fourteen steps, are essentially straightforward and rely on a combination of statistical and human, or cultural, aspects. The principles will be reviewed in turn.

The first three principles, creating constancy of purpose, adoption of a new philosophy and ceasing dependence on mass inspection, may all be seen as focused on the cultural aspects of the organisation. The first principle is aimed at creating a 'team' type of environment

---

Box 6.2   Fourteen Principles for Transformation

W. Edwards Deming:

Principle 1)   Create constancy of purpose to improve product and service.

Principle 2)   Adopt a new philosophy for the new economic age with management learning what their responsibilities are and by assuming leadership for change.

Principle 3)   Cease dependence on mass inspection to achieve quality by building quality into the product.

Principle 4)   End awarding business on price. Award business on total cost and move towards single suppliers.

Principle 5)   Aim for continuous improvement of the system of production and service to improve productivity and quality and to decrease costs.

Principle 6)   Institute training on the job.

Principle 7)   Institute leadership with the aim of supervising people to help them to do a better job.

Principle 8)   Drive out fear so that everyone can work effectively together for the organisation.

Principle 9)   Break down barriers between departments. Encourage research, design, sales and production to work together to foresee difficulties in production and use.

Principle 10)   Eliminate slogans, exhortations and numerical targets for the work-force since they are divisory and anyway difficulties belong to the whole system.

Principle 11)   Eliminate quotas or work standards and management by objectives or numerical goals: leadership should be substituted instead.

Principle 12)   Remove barriers that rob people of their right to pride in their work.

Principle 13)   Institute a vigorous education and self-improvement programme.

Principle 14)   Put everyone in the company to work to accomplish the transformation.

where all are working together towards a common goal. It requires the management to commit to achieving ever improving quality as a primary objective of the organisation.

The second principle, that of embracing management learning and a leadership based style of management, concerns acceptance by the management that the responsibility for developing and achieving the changes is theirs. It requires explicit recognition by management that the workers are not necessarily to blame for quality deficiencies. This may well require a dramatic change in both words and actions on the part of management, particularly if they have been accustomed, as so many are, to pushing the blame down through the hierarchy!

The third principle, ceasing dependence on mass inspection by building quality into the product, requires a further dramatic change in management approach and has major implications for issues such as organisation structure and information management. A simple abandonment of mass inspection not supported by changes in other aspects will potentially be disastrous. A successful example of such a change is the introduction in recent years of multi-disciplinary product development teams in many organisations. These teams include both design and production engineers so that products are now designed with production requirements in mind rather than having to be re-engineered for production. This speeds up the development of new products (Schmied, 1995), reduces manufacturing complexity and leads to improved quality.

The fourth principle, the ending of awarding business on price rather than total cost, is a recognition that the invoiced unit price of a sub-assembly or part is only a fraction of its total potential cost (or value) to the organisation. For example, a part which has the lowest unit cost may carry with it a high level of rejects. This leads to either high inspection costs to identify poor quality parts or to a poor quality of finished product leading in turn to high inspection and rework costs and potential for product failure in the hands of the customer.

Caveat emptor

Apocryphal tales come thick and fast in the world of procurement. NASA supposedly spent millions of dollars to invent a pen that would write upside down in zero gravity while Russian Cosmonauts took a pencil. The Astronaut Alan Shepherd is reported as saying: 'It's a very sobering feeling to be up in space and realise that one's safety factor was determined by the lowest bidder on a government contract'.

Procurement is a big issue, and specification of requirements AND the supplier selection criteria is critical particularly when large (in European Union Member countries that is in excess of €400k) public sector contracts are being let. Typically the supplier selection criteria are across a number of characteristics, including cost and quality. But often the 'quality' referred to is of the submission not of the service, the one being taken as a proxy for the other. Often what then arises is the award of the contract to the organisation that delivers the most compliant bid, rather than the one that will, could, might, deliver the service or product that 'conforms to requirements'.

Because of the need to bid 'inputs' in a very prescriptive way in such circumstances, all we can be confident of at the outset is that there will be a lot of change requests during the course of the contract while the buyer works out what they really wanted to buy and the supplier works out how to deliver it.

A number of aspects need to be considered in the identification of the total cost of a purchased item. These may include unit cost, quality (failure and reject rate), inspection costs, inventory costs (for example the potential for implementing a 'just-in-time' or 'kanban' system) and ease of use in the manufacturing environment – that is the impact of the supplied item on labour and other costs. The other aspect which must be considered is the purchase of items which support the manufacturing process such as machine tools, conveyor systems and control systems. Particularly with these latter items, ongoing running costs are often a far greater part of the total lifetime cost than the initial purchase price, and significant benefits can be obtained by bearing a higher initial cost in order to generate longer-term savings.

Deming also recommends a move towards single suppliers. As with so many things, this approach has both advantages and drawbacks. The principal advantages are that it provides the purchaser with significant leverage in negotiating improvements in product quality and price, it enables long-term relationships based on trust and mutual support and it provides a more secure financial platform for the provider. Conversely, reliance on a single source of parts supply makes the purchaser vulnerable to any failure on the part of the supplier, either financially, or in quality. Such exposure may give cause for concern to bankers and other financiers. A worthwhile approach here would be to consider the use of a single supplier based on Porter's (1980) model for competitive rivalry. Where supplier power is weak (there are many suppliers and the product is undifferentiated or non-critical), a single supplier strategy may bring significant benefits to the company, enabling it to take effective control of its supplier. Where supplier power is strong (there are few suppliers, the product is differentiated or critical), the organisation may maximise its position by supporting more than one supplier.

The fifth principle, aim for continuous improvement if considered appropriate to the customer's needs and industry circumstances, gives greater substance and focus to the first two by focusing attention on productivity, quality and decreasing costs. Objectives at this stage can be made more quantifiable, moving from the ideals of the first principles to a more practical, achievement orientation.

The sixth principle, 'on the job training', emphasises the need to improve competencies and skills in the practical context. While not excluding classroom based training, this principle suggests that the objective of continuous improvement applies at least as much to people as it does to processes.

The seventh principle, 'leadership', is again qualitative and cultural and is closely associated with the eighth, 'drive out fear'. These principles are connected with the management style of the organisation. The objective here can usefully be seen as a requirement to move away from an adversarial style of management towards a collaborative style. Effective management in this way, supported by the SPC techniques, will focus attention on how to improve the individual (special causes) or the system (common causes) rather than on who to blame. The approach will again target curing the diseases rather than convicting the victims.

The ninth principle, 'breaking down barriers', is linked to the fourth. The suggestion here is for the creation of multi-disciplinary teams for product and service development aiming to enhance the development, production and delivery of new products or services. Deming does not discuss how this can be achieved or specifically recognise the difficulties that can be associated with it. There are a number of cultural and professional issues which often emerge in the creation of multi-disciplinary teams and any re-organisation into either a matrix form of management, or project teams, needs to be associated with commensurate changes in reward systems to ensure congruence of individual and organisational goals. Recent developments in Project Management such as 'Business Communications Engineering'

(*The Five Dimensions of Project Planning*, Schmied & Brown, 2009) are intended to address precisely this problem and have been applied very successfully in parts of the European automotive industry.

The tenth principle, 'eliminate slogans, exhortations and numerical quotas', is again more a cultural than a process statement. Here Deming suggests that these features may act more to vex the staff than encourage them. His argument is simple. If through the use of SPC the 'special causes' of failure related to individual machines and workers have been removed, then all other causes of failure relate to the system itself and they are the responsibility of management. No amount of slogans, exhortations and quotas will have any positive effect. Instead, Deming (1986: 67) suggests they will 'generate frustration and resentment'. This principle clearly links to the second, which required management to accept responsibility.

The eleventh principle, 'eliminate quotas, work standards and management by objectives or numerical goals and substitute leadership' seems to be something of a contradiction. Improvement targets must be an inherent part of measuring and monitoring achievement, and statistical process control provides one form of measurement of achievement.

Deming's point is that if the system is stable then its performance cannot be improved by the setting of targets, only by changes to the system. Deming sees the setting of targets and quotas as potentially both meaningless and divisive unless accompanied by specific action to improve the process. This may well mean re-appraising what the system is designed to achieve.

Removal of barriers that rob people of their right to pride in their work is the twelfth principle. Deming distinguishes management and workers from each other here. He sees that annual appraisal or merit review focuses the attention of management on the matters that will be covered in the appraisal or merit system. He implies that they will strive to achieve those things regardless of the impact on quality or productivity. They will do the right thing by the appraisal system, not by the customer!

The workers he sees as being constrained by uncertainty of employment, by lack of definition as to what constitutes acceptable workmanship, by poor quality materials, tools and machines and by ineffective supervision and management. He suggests that if these aspects are corrected, then quality products will follow. Deming (1986: 85) suggests 'Give the work force a chance to work with pride, and the 3 per cent that apparently don't care will erode itself by peer pressure'. He seems to ignore the idea that the whole organisation of many factories, based on the principles of classical management theory, is established (whether or not intentionally) to remove pride in achievement from the workers by fragmenting tasks.

Principle thirteen is to institute a vigorous education and self-improvement programme. This is Deming's recognition that if the organisation is to improve continuously, then the people must also improve continuously. He suggests that future competitive advantage will be achieved through application of knowledge, a conclusion with which there can be little argument.

The fourteenth and final principle is to put everyone to work to achieve the transformation. This suggests that the whole programme can only be successful if a 'total' approach is taken. This will require a strong, unified and cohesive culture within the organisation with commitment from top to bottom. Such a culture can only be achieved when the behaviour of management is consistent with their words, i.e. when they 'walk the talk' and is reminiscent of a very centralised, command and control approach which may not sit well in a Western liberal democracy.

Box 6.3   The Seven Point Action Plan

W. Edwards Deming:

Point 1)   Management must agree on the meaning of the quality programme, its implications and the direction to take.

Point 2)   Top management must accept and adopt the new philosophy.

Point 3)   Top management must communicate the plan and the necessity for it to the people in the organisation.

Point 4)   Every activity must be recognised as a step in a process and the customers of that process identified. The customers are responsible for the next stage of the process.

Point 5)   Each stage must adopt the 'Deming' or 'Shewhart' Cycle – Plan, Do, Check, Action – as the basis of quality improvement.

Point 6)   Team working must be engendered and encouraged to improve inputs and outputs. Everyone must be enabled to contribute to this process.

Point 7)   Construct an organisation for quality with the support of knowledgeable statisticians.

Taken together, these principles can be summarised as proposing wholesale attitudinal change throughout the organisation (a qualitative approach), supported where appropriate by reliance on validated statistical analysis (quantitative).

To enable the principles to be implemented, Deming proposed a Seven Point Action Plan. This action plan is perhaps best interpreted as a series of statements about 'what' to do, rather than the equally important 'how' to do it.

The first three points clearly focus attention on the top management group and are based on attitudes and communication. They suggest that this group must understand what they are trying to achieve, commit themselves to a successful outcome and then communicate throughout the organisation why it is necessary. This has distinct overtones of Crosby's more directly evangelical approach and reflects what can be thought of as the ethical aspect of the programme, the need for quality to be embraced in the values and beliefs of ALL members of the organisation. It can surely be agreed that if the management are not wholly committed to the programme and are unable, or unwilling, to communicate it effectively to the workforce, who must similarly accept it, then it will not work.

The fourth point recognises the process based work flow of many organisations and calls for the processes to be divided into stages. Each stage becomes a clear task with the recipients of its outputs being treated as its customers. Thus at every stage there are customers whose needs must be identified and satisfied. This can be seen as an attempt to overcome the problem of workers in many processes, for example in the manufacture of sub-assemblies who can be unaware of customers and do not recognise the sub-assembly as a product in its own right. It is suggested that this shift of emphasis enables workers to take a pride in their work that is otherwise absent.

The fifth point is simply to implement continuous improvement at every stage through the PDCA cycle. Achievement of implementation in this way implies acceptance, by both management and workers within each process, of responsibility for the process. This in turn implies that higher management must allow them authority to develop and implement the changes.

The next point, participation in team work to improve all inputs and outputs, can be seen to operate at several levels. First, a team culture must be developed within each process to improve it internally. Second, since changes in one area may have implications in another, a team culture must be engendered between process owners (the management) to enable effective communication between them. Third, to be truly effective, a means of sharing and developing improvements across processes must be developed – this links the whole pro-gramme back to top management.

The seventh point, construction of an organisation for quality, is perhaps a further development of the third part of stage six, improvement across processes. The requirement is to build an organisation which reflects and nurtures the achievement of quality. Deming suggests the use of knowledgeable statisticians to support this aspect, perhaps reflecting his own background. It is useful to go well beyond this and propose the support of a multi-disciplined team of management scientists and experts such as cyberneticians, psychologists, statisticians and accountants to work with the management team in the pursuit of the programme. This emphasises the collaborative nature of achieving quality. It is not suggested that the management scientists develop and impose a programme of change; this would be almost certainly doomed to failure. It is suggested rather that the management and workers should be responsible for the whole programme, having both control and own-ership. The role of the management scientists is to use their expertise in a supportive, guiding manner, as experts within the team.

The introduction to Deming's approach is now complete. Statistical Process Control and methodologies for implementing quality will be addressed in the appropriate chap-ters. This section is concluded by reaffirming the view that while initially Deming's approach was rooted in quantitative methods it later came to be supported by more qualitative techniques.

6.4   Successes and failures

While overall Deming can be said to have been very successful in his achievements, there have been both successes and failures. His movement into Japan, for example, was to some extent a result of the early rejection of his ideas by American managements. This perhaps reflects the maxim that 'a prophet is not without honour, save in his own country'. It was only after his substantial successes with Japanese industry that Deming was able to turn his attention again to the problems of industrial America.

Here, what Flood (1993: 14) calls Deming's fundamentally 'mechanistic' approach ran 'into strong workforce resistance, from both the managers and the workers'. Deming, taking account of these issues together with matters of reliance on technology, standards of practice and the cultural issues, substantially revised his methods. This is reflected in the shift in emphasis from quantitative to qualitative approaches and in the codification of the 'Seven Deadly Diseases'.

Adapting from Flood (op. cit.), the principal strengths of Deming's approach are con-sidered as:

- the systemic logic, particularly the idea of internal customer-supplier relationships;
- management before technology;
- emphasis on management leadership;
- the sound statistical approach;
- awareness of different socio-cultural contexts.

There are also significant weaknesses recognised:

- lack of a well defined methodology;
- the work is not adequately grounded in human relations theory;
- as with Crosby, the approach will not help in an organisation with a biased power structure.

Reviewing the strengths, the value of the systemic and logical approach cannot be denied; put simply, it is an organised and systematic rather than chaotic approach. The 'Plan, Do, Check, Action' cycle as a mechanism for organisational learning is recognised in other areas of management as a 'learning cycle'. Handy (1985) for example refers to a process of:

- Questioning and Conceptualisation – fundamental parts of effective planning;
- Experimentation – trying out ideas, the testing and evaluation of hypotheses;
- Consolidation – the alteration of habits, the basis for future action.

Handy sees this as the basis of human learning leading to continuous personal improvement. It is unsurprising that a similar process works for organisations which, after all, have people as their fundamental organisational units. This cycle will be seen echoed in chapter 18 on organisational learning.

Deming's prioritisation of management before technology represents a reversal of the attitudes of many managers. The British adage that 'a bad workman always blames his tools' recognises that the tendency for most managers is to look at external rather than internal factors as responsible for failure. If as Deming suggests 94% of problems belong to the management, then acceptance by them of responsibility is a primary step in enabling change. Equally, even the worst tools can be made to perform better in the hands of a good workman, but a bad workman will not achieve good performance however good the tools.

The recognition of the importance of leadership and motivation can be seen to reflect the development of human relations theory as a major strand of management thinking, although Deming does not draw heavily on the body of knowledge that became established in that area during his productive years.

Regarding the strong quantitative base, perhaps Flood does not go far enough. It is suggested that some form of measurement system, relying on both hard, physical measures and on softer aspects using techniques from organisational psychology, is fundamental to achievement of quality. A simple attempt to 'do better' will always be followed by questions such as 'how much' or 'when'. Vagueness on these issues would be expected to have a dispiriting effect on the participants while a form of achievement target orientation would be motivational. Success is said to breed success, but first of all it must be known that success is being achieved!

The recognition by Deming of different cultural contexts is a vital strength. His failure to draw heavily on the literature of human relations theory for this aspect suggests that his embrace of it was driven by pragmatism rather than desire, perhaps a reluctant recognition that it was necessary to allow the other ideas to work. Nonetheless, the recognition of different cultures and adaptation to them are essential in achieving success. Hofstede (1980) produced the principal work in this area. In the context of quality, the recognition needs to go well beyond the country differences highlighted by Hofstede to recognise the particular culture of organisations themselves, and even sections, functions and departments within organisations. These frequently have unique, perhaps very strong, cultural contexts.

Flood's criticism of a lack of a clear 'Deming method' can be seen as reasonably well justified. Like many gurus and experts, Deming suggests what to do without indicating very precisely how to do it. While perhaps constraining on the one hand, this lack of precision can be seen as potentially disemprisoning and empowering. To find an approach which works, it encourages experimentation and debate within each individual setting rather than using an approach which was developed in another. Perhaps the most important issue is reliance on Deming's principles.

The second weakness having been covered within the strengths, we can examine the third. Deming is criticised for saying nothing about intervention in political and coercive situations, but then perhaps nothing can be said. The second principle and the first three points of the action plan all call on management to accept their responsibility for quality and productivity and to embrace a new philosophy. These remarks are targeted directly at the most senior members of the management team, that is those who hold power in a political or coercive context. If they do not accept responsibility at the outset, they are ignoring the principles, and by default, not following the Deming method. If they seek to impose a quality approach on others, failure will certainly follow. Deming's whole approach rests on the attitude of management!

6.5   Critical review

The foundation of Deming's approach can be seen in his statistical background and his training in physics. The scientific method will have informed the development of his early approaches, and they continued to make a major contribution to work in the field of quality.

The principles and practice of Statistical Process Control have been demonstrated over time to have considerable value to organisations in both the service and manufacturing sectors. They also have value for the workers who use them, providing rapid and personal performance feedback information, enabling them to recognise their own successes and failures and to take corrective action where appropriate, provided always that the outputs are expressed in a language which they can understand.

Deming's work in relation to the softer issues is narrow and underdeveloped, failing to take account of much of the thinking in that area over the period of his career. While he did not claim to be an expert in this field, the value of his approach could have been further enhanced by a clearer focus on it.

The Plan, Do, Check, Action cycle is a clear directive to both management and workers that achieving continuous improvement is the purpose of the quality activity. This contrasts directly with the overtones of a discrete programme suggested in Crosby's work.

Deming makes quite clear reference to the service sector in his work, but again places much emphasis on quantitative aspects of this area. For example, he refers to aspects such as how long a telephone is out of action before it is repaired. While this is of great importance, of equal importance is the tone of voice which a person uses in answering the telephone when it rings. This may be a stronger determinant of how the customer perceives the level of service quality than the number of times that it rings, or even the words that are said – readers will recall the comment on this issue in the previous chapter.

It is often the case that managers take measurements of the things which are easy to measure, rather than the things which, while difficult to measure, are of greater importance. In a world which relies ever more heavily on telecommunications, these will have increasing importance. The reliability and clarity of telecommunication systems are such that these are no longer significant issues, and many businesses are run entirely through them, for example telephone and Internet banking and retailing. Of increasing importance, then, is tone of voice, since technical issues are less problematic and digital technology makes tone of voice transparent to the listener.

It is accepted that Deming has probably made the most substantial contribution to quality management. However, enthusiasm must be tempered with the knowledge that a clearer method, a more explicit and developed recognition of the human aspects and a precise focus on what constitutes quality of service in the contemporary world would enhance the value of his work.

Summary

This chapter has presented the main strands of the work of W. Edwards Deming through the five point critical framework. Readers wishing to develop their knowledge further should read the relevant chapters in part four of this book and refer to Deming's own work, in particular *Out of the Crisis*.

KEY LEARNING POINTS

W. Edwards Deming

Definition of quality:
a function of continuous improvement based on reduction in variation around the desired output.

Seven Deadly Sins and Diseases:

- Lack of constancy;
- Short-term profit focus;
- Performance appraisal;
- Job-hopping;
- Use of visible figures only;
- Excessive medical costs;
- Excessive liability costs.

Five key beliefs:
Quantification, Recognition of failure causes, Systematic approach, Continuous improvement, Constancy

Principal methods:
Fourteen Principles for Transformation, the Seven Point Action Plan

---

Question

Deming suggests that 94% of quality problems are a function of the design of the system (the common causes of error). How would you address these problems?

7 Armand V. Feigenbaum

'Quality is what the user, the customer, says it is'

Armand Feigenbaum, 2014

Introduction

Armand Feigenbaum, who died in 2014, originated the approach to quality known as 'Total Quality Control' (TQC), which has a clear industrial focus. After completing a doctorate at MIT (Massachusetts Institute of Technology), Feigenbaum joined the General Electric Company where he was manager of world-wide manufacturing operations and quality control before becoming Founder and President of General Systems Company. His book, *Total Quality Control*, completed whilst he was still a doctoral student, and his other works, were discovered by the Japanese in the early 1950s. He was also involved with them through his business contacts with Hitachi and Toshiba.

Bendell (1989: 15) states that Feigenbaum presented a case for a 'systematic, or total approach to quality', and it is argued by Bank (1992: xv) that he was the first to do so. Logothetis (1992: 94) suggests that to Feigenbaum 'quality is simply a way of managing a business organisation', while Gilbert (1992: 22) concurs with that and adds that Feigenbaum sees 'quality improvement as the single most important force leading to organisational success and growth'. Pyzdek and Keller (2013) describe it as 'TQC is a system of specialized quality control activities'.

Feigenbaum's contribution has been widely recognised. He was founding chairman of the International Academy for Quality and is a past president of the American Society for Quality Control, which awarded him the Edwards Medal and Lancaster Award for his international contribution to quality and productivity (Bendell, 1989: 15).

7.1 Philosophy

Feigenbaum's philosophy is clearly founded in his early idea of the 'total' approach, reflecting a systemic attitude of mind. He saw it as fundamental to quality improvement that all functions in an organisation should be involved in the quality process and that quality should be built in to the product rather than failure be inspected out.

He earlier defined quality as 'best for the customer use and selling price' and quality control as:

> an effective method for co-ordinating the quality maintenance and quality improve-
> ment efforts of the various groups in an organisation so as to enable production at the
> most economical levels which allow for full customer satisfaction.

Reflecting on Feigenbaum's approach, his philosophy appears systemic, at least in its attempt to embrace the whole. While the work of both Deming and Juran can be interpreted in a systemic manner, Feigenbaum is explicit from the outset that this is vital. In the contemporary, complex world of organisations there is every need to manage through a systemic mindset, recognising and dealing with interactions across internal and external organisational boundaries and at all levels within them as well as with the suppliers, customers and other stakeholders in the enterprise. This approach also respects the economic, social and environmental imperatives for quality outlined in chapter 1.

The issue of building quality in can also be addressed here. This recognises that organisations do not simply manufacture products, they also design and develop them. Feigenbaum appears to be suggesting that many quality problems can be eradicated from both the products and the manufacturing process by paying attention to the quality issue from the conception of the idea, right through to delivery of the first and subsequent items (reflecting Ohno's approach to 'muda'). Basic design techniques here might include colour coding wires so that electronic products cannot be incorrectly wired or varying bolt positions in otherwise apparently symmetrical pieces of metal so that they can only be mounted correctly.

Looking at Feigenbaum's definition of quality, two constraints are discovered which have not previously been seen, 'customer use' and 'selling price'. The first of these is perhaps no different from Deming's 'needs of the consumer', or Crosby's 'conformance to requirements', but it suggests a constraint, rather than an ideal, to aim for. It seems to imply that there are, perhaps, limits to useful quality. The issue of selling price clearly indicates that for any given price Feigenbaum perceives limitations to the expectations of quality. This can perhaps be interpreted as saying that a quality differential, of perhaps longevity, performance or reliability between, say, a car costing US$10,000 and one costing US$100,000 is to be expected and is acceptable. This also implies the need to properly comprehend the use to which a customer will put the product.

His definition of quality control emphasises the integral nature of the quality process, stressing 'co-ordination' of maintenance and improvement efforts across 'groups'. It is notable that he does not say 'functions' or 'departments'. This can be interpreted as a recognition of the human relations aspects of organisations.

Summarising Feigenbaum's philosophy, a commitment to a systemic, 'total' approach and an emphasis on designing for quality and involving all departments is evident. Supporting this is recognition of, and reliance on, the human aspects of the organisation with statistical methods being used as necessary. This contrasts quite sharply with the greater statistical emphasis in the work of Deming.

7.2   Assumptions

Feigenbaum's apparent assumptions about the world reveal a different understanding to those gurus already reviewed.

First is his explicit assumption of a world composed of systems. He works with the interrelationships that he perceives to exist between all aspects within the organisation, and importantly, in its environment or market. He recognises the contribution made by suppliers and the constraints, particularly on performance expectations and price, imposed by customers.

The systemic view is clear again in his second assumption, that human relationships are a basic issue in quality achievement. This concurs with the developments in management thinking, the human relations school, that were occurring at the time of his early work.

In these assumptions he clearly focuses attention on the whole enterprise, from suppliers to users, through every function and to all the groups who are involved in it. The development in more recent times of global businesses serving global markets, of ever more complex and inter-dependent relationships between organisational, social and individual well-being and the emergence of many more virtual organisations based on strategic part-nerships leads to the conclusion that this systemic view must be sustained.

An organisation can today be more clearly seen to exist within an eco-system, comprised of economic and social relationships, in which it will ultimately either thrive or become extinct. Although not explicitly referring to adaptation of the organisation, Feigenbaum's commitment to 'full customer satisfaction' implies constant awareness of customer needs and expectations within the organisation and the need for change to satisfy them.

Feigenbaum further assumes that continuous improvement is both desirable and achievable. Referring again to his definition of quality, we can see the potential for conflict and contradiction. For example, if customer expectations on performance and price are met, then quality, by his definition, has been achieved. However, unless the process of TQC ends, then further improvement will arise. This in turn implies a need for the organisation to interact with its customers, aiming to alter their expectations of quality, perhaps as suggested by Galbraith (1974). There is a danger, therefore, that as with Crosby, Feigenbaum's approach can be interpreted as a finite, ends-oriented and discrete programme, whereas his intent appears to have been for continuous improvement.

7.3   Methods

While Flood (1993: 35) reduces Feigenbaum's philosophy through a four step approach, this (Box 7.1) should be viewed as a simplification of his overall method.

These steps may certainly be seen as capturing the fundamental essence of Feigenbaum's approach, which is intended to lead to a 'Total Quality System'. This is defined by Bendell (1989: 16) as:

> The agreed companywide and plantwide operating work structure, documented in effective, integrated technical and managerial procedures, for guiding the co-ordinated actions of the people, the machines and the information of the company and plant in the best and most practical ways to assure customer quality satisfaction and economical costs of quality.

The Weberian, bureaucratic overtones and dangers inherent in this definition are quite clear, and as Summers (2009) notes, 'experiences are memorable and that it is this emotional connection with a product or service that differentiates one organization from another'. A heavy reliance on documentation and integration of procedures and on co-ordinating the

---

Box 7.1   Four steps to quality

Armand V. Feigenbaum:

Step 1)   Set quality standards;

Step 2)   Appraise conformance to standards;

Step 3)   Act when standards are not met;

Step 4)   Plan to make improvements.

people, machines and information certainly present an opportunity to those 'keener on talking about work than doing any' (Beckford, 1993). Developments in quality management system standards challenge this notion of documentation with a shift from compliance with documented procedures to a focus on customer satisfaction and continuous improvement and with particular attention paid to active management of skills – a change which Feigenbaum would surely have welcomed. It is fair to say that contemporary information technology supports a radically different approach to the availability of information than was possible when Feigenbaum formulated his methods.

To counter the danger, Feigenbaum used in the first sentence the word 'agreed'. This stresses that everyone must be committed to the design of the organisation through effective communication. However, while proposing that gradual development of the programme is preferred, little is said about how agreement is achieved which permits scope for either autocratic or democratic processes to be employed. While Feigenbaum proposes participation as a means of harnessing the contribution of people and encouraging a sense of belonging, it remains the case that the approach need not be used in this participative manner, and Dale et al (2007) note in reviewing Feigenbaum that 'Quality leadership is essential to a company's success in the marketplace'.

A further tool is the measurement of what Feigenbaum calls 'operating quality costs'. These are divided into four self-explanatory categories and have been met before in chapter 3:

- Prevention costs, including quality planning;
- Appraisal costs, including inspection costs;
- Internal failure costs, including scrap and rework;
- External failure costs, including warranty costs
  and complaints.

It can be seen again how Feigenbaum's concept of total quality extends from product development right through to product use, that is, product quality in the hands of the consumer. Bendell (1989: 16) states that:

> reductions in operating quality costs result from setting up a total quality system for two reasons:
>
> Lack of existing effective customer-orientated customer standards may mean current quality of products is not optimal given use.
> Expenditure on prevention costs can lead to a several fold reduction in internal and external failure costs.

The proposal overall is that by measuring quality at each stage the total costs of running the organisation can be reduced. A similar concept is met in the food manufacturing industry, which uses a system called Hazard Analysis Critical Control Points (HACCP) to ensure food product quality and safety at risk points. This would include aspects such as temperature. If, for example, a product must be boiled, then the HACCP system would test it to ensure that boiling point is actually reached. The emphasis on design again stresses the importance to Feigenbaum of designing quality in to the product.

Overall, Feigenbaum's approach is best seen as part of the 'kaizen' management practices, which are management responsibility oriented and involve effective team working across the organisation. These tools will be examined in more depth in the appropriate chapters.

7.4   Successes and failures

Feigenbaum's approach has undoubtedly been successful and has been adopted by a number of organisations. There is little doubt that his recognition of quality as a way of running an organisation, rather than as a secondary activity, was a major breakthrough to thinking in this area, yet even today many organisations continue to consider quality as a bolt on rather than a fundamental of organisational effectiveness. Recent experience with a number of organisations internationally has shown that many continue to focus on pursuit of a quality accreditation rather than on organisational survival through quality products or services.

Southern Paper

Southern Paper is a paper mill with an annual gross capacity of 100k tonnes of recycled paper. The production process for recycling paper has several key stages:

- the liquidising of the inbound fibre and integration of new fibre; colouring the mixture;
- making the paper itself;
- splitting big reels into customer orders.

   In the case of Southern Paper, the process extends to a conversion process in which reeled paper is converted to flat sheets in a wide variety of sizes and colours.

   The quality approach at Southern Paper is dominated by volume. While there is much talk in the boardroom of 'meeting customer expectations', in practice the talk on the shop floor is of the need to meet volume targets rather than quality targets, and those volume targets get dealt with at an aggregate level. Translating, the 100k gross tonnes reduces to about 70k net tonnes of product sold. That equates to about 200 tonnes of saleable product per day. Over time the production staff have come to see a 'good tonne' as a tonne of paper which can be sold. The work required is to help Southern Paper to understand a good tonne as being product of saleable quality for which there is an order. A tonne of good quality paper for which there is no order is no better than waste.

Flood (1993: 36) again provides a summary of the principal strengths and weaknesses of Feigenbaum's approach from which the following is adapted. He sees the main strengths as:

- a total or whole approach to quality control;
- emphasis on the importance of management;
- socio–technical systems thinking is taken into account;
- participation is promoted.

Principal weaknesses identified are:

- the work is systemic but not complementarist;
- the breadth of management theory is recognised but not unified;
- the political or coercive context is not addressed.

It can be added to this critique that the industrial orientation of the approach provides little of real value for service based organisations. Similarly, as with Deming, it lacks clear method; ample instruction in what to do is not supported by guidance on how to do it.

The necessity and contribution of the systemic view proposed has already been acknowledged. Similarly the focus on the importance of management to the process is supported, although as Bendell (1989: 16) suggests:

> modern quality control is seen by Feigenbaum as stimulating and building up *operator responsibility* and interest in quality.

While this is achieved through management commitment, the need for management to *sell* the ideas is stressed, suggesting a certain resistance by employees to accept the concepts of quality. While accepting the value of participation, the question has to be raised again – how is such participation to be achieved? Even Flood's choice of the word 'harnessing' in respect of individual contributions is suggestive of a less than whole hearted commitment, having overtones of compulsion.

Looking at the weaknesses, Feigenbaum's work says nothing about the identification and selection of tools which are most appropriate for a particular organisational or national context. For contemporary managers this issue is of great importance. Many organisations are globally based, and to achieve agreement, which Feigenbaum requires amongst the top management, account must be taken of the varying cultures and expectations of the participants. An approach which works well in Hong Kong may fail completely in Tokyo, Los Angeles or London.

Finally, Flood's comment that nothing is said about political or coercive contexts is valid. Feigenbaum's assumption that people can and will work together for the improvement of the organisation and its outputs is clear in his work. However, his recognition of the need to *sell* the total quality concept perhaps suggests that a degree of political or coercive pressure may, for him legitimately, be brought to bear to achieve the end result. That being said, it is perhaps a little unfair to criticise someone for not offering a solution to a problem he did not set out to address!

7.5   Critical review

There appear to be three founding ideas to Feigenbaum's work. First is his acceptance of the systems paradigm, second is a belief in appropriate measurement, third is the recognition of participation as a means of developing change and encouraging creativity. Feigenbaum's strong academic background in issues of quality control, supported by his extensive practical managerial experience, undoubtedly provided a substantial platform for the further development and successful application of his ideas with considerable success.

The apparent lack of a well developed, clear methodology telling managers how to proceed with his approach is a major drawback. Perhaps leadership and management styles are much greater factors in the success or failure of a Total Quality Control initiative than is normally recognised. Adoption by the most senior management of a collaborative, team-based working pattern is not easily achieved or maintained – especially in a world where, predominantly, rewards are calculated against personal rather than team achievement.

Functionally structured companies usually have power bases within each function. If these are strong, then they may resist the perceived loss of power that arises from any other orientation. Companies are often heard of which are 'production led', 'marketing led' or 'accounting led'. These are companies which are dominated by a particular power group. They perceive the world from a particular standpoint, and perhaps undervalue the contribution of other professions. Adoption of a team based approach where each profession is valued for its contribution to the whole, perhaps in the form of a project or matrix management system, is unlikely. Similar comments can be made about issues such as sexual orientation, gender and race. Professional and other biases must be overcome in the creation of organisations based on expertise, Feigenbaum says nothing of how to achieve this.

The quantitative aspects of Feigenbaum's approach are welcome. Reliance on statistics 'where appropriate' is a useful guide, encouraging managers to use discretion in their choice of measurements. This contrasts quite sharply with the strong emphasis on measurement proposed by Deming. Feigenbaum is quite selective about what it is useful to measure and when. Like Deming he proposes, through the four way division of operating quality costs, a form of customer chain analysis which can be seen to be helpful not simply in identifying the costs of quality but, very importantly, where they arise.

Feigenbaum has made a substantial contribution to work in the field of quality, and certain contemporary aspects of quality management carry powerful influences from his work. Enthusiasm for his approach must be tempered by recognising some weaknesses with respect to methodology and cultural context and the important understanding that his work does not go beyond the industrial sector.

Summary

This chapter has introduced the principal strands of the work of Armand Feigenbaum, presenting and reviewing his philosophy, assumptions, methods and successes and failures. Readers may wish to refer to Feigenbaum's own work *Total Quality Control* (1986) to enhance and further develop their understanding.

KEY LEARNING POINTS

Armand V. Feigenbaum

Definition of quality:
quality is a way of running a business organisation

Key beliefs:
systems thinking, relevant measurement, participation

Principal methods:
the four steps to quality, operating quality costs

Question

The chapter suggests difficulties might arise from Feigenbaum's definition of a 'Total Quality System' with its 'Weberian, bureaucratic overtones'. Critically review Feigenbaum's work in the context of this suggestion.

8   Kaoru Ishikawa

'Wherever they are, human beings are human beings'

Kaoru Ishikawa, 1980

Introduction

Kaoru Ishikawa, who died in 1989, commenced his career as a Chemist, held a Doctorate in Engineering and was Emeritus Professor at Tokyo University. Bank (1992: 74) cites him as the 'Father of Quality Circles' and as a founder of the Japanese quality movement. He became involved in quality issues in 1949 through the Union of Japanese Scientists and Engineers (JUSE) and subsequently became a world-wide lecturer and consultant on quality. Gilbert (1992: 23) suggests that Ishikawa was the first guru to 'recognise that quality improvement is too important to be left in the hands of specialists'. Ishikawa's writings explaining his approach include the *Guide to Quality Control* (1986) and *What Is Total Quality Control? The Japanese Way* (1985), which have both been translated into English. Ishikawa was widely honoured for his work, receiving the Deming, Nihon Keizai Press and Industrial Standardisation prizes and the Grant Award from the American Society for Quality Control.

8.1   Philosophy

Ishikawa himself, cited by Goetsch and Davis (2014), says:

> quality is a broad concept that goes beyond just product quality to also include the quality of people, processes and every other aspect.

Gilbert (1992: 23) and Logothetis (1992: 95) see the philosophical roots of Ishikawa's work in the concept of Company-Wide Quality. Ishikawa himself, cited by Bendell (1989: 18), said:

> The results of these company-wide Quality Control activities are remarkable, not only in ensuring the quality of industrial products but also in their great contribution to the company's overall business.

Bendell (op. cit.) confirms his understanding, saying that Ishikawa defines quality as meaning 'not only the quality of the product, but also of after sales service, quality of management, the company itself and the human being'.

Flood (1993: 33) interprets Ishikawa's approach as involving 'vertical and horizontal co-operation'. It requires communication and co-operation between different levels of managers, supervisors and workers and with suppliers and customers. Ishikawa's first belief is that everyone involved in or affected by the company should be involved in the quality programme. This is similar to Feigenbaum's 'total' approach.

The extent of involvement proposed is also significant. Ishikawa asks that the programme not just be company wide (and beyond) but that it involve '*active*' participation – as opposed to passive tolerance. His approach to participation emphasises greater worker involvement and motivation which Bendell (1989: 19) sees as being created through:

- 'an atmosphere where employees are continuously looking to resolve problems;
- greater commercial awareness;
- a change of shop floor attitude in aiming for ever increasing goals'.

These strands stress three qualitative words, atmosphere, awareness and attitude. These are cultural words and have direct implications for management behaviour.

An 'atmosphere where employees are continuously looking to resolve problems' implies acceptance by management that:

- workers have the ability to recognise both problems and solutions;
- management will either: accept the need for change and implement proposals; or, explain why a proposed change is not possible or desirable in a way which maintains the employees' enthusiasm.

A 'greater commercial awareness' imposes two management responsibilities. First, to facilitate training and education for the workforce, second, to provide accurate, meaningful and timely data about company and competitor performance. These matters should be considered equally important in a public sector or not-for-profit organisation which, rather than profit, will be focused on delivering the 'best' service within a constrained resource.

The third strand, 'a change of shop floor attitude' towards a focus on ever increasing goals – the culture of continuous improvement – again implies management responsibility. Management must align their behaviours and their words in order to enable such a culture. Any inconsistency between words and actions will be destructive. Deming's concern about 'exhortations' is important here, as well as Crosby's promotion through slogans and platitudes.

Clearly Ishikawa believed that effective participation, like effective communication, is a two-way street and as suggested by Hagima Karatsu, Managing Director of Matsushita Communication (cited by Bendell, 1989: 19), 'creative co-operation' between people is an absolute requirement for a quality organisation.

A third element to Ishikawa's work is the emphasis on direct, simple communication. Bendell (1989: 17) states that Ishikawa saw 'open group communication' as critical, particularly in the use of his tools for problem solving. A fundamental part of communication for Ishikawa seems to have been an emphasis on simplicity. For example the book *Guide to Quality Control* was deliberately written as a 'non-sophisticated' (op. cit.) text and Bank (1992: 75) suggests that Ishikawa worked in a 'straightforward manner'. Logothetis (1992: 95) stresses that Ishikawa concentrated on 'simple statistical techniques for data collection and presentation'. The requirement for simplicity covers both the qualitative and quantitative issues.

The emphasis on simplicity and using the language of the shop-floor is considered as empowering, although it could be seen by some as patronising. The workers, having been trained in the appropriate methods, are not obliged to use arcane terminology. Management are unable to hide behind complex approaches and sophisticated language which often seem to betray a lack of real understanding. Since training is given to all levels of employee, a common quality language is spoken by all, which in turn aids and enhances communication.

Three principal strands can be identified in Ishikawa's philosophy. First, in company with Feigenbaum is the systemic or holistic approach advocated by 'Company Wide Quality', an all-embracing view. Second is participation; active and creative co-operation between those affected. Third is the emphasis on communication through simplicity of analysis and method and commonality of language.

8.2 Assumptions

Ishikawa's apparent assumptions about the world will now be explored.

Ishikawa's first assumption is concerned with inter-relatedness, a 'total' or systems view. He explicitly recognises that every aspect of the organisation and the relevant environment must be considered. As with Feigenbaum, it is difficult to argue with his approach, although whether Ishikawa's techniques and methods are systemic will be considered in the next section, since some rely heavily on a reductionist perspective.

Ishikawa's second assumption is that a fully participative approach can be adopted. This implies a belief that every individual within the organisation can, and will, commit themselves to addressing the quality issue. This suggests that a quality belief system must become established and the achievement of higher quality become a superordinate goal, overriding all others. The primacy of this goal, while perhaps accommodating the requirements of the management or owners, seems to assume congruence between the goals of the workforce and those of the organisation. However, little is said about how such a state can be achieved, and Bendell (1989: 19) notes that '[quality] circle members receive no direct financial reward for their improvements'. Commitment to quality then, very like religious belief, is considered to be its own reward! This can be contrasted with Crosby's dictum to reward those who contribute to the quality programme.

A further assumption is that the quality activity takes place in an organisational environment which is free from political or power relations between participants. While this may be an admirable ideal, it must be considered unrealistic. Power structures emerge in all organisations; they may be dominant or subordinate issues in the organisation, but they nonetheless exist. Ishikawa is silent on this aspect and how it may be addressed; perhaps reflecting the strength of his own position, or a lack of awareness of the problems faced by others, less educated, or in less privileged positions. Alternatively, it may simply reflect the strongly collective nature of the Japanese value system.

The third assumption, effective communication, is to some extent associated with the second. Participation relies on effective communication for its success. While the development of a common 'language' for discussing quality issues throughout the company is considered to be a substantial benefit, it is still likely that communication will be inhibited by cultural or political issues which prevent viewpoints from being expressed. For example, respect for age or status or fear of loss of face may prevent an open exchange of views, and no real communication will take place. The 'loser' in the transaction may have a valid viewpoint, but is not heard.

Finally, we can turn to the assumption that 'simplicity' in technique and method is useful. While acknowledging that the sophistication of tools must match that of the people who work with them, Ishikawa's work to some extent may be seen as undervaluing or under-estimating the people in the organisation in assuming that they can only cope with simple concepts and methods.

If we consider the complexity of life for any individual, we must recognise that the majority deal extremely well with a highly complex existence. People cope with accommodation, raising children and managing families (surely the ultimate management challenges), pen-sions, health matters, taxes, driving. All require complex problem solving, communication and organisational skills. These skills are rarely expressly articulated and acknowledged but none the less they exist and are used for the most part very well. To assume, as Ishikawa appears to, that everything must be simplified is perhaps arrogant. Perhaps he underestimates the potential of the workforce and sows the seeds of future discontent.

A second assumption apparently being made is that quality problems are tractable to simple methods. Products and services are increasingly complex, as are organisations and their environments. There are increasing inter-relationships between factors and more factors to be considered. Experience suggests that simple problem solving approaches are unlikely to be adequate in increasingly complex situations. Other, more sophisticated but not necessarily less accessible tools must be used. Despite their increasing availability and prominence, especially in Western nations during Ishikawa's time, he does not appear to have taken account of them. Some, as will be seen later in this book, reflect values in relation to the workforce which accord well with those of Ishikawa and would have enhanced his approach.

8.3   Methods

Ishikawa's overarching method is 'company-wide quality control'. This he sees as being supported by the 'quality circles' technique and the 'seven tools of quality control'. These will be dealt with in turn.

Company-wide quality control has already largely been addressed as the founding phil-osophy of Ishikawa's approach and deals with organisational aspects. It embraces all parts and uses the tools which will be described in the following pages. Bendell (op. cit.) suggests that fifteen effects arise from this approach (Box 8.1).

While acknowledging that these are benefits, it cannot be agreed that they are necessarily consequent upon the company-wide quality control approach being adopted. Perhaps, as Logothetis (1992: 96) suggests, 'kaizen consciousness [implied within Ishikawa's work] can only be established when management changes the corporate culture', an area which is not discussed by Ishikawa.

Quality Circles are Ishikawa's principal method for achieving participation. Composed of between four and twelve workers from the same area of activity and led by a workman or supervisor. Their function is to 'identify local problems and recommend solutions' (Gilbert, 1992). Bendell (1989: 18) identifies three aims:

- 'To contribute to the improvement and development of the enterprise;
- To respect human relations and build a happy workshop offering job satisfaction;
- To deploy human capabilities fully and draw out infinite potential'.

Gilbert (1992: 92) suggests that there are a number of 'cornerstones' to successful Quality Circles (Box 8.2). The first four of which apply universally – management at all levels must

Box 8.1 Fifteen effects of company-wide quality control (Gilbert, 1992)

Kaoru Ishikawa:

Effect 1) Product quality is improved and becomes uniform. Defects are reduced;

Effect 2) Reliability of goods is improved;

Effect 3) Cost is reduced;

Effect 4) Quantity of production is increased, and it becomes possible to make rational production schedules;

Effect 5) Wasteful work and rework are reduced;

Effect 6) Technique is established and improved;

Effect 7) Expenses for inspection and testing are reduced;

Effect 8) Contracts between vendor and vendee are rationalised;

Effect 9) The sales market is enlarged;

Effect 10) Better relationships are established between departments;

Effect 11) False data and reports are reduced;

Effect 12) Discussions are carried out more freely and democratically;

Effect 13) Meetings are operated more smoothly;

Effect 14) Repairs and installations of equipment and facilities are done more rationally;

Effect 15) Human relations are improved.

be committed and workers must be trained and willing participants. The 'shared work background' has some limitations, as it fails to address cross-functional or inter-departmental needs. Solution orientation is a means of ensuring that Quality Circles do not simply descend into complaint sessions where the focus is on what the management, or adjacent processes, could do or not do. Considerable benefit could be gained in using Ishikawa's approach if the notion of the willing participant encouraging willingness had been addressed. In adversarial cultures or where loyalty between the organisation and its employees is limited, as is often found in Western organisations, such participation is often very unwillingly provided.

Recognition of efforts is a difficult area; if there is only effort and no achievement then should this be recognised? To maintain efforts and encourage further attempts, it is probably valuable to recognise the work done. However, the difference between effort and sub-stantial achievement should also be acknowledged.

Minutes and an agenda provide regulatory devices for the circle. They enable the members to consider what has or has not been achieved since the last meeting, to keep track of solutions and to maintain focus within the circle on innovation rather than reiterating old points. The agenda provides the opportunity to control the discussion to give thinking time to the participants before the meeting to consider the issues. Keeping to time is a matter of good discipline which will be supported by the previous two items.

Informing bosses of meeting times is both courteous and good communication practice. He or she may wish to attend or to provide some input to the meeting, either in the form of ideas or implementation progress, or to support the effort in other ways.

Ensuring a non-hierarchical approach is perhaps idealistic. Experience of working within Quality Circles and other team type environments suggests that hierarchy, of some sort, emerges quickly.

Box 8.2   Cornerstones to successful Quality Circles (Gilbert, 1992)

J. Gilbert:

- Top management support;
- Operational management support and involvement;
- Voluntary participation of the members;
- Effective training of the leader and members;
- Shared work background;
- Solution oriented approach;
- Recognition of the quality circle's efforts;
- Have an agenda, minutes and rotating chairmanship;
- Keep to the time allowed for the meeting;
- Members should inform bosses of meeting times;
- Make sure that quality circles are not hierarchical. If seniority plays any sort of part you'll find the MD's [CEO] secretary thinks she's too good to attend the regular secretaries' Quality Forum.

Quality Circles inaction

A retail distributor with several hundred outlets decided to launch a service quality initiative to improve its performance. The organisation, committed to this initiative at its head office, selected 'Quality Circles' as the driving mechanism to be used at the outlet level.

The senior management attended training sessions, which was then extended to the outlet managers. After the training had been completed, the programme was ready to be launched. Staff were informed by letter that the organisation was to adopt Quality Circles and that the local manager would be arranging these events. No-one at the local level was provided with any training.

The local managers then called the staff together – at the end of the working day – and informed them that the first meeting of the Quality Circle would take place at 5pm the following Wednesday; overtime would not be paid and all staff were expected to volunteer to join the circle. At the first meeting the rules would be explained and roles allocated within the circle.

The managers chaired the first meetings and explained the purpose of the circles. They were then thrown open to suggestions from the staff. Discussion in one outlet focused on the number of ashtrays in the customer facing areas. Another focused on opening hours, until the manager ruled the discussion 'out of order'. Opening hours fell beyond the scope of the brief – a constraint applied to many suggested discussion topics. In most cases, the manager's secretary recorded the discussion and produced minutes. The managers edited these and despatched the usually sanitised version to head office as evidence.

While the organisation persisted with these events for around twelve months, no significant or useful ideas emerged or were implemented. No major changes took place in systems and procedures to improve service quality. The whole exercise was a waste – although it could be argued that awareness of quality of customer service was raised amongst the staff, perhaps bringing some intangible benefit.

There were perhaps four major mistakes made by the organisation in pursuing this initiative:

- an absolute lack of training for local staff;
- the structure with managers appointed as QC leaders;
- the attempt to achieve participation was by unilateral dictat;
- the failure by the senior management to understand the organisation structure which determined where problems could be solved.

Any multi-outlet organisation necessarily adopts standardised systems and procedures to ensure continuity and accuracy of service. These are increasingly tied to the capabilities of information systems which dictate what is, or is not, possible to deliver.

This was a classic case of the senior management of the organisation appearing to 'blame' the staff for poor customer service, whilst blinding (or perhaps deafening) themselves to the potential for improvement which lay only within their own power.

Ishikawa suggests that Quality Circles should be an integral part of the quality effort, not an isolated approach. They have met with success and failure in many countries. Bendell (1989: 19) comments that 'Even in Japan, many Quality Circles have collapsed, usually because of management's lack of interest or excessive intervention'. Both Crosby and Juran have questioned their effectiveness in the West, while Crosby is reported to consider that Quality Circles are abused as a cure for poor employee motivation, productivity and quality. Juran suggests that if an organisation's management are not trained in quality then Quality Circles will have limited effectiveness.

The quantitative techniques of Ishikawa's approach are referred to by Bendell as the 'seven tools of quality control' (Box 8.3). Taken together, they are a set of pictures of quality, representing in diagrammatic or chart form the quality status of the operation of process being reviewed.

Ishikawa considered that all staff should be trained in these techniques. They will be explored in part four, as they have a useful role to play in managing quality.

Box 8.3   Seven tools of quality control

Kaoru Ishikawa:

Tool 1) Pareto charts:	used to identify the principal causes of problems.
Tool 2) Ishikawa/fishbone diagrams:	charts of cause and effect in processes.
Tool 3) Stratification:	layer charts which place each set of data successively on top of the previous one.
Tool 4) Check sheets:	to provide a record of quality.
Tool 5) Histograms:	graphs used to display frequency of various ranges of values of a quantity.
Tool 6) Scattergraphs:	used to help determine whether there is a correlation between two factors.
Tool 7) Control charts:	used as a device in Statistical Process Control.

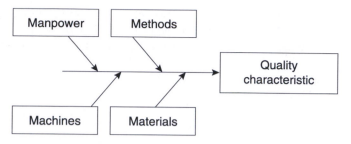

Figure 8.1 The Ishikawa or fishbone diagram.

This chapter will examine only the Ishikawa or fishbone diagram since this is the only technique that originated with Ishikawa. He developed the approach while at the University of Tokyo to explain relationships between factors. It subsequently became part of his quality tools portfolio and has been widely adopted throughout industry.

The Ishikawa diagram, Figure 8.1, is essentially an end or goal oriented representation of a problem situation. The goal or objective is placed at the head of the fish and contributing factors categorised. Gilbert (1992: 111) suggests that major categories such as 'Men, Machines, Materials and Methods' may provide a useful first set of categories; each of these categories is then subdivided again, the 'fishbones' gaining further ribs and sub-ribs as the whole issue of concern is explored. Other forms of categorisation such as processes, technology, knowledge or information systems may also be appropriate. The approach is also useful in enabling and encouraging participants to express their views.

The approach does not carry with it any inherent prioritisation of issues, and ideas are not constrained by any limitations. The pragmatic world of management does impose constraints of issues such as time, technology and capital, and these may affect the value of the approach. Issues emerging, which are not responded to adequately, will cause discontent and perhaps, fragmentation of the quality effort. The diagram can easily be used as a device for apportioning blame instead of one for enabling improvement.

Equally, the approach assumes a linear 'cause-effect' chain of events which does not admit the potential for inter-relationships between causes or dynamic or time-related effects. For example, the inter-relationship between workers and machines, called ergonomics, can have a substantial impact on the ability to produce a quality product or service, whereas looking at either in isolation may produce no clue as to the cause. A successful 'cure' to any problem may mean making adjustments or changes in a number of places to both fix the specific problem and ensure that the whole system remains in balance. Often, changing only one aspect can push other aspects to a point where they may fail.

Summarising Ishikawa's approach, it can be seen to contain both quantitative and qualitative aspects which taken together focus on achieving 'Company-Wide Quality'.

8.4   Successes and failures

Ishikawa's world-wide reputation and the widespread acceptance of his ideas suggest that his approach has met with considerable success. That he is best known for the fishbone diagram should not inhibit appreciation of the value of his other works. Similarly, that Quality Circles have been successful cannot be doubted, notwithstanding the level of failure that has been seen in some organisations. This idea which has been adopted to the extent that Bendell

(1989: 19) reports – 'more than 10 million circle members' in Japan alone – has undoubtedly been useful.

Summarising from Flood (1993: 34–35), the strengths of Ishikawa's approach are:

- emphasis on participation;
- variety of quantitative and qualitative methods;
- a whole system view;
- QCC's are relevant to all sectors of the economy.

The main weaknesses can be viewed as:

- fishbone diagrams are systematic but not systemic;
- QCC's depend upon management support;
- failure to address coercive contexts.

Reviewing the strengths, participation and the development of tools usable by the stake-holders are of undeniable value. They enable people at all levels in the organisation to make a meaningful contribution to the process of achieving quality. Promoting creativity and increasing motivation have value both for the organisation and the individual.

The choice of a mixture of methods and tools, which are both qualitative and quantitative, is seen as encouraging a broader understanding of the organisation than would be achieved with a simple focus on either a single tool, or a purely qualitative or quantitative approach. The 'holistic' perspective proposed is again supported by the view that a systemic approach is vital to contemporary organisations.

While agreeing that Quality Control Circles are in principle relevant to all, there remain considerable reservations as to their practical value. It is rare to discover an organisation where more than 'lip-service' is paid to the QCC movement. It is very often used as a device for allowing workers to feel that they are involved but with little real commitment from managers. That is to say that the theory in practice is rarely as successful as the theory in theory!

As for the weaknesses, it is easy to concur with Flood's view that the 'causal chain' or linear view of problems proposed by the fishbone diagram is useful but limited. It would perhaps be better to recognise that symptoms of problems are often interacting and the relationships far more complex than the fishbone approach will reveal.

The second weakness identified by Flood is that faced when management is not prepared to listen to the ideas of Quality Circles, an aspect which has already been covered. In this case, the organisation is probably facing the third weakness, that is, the approach struggles in a political or coercive context. The view has already been expressed that all human systems are political and/or coercive and a particular tendency currently prevalent in the West seeks 'someone to blame'. In such a culture, genuine commitment and participation in the quality issue is unlikely to emerge, since it implies acceptance of responsibility for both successes and failures. In a 'blame' culture, wholehearted participation will not easily occur, since failure is met with some form of disciplinary action or punishment rather than being treated as an opportunity to learn.

8.5 Critical review

There seem to be three founding elements to Ishikawa's work: an attempt at a holistic view, participation and communication and simplicity of approach.

The first of these should be valued highly, as with the work of the other gurus, however its use is limited by two failures. First, it does not take full account of inter-relationships (the linear view of the fishbone diagram). Second, it fails to break down organisational boundaries in any systemic sense, for example Quality Control Circles are focused on a single area, or workshop, rather than being formed along interacting processes. These represent severe limitations of the approach in the contemporary context.

Participation is highly valued, and the idea of training everybody in the same tools, language and techniques is a sound method to encourage this. However, it relies rather too heavily on a willingness to participate, which is often not easily found. The third strand, simplicity, is criticised for ignoring the complexity and inter-relationships of organisations.

The roots of Ishikawa's approach can be found in his early training and development as a chemist. That is a science which has traditionally been associated with a reductionist 'scientific method' and heavily reliant on analysis and fragmentation of problems. This is clearly carried across into the quality sphere with the use of simple analytical tools and the 'breaking down' of processes into manageable parts.

Similarly, and as with Feigenbaum, there does not emerge from Ishikawa's work an overarching methodology which binds together and integrates all of the different strands of his thinking. Thus, while many of the tools and techniques are useful in isolation, there is no clear means of implementing an 'Ishikawa' programme.

This element may itself explain, to some degree, the failure of Quality Circles in so many organisations. They often stand alone as a device for quality improvement rather than being part of a holistic process of quality improvement. Taken in isolation, they are doomed to failure.

Ishikawa appears to have taken some account of developments in the 'Human Relations' school of management, emerging in the West from the works of those such as Mayo, Maslow and Herzberg. However, he does not give recognition to other developments such as the emergence of the systems approaches.

Finally, recognition must again be given to the multi-dimensional approach espoused by Ishikawa. Unlike Deming, his methods are not predominantly quantitative but incorporate a substantial qualitative element. Aspects such as attitudinal change, participation and communication are seen as vital elements in the management process.

Ishikawa's substantial contribution to the quality movement must be recognised although the lack of a clear methodology is an obvious weakness.

Summary

This chapter has outlined the principal work of Kaoru Ishikawa through the five point critical review. Interested readers should refer to Ishikawa's own works to further develop their knowledge and understanding.

KEY LEARNING POINTS

Kaoru Ishikawa

Definition of quality:
quality of product, service, management, the company itself and the human being.

Key beliefs:
systemic approach, participation, communication

Principal methods:
seven tools of quality control, fishbone diagram, Quality Circles

Question

Quality Circles are Ishikawa's principle method for achieving participation. Critically review the idea of the 'Quality Circle' in the social and political environment of your organisation.

9   Joseph M. Juran

'the principles that are valid, no matter what the product, the process or the function'

Joseph M. Juran & J. A. De Feo, 2010

Introduction

Joseph Juran, a naturalised American, died in 2008. He commenced his initial career as an Engineer in 1924, subsequently working as an executive, civil servant, professor, arbitrator, director and management consultant. His strong professional background supported his first work in the quality field, the *Quality Control Handbook* (1989), which is seen by some as having led to his international pre-eminence in the field of quality (Bendell, 1989: 8). Along with Deming, Juran worked extensively with the Japanese in the 1950s when the focus of his work was with middle and high ranking executives, since he considered that 'quality control should be conducted as an integral part of management control' (op. cit.).

He received numerous awards for his work including, again like Deming, the 'Second Order of the Sacred Treasure' by the Emperor of Japan in recognition of his contribution to Japanese Quality Control and friendship with America.

Juran is described by Bendell (op. cit.) as charismatic, by Bank (1992: 70) as 'perhaps the top quality guru' and by Logothetis (1992: 62) as having made 'the greatest contribution to the management literature of any quality professional'. Juran has published twelve books which have been translated into thirteen languages. Perhaps the most relevant of these is the work entitled *Juran on Planning for Quality* (1988). This is seen as the definitive guide to his thinking on company wide quality planning.

9.1   Philosophy

Juran's philosophy is perhaps best summed up in the saying, cited by Logothetis (1992: 62), 'quality does not happen by accident, it has to be planned'. This reflects his structured approach to company wide quality planning, an aspect already met in the work of other gurus, for example Ishikawa and Feigenbaum. He is considered by Logothetis (op. cit.) and Bendell (1989: 8) to emphasise management's responsibility for quality with the latter quoting him as saying that 'management controllable defects account for over 80% of the total quality problems'. The emphasis of his work is on 'planning, organisational issues, management's responsibility for quality and the need to set goals and targets for improvement' (Bendell: 1989: 8).

Juran's first two beliefs can be derived from this. First, that management are largely responsible for quality. Second, that quality consistently improves only through planning.

Logothetis (1992: 64) notes the avoidance of slogans and exhortations, citing Juran's view that 'the recipe for action should consist of 90% substance and 10% exhortation, not the reverse!' Here is Juran's third belief, that planned improvement must be specific and measurable. Logothetis sees in this aspect a 'formula for results' which consists of four elements:

- Establish specific goals to be reached – identify what needs to be done, the specific projects that need to be tackled;
- Establish plans for reaching the goals – provide a structured process for going from here to there;
- Assign clear responsibility for meeting the goals;
- Base the rewards on results achieved – feedback the information and utilise the lessons learned and the experience gained.

This approach indicates a clear reliance on quantitative methods, rather than vague aspirations to higher quality, what Flood (1993: 19) refers to as Juran's concern that 'Quality has become too gimmicky, full of platitudes and supposed good intentions, but short on real substance'.

Juran's definition of quality constitutes another strand of his philosophy. He defines quality as 'fitness for use or purpose' (Bank, 1992: 71). Bank suggests that this is a more useful definition than 'conformance to specification' since a dangerous product could conform to all specifications but still be unfit for use. This may be compared with Crosby's definition of 'conformance to requirements'; it would probably be reasonable to assume that safety in use would be a requirement for Crosby – although he does not say so!

The final important strand to Juran's thinking is in his trilogy of quality planning, quality control and quality improvement (Box 9.1).

This essentially simple approach encapsulates the demand for substantial action inherent in all of Juran's work. His emphasis is in three areas: changing management behaviour through quality awareness, training and then spilling down new attitudes to supporting management levels. This top-down approach reflects the belief that management is largely responsible for quality problems.

Summarising Juran's philosophy five key beliefs can be identified:

- management is largely responsible for quality;
- quality can only be improved through planning;
- plans and objectives must be specific and measurable;
- training is essential and starts at the top;
- three step process of planning, control and action.

Box 9.1   The quality trilogy

Joseph Juran:

- Quality Planning: determine quality goals; implementation planning; resource planning; express goals in quality terms; create the quality plan.
- Quality Control: monitor performance; compare objectives with achievements; act to reduce the gap.
- Quality Improvement: reduce waste; enhance logistics; improve employee morale; improve profitability; satisfy customers.

9.2   Assumptions

The assumptions about the world which seem to underpin Juran's approach are discussed below.

The first thing to examine is Juran's assumption that there is a quality crisis. It is certainly the case that consumers' expectations of products and services have increased and there is a lower tolerance of faults than was once the case. We all expect our watches to keep time, our cars to start every day and that services will be reliably and consistently provided.

There are at least three potential views of the quality problem. First, it could be argued that the quality gurus 'created' the quality crisis by raising awareness of the quality issue, focusing attention on the negative aspects and driving up consumer expectations which in turn has forced producers and providers to improve. A second argument is that awareness of the costs of poor quality amongst providers and producers increased, leading managements to focus their attention on improving quality which then became a virtue for their product (and bottom line!). A third view is that consumers have driven the quality movement through intolerance of defective or shoddy goods and services.

The truth probably lies in a combination of all of these with many inter-relationships between them. This moves the quality argument away from the linear view of the world, seen in Crosby and Ishikawa, towards a more holistic approach.

Looking at wider issues it can certainly be argued that in relatively mature consumer markets the substantial growth in availability of goods and services must lead to a focus on performance. Poor quality represents a major threat to organisational survival, so achievement of quality becomes a fundamental requirement for staying in business.

A second assumption is that management of both the organisation and quality are processes. This idea has considerable appeal. Management is often thought of narrowly and simplistically as a set of discrete, separate activities. To recognise that management is a process, with all actions and decisions interacting with all others, is a much broader and perhaps more realistic view. There can be little argument with Juran in this respect, especially as much current thinking in management revolves around organisation along process lines (see Beckford, 2016).

A third assumption is of the potential for continuous improvement; this has already been addressed in the chapters on Deming and Ishikawa. Continuous improvement is a reasonable view in a continuous world, but in a discontinuous one it may lose its value. Discontinuity in the environment demands discontinuity in the organisation and a step change in performance – a 'discontinuous improvement' – may be what is required for survival.

The fourth and final assumption to be examined is that relating to quantification. Juran's work focuses very clearly on measurement and specific objectives. As with others, the validity of this approach must be questioned. Many aspects of quality, particularly in the service sector, are difficult to accurately and reliably quantify. Significantly, some aspects are outside the control of the organisation. This leads to two problems. The first is that we measure those aspects which are most amenable, rather than those which are most important. The second is how to measure individual customer expectations which vary each time the service is purchased. The normal response is to provide a standard service and educate the customer to understand what they can expect. A different, and rather more difficult response, is to adapt the service to meet individual expectations.

There is a clear bias towards the use of quantitative methods, which are rooted in Juran's industrial and manufacturing based background. This perhaps provides a certain limitation on the application of his ideas in the service sector.

9.3   Methods

While Juran's 'quality trilogy' of Planning, Control, Improvement offers the guideline to his approach, his overarching methodology for achieving quality is the 'Quality Planning Road Map' (Bendell, 1989: 9). Recognising both external and internal customers, this (Box 9.2) offers a nine step guide.

The first two steps refer to both external and internal customers. These are often seen as identifying the single next step in the process, although a more useful view might be to identify the whole chain and all of the inter-relationships. It could be the case that a particular feature of a product is of no significance to the immediate customer but has enormous impact for one at a later stage of the process. It is therefore important to recognise and take account of the requirements of all possible customers in the chain.

The third step is really about effective communication. A package of requirements expressed in a language unknown to the people in the organisation will be of no help. Obvious examples of this are converting words in general or common usage, the customer's language, into the specific technical 'jargon' of the organisation. Less obvious are internal requirements. Here it is important that the requirements are expressed in terms meaningful to the working group involved, for example a condition expressed in the language of accounting to meet a particular budget in terms of profit and loss may be meaningless to a group of engineers. It is essential that their 'budget' be expressed in relevant terms such as required throughput, machine utilisation or levels of waste.

Developing a product that responds to customer needs takes the quality issue back to its most fundamental aspect – building quality in rather than inspecting defects out. This is one aspect where other gurus agree. It is better and cheaper to establish quality from the outset than to engage in rectification. Optimising the product to meet the organisation's or department's needs as well as those of the customer should ideally be seen as a constraint on the development process of the previous step rather than as a separate issue. It is, or should be, a design constraint that the product meets these requirements simultaneously.

The development, optimisation and testing of a production process is an area that historically has received little attention. Consulting experience suggests that products have often been developed by the Research and Development staff then simply handed over to the production staff with the instruction to make it. More recently many companies are taking account of manufacturing requirements in the development process with ease

---

Box 9.2   The Quality Planning Road Map

Joseph Juran:

Step 1)   Identify who are the customers;

Step 2)   Determine the needs of those customers;

Step 3)   Translate those needs into our language [the language of the organisation];

Step 4)   Develop a product that can respond to those needs;

Step 5)   Optimise the product features so as to meet our [the Company's] needs as well as customers' needs;

Step 6)   Develop a process which is able to produce the product;

Step 7)   Optimise the process;

Step 8)   Prove that the process can produce the product under operating conditions;

Step 9)   Transfer the process to operations.

of manufacture (and designing in low manufacturing or assembly costs) being accepted as a design constraint.

The final step is to transfer the process to operations. Again, historically this has often been done very badly and there is no argument with Juran's proposal. A useful device to assist with this aspect is to create teams for product development which includes operational staff and managers. If the idea of designing for manufacture is adopted, then this step becomes very straightforward.

Supporting this fundamental approach to designing quality into the systems and processes is what Bank (1992: 70) refers to as Juran's 'ten steps' to continuous quality improvement.

Here Juran's philosophy is carried across into practice. The first step begins to establish a quality oriented culture in the organisation through the process of raising awareness of the need and scope – a qualitative approach. The second is quantitative, establishing objectives – goals – for improvement. The third step is an attempt to institutionalise quality, to embed the quality process in the management process so that it becomes an ingrained part of the organisation.

The fourth step takes the organisation forward to train the entire staff. This is seen as helping to make quality an integral part of everyone's thinking.

The fifth and sixth steps, 'carry out projects' and 'report progress', recognise that while continuous improvement is the objective, it must be achieved within visible and measurable elements. The reporting process is seen as enabling experience and learning to be shared and to allow those involved to share their sense of achievement. This also allows the seventh step, 'show recognition', to be actioned. The sixth and eighth steps are linked, 'communicate results' being a call to share the successes (and failures) throughout the organisation.

The ninth step, keeping a record, is an aid to organisational learning. A record may be thought of as an organisational 'memory' to which reference can be made in the future. While Juran suggests that this record should be of successes, it is just as important to remember those strategies and schemes that do not work as those that do. This true form of 'knowledge management' (Hislop, 2013) may enable the organisation to avoid or encourage appropriate actions and behaviour in the future and to understand why changes have

---

Box 9.3   Ten steps to continuous quality improvement

Joseph Juran:

Step 1)   Create awareness of the need and opportunity for quality improvement;

Step 2)   Set goals for continuous improvement;

Step 3)   Build an organisation to achieve goals by establishing a quality council, identifying problems, selecting a project, appointing teams and choosing facilitators;

Step 4)   Give everyone training;

Step 5)   Carry out projects to solve problems;

Step 6)   Report progress;

Step 7)   Show recognition;

Step 8)   Communicate results;

Step 9)   Keep a record of successes;

Step 10)   Incorporate annual improvements into the company's regular systems and processes and thereby maintain momentum.

succeeded or failed. To distil the general principles of success from a specific instance or series of instances is to create a true basis for organisational learning. After all, the specific instance will never arise again – but the principles underpinning the solved problem will almost certainly recur many times – and the practice of problem solving is enhanced by understanding at the general rather than the particular level.

The tenth step is a corporate and public commitment to the achievement of higher quality. This should be seen as reaffirming the quality process in the minds of both employees and customers.

Juran shows awareness of the phenomenon of resistance to change which is so common in organisations. Logothetis (1992: 75) reports Juran's belief that 'resistance to a technological change is due to social and cultural factors'. Juran proposes two principal methods for dealing with this. First, he considers that all those affected by the change should be 'allowed to participate' (op. cit.), second that 'adequate time should be allowed for the change to be accepted'. These approaches provide an opportunity for evaluation and experimentation, promoting ownership of the changes and helping to overcome resistance.

Underpinning the two processes outlined above – 'the road map' and the 'ten steps' – Juran uses a variety of statistical methods. Like Deming, Juran studied under Shewhart and shares many of the same approaches with perhaps one of the best known being Pareto analysis to help separate the 'vital few' problems from the 'useful many'.

9.4 Successes and failures

Like the other gurus, Juran has been hugely successful in developing and promoting his ideas. That his books have been translated into thirteen languages and his ideas accepted and exploited by many organisations in many different countries is a measure of the value of his contribution. However, his work has not been applied universally and can be seen to be less effective in the service sector than in manufacturing.

Adapting from Flood (1993: 21–22), the strengths of Juran's approach are:

- concentration on genuine issues of management practice;
- a new understanding of the (internal AND external) customer;
- management involvement and commitment.

The main weaknesses are perceived as:

- the literature on motivation and leadership is not addressed;
- workers' contributions are underrated;
- methods are traditional, failing to address culture and politics.

Another criticism is that the body of systems knowledge, and in particular managerial and organisational cybernetics, which could have enhanced and enriched Juran's approach, has, like human relations theory, been largely ignored.

The first strength identified by Flood is one with which most people would agree, although a programme which fails to motivate and develop the majority of the workforce is one which may well be seen as consisting of 'hype'.

The second strength, recognising other parts of the organisation as customers, is again welcome. Readers will recall that this can also be found in the work of Deming and is now embedded in the ISO 9000 and other quality management system standards.

The third strength is management commitment and involvement. This is not simply because, by Juran's measure, 80% of the total quality problem resides there, but also because the power, control and leadership reside there. A management which is seen by the workforce to be committed to quality will 'breed' a quality ethos for the organisation. Workers wishing to progress tend to emulate the behaviour and attitudes of their managers. If this occurs then the quality ethos will tend to spill down through the organisation over time.

Turning to the weaknesses, Flood's understanding that Juran fails to adequately incorporate theories of motivation and leadership is accepted. However, Juran is a practitioner; he deals best with the practice of quality, rather than the theory. It might be suggested that the second statement of weakness, that Juran undervalues the contribution of the worker, is countered to some extent by the explicit incorporation of participation.

Flood further suggests that Juran emphasises a somewhat 'mechanistic' view of the organisation, although he does take account of the organisation's environment, that is of its markets. The view is largely evident in the unstated assumption that what is good for the organisation – higher quality – is also good for the individual. This perhaps reflects the thinking of the early management theorists such as Taylor, Weber and Fayol. In the contemporary world of 'knowledge workers', high-technology equipment and increasing emphasis on human rights, quite often what is good for the organisation may appear to be bad for the workers. A company operating in the face of maturing or mature markets and not positioned to exploit emerging markets, with fresh, lower cost base competitors from newly industrialising countries, may be unable to absorb spare capacity through growth. This leads to the need, to use the politically correct terminology, to 're-trench' workers.

The interests of the organisation and the individual worker may come into direct conflict. The organisation wishes to improve quality to preserve and protect its customer base, to reduce its costs and ensure its survival. The workers may recognise that these same attributes can have different consequences for them, for example job losses, pay freezes, reductions in overtime, loss of other benefits. Often it can lead to 'de-skilling' of jobs and the loss of craft skills in which individuals take great, and justifiable, pride. Brynjolfsson & McAfee (2014) explore more fully the implications of changing technology. There is little incentive for the workforce to contribute to the quality programme if a successful outcome for the company threatens their own sense of security.

9.5   Critical review

The founding idea of Juran's work might almost be called 'Design and Build'. His approach stresses planning as the fundamental requirement for quality, followed by action. This orientation towards the setting and achievement of objectives may reflect Juran's engineering and statistical background.

The 'Quality Trilogy', 'Quality Road Map' and 'Ten Steps to Quality' may all be considered as systematic, mechanistic approaches. While Juran established a new understanding of customers (the internal and external), he does not explicitly recognise the importance of the inter-dependence of processes and the interactions between people within the organisation. This prevents his systematic approach from becoming systemic. Juran seems to be making the assumption that improvement in the individual parts will necessarily improve the whole organisation; a view which is challenged by the systems thinking community.

With regard to management, two issues should be stressed. First, Juran views management as a process. Second, he sees management as responsible for quality, having control of 80% of the problems. As regards the first of these, Juran's view is to be welcomed. An organisation which recognises that every action and decision is inextricably linked with every other in a continuous process of management must be considered to be on the verge of a breakthrough in its behaviour. Even today, management in many organisations is fragmented into pseudo-independent functions: marketing is separate from finance which is in turn separate from production and so on. Each of these units attempts to maximise its own function independently from the others. Similarly, even within departments, tasks are often seen as independent, rather than inter-dependent. For example, recruitment is often seen as a separate function within the personnel or human resource function and having no relationship with training and development – and, crucially, no relationship with the units where those recruited will work. In those organisations it is not surprising that there are conflicts, disputes and difficulties in matching people to tasks. A more holistic, integrated and interdependent 'process' view is essential. While Juran moves towards this approach, he does not go far enough.

Turning now to the second issue, management responsibility, perhaps the question that should be asked is why 80%? Deming, for example, has provided statistics suggesting that the figure is 94%, while Crosby's work may be interpreted as suggesting that the bulk of the responsibility lies with the workers. An argument can be proposed whereby management take complete responsibility for quality. If, as Fayol (1916) suggests, it is the responsibility of management to 'Plan, Organise, Command, Control and Co-ordinate', then responsibility should lie with them. The argument is this: management is expected to have control of every aspect of the organisation:

- what is done;
- how it is done;
- when it is done;
- where it is done;
- who does it;
- why it is done.

This suggests that there can be no matter internal to the organisation which is beyond the scope of management to address. Random errors in production, for example, might be eradicable through changes in design or process so that it becomes impossible to assemble a part incorrectly. Human error might be reducible through training, adjustment of work rates, increases (or reductions!) in relaxation time or a range of other variables which could be altered to enable improved performance.

It is suggested that the ultimate responsibility for quality should rest with those who are involved in the production of a good or a service. However, the power to achieve higher quality rests in the hands of those who have authority (power) to change things. If that power is in the hands of the management alone, then they have full responsibility. If on the other hand the power is shared throughout the organisation, perhaps through empowerment initiatives, Quality Circles and other participative approaches, then everyone who shares in that power is responsible.

The strong emphasis by Juran on management responsibility fails to adequately address the needs and aspirations of workers. He does not properly take into account the contribution that they can make to the achievement of quality, nor does he provide mechanisms through which this can be done.

Finally, the issue must again be raised of the applicability of Juran's work. It seems to be most suitable for the industrial and manufacturing sectors. It is suggested that it has limited application in service organisations since it does not adequately deal with human issues.

Summary

This chapter has reviewed the major contribution made to the quality movement by Juran. Students should refer to Juran's (1988) own work to further inform and develop their views.

KEY LEARNING POINTS

Joseph Juran

Definition of quality:
fitness for use or purpose

Key beliefs:
management responsibility, planning, measurability, training, process

Principal methods:
company-wide quality control, the Quality Road Map, the ten steps to quality improvement

---

Question

Why is 'fitness for purpose' important? Who defines purpose?

10 John S. Oakland

'Meeting the customers' requirements'

John S. Oakland & Peter Morris, 2011

Introduction

John Oakland is Executive Chairman of Oakland Consulting plc and head of its Research and Education Division – the European Centre for Business Excellence. John is Emeritus Professor of Quality and Business Excellence at Leeds University Business School, a Fellow of the Chartered Quality Institute and a Member of the American Society for Quality. Oakland's early industrial career focused on research and development and production management. He holds a PhD, is a Chartered Chemist, Fellow of the Royal Statistical Society, the Royal Society for the Arts and the Institute of Quality Assurance, Member of the Royal Society of Chemistry, the Association of Quality Management Consultants and Member of the American Society of Quality Control.

He is considered by many as the British guru of quality. His practice is internationally based, and he has provided substantial support to the development of quality in the UK, particularly to the quality initiatives of the government. The approaches used by Oakland and his colleagues in Oakland Consulting plc are essentially pragmatic and have been used widely in organisations throughout the UK and Europe.

10.1 Philosophy

The philosophy underpinning Oakland's view of quality is perhaps best shown in the emphasis he places on its importance, saying:

> We cannot avoid seeing how quality has developed into the most important competitive weapon, and many organisations have realised that TQM is *the* (sic) way of managing for the future.

> (Oakland, 1993: Preface)

Through this statement, Oakland gives primacy to the pursuit of quality as the cornerstone of organisational success. While organisations which do not achieve quality in their products and services will ultimately fail in the long term, it is more difficult to accept the idea of quality (in isolation) having absolute primacy over everything else. Successful and sustainable organisations are a function of their internal capabilities and their interaction with the dynamic business environment; it is entirely possible for an organisation producing 'quality' products and services to fail as a result of external factors. Purists might argue that if quality pervades the whole organisation then it will recognise such threats and respond effectively to them. This is fair comment – but only applies if quality pervades the whole organisation and not just its productive parts! Although quality has strategic implications (as discussed in chapter 2) and is a strategic issue, it cannot be accepted that it is the *only* strategic issue.

On the other hand the concept of TQM as the way of managing for the future does have considerable value. If TQM is thought of as a way of managing (as seen with Feigenbaum's work), then other management philosophies, methods and tools must be subsumed within it. This idea reinforces Oakland's view that 'quality starts at the top', with quality parameters inherent in every organisational decision. He emphasises seven key characteristics of pursuing TQM (Box 10.1) and these are outlined entertainingly in *TQM: A Pictorial Guide for Managers* (2011).

First is Oakland's definition of quality: *'quality is meeting the customers' requirements'*. This definition is simple and emphasises that quality is a characteristic or attribute defined by the customer not the supplier. Oakland also stresses the importance of the quality chain. He emphasises the internal supplier–customer relationships, stressing in the second characteristic that most problems are inter-departmental – that is, they occur in the interaction between process steps.

The third and fourth characteristics emphasise the purposes of quality control (QC) and quality assurance (QA). These definitions move the focus away from the criticism and blame often associated with these mechanisms and towards the reason for their purpose, to improve quality performance. All too often QC and QA functions in organisations become self-serving, apportioning blame and identifying guilty parties rather than improving the performance. They frequently fall into disrepute and become disregarded by the operational personnel – who focus in turn on not getting caught rather than on not failing. I recently observed an organisation in which managers had a monthly quality day, the day on which they ensured that all the non-conformance reports were resolved. This involved lengthy explanations of why the non-conformance was not their fault; little attention was paid to improvement in quality.

The fifth and sixth characteristics focus on the pro-active nature of the quality drive. The statement that 'quality must be managed, it does not just happen', reflecting Juran's suggestion that 'quality must be planned', sharpens the recognition that quality is not accidental, or achieved through reactive measures. Quality for Oakland, that is meeting customer

---

Box 10.1   Seven key characteristics of TQM

John S. Oakland:

1   Quality is meeting the customers requirements;
2   Most quality problems are inter-departmental;
3   Quality control is monitoring, finding and eliminating causes of quality problems;
4   Quality Assurance rests on prevention, management systems, effective audit and review;
5   Quality must be managed, it does not just happen;
6   Focus on prevention, not cure;
7   Reliability is an extension of quality and enables us to 'delight the customer'.

requirements, must be a parameter of every decision made within the organisation, whether operational, administrative or strategic. Quality must then be inherent in management thinking, which in turn means that it must be part of the norms of the organisation. This view is supported by the sixth characteristic, prevention not cure. Oakland suggests that one-third of all organisational efforts are wasted in error based activity, for example rework, rectification, inspection and so on, with an even higher proportion in service based organisations. Experience suggests these proportions are difficult to argue with and in some cases represent a significant under-estimate. If quality can be achieved at the outset, rather than through detection and rectification, the total costs of the organisation will always be reduced. The limitation to achieving this arises very often from the functionally based budgeting common in organisations, where each manager seeks to reduce current period local costs with no regard to the effect on other parts of the organisation.

The final characteristic deals with quality as more than a momentary attribute. Reliability has two dimensions which are related to the nature of the product itself. The first is reliability in use and relates to durable products such as cars, domestic appliances, watches and so on. In this case, what 'delights the customer' is enjoying the uninterrupted use of the product other than for routine maintenance. A motor car which breaks down will not delight the customer whose requirement is to be able to make a journey without fear of non-completion. This means that each time the service is delivered it must meet the customer requirements. In this context, reliability means consistency, and to achieve consistency of service means there must be a consistent and reliable delivery process.

Quality for Oakland is organisation wide and fundamental, driven by top management commitment and created through reliable, consistent organisational processes.

10.2   Assumptions

The assumptions about the world that seem to underpin Oakland's approach will now be considered.

The first is that quality is the only issue for organisational survival. While this may be largely true of some organisations in fully developed, highly competitive and mature economies (those in which Oakland predominantly operates), it is certainly not true of all. Some organisations will succeed (at least in the short to medium term) because they have established such market dominance (and perhaps customer reliance) that the issue of quality simply does not arise. Customers buy the products or services through lack of alternative rather than through choice. The dominance of Microsoft Windows was perhaps one of these, although this tendency has been challenged by the growth of Apple products and the emergence of other solutions such as Android and Linux with a new generation of users testing alternative systems. Oakland's first assumption can be challenged on the grounds that while perhaps correct as a matter of value, the constraint does not apply across global markets.

The second assumption, that quality must be driven from the top, carries complete support. Unless this commitment is achieved at the outset of a quality programme and maintained, the initiative will fail. The ISO standard focuses on management commitment as a major issue – although many managements can be seen to be struggling to convert the concept into action.

The third assumption is that errors can always be prevented, through planning, design and effective processes. Achieving this requires a substantial shift in the traditional mindset of those in the organisation and a full appreciation of the softer, human issues, particularly in service based organisations. While a process operation can be designed to operate in an error free way, the actual minute by minute delivery of service depends very largely on the personal inter-action between customer and supplier. However robust the technical process may be, there is always scope for error to arise in this context. No standard form of words can cater for the vagaries of mood, sense and interpretation which influence the outcome of such transactions and determine whether customer requirements are met – Oakland's measure of quality.

The fourth assumption is that quality is an organisation wide issue. This is in common with Flood's (1993) call for quality 'across all functions and all levels' and again cannot be argued with. Quality must pervade the whole organisational atmosphere. This suggests that Oakland's approach is systemic. While he makes no direct reference in his work to the systemic approaches to management, there is a systemic as well as systematic attitude reflected in his approach.

Finally, Oakland assumes the involvement of all people through communication, teamwork and participation, in other words through re-developing the culture of the organisation. This view is again supported and reflects a systemic mindset in his approach.

10.3   Methods

While Oakland quite rightly capitalises on the many well established methods, tools and techniques for achieving quality, he does offer his own overarching approach for TQM and some new insight. The overarching method is his 'ten points for Senior Management' (Box 10.2).

Oakland represents the major features of this in his 'Total Quality Management model', Figure 10.1.

Unlike others, Oakland focuses on the total process of achieving a TQM organisation seeking to optimise the mix of qualitative and quantitative aspects. He recognises the necessity of both and, if anything, is slightly biased towards softer aspects as the initial drivers of quality.

The ten point process begins with the absolute commitment of senior and middle management to constant improvement. Oakland suggests that the quality process must start in the boardroom. Adoption of quality at that level is fundamental to its achievement, since it is then a normative decision – a decision about the sort of behaviour that is desired.

Box 10.2   Ten points for Senior Management

John S. Oakland:

Point 1)   Long-term commitment;

Point 2)   Change the culture to 'right first time';

Point 3)   Train the people to understand the 'Customer-Supplier' relationship;

Point 4)   Buy products and services on TOTAL COST (sic);

Point 5)   Recognise that systems improvement must be managed;

Point 6)   Adopt modern methods of supervision and training and eliminate fear;

Point 7)   Eliminate barriers, manage processes, improve communications and teamwork;

Point 8)   Eliminate arbitrary goals, standards based only on numbers, barriers to pride of workmanship, fiction (use the correct tools to establish facts);

Point 9)   Constantly educate and retrain the in house experts;

Point 10) Utilise a systematic approach to TQM implementation.

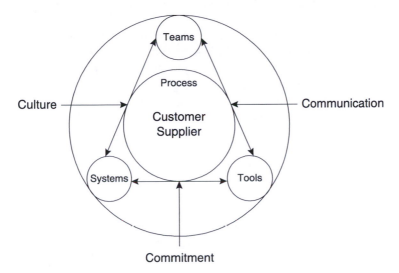

Figure 10.1 Total Quality Management model.

Unfortunately, this is rather more difficult to achieve in practice than is recognised. The Senior Management may say that they are committed to quality, but unless they change their behaviour (that is the decisions they make, the things they say and do, the ways in which they measure and reward performance) then the commitment is not genuine. This will soon be detected at other levels within the organisation.

That'll be a 'no' then?

I was recently engaged by a utility company to work with Directors and develop a new approach to investment in and management of assets.

The client was a regulated business, making investment in plant and equipment to sustain and improve product quality while ensuring that services met the agreed requirements.

An extensive period of research and analysis was undertaken; the asset base is valued in the billions of pounds, the annual maintenance and capital investment programmes running to around £500m. It was worth taking the time and making the effort to do the job properly.

Some information was hard to trace, some was not connected to the relevant asset and historic underinvestment in information systems proved a major drawback.

Nonetheless the job was done and the relevant Director together with the external team invited all those affected by and involved in the work to attend a presentation and discussion of the findings.

These were substantial; it was estimated (and it could only be an estimate at this point) that the organisation could, by working and specifying more precisely, achieve the same outcomes on its capital programme and save around 20% of investment while on operational expenditure a further 15–20% was available.

Delivery of these gains would require a substantial reengineering of business processes, organisational units and job roles and would depend on a substantial

> investment in information systems. The cost of this amounted to 10% of the annual savings available.
>
> All was going swimmingly, the Directors and Senior Managers gently salivated at the prospect of the savings, feeling heroic for having commissioned the study.
>
> Then the penny dropped . . . 'if all THAT is going to happen then that will affect the way I work, the decisions I now make may be made by somebody else, the organisation will be clearly able to hold me to account for my performance'.
>
> The discussion ended with a resounding 'yes, but' and progress stopped.

Arising from the first process, the second requirement is to change the culture of the organisation at all levels to focus on 'right first time'. Oakland sees this as based on awareness of customer needs and teamwork, enabled by participation and use of the 'EPDCA helix'. This is a more dynamic representation of the Deming cycle already seen, with explicit recognition of the need for evaluation before planning. There is much else required in a cultural change as is implied in the ideas of teamwork, participation and customer needs.

The third process represents the orientation of the organisation towards customer–supplier relationships – both externally and internally. Oakland suggests this must be achieved for every one. This is an especially difficult area which will meet with much resistance in many organisations. This is particularly true where the staff of a process or function are traditionally poorly regarded – where there is functional organisation design or a major difference of perceived relative expertise, with the customer regarded by the supplier as being of a 'lower order'. This is a particular concern in organisations where there is a significant perceived difference between the staff member and the client, e.g. doctors interacting with nurses and/or patients, chefs interacting with kitchen assistants. An arrogance based on perceived expertise can easily emerge which inhibits effective communication and team working.

Process four moves away from culture to examine cost. Oakland recognises, like Deming, that initial purchase price is not the sole determinant of the cost of any input. He calls for continuous improvement in everything to reduce the total cost of doing business and recognises that a higher initial cost of purchase may be outweighed by reduced lifetime cost, including operations, depreciation and disposal or recycling costs. For example, a stainless steel machine may be initially more expensive than its mild steel equivalent, but if the maintenance and running cost is significantly lower and the longevity greater, the total cost may be less over time.

Process five calls for the systems used to manage the organisation to be actively managed for improvement. While this may seem like common sense, it is an often neglected area. A key to success is to consider the utility and effectiveness of the systems employed. Many organisations continue to work with IT 'legacy systems', systems purchased and developed over many years and which commonly require substantial investment to replace. Often such systems, like the budget, are functionally owned; that is they reside within a single department which makes effective use of them in its own terms – but the system is not configured in such a way that it can contribute to the whole organisation. Often such systems are poorly understood in the wider organisation, jealously guarded by their departmental 'owners' – but, through lack of integration with the rest of the organisation, are at best failing to add value, at worst causing damage. Often, the replacement cost of such systems is greater, within the individual function, than the business benefit to be obtained from their replacement – making it very difficult to obtain capital funding. Like any other capital investment, IT systems must be recognised as having a useful life and must be replaced at the due time. In choosing the replacement, managers should have regard to the integration of information needs of the whole organisation.

Process six calls for modern methods of supervision and training. This recognises that many traditional supervision and training approaches no longer have great value. These are very often sterile, having no relationship to the particular job undertaken and not being reflected in individual performance expectations. Similarly, the 'kick butt and take names' militaristic approach to performance management is not applicable in a more enlightened environment, but is still surprisingly common.

Process seven calls for organisations to be managed through processes rather than functional silos. While many process based organisations have already achieved this, many still adopt functional orientation as the basis of control. In these there remain many hand-offs (breaks within processes) which extend the range of customer–supplier relationships and create opportunities for the buck to be passed. In the process the consumer (the ultimate customer) is often forgotten. If the organisation is process based this tends not to happen, and communication and teamwork can be encouraged around the process flow, since all parties can visualise and share the team objective(s).

Process eight could be called the elimination round. Here Oakland again reflects the ideas of others. He wishes to see arbitrary goals eliminated, seeing it as useless to call for improvement without supplying the facilities necessary for goals to be achieved and without a formal basis for evaluation. He wants to end standards based only on volumes. Purely volume based output measures will always lead to quality problems. As a minimum it is essential to measure quality performance as well – and to recognise that this may mean a lesser initial output – but that the output received should all be perfect! His third requirement is to eradicate barriers to pride of workmanship. Apart from purely measuring output volume (which is one barrier) – this means the design and redesign of jobs, as suggested in the quality and HR literature (e.g. Torrington et al, 2008), to enable people to have pride in the completion of a meaningful task. Lastly, he calls for reliance on facts not fiction, proposing costs of quality and level of fire-fighting as measures of internal health. The important characteristic here is for measurements that are both meaningful and factual – that is numbers which cannot be (easily) manipulated to present a particular picture. While doctors bury their mistakes, managers frequently reclassify theirs, even to the extent in one factory of making for reject to maintain production efficiency.

Stating that 'the experts . . . are the people who do the job every day', Oakland calls at process nine for constant education and retraining. The dynamics of contemporary business and rapid changes in the business environment render this essential. Training must be related back to job performance and expectations; that is, it must link to further improvement. This is a particularly strained point in many organisations, especially in times of economic downturn – the first budget items to suffer are normally the Training and Research and Development budgets!

Finally at process ten, Oakland calls for a planned, systematic approach to the operational implementation of TQM to realise the vision. Again, this seems like a sound platform for improvement. However, such systematisation and planning must not preclude capitalising on spontaneous and unexpected successes. The potential opportunist gain must not be lost through rigid adherence to a particular plan.

To support the implementation process, Oakland predominantly relies on standard tools for achieving quality, e.g. statistical approaches, quality circles, process analysis and review and so on. He does however enrich his approach by capitalising on particular developments in the pursuit of quality.

First of these is 'quality function deployment'. This is a systematic approach to the design of a product or service around the expressed requirements of the customers. It involves members from across the organisation in converting customer requirements to a technical product or service specification. The QFD process is based around seven activities (Box 10.3) and is intended to ensure that the product or service meets the customer requirements first time and every time. Oakland stresses the importance of recognising the design input of those whose jobs do not include an evident design element.

Second, Oakland stresses the importance of teamwork in his approach and draws extensively on the established literature in this area to explain and elaborate his approach.

This chapter is intended only to provide an introduction to Oakland's overall approach. Methods, tools and techniques will be elaborated in part four. This section has introduced Oakland's primary method, which relies heavily on absolute management commitment and leadership of the quality process supported by a wide selection of tools and techniques.

10.4   Successes and failures

The use of Oakland's approach to TQM by many companies speaks volumes for its utility. Quite simply, no programme could achieve such sustained success without substantial benefits being delivered to many customers. The establishment of the European Centre for Business Excellence and of Oakland Consulting plc further confirms that Oakland's approach adds value to quality practice.

A number of strengths and weaknesses can be identified in Oakland's approach. The strengths are:

- Systematic, methodical approach;
- Process based view of organisations;
- Capitalises on developments in quality practice;
- Participative approach which utilises ideas from the literature on teamwork;
- Stresses the importance of management commitment and leadership.

The weaknesses are:

- Ignores many developments in organisation theory, especially the systems literature;
- Fails to offer assistance in coercive contexts;
- Justifies quality in terms of developed economies (the focus on competition);

Box 10.3   Quality function deployment activities

John S. Oakland:
- Market research
- Basic research
- Invention
- Concept design
- Prototype testing
- Final product or service testing
- After-sales service and trouble-shooting

- Ignores other aspects of strategy formulation;
- Does not explain how to obtain the commitment from Senior Management on which the whole process relies.

The systematic and methodical approach provides a straightforward, coherent platform for the quality initiative. Unfortunately it assumes that there is established agreement about the need for quality. Second, the process based view adheres to current developments in the understanding of how organisations actually function and how effectiveness is improved. Third, capitalising on current developments in quality practice ensures that 'best practice' is achieved – a fundamental characteristic of quality.

Oakland's emphasis on team working, and in particular his utilisation of the literature on effective team working, is to be admired. This shows that he has moved outside the relatively narrow discipline of pure quality to embrace other ideas which support his activities.

The final strength, emphasising the importance of management commitment, is again fundamental to effective pursuit of quality. It is unfortunate that (as suggested by the weaknesses) he says little about how such commitment can be achieved. If senior management are not passionately committed to the achievement of quality throughout every aspect of the organisation, then it will not happen. Unfortunately, Oakland does not advise on how to achieve this passionate commitment, nor how to overcome the many functional and professional barriers which may obstruct it.

Turning to the other weaknesses, the failure to explicitly incorporate other aspects of organisation theory and especially to have ignored the value to be derived from a systems based understanding of organisation (together with the associated methodologies) detracts substantially from Oakland's work.

The failure to deal with coercive contexts is common to all quality approaches and is perhaps a little unfair as a criticism. Nonetheless, there are many organisations in the world which are characterised by potentially abusive power relations. One responsibility of the management guru or scientist must include attempting to ameliorate such conditions.

Perhaps because Oakland's practice is centred on Europe, the focus of his justification for pursuing quality is, if not entirely euro-centric, at least based on a perception of the problems and opportunities facing Western organisations in developed economies. These economies are dominated by industrial oligarchies, and it can be argued that, at least in some industries, effective competition on strategic issues has almost disappeared and been replaced by a high degree of collaboration and, to some extent, a tacit acceptance of established market shares.

Developing economies, on the other hand, often experience much lower levels of consumer and producer sophistication, which means that the customers are perhaps less discriminating in their purchasing choices, placing a lesser credence on Western perceptions of quality. These countries often have much more diverse industrial bases with a greater proportion of small to medium sized businesses and less dominance by major players.

These two factors taken together generate scope for strategic advantage to be obtained through routes other than quality.

10.5   Critical review

Overall the foundation to Oakland's work can be seen in his professional background and practical experience of quality. The approach is broadly based enough to be regarded as reflecting a systemic as well as systematic view, but it fails to explicitly capitalise on developments in systemic thinking.

Oakland is clearly concerned about management commitment with his calls for passionate leadership, but the approach falls down in not proposing a method for establishing this. Fear of competitive failure may be enough to stimulate this response, but that is to rely on people running away from something – a negative reaction, rather than running to something – a positive reaction. Running away will stop as the stimulus is relaxed, the negative response will cease and with it the passion for quality. There is clearly a need to develop an ethos where management want quality as a means to a positive end rather than as an alternative to failure, but Oakland makes no tool available to support this.

One very positive feature is that the generality of Oakland's overarching methodology renders it potentially useful in the service as well as the manufacturing industry. While he says little of the public sector, it is quite clear that the method may also work there.

In summarising, support has to be given to Oakland's approach, while recognising that it relies very heavily on well established techniques with all the drawbacks those entail. On the other hand he has capitalised on recent developments and drawn on at least part of the relevant management literature to support and enhance his work. The practical success speaks for itself.

Summary

This chapter has presented the quality approach of John Oakland through a five point critical framework. Readers may wish to refer to Oakland's own work *Total Quality Management*, 1993, second edition, and *Total Organizational Excellence*, 1999, to further develop their understanding and knowledge.

KEY LEARNING POINTS

John S. Oakland

Definition of quality:
quality is meeting the customers' requirements

Key beliefs:
quality is the only issue, quality from the top, errors can be prevented, quality is an organisation wide issue, quality involves everybody

Principal methods:
ten points for senior management, EPDCA cycle, TQM model, quality function deployment

---

Question

Oakland proposes that 'Quality is the only issue for organisational survival'. Discuss this proposal in the light of the contemporary challenges facing organisations.

11 Taiichi Ohno

'All we are doing is looking at the time line ... from order ... to cash ...
and reducing that time by removing the ... wastes'

Taiichi Ohno, 1988

Introduction

Taiichi Ohno, who died in 1990, is perhaps less well remembered than his work. He was the creator of the demand driven, 'just-in-time' Toyota Production System which has morphed into 'Lean Manufacturing'. Born in China in 1912 and a graduate of Nagoya Technical High School, he worked initially with Toyoda Spinning before joining the vehicle business in 1943 where he completed his career, eventually working primarily to develop Toyota thinking in suppliers to the business.

His most widely read work is *Toyota Production System: Beyond Large Scale Production*, originally published in Japanese in 1978, and in English by Productivity Press in 1988. In a foreword to that text, Muramatsu Rintaro describes Ohno as 'a determined man' who 'always challenged existing concepts' and 'able to conceive of and apply improvements that are both accurate and swift'.

11.1 Philosophy

Arguing that, 'The world has already changed from a time when industry could sell everything it produced to an affluent society where material needs are routinely met', Ohno, inspired by Toyoda Sakichi and Toyoda Kiichiro, saw the objective of the Toyota system as being the consistent and thorough elimination of waste, combining that objective with 'respect for humanity'.

Ohno (1988) states that 'The Toyota Production System ... will reveal its strength as a management system adapted to today's era'. His belief seems to have been that by re-engineering production processes to enable 'small quantities in many varieties' (contrasting with the Western high volume, long run, single product approach), Toyota could compete more effectively in challenging markets.

He demonstrates three clear beliefs; the first is in an ordered, disciplined, systematic approach to eradication of waste. The second is that individual workers will, willingly, contribute to this improvement, given training and opportunity. Third, he uniquely emphasises the role of the customer, suggesting that far from organisations 'pushing' their goods into the marketplace, the underpinning belief in the West, customers now:

> pull the goods they need, in the amount and at the time they need them.

Taken together these translate to a belief in industrial engineering to resolve the challenges of improvement, in the value of human beings as contributors to success and, ultimately, in the power of consumers to determine the fate of a company and its products.

Although not explicit about this, he clearly views the management as having a 'top down' responsibility to drive changes. When he writes about the workers, and notwithstanding the preceding comments about humanity, he writes about initial resistance to his work and of using 'authority to encourage them' – a clear recognition of traditional power relations. Indeed, it is reported by Dennis (2007) that in establishing the first initiatives in the Toyota Production System it was necessary to terminate a quarter of the existing workforce while promising a guarantee of lifetime employment to the rest along with pay rated to seniority. It should be no surprise that this brought a compliant workforce – though whether through fear or genuine commitment is impossible to establish at this distance in time and space.

He states that authority needs to be focused into the area under control saying, 'I could yell at a foreman under my jurisdiction, but not at a foreman from the neighbouring department'. Here we can see both the determination of Ohno to see the innovations succeed, but also a limit to personal tolerance, perhaps a measure of his personal drive and ambition which conflicts with the team working and respect written about elsewhere.

The Sisters of Nazareth (renewed)

In 2006, the newly elected Superior General of the Congregation of the Sisters of Nazareth recognised that the Order needed to change the way it worked if it was to survive into the future and continue the mission of the foundress, Victoire Lameniere. Successful for over 150 years, the Congregational Mission was threatened by both legislative changes and the emergence of strong lay organisations offering similar services.

Particular concerns were brought into focus by the significantly increasing average age of the members of the Congregation and falling new vocations (a factor affecting every religious order). These were the challenges of progressively introducing senior lay management and the need for the order to come to terms with the prospect of withdrawal from operational management, together raising the further challenge of the members of the Congregation needing to learn how to act in a governance capacity, more as owners than operators. This, probably the most significant change of role in their history, compelled the engagement of the whole community.

The Superior General and her Council (equivalent to the Board of a company) engaged with a firm of consultants to support them in renewing the spiritual life of the Congregation, enhancing their stewardship of the assets on four continents (principally care homes for the elderly but including schools, orphanages and outreach programmes) and leading their religious and lay communities to a more certain future.

Recognising themselves as being a 'community of will', persisting only by the choice of the Sisters and the commitment of their lay staff, the General Council knew that any programme of change required the full engagement of everybody associated with the Congregation. Working with the consultants, they devised a series of engagement events. The first events, delivered in each of the regions, brought together the sisters superior for each region to examine and understand the opportunities and threats facing the Congregation and to make some decisions about the future. These included making plans to react to significant challenges to their survival – financial, organisational and human (including falling numbers of vocations). The outputs from these events were considered by the General Council and shared, in full, with every one of their communities.

With a new shared understanding, the regional superiors were asked to work with their houses to develop regional plans which addressed the challenges and threats for that area and aligned with the agreed plans for the global congregation. With those plans in first draft, the Superior General, working throughout with at least one member of the general council and the regional superior, undertook a second round of regional meetings to review the plans, to provide the opportunity for everyone to contribute, to share their feelings and offer guidance based on experience and knowledge gained through the process. The outputs were again brought together, reflected upon and shared widely through the organisation.

Finally, a third global tour was undertaken, presenting back to each of the regions the findings and proposals arising from the discussions – covering the global, regional and individual house plans. These workshops provided again the opportunity for all members of the community (religious and lay) to engage in the change process. Emerging from this final round was a plan to transform the congregation and its various care operations over the subsequent four years.

Although this was a hugely time consuming process for the 'senior management', this approach enabled the general council to ensure that as decisions are taken and implemented, the whole organisation was aligned behind them and the chances of success were greatly increased. Involving over 80 meetings in a twelve month period, every religious member of the community and probably over half the lay management, this was senior management commitment writ large.

In addition to the success in engaging the community, the Congregation has begun to be a learning organisation. Each step in the process has been iterative – the questions have been posed, the answers developed, tested and reflected on – and only then has action been taken. This learning has also occurred at the individual level. One example of this is that of the 80 plus meetings, 42 of them were conducted by the Superior General with the representatives of individual houses. In the first of these meetings, the Superior General provided a two minute introduction with the assisting consultant giving ten minutes. By the forty second meeting, the Superior General was providing a ten minute introduction and the assisting consultant was pretty much redundant!

At the time of writing in 2016, this organisation has persisted with the changes for nearly ten years and the fruits of their work are clear. The mission, the reason for their existence, is in good health, with more people being served than was the case at the outset. The financial performance is strong and Regions are improving and rebuilding the Houses. The Congregation is supporting and enabling this process while the Sisters are better able to devote their energy to their spiritual lives.

Ohno acknowledges the contribution of Taylor's 'scientific management' to his work, which aligns very closely with the 'machine' view of organisations potentially having the same limitations, particularly a reliance on the 'rightness' of the designer of the organisation.

While Ohno's approach increases the low level and local adaptiveness of the organisation, it arguably reduces it at the corporate one.

Ohno argues that the traditional 'cost–plus' model of pricing:

selling price = profit + actual cost

is outdated and inappropriate. Today organisations have moved away from this model towards value based pricing. Increasing competition and market growth, at rates lower than growth in production capacity, have forced businesses to look in this direction. Ohno argues that:

> Our products are scrutinized by cool-headed consumers ... where the manufacturing cost of a product is of no consequence

and hence the

> question is whether or not the product is of value to the buyer.

Increasing value can, in that competitive environment, primarily be derived by driving down the cost of production and hence the focus on elimination of waste. This is also consistent with imposing least possible cost on the supply chain, the environment and the customer.

Ohno might be thought of as Shaw's 'unreasonable man' – adapting the world to himself rather than adapting himself to the world. Clearly a practical man of courage, determination and intelligence, Ohno's 40 year mission at Toyota is undoubtedly having a long-term impact not only on Toyota but on management globally. As this is written, more than 25 years after Ohno's death companies globally are still learning and adopting his methods.

'Lean' is becoming a common approach, albeit it is often 'old wine in new skins' in that much of what is presented as 'lean' is more closely adherent to Taylor's work than Ohno's, adhering as it does to the 'production push' mentality of the West rather than the 'consumption pull' thinking that drives Toyota. It is perhaps a tragedy of much thinking, not just in the management field, that the desire to acquire the benefits of applying new ideas is not matched by a willingness to invest in fully appreciating their richness, complexity and subtlety. Too often they are reduced to a series of procedural steps to be learned and repeated, the effect of which is to reduce or eliminate their value (see Beckford, 1998).

11.2   Assumptions

What assumptions about the nature of the world does Ohno seem to be making?

There are several; first, and perhaps most dominant, is that the conventional model of mass production (Ohno cites the then Ford production method) is inappropriate for contemporary businesses and markets. Ohno claims that in 1949, Toyota produced around 25,000 vehicles – of which only about 1,000 were passenger cars. At the same time the American manufacturers were both the most advanced in production methods and the largest. More recently Toyota and Volkswagen have been vying to be the world largest manufacturer, each producing in the order of 10m vehicles.

It is fair to say that there is a significant range of differences, other than the Toyota Production System, that separate Toyota from its Western competitors. In the 1940s, the

Western organisations were working with a legacy of established investment in manufacturing plant, with established, powerful, functionally oriented and disparate Unions and succeeding with their products in the market-place. Where was the incentive to change? Toyota, on the other hand, was building a new business and seeking to compete with Western producers, investing in new plant and new markets. Supported particularly by American industrialists and consultants, it was able to study and learn from the challenges facing the Western manufacturers and had a less adversarial industrial relations environment. Culturally, Japan was very different to the West, apparently having a much more disciplined and homogeneous culture, whereas individuality was beginning to assert itself more strongly in the West. It is appropriate to wonder if under alternative conditions the Western manufacturers might have evolved differently.

In addition to 'demand-pull', the assumption that 'multi-kind, small quantity', just-in-time production is more cost-effective over time was the fundamental operating difference between Toyota and its competitors. The current situation suggests that, at least for now, Ohno was right. The ultimate expression of this approach might be reflected in work on Mass Customization (Pine, 1993) and is very evident in those products sold almost as fashion accessories, the customer can specify a very high degree of individualisation. Examples abound in the motor industry where, at the luxury end such as Rolls-Royce or Bentley, every car is essentially made (using a platform and crash structure shared with many other vehicles from the owning groups) to specific customised order including one-off variations (for example a unique colour or finish) to the super-mini market where, whilst mass produced, the customer is able to specify a wide range of product characteristics from a generous but limited range.

Ohno's second assumption appears to be about the responsibility of management – not just for quality (which he hardly mentions) but for the whole process of managing the organisation and driving continuous improvement in the eradication of waste, in achieving consistency and in minimising costs. In this regard, although acknowledging the inspiration of the Toyodas, it is apparent in his writing that Ohno sees himself as battling persistently against the established methods and norms whether with the executive, from whom he undoubtedly had significant support at the highest level, or with the production workers whose established practices he (apparently successfully) worked to change. This 'top down' approach is not unusual in organisations and does perhaps challenge the reputation of Japanese organisations as being much more participative. Dennis (2007) notes that the engagement culture seen in Toyota is not reflected across the whole of Japanese industry.

Whilst effective, trained workers are recognised by Ohno as fundamental to success, he clearly sees them as necessary rather than desirable – and their contribution, whilst perhaps wider than their Western equivalents, is constrained to their own working area. There is no scope in his system for them to query whether or not something should be done – just to think about how the given task might be done faster, cleaner and cheaper than before. To a large extent this is no different to many Western organisations – but it does not fully reflect a 'respect for [their] humanity'. Ohno writes about the necessity of effective team-working; 'Teamwork is Everything' and the benefit that can bring 'not how many parts were machined or drilled by one worker, but how many products were completed by the team as a whole'. He acknowledges that this may mean less than optimal performance from some individuals – 'distribute force equally … and at the same depth'. There is clearly a slight clash here with the notion of 'eliminating waste' since he seems to be accepting as part of the necessary functioning of the team, that some talent or strength may not be fully utilised in the creation of the product.

The centralised, 'command and control' organisation implied by this approach has already been critiqued (part one) and whilst encouraging low level process improvement, it says nothing of the ability of the organisation to adapt and change at a more strategic level.

A third assumption appears to be that workers will contribute 'as directed' and sacrifice themselves for the good of the business. The 'as directed' again points to a requirement for individuals to follow instructions whilst offering contributions to performance improvement which ultimately may not be in their interests. It has been argued elsewhere (see chapter 1) that jobs cannot be protected by the perpetuation of inefficient work practices. In a competitive world, efficiency or productivity gains are essential for an organisation to remain in business. As Toyota demonstrates, the relentless pursuit of process efficiency is at least one key to continued success – and provides some competitive advantage in a global economy where 'there is a surplus of everything' (Peters, 1992). However, an expectation that the average production worker will actively seek to bring about changes that lead to his or her own redundancy must be considered, at best, optimistic. Whilst working in a predominantly growing business, Toyota employees may have considered themselves relatively immune from loss of employment. This can no longer be considered to be the case. Notwithstanding the emergence of China and India as major growth economies, the mature, product replacement cycle markets must offer limited demand growth. In the medium to long term this may threaten employment numbers in the East.

11.3   Methods

Unlike the other gurus discussed, Ohno does not offer a quality programme or method for a quality project, but a business management philosophy that gives primacy to satisfying the needs of customers. This designs the production system around a 'demand-pull' rather than a 'production-push' approach. Ohno argues that this approach works to eliminate waste as only those things which are demanded by customers are produced. Simple to say, this philosophy requires a complete reversal of the thinking that drove the development of the Western economies. It is not a philosophy that can be adopted in part, or from which the 'juicy bits' can be extracted and applied, it is very much 'all or nothing' if it is to be successful.

The key elements to Ohno's thinking, the fundamentals of the Toyota Production System, seem to be:

Learn:	Citing Toyoda Kiichiro, then Toyota President, saying 'Catch up with America in three years. Otherwise the automobile industry of Japan will not survive', Ohno saw that learning from and about competitors was fundamental to success.
Revelation:	A different understanding of the world which, in effect, denies the existence of a mass market to focus on the customer as an individual.
Flexibility:	Recognition that a 'slow-growth' economy demands cost-effectiveness in small batch sizes and frequent tool changes in contrast to the traditional 'long-run, large batch' mentality.
Waste:	Elimination of waste and reduction of cost as the basis of survival and efficiency enabled by the 'just-in-time' meeting of needs and the development of autonomic systems which generate self-control in the production flow process – which becomes the basis of organisational design. Ohno sees price as value based rather than cost based – and value is determined by the consumer not the producer.

Information: The idea of 'kanban', a communication device for the production process which informs the preceding step AND controls its rate of output, is start-ling in its simplicity and effectiveness. 'Kanban' eliminates a mass of plan-ning, reporting, controlling activity and information systems that impose enormous costs on traditional organisations. Information also manages the essential process flow – from customer demand backwards to supplier man-agement and is used to smooth or 'level' demands to minimise peaks and troughs.

Autonomation: Rooted again in the notion of self-control, 'autonomation' (Ohno, 1988) requires that machines be designed in such a way that they monitor their own performance and stop themselves if they are not performing within preset parameters or are producing defective product. This cybernetic thinking eliminates waste in three ways:

> no more than one defective part is produced (eliminating scrap and rework) because the machine monitors itself;
> human talents can be put to more effective use than 'machine-minding';
> final products are not assembled using defective parts.

Coaching: With autonomation taking over much of the role of production super-vision, the Supervisor and Manager are freed to focus their attention on developing the skills and talents of the workers and in supporting their development as multi-skilled workers able to carry out a range of tasks.

Needs: In the Toyota Production System innovation and improvement are based on identified need, drawing on the information generated by the system. The need is used to drive thinking about the change – so management is not fad or initiative oriented but is consistently focused on understanding the ongoing need for improvement, on identifying through accurate infor-mation the opportunities for it and on taking deliberate action to achieve it.

Dennis (2007) suggests that lean requires focusing on understanding the organisation as a system stating that:

> A system is an integrated series of parts with a clearly defined goal

continuing:

> a car is a system whose goal is to provide transportation.

He suggests that systems have the characteristics outlined in Box 11.1:

What Dennis does not refer to is the notion of 'emergence', characteristics or properties which emerge only from the whole system and which cannot be found in any of the parts. This idea will be explored further in the third part of the book.

Dennis proceeds to represent a core image of lean production as a temple. Built on the foundations of standardisation and process stability, the roof is supported on the joint pillars of 'just-in-time' and 'Jidoka' with the filling provided through the engagement of people – an issue we have already discussed.

Box 11.1   System definition

Each part of a system has a definable purpose;
The parts of the system are interdependent;
We can understand each part by seeing how it fits into the system. But we
cannot understand the system by identifying the unassembled parts;
To understand the system we must understand its purpose, its inter-dependencies
and its interactions.

'Just–in–time' requires a system, integrated as far back up the supply chain as possible, which produces the 'right item at the right time in the right quantity' (Dennis, 2007).

Jidoka refers to 'automation with a human mind' and demands that intelligent workers and machines identify errors and rapidly correct them. Dennis (op. cit.) goes on:

> I came to understand that Jidoka means making defect-free processes by continually strengthening:
> Process Capability.
> Containment. Defects are quickly identified and contained in the zone.
> Feedback. So that quick countermeasures are taken.

This idea of Jidoka extends the 'lean' idea from the constrained Tayloristic machine type model to embrace notions of organisational learning (Senge, 1990) and adaptation (Beer, 1966), at least at the operational level, which are not reflected in the philosophy.

Ohno offers a mechanism (Figure 11.1) for the complete analysis of waste – moving beyond traditional measures of 'yield' or 'scrap' suggesting that:

Present capacity = work + waste

and identifying waste in the following ways:

- overproduction;
- time on hand (waiting);
- in transportation;
- processing;
- of stock on hand (inventory);
- of movement;
- of making defective products;

For Ohno then, the focus on waste emphasises that 'the ratio of value-added work is lower than most people think'. The elimination of waste might then be thought of more positively as increasing the proportion of value-adding work – which for Ohno means 'actually advancing the process towards completing the job'. Whilst there has been much work on process improvement in many companies over recent years, there is still a surprising amount of 'waste' in many if Ohno's definition is accepted. For example, a project undertaken to improve performance in the management of a sterile supply chain revealed that for some products, the proportion of overhead in terms of process time was 94%, i.e. for 94% of the time the product was 'waiting' whilst in terms of the non-value adding work, this ranged

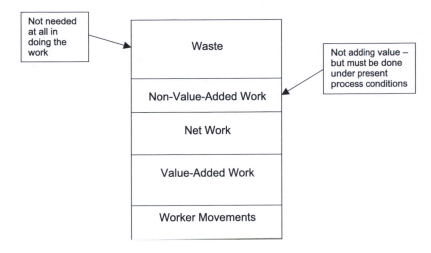

Figure 11.1 Understanding waste (adapted from Ohno, 1988).

from 36% up to 67% depending on the proportion of fixed to variable elements in the product. Redesigning the process to eliminate these both significantly reduces process cost and dramatically improves process output. The benefits of this are realised in financial terms and improvement in customer service.

In 1988, Ohno proposed that Toyota, having already achieved substantial performance improvement (reduction in waste), was able to focus on the 'Order to Cash' time line, reducing it by 'removing all the non-value-added wastes'. For a capital intensive industry such as motor manufacturing, reductions in the order to cash cycle substantially reduce the working capital needs of the business. This focus is not available to organisations that have not already largely eliminated waste or slack in their production facilities.

For a fuller exposition of the specific tools, techniques and methods of the 'lean manufacturing' movement, readers are referred to the work of Dennis (2007), Feld (2001), Levinson (2002) as well as that of Ohno himself.

11.4   Successes and failures

That Ohno's work has had major impact is unarguable – it has been adopted and adapted under the 'lean' label by many large organisations and is researched and taught in University Business Schools and by employers. The growth of Toyota vehicle manufacturing to become first or second in the world can, at least in part, be credited to the adoption of Ohno's work. No doubt there have been many other factors that have affected this such as the vision of the Toyoda family, the availability of low cost labour in a number of Asian countries and the favourable economic conditions that prevailed for much of the period from the late 1940s through to the turn of the century.

As a manufacturing approach, Ohno's methodology works well. However, it is not without its limitations. Particularly in an established organisation and supply chain, the adoption of parts of the Toyota process can be problematic – and even inappropriate where the supplier technologies or worker capabilities are not aligned. While the implementation of this method on a new or growing facility is relatively straightforward, the difficulty of application and use in an established factory should not be underestimated.

The idea of 'autonomation' applied in a production environment works well; employed in a service environment it is inadequate – an automated (or autonomated) system cannot deal with the infinite variety of human behaviour. If you doubt this, think about your last experience of dealing with an automated telephone call handling system or buying online.

Human behaviour also exposes another significant weakness. Although Ohno expressly includes the workforce within the methodology, it is as small-part players – expected to contribute to their part of the grand central design – but not to be full participants in the decision processes. The core ownership of the ideas is clearly reserved for the directors and senior managers with workers expected to follow that lead. That said, the emphasis placed by Ohno on the customer (as the focus of the process), places the whole organisation at the mercy of customer desire – and he says nothing of how the organisation can and should seek to understand the customer – nor how the customer should be influenced to want what the organisation has to offer.

The focus of lean has been on manufacturing and although some (Seddon, 2008) have revised the approach to focus on the service sector, its success is very much more limited in circumstances where the process is less influential than the human interaction. Considering organisations which are predominantly service based, where manufacturing is only one part of the process or where the process is only a small part of the whole transaction, the idea of 'lean' attracts new and difficult challenges. If 'process' is a smaller element of the whole then skills and behaviours increase dramatically in importance.

Dennis (2007) suggests that 'involvement animates the Toyota system' and describes how the tools of lean are intended to be used in a shared, collaborative environment. However, whilst this might inform the approach to providing people with problem solving skills, it neither addresses the culture and behaviours required in the organisation nor indicates how the management must develop a collaborative approach. Looking at the early experiences it could be argued that workers were coerced into compliance while, over time, the default of engagement (however it may actually be practised) has become a cultural norm; people know that if they work there then they must become involved.

The output end of the service chain, though, is much more challenging. If production has been systematised to the point of producing standardised, systematised physical product (as is the case for most manufacturers) the challenge to sustain value rests in human interaction and an understanding of what value means to the customer.

In a 'lean' process it would be not unusual for the precise form of words to be used in each customer engagement to be prescribed – 'do you want fries with that?' – while other, muda generating words may be proscribed. That, while efficient (and I am being deliberately obtuse), reduces the engagement to the minimum essential process and yet it still leaves ample room for error. Suppose the right words are used with the wrong tone of voice or the customer is partially deaf? Maybe the customer is in a friendly mood – or unfriendly. The person providing the process must be able to adapt, in real time, to the emotional tone of the engagement so must have BOTH the skills AND the freedom of choice to exercise judgement in how they deal with the customer if the relationship is to be sustained (the objective of effectiveness). This cannot be done where process efficiency overrides human engagement.

Similarly, whilst the customer 'drumbeat' is driving the pace of the production system (demand–pull), what constitutes value for that customer needs to be understood. When, as is now so often the case, the product characteristics in any given market are so alike as to be immaterial to customer decision, then the 'service' is what can differentiate. When the products are all (nearly) the same it is service that informs the customer drumbeat. At the time of writing I have been fortunate enough to be able to order a new Jaguar car from a dealership, but why a Jaguar? In the particular segment of the market to which my budget takes me there are three dominant European manufacturers – Mercedes, BMW and Jaguar. All provide big, comfortable saloon cars (in a remarkably similar range of colours, engine sizes and so on) all of which are more than capable of fulfilling my core requirement for a long-distance, economical and respectable 'work car', a vehicle that will help me earn my living for the next five years or so. So why a Jaguar? The dealership sales and service staff. Very simply, I have sampled the 'customer experience' at outlets for all three, I even believe that one of them builds a vehicle which is slightly better suited to my needs (though it is marginal), but it is the Jaguar dealership that I feel most welcome in, it is the staff at the Jaguar dealership (NOT the processes) who consistently demonstrate empathy with my interests and needs that give me confidence that I will be valued and looked after for the whole of my period of ownership. It is that sense of support and confidence that I am buying into far more than the physical product.

If 'lean thinking' is going to successfully move from the manufacturing to the service sector it needs to develop (or adopt) tools and ways of working that will genuinely embrace the inherent variability of people based processes.

11.5   Critical review

Ohno's core idea might best be characterised through the call to eliminate waste of all types. With its roots in the desperate straits of post-war Japan and the urgent need to maximise value from every aspect of the economy, this makes much sense. It is also very supportive of the more contemporary need to minimise environmental impact caused by business operations and the use of products.

The adoption of the ideas throughout the world are testament to the value and resilience of the approach under changing circumstances – but that adoption has in many cases been somewhat partial with organisations attempting to cherry pick the parts that they want (usually those that appear to immediately save money). It is noticeable that investment in training for workers has, certainly in the West, been more challenging to achieve than the implementation of kanban type systems.

Ohno, bizarrely, does not offer a systematic methodology for the development and adoption of the Toyota System – though this is derivable from his work (Ohno, 1988). He says little or nothing of how to commence the implementation process – and in particular nothing of how to engage the hearts and minds of the company directors whose support, encouragement and funding will be necessary for successful implementation. Inspiration for a systematic methodology can be drawn from other areas. For example, there is now a substantial literature on the subject of 'lean production' – with authors such as Feld (2001), Levinson (2002), Dennis (2007) and Junewick (2002) who, each in their own way, seek to systematise, organise, synthesise and homogenise the Toyota System. Each brings a slightly different perspective. Secondly, the underpinning method that drives improvement in the Toyota method is the use of 'feedback control'. There is a whole body of knowledge – cybernetics – of which feedback control is but a small part and this ranges from Wiener (1947) through Beer (1959, 1966, 1979, 1981) and more recently Beckford (1993, 1998, 2002, 2016) and Dudley (2000).

The focus on 'method' in Ohno's work, the science, perhaps understates the nature of power relations in Japan generally and Toyota in particular (at least at that time). It is likely to be the case that in countries and businesses with different power structures and relationships, the same success may be harder to achieve.

Summary

This chapter has introduced the work of Taiichi Ohno and considered his substantial contribution to the global quality movement. Students are encouraged to read Ohno's own work to further inform and develop their views.

KEY LEARNING POINTS

Taiichi Ohno

Father of the Toyota Production System and Lean Manufacturing
Focus on the elimination of waste

Scientific Methodology
Very successful in manufacturing organisations
Adopted by many businesses worldwide under the 'Lean Production' banner
No clear methodology for engagement and implementation

Question

Consider what challenges would be faced by a traditionally managed organisation in adopting the Toyota Methodology. Identify tools from all the gurus that might help overcome them.

12 Shigeo Shingo

'It is a waste and you, the customer, should not have to pay for the waste'

Shigeo Shingo (attrib.), 2016

Introduction

Shigeo Shingo, who died in 1990, is perhaps the least well known in the West of the Japanese quality gurus. Educated as a mechanical engineer, he became a consultant in 1945, subsequently working with a wide variety of companies in many industries. These companies included Toyota, Mitsubishi, Matsushita and Sony. During his later career he became involved with a large number of Western organisations. Norman Bodek, President of Productivity Incorporated, in the Foreword to *The Sayings of Shigeo Shingo* (1987), cited by Bendell (1989: 12), says:

> If I could give a Nobel Prize for exceptional contributions to world economy, prosperity and productivity, I wouldn't have much difficulty selecting a winner – Shigeo Shingo's life work has contributed to the well-being of everyone in the world.

He is regarded by Gilbert (1992: 24) as 'one of the 20th century's greatest engineers' and he made a number of significant contributions in that area. He wrote fourteen major books with several translated into English and other European languages.

12.1 Philosophy

Shingo's early philosophy embraced Taylorist (1911) 'scientific management' ideas. The approach was adopted extensively by Shingo until in mid-career he became aware of the methods of 'Statistical Quality Control'. He adopted these methods until in the 1970s he was 'finally released from the spell of statistical quality control methods' (Bendell, 1989: 12). The breakthrough in his thinking arose when he came to believe in defect prevention. This led to his major contribution to the quality debate.

Dale et al (2007) suggest that Shingo argued that 'using statistical methods is tantamount to accepting defects as inevitable'. Essentially, they, with Flood (1993), suggest he believed 'statistical methods detect errors too late in the manufacturing process'. He proposed that instead of detecting errors it was better to engage in preventative measures aimed at eliminating their sources. Gilbert (1992: 166) suggests that Shingo meant that we need to change our 'attitude of mind' and 'to organise and then behave in a way' which allows mistake proofing to happen.

Thus, over time, Shingo effectively rejected the scientific management 'economic man' theory with all its attendant difficulties; rejected control after the event and focused on prevention. He became concerned with the total manufacturing process and Gilbert (1992: 24) cites him as saying that:

> he would prefer to be remembered for his promotion of the understanding necessary behind the concepts of looking at the total manufacturing process and the elimination of transportation, storage, lot delays and inspection.

Much of this approach has become embedded in the 'kanban' systems, often called 'just-in-time'.

Shingo continued to believe in mechanising the monitoring of error, considering that human assessment was 'inconsistent and prone to error'. He used people to identify underlying causes and produce preventative solutions.

There is a clear belief, like Crosby, in a 'zero defects' approach. However, unlike Crosby who emphasises worker responsibility, exhortations and slogans, Shingo's approach emphasises zero defects through good engineering and process investigation and rectification. Bendell (1989: 12) reports that Shingo shared the concern of Deming and Juran that 'posting defect statistics is misguided, and that instead the defective elements in operations that generate a lot of defectives should be hunted down'.

12.2   Assumptions

The assumptions about the world that seem to underpin Shingo's approach will now be reviewed.

Perhaps unsurprisingly, given his mechanical engineering background and training, Shingo adhered to a mechanistic approach to organisation throughout his career. From engineering jobs and people in the scientific management approach of his early work, he moved to the quantitative methods of statistical quality control and, finally, to error prevention through engineering.

The mechanistic view of organisation has been challenged by many management theorists and practitioners. It is criticised for failing to take account of human needs and desires, failing to recognise the interactions within an organisation and between the organisation and its environment. Further criticisms have been aimed at the reductionist nature of the approach which tends to fragment organisations, their systems and processes, rather than deal with them as wholes. An approach which does not take account of these factors in an increasingly inter-related world must be flawed.

The adoption then abandonment of statistical methods rests on the belief that it is possible to develop processes which are error free. While in an engineering context it may be possible to achieve the zero defects objective, it is considered unlikely that the same can be done in other sectors. Food production relies on natural processes which cannot (yet) be engineered to achieve absolute reliability. While materials and yields may be improved, the processes are still outside the control of the organisation and its people, for example temperature, humidity, wind, soil condition, crop diseases. Similarly in the service sector, as has previously been discussed, there are many variables which cannot be controlled to the extent that Shingo's approach requires.

It has been consistently argued in this book that an appropriate balance of both qualitative and quantitative approaches is most useful. Here Shingo's assumptions must be challenged by suggesting that ignoring the human relations aspects of organisation and abandoning statistical methods largely limits the potential applications to the manufacturing sector.

12.3   Methods

Shingo could be considered as the first management thinker and practitioner to engage in what has recently come to be called 're-engineering' (Hammer & Champy, 1993), although the term was used in Operations Research as early as the 1940s (Wiener, 1947). His achievement in reducing hull assembly time from four months to two months at Mitsubishi, and the development of the SMED System at Toyota (Single Minute Exchange of Die) as part of the 'just–in–time' concept, were both substantial contributions in their own right.

However, his principal contribution to the quality field is mistake proofing, 'Poka–Yoke'. This approach stops the production process whenever a defect occurs, defines the cause and generates action designed to prevent recurrence. Alternatively, 'on–line' adjustment to the product or process may be made, enabling continuous processes to be managed. For example, in the chemical and steel industries it may be both impractical and expensive to stop a production process.

Poka–Yoke relies on a process of continuously monitoring potential sources of error. Machines used in the process are equipped with feedback instrumentation to carry out this task as Shingo considered that human personnel are 'fallible' (Bendell, 1989: 12). People are used to trace and resolve the error causes. Installation of the system is expected to lead over time to a position where all likely recurring errors have been eradicated.

Cybernetic systems

The idea of Poka-Yoke is similar to the concepts employed in cybernetic systems – systems which in the process of going out of control put themselves back in control again. The simplest and commonest form of cybernetic system is a domestic heating system which on receipt of 'feedback' information about the air temperature from the thermostat turns the heating system on and off in the attempt to maintain a set temperature. A similar example is the cooling system on an engine where the thermostat opens and closes to control the flow of water through the radiator, keeping the engine at its optimum operating temperature.

The 'goal' of these systems is a particular temperature. In the case of 'poka-yoke' the goal of the system is zero-defects. In each case the goal is determined outside the system – by the design engineer for the car, the house occupier in the case of the heating system or the factory management in the case of a production process.

The concept is now widely employed in industrial control systems for production processes. For example, the baking industry uses a system of this type to control the chamber temperatures in travelling ovens aiming to ensure that the product is appropriately heated at each stage of the cooking process.

The employment of these techniques can reduce or eliminate the need for human monitoring of processes and, as Shingo suggests, enhance reliability. Advances in information technology and approaches to information management make the application of these techniques much simpler. Systems which operate in 'real-time' and are capable of both detecting errors – and, perhaps more importantly, anticipating errors (on the basis of the information being received) and stopping the line before the error occurs are now common place while 'smart' infrastructure is being created with embedded 'intelligence' which can both manage and self-optimise. These capabilities will become increasingly important in the age of 'the internet of things'.

A common failure amongst organisations is to fully appreciate what it is now possible to achieve in this regard and to stay with outmoded techniques of management. In pursuit of quality it is useful to adopt proven, reliable techniques, but it is essential to embrace those new approaches which have the latent capability to bring about substantial improvement.

The concept has been adopted to some extent in the food processing industry through the system known as 'HACCP' (Hazard Analysis Critical Control Points) which has already been outlined. Clearly it would be unacceptable for even one defective food item to move through a system where that generated risk to health. However as is regularly seen, even such rigorous systems cannot entirely remove the risks.

12.4   Successes and failures

There is no doubt that Shingo's ideas have made a substantial contribution in a variety of areas. The adoption of all or some of his methods by companies throughout the world and his extensive consulting in many countries stand as testament to his success. There are, though, apparent limitations.

While Gilbert (1992: 166) suggests that the Poka-Yoke concept can be applied equally to administrative procedures and production processes, this is, at best, arguable. A production process may well be fully or extensively automated, minimising the opportunity for human or machine error. Administrative and book-keeping procedures, which rely for the most part on the communication and transcription of information, cannot be automated to the same extent, allowing scope for error. An error rate of 2% (two keystrokes in 100) is regarded as normal for a competent keyboard operator. Human interaction and intervention in the system is inevitable, and as Shingo himself said, humans are fallible. A second strand to this is the potential for misinterpretation of data. Language relies on two levels of understanding, the syntactic (signs) and semantic (meaning). While syntactic understanding can be relatively reliably conveyed, even automated, semantic understanding cannot be guaranteed. It is not therefore possible to build an administrative system which can guarantee that the message, including its meaning, transmitted by one party is received and understood in the same way by the other party.

Flood (1993: 29) provides the basis for the main strengths of Shingo's approach:

- On-line, real-time control;
- Poka-Yoke emphasises effective control systems.

The main weaknesses are:

- Source inspection only works effectively in manufacturing processes;
- Shingo says little about people other than that they are fallible.

Considering the first of these points, there is little doubt that in a fast moving and rapidly changing world, on–line, real–time information is not just desirable but essential. However, many production processes are difficult to halt (anything with continuous flow rather than discrete products such as steel, oil, paper) and hence error must be designed out and/or error correction capability embedded in the running system.

The use of automated feedback and control mechanisms is a sound starting point for the control of a process in operation and is to be welcomed. However, little is said about the management attitudes towards accountability and responsibility that must go with it. It could be argued that a management unsupportive of this approach would not implement it. However, a technical system of this sort provides information which an autocratic management could use in a way which might be considered inappropriate – as a stick with which to beat people rather than a tool for improvement. Nonetheless, as Wiener (1947) stated in the early stages of the development of modern cybernetics, there are 'great possibilities for good or evil' and it is up to managers to use the knowledge wisely.

Turning to the weaknesses, the applicability of the ideas to the service sector has already been questioned. Regarding the attitude to people, it is clear that Shingo's work assumes a willing, co–operative workforce although he says nothing of how this state can be achieved and maintained. Shingo does not take into account the body of literature concerning this topic which has arisen during the middle and later years of the 20th century.

12.5   Critical review

There appear to be some consistent themes to Shingo's views, despite the apparent developments in his thinking – from scientific management through statistical quality control to mistake proofing.

He seems to have adhered, in the main, to an 'economic man' view of the people involved in the organisation. The wisdom of this view, and his failure to address the body of theoretical and practical knowledge which challenges it, has to be considered a major weakness of his work. While in some Eastern cultures there remains a strong allegiance to collective societal values, other nations are more individually oriented. This often translates into the pursuit of individual rather than corporate benefit from work – often reinforced by the style of corporate rewards offered. In a situation where that is the case, the individual may not be willing to contribute in the way that Shingo's work suggests is necessary.

A second clear and consistent theme has been the concentration on good engineering. This is unsurprising given Shingo's background, and his contribution must be considered substantial in this area. However it does limit the application of his ideas to organisations and processes where the concepts are most readily applied.

The concept of mistake proofing (and inevitably sitting comfortably with the work of Taiichi Ohno) by refining and redesigning processes is of great importance. While it will generally be most easily applicable in the manufacturing sector, there is little doubt that the concept if not the practice can be carried across into service organisations. The danger is that it may give rise to additional administrative, auditing and checking procedures which, far from reducing costs and speeding up processes, may well serve to increase costs and slow down service, increasing waste. Associated with this is that the procedures may become 'institutionalised', inhibiting or preventing adaptation and learning by the organisation. Manual methods, once ingrained, can become the fabric of each individual's daily task – and very difficult to change. Nonetheless, the underlying emphasis on prevention of error is to be welcomed.

Summary

This chapter has reviewed the major contribution of Shigeo Shingo to the quality movement. Students should refer to Shingo's (1987) own work to develop and enhance their own understanding.

KEY LEARNING POINTS

Shigeo Shingo

Definition of quality:
defects in process

Key beliefs:
defect prevention through eradication of defective processes, human fallibility, 'mechanistic' view of organisations, real-time information processing

Principal method:
poka-yoke (zero-defects)

Question

Consider how you might pursue 'mistake-proofing' in a service organisation.

13 Genichi Taguchi

'Cost is more important than quality, but quality is the best way to reduce cost'

Genichi Taguchi (attrib.)

Introduction

Genichi Taguchi, who died in 2012, trained as a textile engineer prior to his service in the Japanese Navy. He subsequently worked in the Ministry of Public Health and Welfare and the Institute of Statistical Mathematics. In that post he learned about experimental design techniques and orthogonal arrays. He began his consulting career whilst working at Nippon Telephone and Telegraph. His early work in the field of quality was mainly concerned with operational production processes – the shift to a focus on product and process design occurring during the 1980s. It was during this period that his ideas began to be adopted in the USA. Logothetis (1992: 17) describes Taguchi's contribution as an 'inspired evolution' in the quality movement, by eliminating the need for mass inspection through his process of building quality into the product at the design stage. Taguchi (1986), cited by Pyzdek & Keller (2013), had a concern that 'increased variance translates to poorer quality and higher cost'.

Taguchi was awarded the Deming prize and the Deming award for literature on quality. His best known work is *Systems of Experimental Design* (1987).

13.1 Philosophy

The two founding ideas of Taguchi's quality work are essentially quantitative. First is a belief in statistical methods to identify and eradicate quality problems. The second rests on designing quality in to products and processes from the outset. Logothetis (1992: 13) sees Taguchi's view of quality as a negative, the cost of non–quality, meaning 'the loss imparted to society from the time the product is shipped'. Taguchi's prime concern is with customer satisfaction and with the potential for 'loss of reputation and goodwill' associated with failure to meet customer expectations. Such a failure, he considered, would lead the customer to buy elsewhere in the future, damaging the prospects of the company, its employees and society. He considered that losses occurred not only when a product was outside its specification but also when it varied from its target value.

Flood (1993: 30) suggests that Taguchi's view 'steps back one further stage on the technical side', pulling back quality management into design. This is achieved through a three stage prototyping or 'experimental design' (Dale et al, 2007) method (Box 13.1).

Box 13.1　Three stage prototyping method

Genichi Taguchi:

- System Design;
- Parameter Design;
- Tolerance Design.

The first stage is concerned with system design reasoning involving both product and process. This is an attempt to develop a basic analytical, materials, process and production framework. The framework is carried forward into the second stage, parameter design. The search at this stage is for the optimal mix of product variation levels and process operating levels, aiming to reduce the sensitivity of the production system to external or internal disturbances. Tolerance design, the third stage, enables the recognition of factors that may significantly affect the variability of the product. Further investment, alternative equipment and materials are then considered as ways to further reduce variability.

Here a clear belief can be seen in identifying and, as far as possible, eradicating potential causes of 'non-quality' at the outset. This ties in with Flood's (1993: 32) view that Taguchi's work perceives quality to be a 'societal rather than organisational issue'. He further recognises that Taguchi's method relies on a number of organisational principles (Box 13.2).

Clearly, Taguchi recognises organisations as 'open systems' – that is, systems which interact with their environment, influencing and being influenced. The emphasis on communication and control – the systems view – recognises inter-dependence between processes, something which he has been criticised for ignoring. Logothetis (1992: 340) considers this unreasonable and says that 'Taguchi, contrary to common opinion does recognise interactions' – saying:

> If one assumes a linear model thinking it correct, then one is a man removed from natural science or reality, and commits the mistake of standing just upon mathematics which is nothing but idealism.

Summarising, there appear to be several beliefs. The first is in quantitative methods, providing measurements for control. The second is in the eradication, as far as possible, of causes of failure at the outset. The third is in the societary cost of non-quality. The fourth perhaps

Box 13.2　Organisational principles

Genichi Taguchi:

Principle 1)　Communication;
Principle 2)　Control;
Principle 3)　Efficiency;
Principle 4)　Effectiveness;
Principle 5)　Efficacy;
Principle 6)　Emphasis on location and elimination of causes of error;
Principle 7)　Emphasis on design control;
Principle 8)　Emphasis on environmental analysis.

reflects the third, and is the systems view of inter-dependence and inter-relationship both within the organisation and with its environment.

13.2   Assumptions

Taguchi's first and quite critical assumption is that quality can always be controlled through improvement in design. While this may be the case for many aspects of manufacturing, its validity in the service sector must be questioned. Similarly, where products exhibit either natural properties – as in the case of food – or contain aspects of 'craft' skill – cabinet making, pottery or precious metal work – this may be inappropriate.

A second assumption relates to his attitude to people. While it will be clearly seen that he values their creative input to the design and development process, they are perhaps not considered a significant factor in the production of quality goods. Little or nothing is said about them or the management process.

It has already been mentioned that the work has a clear focus on the manufacturing sector. Nothing is said about how to manage the quality process in service industries.

The next assumption is again quite critical. Taguchi seems to assume that the organisation can wait for results – that delays between product conception and production will be acceptable. While these delays are to some extent inevitable, contemporary market demands are such that delays need to be minimised. 'Time to market' has become an absolutely crucial element in success for many organisations. In pharmaceuticals the first in the market with a new therapeutic becomes the market leader and the position is often unassailable. A similar situation arises with information technology where the most recent innovation tends to act as a key attractor for the 'early adopters' – and the innovator does attract a significant degree of loyalty. It is essential therefore if Taguchi's ideas are to be fully implemented that they are not additional to but an integral part of the product development process and that the process is designed in such a way that 'time to market' is a key consideration. A conflict may arise between the business need to be fast into the market and the business need to achieve high quality. Adopting the Taguchi method after initial product design must be seen as unacceptable. It is suggested that quality parameters should be as much a part of a basic design brief as timing, markets and prices.

It is easy to see that much of Taguchi's work has been informed by his background in engineering and quantitative methods. What is less obvious is how his 'systems' perspective arose. The adoption of a systemic view, while not apparently extending to the management process of the organisation, is certainly a step forward from the work of many of his fellow gurus.

13.3   Methods

The principal tools and techniques espoused by Taguchi centre around the concept of 'kaizen' thinking, continuous improvement. His backward step into the design process helps to ensure a high basic quality standard. Other than the 'quadratic loss function', the other statistical methods are common to many thinkers and will be reviewed in the appropriate chapter. This section will consider:

- Suggested steps for experimental studies;
- Prototyping;
- Quadratic loss function.

The suggested steps (Box 13.3) fall into the 'parameter design' (Logothetis, 1992: 306) stage of product development. It is within this process that Taguchi utilises people. This scientific method is very reminiscent of Deming's 'Plan, Do, Check, Action' cycle. This should perhaps not be surprising given their common background in statistics.

The first stage is concerned with developing a clear statement of precisely what problem is to be solved. Taguchi considers it of great importance that the experiment should be exactly targeted. The second stage links with the first. It is important to determine what output characteristics are to be studied and optimised through the experimental process, and what measurements are to be taken. It may be necessary to run control experiments in order to validate results.

The third stage is brainstorming. At this point, all the managers and operators related to the product or process are required to come together and determine the controllable and uncontrollable factors affecting the situation. Here the aim is to define an experimental range and suitable factor levels. Logothetis (1992: 306) suggests that Taguchi prefers to consider as many factors (not interactions) as is economically feasible. Whether this represents a sufficient involvement by people in the solution development process is debatable; perhaps they should be involved at all stages. Nonetheless, their involvement in experiment design, and their contribution of knowledge to the debate, must be considered invaluable. It is normally the case that those who perform a job know it better than anybody else. The opportunity for them to articulate that knowledge in an informal session such as brainstorming is to be welcomed.

The fourth stage is experiment design. At this point the controllable and uncontrollable (noise) (Silver, 2012) factors are separated for statistical monitoring purposes. This is followed by the fifth stage, the experiment itself.

The sixth stage is to analyse the performance measures recorded, using appropriate statistical methods. This is followed by interpretation of the results at the seventh stage. This aims to identify optimal levels for the control factors which seek to minimise variability and bring the process closest to its target value. Prediction is used at this stage to consider the performance of the process under optimal conditions.

The eighth and final stage is to validate the results so far obtained by running further experiments. Failure to confirm results by further experimentation generates a need to revisit stages three through eight.

This whole process may be regarded as similar to the 'black box' technique used in cybernetics. In that case, altering inputs and monitoring the effect on outputs is an

---

Box 13.3   Eight stages of product development

Genichi Taguchi:

Stage 1)   Define the problem;
Stage 2)   Determine the objective;
Stage 3)   Conduct a brainstorming session;
Stage 4)   Design the experiment;
Stage 5)   Conduct the experiment;
Stage 6)   Analyse the data;
Stage 7)   Interpret the results;
Stage 8)   Run a confirmatory experiment.

experimental device or method for determining the function of a unit. This technique could be used from a 'macro' perspective in a production or manufacturing facility, to determine areas of maximum concern for detailed analysis through the Taguchi methods. Interested readers should refer to the work of Beer (1981) for a more detailed discussion of this approach.

Prototyping is the technique which Taguchi uses to develop what Gilbert (1992: 24) calls the 'up and limping' prototype. This has already been seen in the review of Taguchi's philosophy. The technique consists of three stages. The first, System Design, is aimed at applying scientific and engineering principles to the development of functional design. It has two elements, product design and process design. The second stage is Parameter Design. This looks at establishing process and machine settings that minimise performance variation. A distinction is made at this stage between controllable and uncontrollable factors (parameters and noise). The specification criterion is for optimisation and is usually expressed as monetary loss arising from variation. The third stage is Tolerance Design. This is aimed at minimising the total sum of product manufacturing and lifetime costs.

The quadratic loss function is Taguchi's principal contribution to the statistical aspects of achieving quality. The aim is to minimise the cost of a product or service. In this, a particular quality characteristic (x) is identified and a target value (T) set for it. Proximity to the target value is expressed as $(x-T)$. The result of exceeding or failing to achieve T is a financial loss to the organisation, hence the result must always be positive. This is achieved through squaring the answer, $(x-T)^2$. This result is multiplied by a cost co-efficient (c) which puts a cost on failing to meet the target (T). A further co-efficient (k), representing the minimum loss to society with a value always greater than 0, is added. The sum represents the total loss (L) to society. Thus:

$$L = c(x - T)^2 + k$$

This may be viewed, in some respects, as a measure of efficiency and of effective utilisation of resources. Of critical importance to its use are the correct selection of criteria and the accurate development of the co-efficients c and k. If any of the values selected for the calculation are incorrect, then the whole process becomes useless.

13.4 Successes and failures

As with each of the other gurus reviewed, Taguchi is accepted as having made a substantial contribution to the field. His books, and his consulting, indicate the wide acknowledgement of the utility of his approach.

Adapting from Flood (1993: 32–33), the following strengths to Taguchi's work are suggested:

- quality is a design requirement;
- the approach recognises the systemic impact of quality;
- it is a practical method for engineers;
- it guides effective process control.

The principal weaknesses are:

- usefulness is biased towards manufacturing;
- guidance is not given on management or organisational issues;

- it places quality in the hands of the experts;
- it says nothing about people as social animals.

Looking at the strengths, it can again be argued that Taguchi does not go far enough backwards into the design process. Quality parameters are to some extent already determined once the product has moved beyond the initial concept stage, since certain factors such as market and price range will often be decided at that point.

The recognition of the total cost to society of defective products is useful – and particularly relevant in the light of legislative and regulatory changes concerning corporate social responsibility and environmental impact. However since, as Flood suggests, little account is taken of the people or management process in the organisation, the definition of 'total cost' has to be open to question.

That the method is developed for practising engineers, rather than theoretical statisticians, perhaps serves to make it useful. However, the validity of the quadratic loss function should be questioned if each application is not properly understood and underpinned by a validated statistical base.

Turning to the weaknesses, Flood's assessment, that the model is of no use where measurement produces no meaningful data, stands. This perhaps limits its usefulness outside the manufacturing sector. That nothing is said about managing people and the organisation is also agreed and is considered to be a major drawback to the whole approach.

Taguchi's failure to recognise organisations as social systems contrasts quite sharply with his recognition of quality as a societal issue. There is no explanation in his work for this. He appears to consider the people within the organisation as 'machine parts' who will perform whatever function they are allocated to. No account is taken of human variability in the measurement of processes; perhaps he regards this, unsympathetically, as noise!

13.5   Critical review

There can be little doubt that Taguchi's work makes a substantial contribution to the quality movement. This contribution has, however, been focused very narrowly.

His engineering and statistical background quite clearly underpins the approaches which he espouses and this, to some extent, has limited the value of his work. He relies absolutely on quantitative measures of quality, and this makes his approach quite unsuitable for application to the service sector where quality is often defined by observers at a much more subjective level.

Contrasting with this, his emphasis on quality of design and the process of prototyping are invaluable, even if perhaps not far reaching enough. The impact on total (organisation) cost of developing quality products and processes must not be underestimated. They will enable substantial reductions or even complete eradication of processes of inspection, re-work and reject. Each of these items substantially impact on the operating costs of many organisations and are often directly related to the inadequacy of the design and development work.

Taguchi's lack of concern with people and managing organisations must be considered the second major flaw in his approach. He says nothing of how to implement his approaches, which would meet major resistance in many organisations. The necessary re-organisation and alteration of corporate structures, the shifts in power and perhaps the change in budgets associated with his method would all be expected to generate substantial resistance within the organisation. Handling this resistance is not addressed.

Summary

The review of the work of Genichi Taguchi is now complete. Readers should refer to his original work (Taguchi, 1987), in order to develop their own appreciation of his contribution.

KEY LEARNING POINTS

Genichi Taguchi

Definition of quality:
the loss imparted to society from the time the product is shipped

Key beliefs:
statistical methods, quality as inherent in design,
quality is a societal issue

Principal methods:
prototyping method, eight steps of parameter design,
quadratic loss function

Question

Taguchi believes that quality is a societal, rather than an organisational, issue. Debate the merits of this belief.

Part three

Contemporary thinking

User guide

Part one showed how quality has become a major organisational issue and placed it in the broader context of early management thinking. In part two the work of the quality 'gurus' and its relationship to that thinking was considered. In part three the aim is to bring quality thinking up to date by placing it in the context of the contemporary appreciations of management.

Management thinking has developed substantially in recent years although the dominant literature about quality has not, for the most part, explicitly embraced the potential benefits emerging from that development. It was shown in part two that the work of the quality gurus relies principally on the 'machine' view of organisation, with some writers moving towards 'human relations' theory but failing to take full advantage of the substantial body of work in that area. For example, Ishikawa emphasises participation and provides a potentially useful tool for achieving it, but says nothing of the aspects of human behaviour which enable or inhibit meaningful participation. Similarly, the value of holistic or systemic thinking about organisational issues is achieving increasing prominence in other areas of problem solving (for example Senge's *Fifth Discipline*) but is largely ignored in the quality literature.

This part of the book commences by considering quality management systems and standards then explains systemic approaches to understanding organisation. Systemic thinking moves away from treating quality as a technical exercise in improving production performance and product quality to embrace less mechanistic, softer issues of culture, stakeholder relations and organisational politics as well as offering assistance on the technical aspects. Whilst quality purists might argue, from a systemic perspective the pursuit of the traditional, narrow interpretation of quality is just one of many strands in the achievement of organisational effectiveness. Systemic thinking is as much concerned with the interaction between elements of production as with the performance of the elements themselves since it is the interaction which is considered to create 'the system'.

The chapters in this part commence with consideration of ISO 9001:2015 and EFQM. Thereafter the idea of organisations as systems is introduced, progressing through some well established problem solving methodologies to consider re-engineering (including six-sigma), notions of organisational learning and lastly service quality management.

14 Quality management systems standards

'Sincerity – if you can fake that you've got it made'

George Burns

Introduction

I was unsure whether this chapter should close the last section or open this one. I opted for the latter because, while the ISO 9001:2015 Quality Management System Standard essentially summarises many key procedural elements of the work of the gurus, it thereby provides a platform upon which new thinking should build. Although some of the gurus' thinking may not be wholly appropriate to contemporary needs, quality management systems adherent to ISO requirements are essential to continued trading for many organisations.

The fundamentals and vocabulary of quality management systems (QMS) are set out in ISO 9000:2015. However, the primary focus of the first part of the chapter will be the ISO 9001:2015 QMS requirements. The third part of the trilogy, ISO 9004:2015, offers guidance for organisations wishing to pursue 'sustained success'; an odd document; when continuous improvement is already embedded in ISO 9001:2015 arguably ISO 9004:2015 is redundant.

The review will broadly follow the pattern of the standard itself, identifying a number of key areas for interpretation and discussion and will also look briefly at the complementarity between this, the Environmental Standard (ISO 14001:2015) and the Occupational Health and Safety Management Systems Standard (BS OHSAS 18001:2007).

In the final part of the chapter the EFQM Business Excellence Model will be considered.

14.1 ISO 9001:2015 principles

ISO 9001:2015 is the latest evolution of a QMS standard which began with consistency of specifications and standards in the defence industry. NATO (North Atlantic Treaty Organization) began developing these in the late 1940s to enable harmonisation between co–operating military forces. These standards were consolidated and revised in 'DefStans' (Defence Standards) 05–08, 05–25 and 05–28 between 1951 and 1973. Standards systems which were once dominant in the civil world such as BS5750 (the British standard) and EN29000 have largely been subsumed in the ISO system.

The introduction to ISO 9001:2015 states that:

> The adoption of a quality management system is a strategic decision for an organisation that can help to improve its overall performance and provide a sound basis for sustainable development initiatives.

The requirements document sets out seven underpinning quality management principles (Box 14.1).

These principles reflect the breadth of the approaches proposed by the various gurus but are important in emphasising some aspects. The principle of customer focus, reflecting Ohno, Crosby and Feigenbaum, is crucial; the true arbiter of quality is always the customer. Similarly the process approach when coupled to both an improvement orientation and evidence based decision making, reflective of Deming, Ishikawa, Juran and Shingo, is fundamental to achieving consistency. Leadership, engagement and relationship management reflect Oakland and Crosby and Taguchi's perspective on quality as being a societal issue. We can see that, explicitly or not, the principles underpinning the standard are now substantially shaped around the core ideas of the key writers and practitioners in the field.

In describing the 'Process Approach' the introduction makes specific reference to 'understanding and managing interrelated processes as a system'. While this is encouraging in itself, the next part of the paragraph undermines it by emphasising that this 'enables the organization to control the interrelationships and interdependencies amongst the processes of the system'. This emphasis on control suggests that the authors of the standard have yet to grasp the nature of dynamical systems (see Beckford, 2016) and the particular challenge of 'control' in the service sector in which the influence of human behaviour (of both provider and customer) is critical in service transactions and relationships. However rich the process these are not susceptible to control in the conventional sense.

The description then moves to talk of the 'systematic definition and management of processes and their interactions' suggesting that 'management of the processes and the system as a whole can be achieved using the PDCA cycle'. Being systematic in definition of inputs is highly important, but it does emphasise an input orientation to the thinking, whereas if customer requirements are to be truly met, the process needs to focus on the customer outcome rather than the outputs and inputs. That is not 'did the process do what we specified it to do', but, 'did we co-produce with the customer the desired outcome'. In manufacturing to some degree, but very clearly in services, the customer is not a passive beneficiary of the process but an active participant.

There is a fundamental difference between the manufacturing orientated notion of process compliance and the service oriented notion of customer satisfaction. Of course the achievement of the latter is rooted in process, but it relies on the technical and inter-personal skills of the service deliverer and their behaviour; the application of their emotional intelligence to the service relationship in such a manner as to ensure satisfaction. Applied emotional intelligence by both the organisation and its customer can absorb the shocks of variability in service processes.

Box 14.1   Quality management principles ISO 9001:2015

Customer focus

Leadership

Engagement of people

Process approach

Improvement

Evidence-based decision making

Relationship management

It seems to me that, although a significant advance on the previous versions, the authors of ISO 9001:2015 have not yet grasped the full meaning of a systemic understanding of the world nor have they come close to properly considering the behavioural aspects of service quality, remaining rooted in the 'manufacturing specification and standards' mindset.

14.2 ISO 9001:2015 requirements

14.2.1 Scope

The standard requires that any organisation applying the standard is able to:

- Demonstrate the consistent ability to provide products and services that meet both customer and regulatory or statutory requirements;
- Use the QMS to improve customer satisfaction;
- Use the QMS to improve the QMS itself.

14.2.2 Organisation and context

The organisation needs therefore to demonstrate that it has a current knowledge of those internal and external factors that are relevant to fulfilment of its purpose and strategy as they impact on its achievement of intended outcomes. Consistent with this, the standard requires the organisation to identify and understand the requirements of stakeholders in as much as they are 'relevant to the quality management system'.

This is an interesting constraint, as it suggests that the QMS need not embrace the total organisation nor all of the interests of all of the stakeholders. This conflicts with the notion of 'Total Quality Management' adopted by many organisations and continues to place 'quality' in a functional box separate from other aspects of organisational performance. This constraint continues with the consideration of the scope of the QMS. Here the standard invites the organisation to determine the limits to the system in the light of the interests of the stakeholders it has identified. There is no objective or operational definition of how these stakeholders and their interests should be defined or selected. The potential exists for an organisation to pursue accreditation to the standard through a very narrowly drawn set of boundaries which may lead to misleading claims.

14.2.3 QMS and processes

The QMS itself can be characterised as based on a straightforward, input driven, output oriented, process description with supporting documentation. It requires determination of inputs and outputs, statement of the process, sequencing, methods, monitoring and control, resource, responsibility and authority allocations, risk and opportunity assessment and evaluation and improvement of process performance. This is all good but is limited by the focus on output rather than outcome. It is entirely possible, and particularly in services, for a process to achieve a compliant output (that is a successful transaction) but leave the customer dissatisfied with the outcome; an inadequate emotional engagement.

14.2.4 Leadership and commitment

The standard then discusses the joint notions of leadership and commitment although it says nothing of how 'leadership' (a behavioural construct) should be exercised. In this respect it rightly calls for key aspects of good administrative management, accountability, alignment, integration into business processes (something the section on process management does NOT include), promotion of the process, risk and opportunity understanding, improvement, resource allocation and engagement of others, communication and, to some extent repeating its own opening requirement on accountability, ensuring that intended results are achieved. In other words, it simply delineates the process accountabilities of management, saying nothing of the skills or behaviours that will be required. Similarly, the section on customer focus adds nothing new, simply asserting the obligation of management to ensure that this exists.

14.2.5   *Policy*

The requirements demand that what it calls 'Top Management' 'establish, implement and maintain' a quality policy that meets the QMS requirements and communicate that policy to others. It requires that responsibility and authority to implement, monitor and control a compliant QMS are assigned, communicated and understood. This is all very reasonable, however, one particular clause gives cause for concern. Clause 5.3b introduces an organisational conflict and confusion which, for me, rests at the heart of many of the challenges of implementing a QMS, saying:

> Top management shall assign the responsibility and authority for . . .
>
> b) ensuring that the processes are delivering their intended outputs

This can be interpreted in at least two ways:

1   The responsibility for processes delivering their intended outputs must be assigned to the person responsible for the process;
2   The responsibility for processes delivering their intended outputs must be assigned to the person responsible for the QMS.

Either interpretation is perfectly reasonable, i.e. there are arguments for either. Many, if not most, organisations, thoughtfully or not, take the second interpretation. Hence, in so many organisations conflict and tension exist between the people making the product or service and the people managing quality. Conflict has been institutionalised, since their typical interests (volume versus quality) are not aligned.

A simple reallocation of responsibility is needed. The process manager must be the recipient of the responsibility and authority outlined in clause 5.3b. The Quality Manager must be responsible for the design, implementation and operation only of the Quality Management System. He or she must make sure the QMS is available, compliant and provides the information the process manager needs. The process manager must take responsibility for using that system to manage and improve the quality of goods and services.

14.2.6   *Planning*

The next requirement is for the organisation to make a plan to address risks, opportunities and quality objectives. This focuses on the avoidance of error and the pursuit of improvement through deliberate action coupled to measurement and evaluation of performance including planning for improvement in the QMS itself. This embeds in the organisation two levels of improvement – improvement in the process generating the product or service and improvement in the QMS process. What it does not explicitly do is loop that back to any higher order or more broadly based organisational learning capability. The improvement thus embedded is limited to doing the same thing better rather than doing better things. The potential gains implied are constrained to incremental improvement of what already is and do nothing to stimulate thinking about what could be. In anything other than the relatively short term, this will limit organisational performance and impart a threat to the sustainability of the organisation, yet sustainable development is explicitly called for in the opening lines of the standard.

14.2.7 *Support*

The standard demands that the QMS be appropriately supported with people, infrastructure, organisational environment and resources for monitoring and measurement (including traceability). In some respects it might be considered to be straying into territory which is beyond its competence and subject to wide interpretation on different national and cultural contexts. It is asking for characteristics of the system to reflect social, psychological and physical norms which have a post-industrial mature economy bias and may (and I stress may) not be achievable or appropriate in some organisations. These requirements represent an ideal state with which any one of us may or may not be in sympathy. It seems to me that they may go beyond the brief of a technical standard, reflecting the personal and political pre-ferences of the authors rather than being objective statements of a requirement.

The standard calls for both organisational knowledge and competent persons. Each must be demonstrated through documentation and the standard demands that it be 'maintained'. This is a challenging area and again more so for service organisations than for manufacturing. In both cases and however well and thoroughly documented the process and the supporting knowledge and skill sets, there will nearly always be a body of tacit or implicit knowledge (know how as opposed to know what or when) which cannot be easily codified in docu-mentation. It may well be recognised, observed and experienced but difficult to capture. It is encouraging that the standard recognises 'experience' as a basis of competence but it is important to organisations pursuing a compliant QMS that they find a cost-effective means of capturing and maintaining records of competence. The risk of a bureaucratic overhead is substantial here, as is that of simplifying or reducing the complexity of human interaction to a skill acquired rather than a behaviour demonstrated.

It is also a requirement that individuals are made aware of the quality policy, objectives and so on and that they understand how they contribute to their achievement. The standard is oriented in discussion of communication around the transmission of messages – what, when, recipients, how, senders – but says nothing of response. Beer (1985) suggested that we know communication has happened when something changes. A protocol entirely built around transmission with no requirement for listening is unlikely to communicate anything.

14.2.8 *Operation*

This section of the standard is concerned with the application of the QMS to the product or service processes themselves, i.e. the planning, quality performance criteria, resourcing, control and documentation of both process compliance and product or service conformance. Here the standard sets out requirements for communication with customers, in this instance looking for what it, incorrectly, calls 'feedback' (it simply means customer comments and complaints). It also suggests that the organisation should ensure it has the capability to deliver what is required and that, surely, is part of the purpose of adopting the standard?

The standard goes on to discuss the development and maintenance of processes and records for both ensuring internal control and engaging effectively with external influential processes such as those of suppliers of goods and services. This extension of the organisation's processes backwards down the supply chain is consistent with Ohno's work and the Toyota Production System.

14.2.9   Performance and review

Section 9 of the standard requires the organisation to evaluate its performance and that of its QMS. This is consistent with the earlier requirement to manage the process and manage the process that manages the process! Again, consistent with the adoption of the PDCA cycle, the organisation is required to evaluate each of the key aspects of its performance in terms of both compliance and customer satisfaction and to plan corrective and improvement actions based on the differences. This evaluation extends to suppliers. No prescriptive guidance is given as to methods of measurement or evaluation.

Section 9.3 is concerned with the review by what the standard calls 'Top Management'. This requirement is essential to ensure that the QMS is doing what it should, is being applied appropriately and is resourced adequately to achieve its aims. It should also ensure that risks are being appropriately identified and mitigated and opportunities for improvement pursued. The outputs of the review need to be documented and actions taken.

14.3   Reflection

Readers should of course study the standard for themselves and make their own interpretation. I cannot help but think that, for all that this version is a step change from its predecessors, the standard remains trapped in a manufacturing rather than service oriented view of the world. In addition, while the emphasis on planning is to be welcomed, it remains somewhat obsessed with documentation. Even if this is captured electronically, it can impose a substantial operating burden on the organisation. If embedded in process oriented computer software it can act as a brake on innovation and change because of the cost and disruption associated with changes to such programmes.

The trick, as ever, is to focus on getting an appropriate balance between freedom and control, to design and implement a system which only controls and documents those things which it must do and no more. There is always a case for just a little more documentation, just a little more control, just one more measurement point or device. Meanwhile the customers are shopping with your competitors who may not have such well documented processes but whose staff enjoy authentic, empathetic exchanges in which the warmth of human engagement outweighs the odd process failure!

Meanwhile the models proposed continue to separate the process of doing from the process of managing (the standard separately contains a process model and the PDCA model). This failure to embed control in the process itself prevents control becoming integral to it contrary to the proposals of Deming, Ishikawa and Shingo. A system designed in such a way will never be able to progress from error detection and correction to error prevention, which should surely be the objective of any QMS.

The other major challenge to the standard continues to arise from its failure to address the true challenges of the service sector. The need to shift from the process focus of a transaction to building empathetic relationships capable of absorbing process variability is not even considered. The assumption underpinning the standard is that the 'human' dimension can be resolved through ensuring 'skills', but this fails to accept that variability in human inter-actions is inevitable, even desirable. If service organisations are going to be sustainably successful it will not be enough that they have good documented processes and competence frameworks for their skills. They will need to build authentic, trusting relationships between staff members both horizontally and vertically before they can also build trusting relation-ships with their customers or clients.

14.4   ISO 14001:2015 and BS OHSAS 18001:2007

ISO 14001:2015 sets out the requirements for Environmental Management Systems while BS OHSAS 18001:2007 sets out the requirements for Occupational Health and Safety Management Systems. It is anticipated that this latter standard, in final consultation at the time of writing, will be replaced by ISO 45001 in October 2016.

An environmental management system (EMS) standard is one designed to assist an organisation to achieve a sustainable balance between environment, society and economy without compromising the ability of future generations to meet their needs.

An occupational health and safety management (OHS) system is designed to assist an organisation to demonstrate appropriate OHS performance by controlling risks in line with policies and objectives, to comply with relevant legislation and develop financial approaches which support sound OHS.

Dick Hortensius (2013), writing on the ISO website, says:

> Although worded differently, all MSSs (Management System Standards) are based on the same fundamental concepts:
>
> * Process management and control: to ensure that processes deliver the intended results and that applicable requirements are complied with;
> * Plan–Do–Check–Act approach to management process and control: establish objectives, define the processes needed, monitor progress and compliance, take action where necessary and consider improvement opportunities;
> * Risk management: identify the risks that provide threats and opportunities and implement controls to minimise negative effects on performance and maximise potential benefits.

The significant difference between these standards and QMS is in their specific technical content rather than in their approach. This suggests that, organisationally, significant benefit could be obtained through the integration of the QMS with the EMS and OHS into an Integrated Management System (IMS). This could be achieved through a number of relatively simple procedural and organisational changes but with one major internal obstacle and one external.

As I suggested in section 14.2.5 the organisational policies which underpin the adoption of these standards are interpretable in two ways:

1   The responsibility for processes delivering their intended outputs must be assigned to the person responsible for the process;
2   The responsibility for processes delivering their intended outputs must be assigned to person responsible for the QMS.

If the organisation is to pursue integration of the standards into an IMS then it must organise itself to think in terms of option 1 whereas most, as already stated, think in terms of option 2.

Option 1 would mean that the line managers responsible for the operating processes that generate goods and services would ALSO have to take responsibility for quality, health, safety and environmental aspects. That is, the scope and scale of their roles would need to expand to take full delegated responsibility and accountability. The manager responsible for the IMS would be charged with ensuring that the IMS itself is fit for purpose and operated in accordance with the requirements of the various standards.

From an organisational overhead and cost perspective, the integration would be expected to lead rapidly to a lower overall cost of system provision. It would also lend itself much more readily to the adoption of a computer as opposed to paper based system, i.e. all the 'documentation' would be electronic. The unit providing the IMS would continue to need people expert in the technical content of the areas integrated, but there would be a significant shift in responsibility.

In the operating processes of the business there would be a similar, perhaps in some cases even more profound, shift, and that would be in the breadth of accountabilities of the process managers. The change would require them to be subject to a performance and review regime which embraced all of the relevant performance dimensions including, at least, productivity or efficiency, quality, safety and environmental parameters. Their decision making would need to be informed not by achievement of a single parameter of performance but by operating the whole within a performance envelope in which they optimise performance across all dimensions. Beckford (2016) proposes a methodology for capturing this complex performance regime.

The corollary to that change, apart from the organisational resource allocation, is a shift in autonomy. It would be essential, to go with the greater responsibility and accountability, to increase the autonomy of the affected individuals, to allow them freedom to decide and to act commensurate with the needs of the task. This contrasts quite sharply with the tendency observed in many organisations (and frequently appearing in the press) where one part of the organisation in pursuit for example of revenue overrules another part in pursuit of quality. Deming (1986) refers to this tendency saying:

> Anyone can boost the dividend at the end of the quarter. Ship everything on hand, regardless of quality: mark it shipped, and show it all as accounts receivable. Defer till next quarter, so far as possible, orders for material and equipment.

With an integrated IMS, the line managers would need to be fully responsible for all aspects of performance. The IMS managers would need to understand that their responsibility is limited to the provision of the system and its operation, not to the achievement (or not) of the objectives of the system. Their job, like any other supplier, would be to ensure that the system meets the needs of the customer.

The external obstacle is the system suppliers, evaluators and auditors and the various regulatory organisations with which the organisation engages. It would be essential for the organisation proposing an IMS to engage all such organisations in the change process (to engage them just as if they were customers) to ensure that, when it comes to verification, regulatory compliance and, in the worst case, defence in litigation, that they would accept the contents and process of the IMS as sufficient and adequate to their needs. Although the IMS should appear as an obvious thing to do, recent observation of regulators and auditors of such systems confirms that while it may be obvious to some, it is not to all!

14.5   The EFQM Excellence Model 2013

While the focus has been on the ISO standards, there are other approaches to the management of quality which, whilst perhaps not carrying the same global authority, have delivered significant value to their adopters.

The Business Excellence Model, updated in 2013, is sponsored by The European Foundation for Quality Management. The EFQM Excellence Model 2013 is intended to provide a framework for addressing the complexity facing organisations in dealing with inter-dependencies, increasing competition, innovation, improvement and meeting the needs of customers and other stakeholders. Argued as 'pragmatic and practical' it is intended to stimulate continuous improvement.

The EFQM Excellence Model 2013 purports to assist users to understand the 'cause and effect' relationships between the things done by the organisation and the results arising. It has three core elements:

- The fundamental concepts of excellence
- The criteria
- The RADAR

These will be discussed in turn.

This model is developed from the belief that contented customers, satisfied staff and positive societal impact can only be achieved through effective leadership. Leadership in turn steers both organisational policy and strategy in relation to organisational processes and human resource actions. Taken together, this integrated approach is considered to drive the organisation towards excellence in business. Whilst the model refers to business, the BEM has been widely adopted in the public sector and can be used in any sort of organisation.

14.5.1   The fundamental concepts of excellence

There are eight fundamental concepts of excellence outlined in the model, and these are considered essential by the EFQM for achieving 'sustainable excellence in any organisation'. They are:

- Adding value for customers
- Creating a sustainable future
- Developing organisational capability
- Harnessing creativity and innovation
- Leading with vision, inspiration and integrity
- Managing with agility
- Succeeding through the talent of people
- Sustaining outstanding results

These are largely both reasonable and self-explanatory, although 'Creating a sustainable future' requires that the organisation be 'advancing the economic, environmental and social conditions'. While this is consistent with the quality imperatives outlined in the first chapter, it is hard to see how some organisations could ever be considered to be environmentally beneficial. The best they could hope for is to minimise damage.

14.5.2   *The criteria*

Using the BEM, the organisation assesses itself against nine performance criteria divided into two sets. These are 'Enablers' – those aspects of the organisation which provide the foundation for excellent performance, and 'Results' – the impact of those enablers on staff, customers, society at large and ultimately on business performance.

- Enablers:
  - Leadership
  - Strategy
  - People
  - Partnerships and resources
  - Processes, products and services

- Results:
  - Customer
  - People
  - Society
  - Business

'Leadership' considers how effectively those who manage the organisation act in relation to the drive for excellence. 'Strategy' examines how those aspects of the organisation are oriented towards the achievement of total quality and how it goes about delivering them. 'People' explicitly recognises that quality is ultimately delivered by people, to people, through people. It is a major factor in achievement of the award and considers how the organisation works to realise the capabilities of its employees in driving improvement.

'Partnership and resources' is focused on the effective use and maintenance of the organisation's physical assets (buildings, finance, information, technology, suppliers and materials). 'Processes, products and services' is concerned with the design, development, production, delivery and service processes which add value to the organisation. The BEM examines how these processes are identified and managed to achieve improvement.

Results criteria focus on Customer, People, Society and Business. This category attempts to compare the organisation's actual achievements with its internal standards, with its competitors' performance and with those organisations considered to be the best in the market. Results are generally presented quantitatively using time-series graphical representation – charts!

People satisfaction attempts to determine the degree of satisfaction of staff in terms of how the employees feel about the organisation in relation to issues such as morale, terms and conditions of employment, management behaviours, development, the work environment and participation in the quality programme. Objective measures include issues such as staff turnover, development activity, absenteeism and numbers involved in suggestion schemes and improvement programmes.

Customer satisfaction considers the response of customers to the goods and services provided. Again the results are split between customer perceptions of performance on delivery, reliability, service levels, complaints, warranty and accessibility of staff, and objective measures based on error and rejection rates, actual delivery performance, numbers of complaints and warranty claims and, significantly, numbers of repeat customers.

The impact on society examines many of the issues which would be considered under ISO 14000, such as environmental impact, impact on quality of life, preservation of resources and internal measures of resource utilisation efficiency. The model looks at external perceptions, that is, how well the organisation represents itself to its community; and objective internal measures such as employment, recycling, waste reduction, pollution and complaints.

Finally, the BEM addresses the 'Business Results' – the success or otherwise of the organisation in meeting the expectations of its financial stakeholders and in meeting business objectives. This section is considering objective aspects of business performance focused on the range of measures traditionally associated with business success. These include statutory accounting information (profit and loss, margins, sales, net worth), cash flows, share prices and ratings, dividends, productivity and returns on investments. Other aspects may include market share, performance of suppliers, error rates, process performance and cycle times.

The EFQM suggests that organisations should:

- Develop KPIs in relevant areas;
- Set targets;
- Break down results to specific areas;
- Sustain results over time;
- Demonstrate understanding of the drivers of results;
- Have confidence in the future based on that understanding;
- Be able to compare themselves with others.

The EFQM Excellence Model award process engages external assessors in evaluating the performance of the company against the award criteria in competition with other organisations also pursuing the programme.

Overall the EFQM is suitable for companies which have already made significant progress towards excellence in all aspects of their operations. It is unattainable to those organisations which have not already been pursuing meaningful quality initiatives for some time. It can be thought that the EFQM is a target to work towards for organisations which have already achieved the ISO standard.

14.5.3   The RADAR

The RADAR is held out within the EFQM as 'a dynamic assessment framework' to provide a structure for understanding the performance of an organisation. It has four elements which, although re-titled, in effect represent the familiar PDCA cycle. These elements are:

- Required results
- Plan and develop approaches
- Deploy approaches
- Assess and refine approaches and deployment

This cycle can be used to assess current capability and to support development of an improvement plan.

14.5.4   Critique

The key limitations of the EFQM are that it relies rather heavily on many self-assessments and perceptions rather than on ongoing objective measures. It has been found by some organisations to be cumbersome and bureaucratic in use (especially in the public sector), and its reliance on self-assessment leaves creative managers free to evaluate their performance (at least initially) at a lower level than is actually being achieved, enabling them to demonstrate improvement at the next evaluation – without changing anything. Whilst this criticism may seem unfair (and is necessarily difficult to prove) it is undoubtedly the case that the strategy is frequently employed.

The second major criticism relates to the lack of real dynamism in the model itself. Considered as a foundation for a management system, the EFQM framework has the potential to represent a network of inter-related enablers and results. It could be used, with appropriately objective performance measurement, to drive a dynamic business model in which the impacts of change on other areas could be usefully assessed before being made, rather than reflected upon after the event.

For an organisation which is mature on its journey towards quality, it may well be that pursuit of EFQM will provide a new focus and energy. For organisations starting in that direction, it will be too demanding organisationally and culturally.

Perhaps the biggest benefit of EFQM, and it has been in use for 25 years with 30,000 or thereabouts organisations using it, is the ability to promote their excellence to others against a set of criteria which are not simply measuring compliance to a standard (as does the ISO award) but genuinely reflect the achievement of excellent results.

Summary

This chapter has introduced and critiqued the ISO 9001:2015, ISO 14001:2015 and BS OHSAS18001:2007 management system standards before considering the substance of the EFQM Excellence Model.

It is important to reflect how these management approaches bring together in coherent frameworks the core element of the quality gurus' work. They thereby validate the utility of those approaches in delivering quality performance gains. This work will now be treated as a platform summary for the introduction of more contemporary approaches to management and, in particular, to service quality.

KEY LEARNING POINTS

Quality management systems

Key definitions:

the ISO 9000 series is the internationally accepted standard for quality management systems

the ISO 14000 series is the internationally accepted standard for environmental management systems

Quality Management System:

a formal record of an organisation's method of managing the quality of its products or services

needs a systematic, ordered approach, leading to third party certification of the system, not the quality

Purpose:

provides a basis for measuring and monitoring quality performance

European Foundation for Quality Management Excellence Model 2013

Framework of performance criteria for the achievement of the European Quality Award

Question

Compare the requirements of EFQM with the work of any of the quality gurus.

15 Organisations as systems

'Life is what happens to us while we are making other plans'

Allen Saunders, 1957

Introduction

Systems thinking emerged in the West after the traditional and human relations models and is fundamentally different to the reductionist thinking on which much of the quality approaches rest. The shift in thinking is 'not a gradual evolution, but a discontinuity' (Singleton, 1974: 10–11), a total change of paradigm and a complete break from traditional, reductionist approaches. Systemic thinking demands stepping back from the individual parts and understanding the organisation, its behaviours and the interaction of its parts as a whole.

Systemic thinking considers the organisation as arising from a complex but bounded network of elements and relationships in interaction with the environment in which it is contained. Thinking about organisations as 'systems' builds upon the early work of Barnard, Selznick and von Bertalanffy and has become significant for management thinkers and practitioners. While the 'language' of systems is now being widely used, understanding and application lag far behind. Thinking systemically has profound implications for individuals and organisations, but is not easy to embrace for those educated in a reductionist approach to the world. Many have adopted the idea of holism, dealing with the whole system of interest, but not yet the notion of emergence, the synergistic effect of interactions.

If we remove the engines from a jet aircraft, neither they nor the aircraft will fly; flight is a systemic product of their interactions, a synergistic outcome. It is a property which belongs only to the complete aircraft and none of its parts. Properties such as this are called 'emergent' – they 'emerge' from the interaction of the various system elements. Whilst observable, they may be both hard (flight) and soft (culture) and, like Taleb's Black Swan events (2010), difficult to define or predict in advance.

To understand the performance of an aircraft we must look at it in its totality, not just at its components, since the whole aircraft has properties (exhibits characteristics) not found in any of the components. Equally, the parts may have properties not found in the whole. The turbine of a jet engine rotates at high speed while the engine as a whole does not. Similarly, where is the voice in a radio, or the picture in a television? These things are observable outputs of interactions within such systems and with their environment (the reception of radio or television signals) but cannot be found by reductionist examination or analysis of them.

Ackoff (1981: 18) offers the most lucid explanation of thinking systemically:

> suppose we bring one of each of these … [types of automobile] … into a large garage and then employ a number of outstanding automotive engineers to determine which one has the best carburettor. When they have done so, we record the result and ask them to do the same for engines. We continue this process until we have covered all the parts required for an automobile. Then we ask the engineers to remove and reassemble these parts. Would we obtain the best possible automobile? Of course not. We would not even obtain an automobile because *the parts would not fit together*, even if they did, *they would not work well together. The performance of a system depends more on how its parts interact than how they act independently of each other.* (sic)

This chapter briefly focuses on the theoretical development of systems thinking starting with contingency theory.

15.1   Contingency theory

Contingency theory initially arose from the body of work concerning leadership and motivation. The principal proponent of this psychology based approach is Fiedler (1967) who suggests that the best leadership style depends on the circumstances of the organisation. He identified two leadership styles, 'relationship-motivated' and 'task–motivated' which were equally valid under different conditions. The first he sees as appropriate when the technical task is relatively easy but relationships are difficult to manage, while the second is appropriate to the opposing circumstances. There is a continuum of variations between these two extreme positions. Overall, Fiedler suggested, unlike earlier writers, that there is no 'one best way' of leading or managing.

During the 1970s contingency theory developed from its roots in leadership and motivation theory to become a common approach to organisation design and management. It reflects some of the developments of systems thinking but is based on observation and practice rather than theory and has been superseded by other developments.

Contingency theory (figure 15.1) sees an organisation as an interacting network of functional elements bound together in pursuit of a common purpose. Each element is essential to the effectiveness of the organisation and contributes to meeting its needs, the balance continuously shifting to reflect changing demands. Stability relies on continued dynamism. Like systems thinking, but unlike the classical and HR theories, contingency

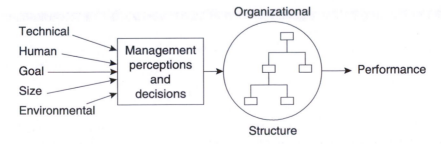

Figure 15.1 The contingency perspective (adapted from Jackson, 1990).

theory recognises that the organisation is set in an environment with which it interacts, both influencing and being influenced.

Burns and Stalker (1961) proposed that 'organic' organisation structures and systems were most relevant to organisations in a dynamic state where conditions and requirements were continually changing. They identified the key variables influencing the structure as being the product market and the manufacturing technology. Joan Woodward (1965) studied the relationship between technology and organisation design. She found that there were sub-stantial variations between the organisational characteristics of different firms with notable differences in the span of control, the number of levels of management and the formality of communication. Woodward identified that a key factor in these differences was not the size of the organisation, as was originally assumed, but the technology employed and the pro-duction method. This led to the suggestion (Pugh & Hickson, 4th Ed., 1989: 16–21) that the 'objectives of a firm ... determine the kind of technology it uses' and this in turn may be seen as driving the organisational structure – that is, the design of the organisation is to some extent 'contingent'. It could be argued today that for information based businesses such as Google, Microsoft and Amazon, the technology 'IS' the organisation.

Jackson (1990) considers that there are five 'strategic contingencies', sub-systems, which affect each other and influence the choice of organisation structure. They are:

- Goals;
- People;
- Technical;
- Managerial;
- Size.

The goal sub-system is concerned with the survival of the organisation in both the long and the short terms, with normative, strategic and operational objectives. These goals need to meet the aspirations of the stakeholders, to match the dynamism of the organisation's environment and to be reflected in the decision making structure. Contemporary mantras such as 'think global, act local' reflect this demand for appropriate autonomy in goal setting.

Goals are determined within and by the organisation, although the normative goals (decisions about the nature of the organisation) are strongly influenced by the socio-economic context in which the organisation exists. All goals must be dynamic and evolutionary, some-times revolutionary, to avoid the danger of complacency. It can be argued that the 'economic crisis' of 2008 was, to some degree, driven by a complacent attitude to espoused goals and their inter-relationship with the business environment – perhaps the definition of a bubble?

Goals are driven by a number of aspects. The expectations of the managers and workforce of the organisation are as significant as the community of shareholders and other stakeholders surrounding the organisation – recalling again the idea of Corporate Social Responsibility. It may be argued that CSR has really arisen amongst those thinking differently about organisational goals and objectives – and they are perhaps thinking systemically.

The people or 'human' sub-system is concerned primarily with the evolving needs of the employees of the organisation. These needs must be met if people are to be content within the organisation, to be attracted to it and to be fulfilled by their work. It is reasonable to suggest that needs will vary with the employment context; the requirements of London based employees may be very different to those in New York, Melbourne or Hong Kong. If it is to be survival worthy the design of the organisation must take account of the needs and capabilities of the staff.

While Jackson emphasises a boundary reflecting differing perspectives for people within the total system to those outside in the 'environment', the boundary is itself arbitrary. Traditionally reflecting legally established relationships, for the most part it will be porous, it will allow transduction to take place.

Reflecting briefly on the work of the gurus and others, the notions of 'supplier development', the 'value chain', the 'internal supplier–customer chain' and 'customer feedback' all imply a very close relationship between the system and its environment, almost to the point that the boundary ceases to exist. Perhaps as Beer (1979: 94–95) suggests, this creates a 'diffusion' of information within the larger system. The relationships may be seen as symbiotic, interaction for mutual benefit. While a distinction may be drawn between suppliers, staff and customers, it may be more appropriate to see staff as both *in* and *of* the system; they work within it and are largely loyal to it. Customers and suppliers are *in* but not *of* it. They work *with* or *buy from* the system but not for it; their primary loyalty lies elsewhere. They do not necessarily directly share in or benefit from the system's objectives.

Increasingly today the boundaries of organisations are blurred and amorphous. Growth in the number of small businesses, often working in partnership with other small businesses, means that many 'virtual' organisations now trade. They do not conform to the norms of traditional organisations, they are organised on collaborative lines and their mechanisms of structure and control are rooted in relationships and contracts rather than in conventional bureaucratic and hierarchical forms.

The technical sub-system refers to the technology employed by the organisation in carrying out its work. As already stated, it was found by Woodward (1965) that organisations employed different forms of organisation according to their size and production technology. She discovered that 'typical' organisational forms had developed within particular industries and that the most successful firms employed these structures. To some extent this may be regarded as a predictable result – the practice now called benchmarking is not new. Although the more formal exchanges which take place today may be more rigorous in their use, there is little doubt that there has always been a fluid movement of ideas between participants in the same industry, particularly when there is high mobility of labour and low job security. Equally, if a particular technology is appropriate to production of a product or product group, it should be no surprise that the organisational form which succeeds with manufacturing and servicing the product for one business will also work for others. Interestingly, breakthroughs in organisational form and in process, utilising new or emergent technology, is often the catalyst for change in a mature industry. The emergence of so called 'low-cost airlines' was enabled by process-change and information technology. Like the supermarkets before them, these budget airlines have used process change to outsource some of their costs to their customers. Today you will perhaps carry your own bags or have no seat allocation, market price differences are exploited (arbitrage) to secure lower landing fees (essentially by using less popular airports and outsourcing the additional travel costs to their passengers). Advances in information technology are exploited to eradicate other costs (e.g. ticketless travel eradicates paperwork and distribution costs of tickets).

The role of the managerial sub-system is to co-ordinate and enable the activities of the others. Current thinking recognises that the management of an organisation can enable it to respond to developments in the environment through the implementation of strategic choices. Thus, rather than being at the mercy of the environment, the organisation can, through its management decisions, actively address it. Since the scope for the organisation to influence the environment is recognised, to some extent the management sub-system as observer can create the environment through its observations and its interventions (Dudley, 2000).

Jackson (op. cit.) suggests that what he calls the deterministic origins of contingency theory are flawed and that the managerial sub-system is an important determinant of organisational success. This criticism pushes the argument away from the 'mechanistic' view of Woodward – 'technology determines structure' – towards a more organic, interactive view.

The importance of size as a factor in organisational structure was recognised by Pugh and the Aston group in studies (Pugh & Hickson, 1976; Pugh & Hinings, 1976) which considered larger organisations than those studied by Woodward. Their work showed that increasing size reinforces the need for delegation and decentralisation of decision making, while simultaneously increasing the need for structured, formal activities. This can be linked to Fayol's call for an appropriate balance between centralisation and decentralisation and is reflected in Beckford's (2016) take on managing autonomy.

While not specified by Jackson, the environment is important to the effectiveness of any organisation. Differing environmental demands and constraints require different organisational formats to be employed. Overall there appears to be a correlation between the level of environmental complexity and turbulence and the adaptability or flexibility of an organisation. To ensure the survival of the organisation, it must be capable of responding at an appropriate rate to changes in its environment and, perhaps through marketing and other activities, of influencing the environment in favour of itself.

15.2   Is quality contingent?

This question has two distinct dimensions. The first is concerned with quality as an output measure of the organisation's performance. The second is concerned with defining quality itself.

Dealing with the first dimension, the answer must be yes. The quality of any product or service is a function of the interaction of all of the elements of the system itself and its environment. If any of the inputs, procedures or processes of the organisation are flawed, if the demands or influences of the environment are not appropriately responded to, or if the expectations of the customers in the environment are not understood, then the product or service may fail to meet expectations. Therefore, achievement of quality is contingent upon the effectiveness of every part of the system. This perception demands a holistic approach to creating and managing the organisation to achieve quality.

Dealing with the second dimension is much harder, since this is concerned with the definition of 'quality' itself. The gurus reviewed in part two of this book each offered definitions of quality resting on well defined, measurable characteristics of a product or service. These are expressed in the form of 'the one best way'. They state that *this is quality* (the definitions) and *this is how it is achieved* (the different methodologies). It is clear that there are substantial differences between them, for example Deming's statistically based approach compared with Ishikawa's participative approach and the internal evangelical focus of Crosby's work compared with the societal concerns expressed by Taguchi.

Are they ALL right, or are NONE of them right? *What is quality?* For Crosby it is 'conformance to requirements', for Deming and Shingo it is eradication of error, for Feigenbaum 'best for customer use and selling price', for Ishikawa it is the product, service, management, the company and the people – very near to the contingency view of organisation. Juran sees quality as a function of planning, while Taguchi focuses on the cost imparted to society.

It is suggested that, in the contemporary dynamic and turbulent organisational environment, quality cannot be adequately defined in these absolute terms as something fixed and always traditionally quantifiable. Perhaps as Hume (1777, Of Tragedy, *Essays*) suggests, quality is like beauty, 'Beauty [quality] in things exists in the mind which contemplates them'. Perhaps customers experience rather than receive quality of service or product. As each customer has different expectations, they continually redefine quality in terms of their past experience and their changing expectations. This means of course that the pursuit of quality, like the hunt for the Loch Ness monster, the American Bigfoot or the Yeti, is doomed to failure because, like the monster, quality is mysterious and ethereal rather than substantial and absolute. Quality then IS contingent, but upon the customer, NOT the organisation, its products or services.

This perspective on quality poses a problem for organisations pursuing quality programmes. If quality is not an absolute, then what are they aiming for and how do they know when they have achieved it? The answer seems to be that the quality target is continually shifting and that organisations must pursue 'rightness' or 'appropriateness' in their products or services. Products and services must fulfil the varying purposes for which they are purchased. They, and the processes and procedures by which they are produced, must be error free – within the limits of expectations already created in the customer's mind. Those processes and procedures must minimise cost (land, labour, capital and entrepreneurship – the four factors of production), and crucially every aspect and activity of the organisation and its management must be focused on doing the right job right.

The key to success in such a scenario rests on communication both within the organisation and between the organisation and its environment. If internal communication is defective, then staff may do the right job wrong, or the wrong job right. Communication with the environment rests in understanding the expectations of customers (communication into the organisation) and creating or modifying the expectations of customers (communication out to the market). If this communication is not effective then there will be flawed understanding on either (or both) sides and hence there will not be quality – because however technically good the product or service may be, the expectations of one party of the other will not be met.

15.3   Systems thinking

Parsons and Smelser (1956) attempted to 'elaborate four functional imperatives to be fulfilled for a system, by its sub-systems, if that system is to continue to exist' (Box 15.1). The imperatives they identified are adaptation, goal-attainment, integration and latency (pattern maintenance) and make up the AGIL mnemonic.

Jackson (1990) interprets this somewhat differently, seeing four primary sub-systems of an organisation as essential prerequisites – goal, human, technical and managerial. These reflect his contingency theory perspective. He considers that effectiveness and efficiency are attained through the interaction of the sub-systems in pursuit of the purpose of the system in its environment.

The goal sub-system is concerned with the purpose of the system and the means of achieving that purpose; the human sub-system deals with the people and their management and motivation; the technical sub-system handles the operations (that is, input – transformation – output); and the managerial sub-system co-ordinates and manages each of the others, balancing the relationships and attending to the environmental interaction.

The systems model adds value to thinking about management by demanding explicit recognition of the environment and of internal organisational interactions. The generic

Box 15.1   Functional imperatives of a system

Parsons & Smelser:

Imperative 1) A =   Adaptation; the system has to establish relationships between itself and its external environment.

Imperative 2) G =   Goal-attainment; goals have to be defined and resources mobilised and managed in pursuit of those goals.

Imperative 3) I =   Integration; the system has to have a means of co-ordinating its efforts.

Imperative 4) L =   Latency (or pattern maintenance); the first three requisites for organisational survival have to be solved with the minimum of strain and tension by ensuring that organisational 'actors' are motivated to act in the appropriate manner.

system model is of great utility as a descriptive tool enabling the elaboration of the system elements and interactions. However, while this enables diagnosis of faults and failures in connectivity, it does not offer a prescriptive model for improvement or change based on an organisational ideal. The basic systems interpretation perhaps underplays the essential, purposeful role of individuals within organisations and the extent to which human inter-actions affect outputs.

The systems model takes account of the environment and focuses on the generality of survival rather than specific organisational objectives. It does not attempt to quantify the success of an organisation, and says little about mechanisms of adaption. The potential for relative autonomy is not explored and little advice is offered in terms of specific, general remedies for ineffective organisations.

The emphasis in this view is on harmonious internal interaction, whereas conflict and coercion are often present amongst the human actors. Change is perceived as being environmentally driven, rather than initiated by the organisation.

15.4   Systems thinking and quality

The shift from classical management theory to the human relations school represented a change of emphasis within the reductionist paradigm; from a focus on the needs of the

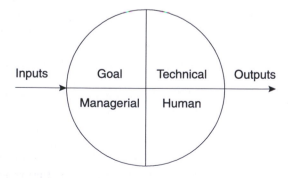

Figure 15.2 The organisation as a system.

organisation to that of the individuals and groups within it. This shift in thinking has not been strongly reflected in the quality literature, although the quality gurus do generally recognise in their work the importance of the commitment of all staff to quality initiatives and some acknowledge the importance of dealing with the totality of the organisation. The shift from reductionist to systemic thinking about quality is much more fundamental, involving the acceptance of a new paradigm, a re-framing of the entire way in which we think about the world. The impact on thinking about quality is substantial.

When thinking systemically about quality, the focus on improving the performance of individual parts of an organisation shifts to their total interacting performance. This means examining not just the performance of functional units such as production, sales, finance, personnel (as would be the case in a reductionist approach) but, crucially, how the performance of those parts is enabled or inhibited by other parts, that is, how they interact to produce goods or services and the impact of change in one part on each of the others.

Traditionally quality initiatives have focused on the technical performance of production systems, whether for products or services. They examine in detail the characteristics of machines (Shingo), they study the accuracy and reliability of the human and technical inputs to the production system (Deming's special causes of error) and they sometimes look at the internal supplier-customer relationships. Few quality programmes go beyond these technical aspects in any substantial manner; indeed it can be difficult in organisations to get those 'in charge' to recognise that the source of improvement may be themselves.

Systemically the examination needs to step back and consider how each of the parts of the organisation interact with every other. So for example, financial objectives, recruitment and training policies and inbound logistics all impact on production capability and the ability to meet quality targets. Similarly, the sales function and the commitments given to customers by sales personnel are strong determinants of the level of after-sales service, which must be provided to meet customer expectations, and of the cost of providing it. These sales commitments also interact with the production elements of the organisation, creating demands which need to be met. Overlaying all of these aspects are the internal politics of the organisation, that is the ways in which people interact, the coherence or otherwise of their behaviour, the degree of mutuality in their objectives given that individuals tend to compete for preferment within the organisation – and sometimes at its expense.

Complicating the situation further is the issue of measurement (and the associated rewards and punishments). It has already been suggested that in general 'we get what we measure' and for many organisations, and the individuals within them, the measurements are narrow, simple and taken in isolation at a single level. Such systems tend to lead to a focus on one aspect of performance at the expense of others. So for example, if the measurement system (or the Boss) emphasises production efficiency, that is what the management will aim for. Systemically, production efficiency cannot be measured in isolation but must be related to the demands of the marketplace, the availability of inputs to the system (land, labour, raw materials) and to the capacity of the organisation to provide financial support. We cannot simply measure one dimension of the organisation, but must measure many simultaneously, and produce an integrated understanding of the performance of the whole. We must measure organisational effectiveness, not just quality, productivity or efficiency.

Systemically, quality is not something which can be achieved through enhancing independent functional units, however effective they may become individually. Equally, quality cannot be measured in purely technical terms by some physical characteristics of the product or service such as size, shape, colour or conformance to requirements. Systemically, quality must be recognised as a property of the total organisation and measured both quantitatively and qualitatively. Note this is not 'either/or'; it is 'and'.

Quality must be inherent in each process and each interaction within the system and must persist in the organisation's dealings with its environment. The products or services of a company may be admired for their apparent quality. However, if the process by which they are made is unnecessarily environmentally damaging or the management system abuses the employees within the organisation, then it cannot be considered a quality organisation – except by that single output measure of operational performance. In the event that the processes are environmentally damaging or abusive of people, then quality is achieved at some other cost which may not be acceptable at a societal level. The growth in the measurement of environmental impact and the demands for demonstrably greater commitment to Corporate Social Responsibility reflect the increasing importance of these aspects – and they are not 'instead of' other measurements but additional to them. The complexity this generates demands a whole new approach to measurement and reporting.

Summary

This chapter has briefly introduced the concept of the contingency and systems views of the world. The emergence and background of contingency theory was explored and its roots in the empirical study of organisations explained. The implications of systems thinking for quality have been addressed. In subsequent chapters the development of organisationally systemic thinking will be explored.

KEY LEARNING POINTS

Contingency theory

Definition:
organisational effectiveness is the product of the adequacy of managerial response to five key effectors on the organisation: technology, human, goal, size and environment.

Key belief:
there is not one best way of structuring an organisation

Contingency and quality:
quality is contingent upon the expectations of the customer, not on the products or services offered

Organisations as systems

Key definition:
the study of organisations and their interactions as wholes, not as an assembly of individual parts.

Key beliefs:
the 'system' exhibits behaviour which is not exhibited by any of the parts and has 'emergent' properties which belong to none of those parts individually.

Implications for quality:
shift of focus from just the individual parts to embrace the interactions between those parts, recognition of the internal customer chain as creating the organisation, quality must be recognised as an emergent property of the system rather than just a technical measure of output.

Question

What do you think might be the 'emergent' properties of a University? Why?

16 Systems methodologies

'The truths of cybernetics are not conditional on their being derived from some other branch of science'

Ashby, 1956: 1

Introduction

This chapter will briefly consider three different ways of applying systems thinking to organisations, each informed by a different philosophical underpinning. The aim is to be illustrative rather than definitive and to convey an overall understanding rather than a deep knowledge of each of the approaches.

Organisational cybernetics

Through Norbert Weiner, cybernetics emerged as a branch of management science during the 1940s working primarily on machine systems now developed extensively by others as robotics. Weiner's group was inter-disciplinary, bringing together mathematicians, biologists, operational researchers and physicists in a ground breaking approach to developing a unified science for solving complex problems.

From the 1950s, Stafford Beer, who died in 2002, led the application of cybernetic principles to the study of organisations developing what we now call 'management' or 'organisational' cybernetics. Development continues, not least in my own work on *The Intelligent Organisation* (Beckford, 2016). Beer defined cybernetics as the 'science of effective organisation' – something essential to quality.

Organisational cybernetics conceives any organisation as a social system composed of people, processes and information existing as the product of their interactions. Early work, from which the cybernetic principles were developed, addressed such diverse fields as automation, computing and radar and built upon earlier discoveries such as Watt's steam engine governor, which are used to illustrate what Jackson (1991) has called 'management cybernetics'.

Organisational cybernetics builds upon and draws ideas from that fundamental work, but 'breaks somewhat with the mechanistic and organismic thinking that typifies management cybernetics' (Jackson, 1991: 103). The distinction is drawn by Jackson on the basis of two differences between the work of Stafford Beer and that of others in this field. First, in *The Heart of Enterprise* Beer (1979) builds a model of 'any organisation' from first principles of cybernetics. Second, he pays significant attention to the role of the observer whose presence influences the situation observed. Accepting the intellectual insights of Beer, we can use the principles of cybernetics without relying on analogies between the organisation observed and other natural phenomena. The existence and behaviour of any organisation is, to some degree, a function of the perceptions of the observer.

Cybernetics helps the manager (any person legitimately attempting to command and control an organisation) to understand:

- how an organisation works (or doesn't work);
- why it works that way;
- what to do to improve it.

This is because 'Cybernetics ... treats, not things but *ways of behaving*' (Ashby, 1956).

16.1   Cybernetic systems

This section deals with the major characteristics of systems susceptible to cybernetic diagnosis and improvement. In taking account of the observer they reflect the essentially cybernetic operation of those natural systems which have been studied. The principles of cybernetics can be observed operating in nature (viz.: Gell-Mann, Gleick, Lovelock, Hawking, Penrose) and are concerned with 'general laws that govern control processes, whatever the nature of the system under governance' (Jackson, 1991: 92) and that includes quality systems. Beer (1959) considers that, in order to be a worthwhile subject for the application of the cybernetic approach, the organisation will be likely to demonstrate three characteristics (Box 16.1).

Beer (1959: 12) designates as 'exceedingly complex' any organisation which is so complicated that it cannot be described in a precise and detailed fashion. To explain this point, the wiring loom of a car is, in Beer's terms, 'complex but describable'; its design and connectivity can be completely documented. An exceedingly complex organisation would perhaps be an interaction between two people in a meeting. This transaction, while apparently simple to observe and record, would not be describable. The varied interpretation of words, inflections of speech, degree of eye contact and bodily postures adopted, all form a part of the interaction. The recognition of this complexity helps us to understand why managing service quality, which is about human interaction, is so different from managing product quality.

Self-regulation describes the ability of an organisation to 'manage' itself towards its purposes or goals while responding to environmental disturbance. The temperature control system in the bodies of people and animals is autonomous; it needs no active direction or management from the brain although the brain is where the '*rules*' of temperature control are generated.

Box 16.1   Characteristics of cybernetic systems

Stafford Beer:

Characteristic 1)   extreme complexity;
Characteristic 2)   a degree of self-regulation;
Characteristic 3)   probabilistic behaviour.

Box 16.2   Tools of cybernetics

Tool 1)   the *black box* technique – to address extreme complexity;
Tool 2)   *feedback* – to manage self-regulation;
Tool 3)   *variety engineering* – to handle probabilism.

Probabilism exists where there is some randomness in organisational behaviour. Returning to the example of the car wiring loom – it is not only 'complex but describable', it is also 'deterministic'. In the absence of a fault, its behaviour is known in advance; any given input will generate a precisely predictable outcome while the outcome of the meeting between two people would be 'probabilistic'. This is because, while the agenda for discussion may be known in advance and a 'most likely' outcome predicted, the variables in the meeting, such as mood, posture and experience of the parties separately and together, make the outcome uncertain.

16.2   Tools of cybernetics

There are three principal cybernetic tools for dealing with these exceedingly complex, self-regulating, probabilistic organisations (Box 16.2).

Complexity is dealt with by the black box technique. Schoderbek et al (1990: 94) consider that complexity is a product of the interaction of four main aspects – the number of elements, their interactions, their attributes and their degree of organisation.

The interaction of those four 'determinants', because they are factorial not linear, can generate what would be an exceedingly complex organisation. That does not lend itself to the reductionist analyses of the classical or human relations view; those approaches break down the organisation, and the emergent properties disappear.

Studying the organisation while interfering minimally with its internal operation leads to the black box technique. This is a way of gaining knowledge about the operations of an organisation without the need to reduce it to its component parts. The black box technique involves manipulating the inputs to an organisation, observing the effect on its outputs to establish patterns or regularities in its behaviour. As knowledge or understanding of the organisation's behaviour is acquired, the manipulations can become more structured. The black box technique is shown in Figure 16.1.

Everyday black boxes

All of us are familiar with and deal with complex black box organisations in our daily lives without ever needing to know or understand how they work. Indeed, the black box technique will never reveal how the transformation process works or how efficient it is.

Finally, parents learn to manage their children (and children their parents) long before they have a common spoken language with which to communicate and explain their actions. Nobody would propose a reductionist analysis of a baby to 'find out how it works' in order to control it – it is simply managed as a black box.

Managers in organisations unconsciously adopt the black box technique because it is not possible to grasp the full complexity of their organisations. They work by manipulating inputs to the organisation, recording outputs and deducing patterns of response. These patterns inform future actions. Measurement of the effect on output of changes in input is critical. Unfortunately most managers and the performance management systems on which they rely are not integrated so deny the black box its effectiveness. Some readers will recognise this reflective cycle as being similar in principle to the Deming or Shewhart Cycle but adding to that a richness in the content.

Feedback is the process which makes self-regulation possible and describes 'circular causal processes' (Clemson, 1984: 22). An exceedingly complex probabilistic organisation to some extent regulates itself and how this occurs must be understood to enhance predictability of the outcomes of managerial actions. Self-regulation generates a degree of stability which can be disturbed through interventions undertaken in the organisation or the environment. If the 'circular causal chains' have not been adequately understood then the intervention may produce unmanageable instability.

The simplest feedback occurs when two elements continuously interact with each other such that the output of one determines the next action of the other. There are two types of this 'first order' feedback behaviour. In the first, negative feedback or goal seeking, the organisation will resist disturbances that take it away from its goal; the reaction of each element is to inhibit the change in the other. A common example of first order feedback behaviour is the thermostatic control of a heating or air conditioning system.

The opposite of negative feedback is positive feedback in which deviation by one element is increased by the other. These systems whilst potentially highly unstable are also useful. A good example of this is the level of interest acting on a bank account. Positive feedback results in the interest compounding – in effect, running away out of control.

A second order feedback system is capable of choosing between a variety of responses to environmental changes in order to achieve its goal, for example the 'climate control system'

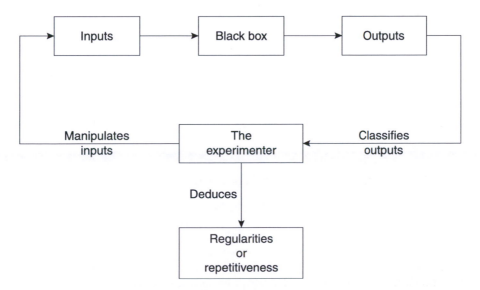

Figure 16.1 The black box technique.

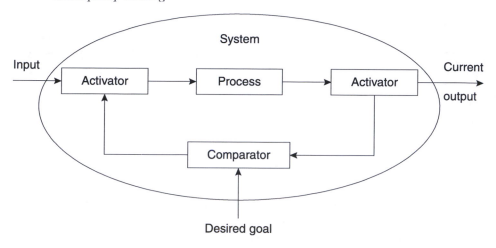

Figure 16.2 A closed–loop first order feedback system.

in a car can choose between activating the heater or the air–conditioner in order to achieve its goal of a particular temperature. A third order system is even more sophisticated. It is capable of changing the goal state itself in response to feedback processes, determining the goal internally as opposed to externally, as in the first and second order systems. Figure 16.2 shows an example of a closed-loop feedback system.

In organisations the feedback systems are highly complex, containing large numbers of elements connected in a number of ways and consisting of both positive and negative loops. At any time the 'sum' of the loops may operate in a positive or negative manner and in human systems (such as organisations) they need not be physical.

Clemson draws from this that:

> there is nothing structural or in the 'essence' of the system, about whether the loop is positive or negative.

Ultimately, systems that include feedback loops are capable of demonstrating exceedingly complex behaviour, and large changes in that behaviour may be brought about by small changes in the direction or extent of internal relationships. Chaos and complexity theories both rely on this notion of feedback.

There are several key criteria for the design of effective feedback mechanisms (Box 16.3).

Box 16.3   Design criteria for feedback systems

Criterion 1)	All the elements of the system must be working properly, and the communication channels between them must be adequate.
Criterion 2)	In an organisation, responsibility for action (which carries with it accountability) must be clearly allocated.
Criterion 3)	Controls must be selective.
Criterion 4)	The control must highlight the necessary action.

Variety is the measure of complexity in an organisation; the number of possible states it can exhibit. Probabilistic behaviour exists when the behaviour of some of the elements of the organisation is considered to be at least partly random. A principal argument of cybernetics is that the mechanisms that are used to manage this complexity must answer to Ashby's 'Law of Requisite Variety' which states that 'only variety can destroy variety'. This means that, in order to effectively manage a situation, the management must generate as much variety as the operation(s) it seeks to control.

Variety engineering consists of the two prime methods of achieving this control, either reducing the variety of the organisation to be controlled (variety reduction) or, increasing the variety of the management (variety amplification). Variety is a property of the system so it can neither be absolutely reduced nor absolutely increased, only managed (Box 16.4). This must be undertaken appropriately to the particular organisation and should contribute to the achievement of its goals. There are a number of management techniques which may be seen as the tools of variety engineering if used thoughtfully, and with full awareness of their possible consequences, rather than randomly, or politically, as often seems to happen in organisations. Actions or processes that work to reduce the variety faced by managers are known as filters or attenuators, whilst those which act to increase the variety of the manager are amplifiers.

Recursion is the final topic for this section. In this context recursion refers to the 'organisational and interactional invariance'. Beer (1981: 72) argues that each level of an organisation contains all the levels below it, and is contained in all the levels above it such that it exists in a chain of embedded systems (Figure 16.3). The principle structural elements necessary for decision, information flows and interactions within the organisation are perceived as identical at every level. This invariance offers great ease of understanding of the structure at every level and enables the determination of the relevant autonomy of the system studied. Each level of organisation manages surplus variety from its contained levels and enjoys a degree of freedom in managing variety at its own level constrained by its membership of the next higher level.

16.3   Cybernetics and quality

While the 'systems' and 'contingency' approaches to management progress well beyond the clear limitations of the 'classical' and 'human relations' schools of thought, they are primarily

---

Box 16.4   Variety reduction and amplification techniques
Variety Management

Reduction:

Structural:	delegation (autonomy or decentralisation), functionalisation or divisionalisation;
Planning:	establishing objectives and priorities;
Operational:	budgeting, management by exception;
Rules/policies:	instructions and 'norms' of behaviour.

Amplification:

Structural:	team work and groups;
Augmentation:	recruit/train experts, employ independent experts;
Information:	management or executive information systems (which may also act as attenuators).

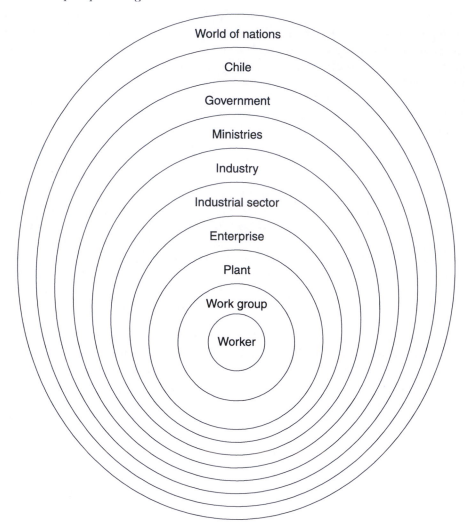

Figure 16.3 Recursions of a system.

descriptive. The ability to describe a situation or problem does little to improve or solve it. The cybernetic model can be simply descriptive, but Beer's work adds to this the capability to diagnose organisational faults and provide a prescription of changes to enhance performance. The cybernetic approach then, through Beer's Viable System Model, can be used to provide a description, diagnosis and prescription for any organisation.

The adoption of cybernetic principles generates several challenges to the established ways of thinking about organisations and achieving quality. First, the cybernetic model of organisation relies on appropriate distribution of information, that is that information is held at the lowest level in the organisation where it is relevant. The design of the information system ensures this and provides the opportunity for local decision making – metaphorically the equivalent of reflex reactions in the human body. Information received locally may be reacted to locally, provided that reaction is consistent with the needs of the whole organisation. Every feedback loop contains a comparator which implies the capacity for making decisions.

The organisation provides as much autonomy as is consistent with organisational cohesion. Therefore, the local operation may not undertake activities or engage in reactions which are different from its agreed role or which challenge or threaten the organisation, but does have the freedom to react to those matters which are only of concern to itself.

This raises the second issue. If information is distributed, then power is distributed. It is common in organisations for power (authority to make decisions) to be relatively highly centralised. Beer, using the expression 'dysfunctional overcentrality', contends that in many organisations decisions are taken at higher levels than is necessary or desirable for their effective functioning. He suggests that this is highly inefficient and wasteful of resources and reduces the adaptability and flexibility of the organisation, inhibiting the ability to react to threats and opportunities. In some cases the result of this is organisational demise, since failure to respond appropriately and rapidly to a threat may lead to liquidation, receivership, bankruptcy.

A third issue directly challenges a key assumption which underpins much of early management thinking concerning the abilities of workers. Taylor (1911) provided a prime example of this thinking when he suggested that 'no man suited to the task of handling pig iron is capable of understanding the science that applies to it'. This negative view of the capabilities of workers suggests, of course, the opposite view of management – omniscient, 'god-like' creatures of a higher order of intelligence than workers. Whether this view had validity in Taylor's time may be considered open to debate. Its relevance to the contemporary world is highly questionable. The generally higher levels of education now in evidence, coupled with the technology driven move towards 'knowledge industries', have created a situation where Taylor's view is clearly unacceptable.

This generates a significant difficulty. The adoption of cybernetic principles in organisation design demands that those who currently hold power in organisations must release it. Thus the solution to many problems rests in the hands of those least likely to use it. This is a major criticism of cybernetic thinking. In a highly political or coercive situation the solutions which cybernetics proposes would not be applied. The approach is also criticised for being open to abuse by those with autocratic intentions. It is certainly the case that the concepts and principles underpinning cybernetics may be used in this way. Such applications, though, would be to corrupt the intent of the work of cyberneticians and in the medium to long term would be likely to fail. They would in any event be highly inefficient, demanding a high level of inspection or 'policing' to maintain themselves.

Comparing the cybernetic approach with the various approaches to quality, a number of parallels are revealed – most clearly and transparently with Ohno's (1988) Toyota Production System. Ohno's use of information and feedback to control production and prevent error directly reflects the necessary cybernetics.

The cybernetic demand for distributed information, coupled to devolution of decision making, reflects the demand in the quality literature for participation and improvement centred on the particular process or workshop. The idea of 'knowledge workers' supports the concept of Quality Circles – the assumption that the workforce do have the capacity to bring about sustainable, substantial and constructive improvement in quality performance. Cybernetics demands that power be distributed throughout the organisation and utilised by those who have the information to make a decision, rather than those whose position in the hierarchy grants them power. This in turn reflects the quality call for management commitment. A management which is serious about the pursuit of quality will facilitate and encourage this distribution of power, recognising that it is both necessary and desirable. If their managerial actions and behaviour do not support their open calls for improvement, then the psychological feedback loops inherent in any organisation will act to inhibit quality performance improvement.

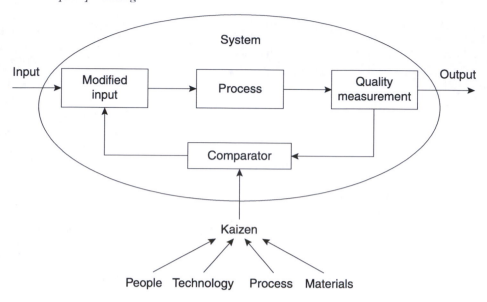

Figure 16.4 A closed-loop quality feedback system.

The achievement of quality itself may also be seen as a cybernetic function. Any production process (whether for goods or services) will include a feedback system of the type shown in Figure 16.2. This was a model of any feedback system. In Figure 16.4 the same model is used but this time modified to be explicitly about quality improvement. In this more specific model it can be seen that the input to a process is modified to reflect some desired quality improvement. The output of the process is measured in some way and the results fed back to a comparator. This compares the actual output with the desired output. The desired output is itself being continually modified by the kaizen process. Results are used to further modify the input to bring the actual output closer to that which is desired. The kaizen process itself consists of a further and similar set of feedback systems dealing with people, technology, processes, materials and so on. Each time a quality improvement is made in one of those aspects, there is a consequent change in the desired output.

The cybernetic view considers organisations as made up of closely interacting feedback systems. The action of each system is continually modified by the actions, changes and outputs of each of the others. This conception of organisation serves to bring the organisation 'alive' – it can be imagined as constantly active – engaged in a continual process of self-maintenance and self-improvement, steering itself towards a better future rather than as the static, management driven and controlled machine of earlier views.

16.4   Soft systems thinking

Every venture has a fundamental reliance on human input for control and development, no matter to what extent it is automated and its products or services are believed guaranteed by the excellence of its technical artefacts. If there is an aim to create a quality organisation, then it is vital that the people, whether they are relatively unskilled workers or highly qualified experts in a consultancy or research organisation, are committed to that aim. This cannot be

achieved if they are excluded from the development and decision processes of the organisation or its quality programme. They may tolerate the programme or accept it at a
superficial level, but they will not take ownership of it, regard it as their own and drive it
forward. A programme for quality which is not actively supported at every level in the
organisation will fail.

16.5   Soft systems explained

Organisational cybernetics is often considered by those not fully familiar with its breadth and
depth as applicable to 'hard' problems – those where the end – the objective – is known and
any debate is about means. Soft systems thinking, largely represented in the work of Peter
Checkland (1981), proposes the study of human activity systems, those 'soft ill-structured
problems of the real world'. Checkland suggests that in 'soft' problems, identifying the 'end'
is the challenge. His work focuses on defining a systemic methodology to help participants
understand social systems.

The study of 'soft systems' is ends orientated. It is concerned with discovering the purpose
of the system, as defined by the stakeholders. It presumes that the problem of what to do must
be solved before the problem of how to do it can be addressed.

Considering hard systems thinking, Checkland (1978) suggests that the problem to be
tackled 'is to select an efficient means of achieving a known and defined end', a criticism
often levelled at the cybernetic understanding already discussed. Soft systems thinking
supposes multiple perceptions of reality. This simply means that reality is not assumed to be
the same for every observer. The existence and purpose of the organisation are considered to
be functions of the observer rather than objective statements of fact. Contrasting with the
hard approach, the desired end needs to be defined because only limited agreement about it
is believed to exist.

A rainbow appears as a result of the action of light through water droplets suspended in air,
but it can only be observed from the outside and from specific angles. When approached, it
disappears; it is a mirage. While we cannot grasp or physically handle a rainbow, we can
describe it and understand how it is structured even though from a different perspective,
literally a different angle in this case, the rainbow simply isn't there! Consider an entity such
as the City of Kowloon in Hong Kong. There is only one Kowloon and all parties can agree
about its objective existence. However, consideration of Kowloon from vantage points on
the eight hills surrounding it would generate different descriptions of that objective existence. Each of the descriptions would be 'right' for the particular observer and viewpoint, but
each would describe a different reality.

Similarly, each observer's perception is informed by past experiences, personal desires and
expectations; each observation is unique. This means that even if the same organisation is
studied from precisely the same physical viewpoint by a variety of people, differing aspects of
the organisation will be highlighted. Examining Kowloon through a fixed set of binoculars
from a hilltop will reveal different sights to different people – an architect may see the
buildings, a town planner the roads, an anthropologist the people and an entrepreneur the
profit opportunities.

Accepting this very different, 'interpretive' (Burrell & Morgan, 1979) perspective on
organisations demands a completely different approach to problem solving and organisational management. The nature and existence of an organisation and its purposes can no
longer be taken as facts within an established framework; they must be negotiated through a
discussion between those observing it. The first step in any problem solving or improvement

process then becomes developing consensus about the existence and nature of the organisation and the problems or issues to be addressed.

The adjective 'soft' does not refer to a characteristic of the system itself, but is a function of the perspective on the system of those who set themselves up as its problem solvers. It reflects their particular social philosophy of how organisational problems should be solved and makes some challengable assumptions about the nature and distribution of power. Soft systems thinkers propose that the dominant element in a problem solving situation is generating agreement amongst the participants, with this agreement itself leading to improvement in the situation. The generation of agreement will highlight aspects of the organisation which do not meet the terms of that agreement and must therefore be modified to fit.

16.6   Tools for soft systems

At a fundamental level, the tools of soft systems may be seen to be cybernetic in their nature. Effective communication between members of a group may be interpreted as operating through positive and negative feedback loops, using comparators of achievement against expectations and adaptation or modification of attitudes in order to work towards defining goals. The processes by which this takes place, though, make more explicit use of interpersonal action and debate.

For example, in Strategic Assumption Surfacing and Testing (Mason & Mitroff, 1981) there are four phases (Box 16.5).

Each of these phases relies heavily on open, effective communication (speaking AND listening) between the participants. Phase one is concerned with structuring groups on the basis of some common ground. Phase two involves the individual groups developing an agreed perspective on the problem. Phase three is based on advocacy with each group presenting its approach and explaining the assumptions which underpin it. Dialectical debate, that is debate based on logical argument, oriented around the underpinning assumptions of the respective arguments follows between the groups. At phase four, the attempt is made to converge the two different views into a consensus view shared by all the participants. Reiteration of the process with additional information is encouraged where consensus cannot be achieved. It can be seen that this process relies on a number of key characteristics:

- Agreement by the participants to open debate;
- A common language – both syntactic and semantic;
- Freedom of expression;
- Advocacy skills;

Box 16.5   Four phases of SAST

Mason & Mitroff:
Phase 1)   Group formation;
Phase 2)   Assumption surfacing;
Phase 3)   Dialectical debate;
Phase 4)   Synthesis.

- The capacity of the individuals to express themselves, hence freedom from fear;
- Sufficient commonality of opinion at the outset for agreement to be a feasible potential outcome.

Checkland's (1981) 'Soft Systems Methodology' offers an approach which enables the engagement of small groups of stakeholders in developing understanding and agreement about outcomes desired.

The tools then are the tools of human communication, perhaps best understood and expressed through the discipline of psychology. Whilst admirable in theory, some of the characteristics of debate outlined above can be difficult to achieve in practice.

16.7   Soft systems and quality

The traditional approaches to quality predominantly focus on its technical aspects, paying relatively little attention to the human side. They are 'hard' approaches which assume that the pursuit of quality necessarily leads to improvement. However, this examines quality only from the perspective of the owners or managers of the organisation. If quality means less cost and higher profits, then in a profit oriented world, quality is good for managers and owners. The assumption which underpins those approaches is that 'economic man' will fall in line with the corporate expectations.

However, as has been discussed by numerous writers, the theory of man as purely economically motivated does not necessarily stand up to practical examination. People work for many different reasons and while for some, money is a strong, extrinsic motivator, others derive the greater part of their value from the intrinsic value of the work itself. From yet another perspective it is argued that people work simply because man is a social animal and needs both company and work for social and psychological reasons.

If the motivation underpinning an organisation's drive for quality is simply economic (as it so often is), then the probable outcomes include reduced numbers in the workforce (assuming a stable output) and changes to working practices and the established social mores of the organisation. If management does not appreciate the differing perspectives of the other members of the organisation and accommodate them within their mental models of what is to be achieved, then they will meet varying degrees of resistance to those changes. This resistance will arise from the different interpretations which the individuals put on the organisation and its actions.

When resistance to the quality programme is met, the programme will almost certainly fail to fulfil all its stated objectives. Blame will be placed on the 'workers' – 'they failed to make it happen'. The soft systems thinker will immediately recognise that the failure belongs to management because it failed to create the conditions which would have made it possible for the programme to succeed. The management have failed to discover and accommodate the different viewpoints within the organisation.

This thinking re-emphasises the points made in earlier chapters about the need for effective communication and is a reminder of the comments made by various gurus that most of the responsibility for quality lies with the management.

16.8   Critical systems thinking and quality

'Critical systems thinking' (Flood & Jackson, 1991) has great relevance to the quality movement. Simply, critical systems thinking rejects the idea of 'one best way' of solving any problem (whether or not a problem of quality). It proposes instead that each method has potential utility in those contexts which reflect the theoretical assumptions that underpin the approach being applied and that human freedom and well-being must be respected. In the quality context this suggests that, far from any one quality guru being absolutely right and the others absolutely wrong, they are all right *and* all wrong, as are the various strands of thinking being introduced.

This suggests that, in a certain situation, the statistically based approach espoused by Deming may be most appropriate, while in another the participative approach preferred by Ishikawa may have greater utility. Equally, at a higher level of intervention, both of those approaches may be rejected in favour of a systems based approach which embraces the whole system of interest in the pursuit of quality.

A word of caution is appropriate at this juncture at the risk of offending some readers. It is not only quality methodologies and ways of thinking about the world that have different value in different contexts. These differences also apply to the words which we choose to use and the concepts which we attempt to apply. Thus such concepts as freedom of choice, participation and emancipation have different meanings and value in different contexts. These ideas are essentially products of Western thinking, reflecting primarily what philosophers consider important in societies which are relatively complex in both the economic and the social senses. They are aimed at furthering the interests of those parts of societies already supposed capable of exercising substantial political and economic choices and accustomed, even if for relatively short periods of history, to making those choices. Such parts of societies may be thought of as enjoying significant psychological maturity.

Other societies operate under different sets of opportunities, demands and constraints; they may be considered less psychologically mature. Thus, while in a mature society the idea of participation in process design and improvement may be wholly applicable, in other contexts the members of the society may not be familiar with the notion of being employed. Consequently they may require a totally different (although not dictatorial) management approach, perhaps placing greater emphasis on the parental role of the manager. This difference in approach does not apply solely to emerging or developing economies but also to those parts of Western economies which have suffered high levels of unemployment over many years. There are significant numbers of people in post-industrial societies to whom the concept of a job is wholly unfamiliar since work has been unavailable to them, in some cases for two or more generations. This might be thought of, in part, as a product of the failure of employers and employees to embrace changes in management thinking and practice which might have enabled organisational survival. Critical systems thinking enables the thoughtful manager to recognise and reflect upon these aspects of the circumstances in which he works and to choose quality implementation methods accordingly.

16.9   TQM through TSI

Flood (1993) explored Total Quality Management through the ideas of critical systems thinking, seeking to establish a sound platform for the theory and practice of TQM.

He defines quality as:

> Quality means meeting customers' (agreed) requirements, formal and informal, at lowest cost, first time every time.

Box 16.6   Ten principles of TQM

Robert Flood:

Principle 1)	There must be agreed requirements, for both internal and external customers;
Principle 2)	Customers' requirements must be met first time and every time;
Principle 3)	Quality improvement will reduce waste and total costs;
Principle 4)	There must be a focus on the prevention of problems, rather than an acceptance to cope in a fire-fighting manner;
Principle 5)	Quality improvement can only result from planned management action;
Principle 6)	Every job must add value;
Principle 7)	Everybody must be involved, from all levels and across all functions;
Principle 8)	There must be an emphasis on measurement to help to assess and to meet requirements and objectives;
Principle 9)	A culture of continuous improvement must be established (continuous includes the desirability of dramatic leaps forward as well as steady improvement);
Principle 10)	An emphasis should be placed on promoting creativity.

Flood sees ten principles (Box 16.6) emerging from this definition. These are to some extent a distillation and synthesis of the work of the gurus already explored in part two of this book.

The first principle, the call for agreed requirements, implies a need for a high degree of communication both within the organisation and with the customers in its environment. The demand for agreement implies that the communication must be focused on discourse not dictat – it must be a two way process of finding out and informing rather than a matter of giving orders. To be effective there must be understanding and genuine consensus.

The second principle of 'first time, every time' reflects Crosby's call for zero defects. The clear implication is that there is no benefit to be gained from failing to meet customer requirements and that achieving quality is a matter of consistency. Third is the belief that 'quality improvement will reduce waste and total costs'. The important issue here is the positive nature of the statement. Note that Flood uses the unconditional 'will' rather than may, could or should. This is of great importance as a belief, since many quality improvement programmes, initially at least, produce solutions which seem to have the opposite effect; increasing costs and waste in the short term while new techniques or processes are learned and embedded. Often managements not fully committed draw back from the changes in response to this negative short-term effect and hence fail to achieve any of the expected benefits.

The fourth principle 'focus on prevention' again reflects ideas of the mainstream gurus and is fundamental to achievement of quality. If the previous principle is to hold good, then clearly the process of achieving quality has to start with error prevention, since when an error occurs, extra cost is incurred in rectification, rework or after-sales support. As Crosby suggests 'It is always cheaper to do it right first time'. This links neatly to the fifth principle, 'planned management action'.

Planning is at the root of success in all manner of activities in life. Planning implies intent, a commitment to a particular course of events. All too often managements attempt to deal with some form of operational organisational crisis (usually a cost based crisis) by trying to achieve 'quick wins' through an instant TQM programme. This is sure to fail, since the focus is wrong. The banner headline may read 'Quality' but the sub-text reads 'save money' and, since the latter is much easier to understand and measure, that will become the focus of the exercise. Some money may be saved in the short term, what is almost certain is that greater quality will not be achieved. A commitment to quality improvement is long-term, and planning is key to success.

The sixth principle, 'every job must add value', is perhaps a recognition of the extent to which organisational processes are characterised by tasks which do not add value, being either unnecessary or obstructive to the process. It is interesting to note that 'every' does not just apply to production focused jobs but to every job in the organisation – from the Board downwards! This again links to the seventh principle – 'the involvement of everybody' – all levels and all functions. This takes the responsibility for quality away from the quality assurance or inspection department and places it firmly in the hands of those responsible for actually doing the job.

The eighth principle – 'emphasis on measurement' – is not taken as a call for reliance on purely statistical methods, but as a recognition that without some form of measurement there is no effective basis for evaluation of performance.

The ninth and tenth principles can be taken together – 'calls for continuous improvement and the promotion of creativity'. The first of these relies on the second. Flood specifically recognises in the ninth principle that continuous improvement should include 'dramatic leaps as well as steady improvement'. In this case we can argue with word choice and suggest that 'continual' improvement implies a more dynamic frame of reference for these 'dramatic leaps' than 'continuous', with its implications of incremental behaviour. Figure 16.5 attempts to highlight the difference between continual and continuous improvement.

Quality is then considered by Flood as a function of effective communication between the organisation and its customers. This communication clarifies expectations and is

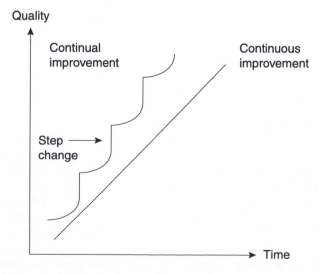

Figure 16.5 Continual and continuous change.

supported by consistent effort from all those within the organisation to meet those expectations. This necessitates meaningful measurement and a creative approach to continual improvement.

16.9.1   Assumptions

Flood's assumptions about the world in the quality context will now be explored.

Flood assumes willingness on the part of organisations to communicate and negotiate with their customers. This suggests recognition of equality of power between the supplier and customer. In practice, such equality of power is rare, with one party or the other normally assuming a dominant role in the relationship. When power is unequal, one party is reliant on the other for its continued existence or financial well-being, it is unlikely that equality will be maintained in negotiations about quality. It is often the case in the motor industry that component or sub-assembly manufacturers rely on orders from a single manufacturer for the majority of their business which means that the buyer can dictate quality standards and prices. Similar behaviour is seen in the food industry where the major supermarket groups exercise enormous power over their suppliers. The banking and telecommunications industries often demonstrate similar characteristics in relation to their customers.

Flood's approach also assumes a willingness within an organisation to distribute power; this is the clear implication of involving 'everybody, at all levels and across all functions'. Again, the relatively low power held by many employees, and their general vulnerability to loss of employment, makes it more likely that managers will behave autocratically, dictating how things will be. This will not lead to full commitment and co-operation, which Flood requires, but does more accurately reflect the power relations in many contemporary organisations. This assumption is also implicit in the ninth principle – the culture of continuous improvement. It suggests again effective sharing of power within the organisation.

Flood's third assumption is that it is possible to be 'right first time, every time'. While in the manufacturing context this is not so unreasonable, in the service and public sectors it is arguably extremely difficult. The technical aspects of any transaction are of course no more difficult to get right than the technical aspects of a physical product. Where the service and public sectors will always have difficulty is where the organisation meets the customer. While the technical aspects of any particular transaction are constant, each transaction is unique in its dependence on the mood and expectations of the customer and the member of staff at the particular time. There are three variables within any given transaction which are largely beyond the scope of the organisation to control; it is inevitable that there will be an occasional mismatch between expectations and delivery.

The final assumption which distinguishes Flood's work from that of others is the whole hearted embrace of the systemic approach. This comes through in his recognition of both external and internal customers and in the use of the word 'every' in relation to meeting expectations, to jobs adding value and to the involvement of all levels and all functions. He does not preclude the involvement of customers in this – although he does not specifically require it.

Overall, Flood's principles rely on a systemic worldview in which people behave as if they are in partnership. Power is distributed, with those having the information making the decisions, and collaboration rather than competition as the keynote of success. This is a rather different world to the one which many people experience each day.

16.9.2   *Successes and failures*

It is too early to make properly informed judgements about the success or failure of this approach as, unlike the approaches reviewed in part two, it has not had the benefit of extended development and empirical study. It is reasonable, though, to attempt some preliminary evaluation of this work. The probable strengths are:

- It attempts to be truly holistic;
- It is systematic, methodical and iterative;
- It embraces much of value from the established approaches, overcoming some weaknesses previously recognised;
- It is rooted in a substantial appreciation of management and organisation theory.

Perceived weaknesses include the following:

- The theory and practice of TSI is not yet accepted as part of mainstream management theory;
- TSI is regarded by many practitioners as too complex in itself;
- There is a lack of widely reported case studies in the literature;
- Substantial empirical development has been principally undertaken by Flood himself;
- As with the other approaches already considered, the approach is of limited value in a coercive context.

The holistic view stems from the meta-methodological, complementarist framework of TSI which underpins the approach and tries to avoid the isolationist, pragmatist and imperialist criticisms made of other methods. The systematic, methodical and iterative process provides a heuristic aspect which reflects the Deming or Shewhart cycle of learning. The embrace of established approaches recognises that there are strengths in them and supports them with a broader conceptual framework, increasing their potential utility. Finally, the appreciation of management and organisation theory recognises that quality is only one aspect of organisational effectiveness, and opens the pursuit of quality to the importation of ideas from other frames of reference within the total knowledge set.

With regard to the weaknesses, the lack of acceptance of TSI amongst mainstream theorists is not necessarily a fault of the approach itself, but a function of the different paradigms within which people are educated and work, and the complexity of the world itself. Unfortunately, contemporary problems cannot always be addressed through simple techniques. In fact it could be argued that many of the failures of problem solving approaches rest on their simplicity, rendering them inadequate for the problems which they attempt to address.

The lack of available case studies continues to be a problem for the approach, which has seen no significant development in theory practice.

The final weakness, limited value in truly coercive contexts, is common to all the quality methodologies reviewed (and indeed to other problem solving approaches). This weakness is one which no adequate methodology exists to address. For many practical purposes this may be regarded as relatively unimportant. Power relations in most organisations are distorted to some degree, but in most contexts there are practical limits. If the organisation becomes too oppressive the people will leave, thus the power of those in charge is finite. Employees in many contexts do have choices.

There are situations, in fully developed as well as developing countries, where a considerable degree of practical oppression does exist, where the employees do not have effective choices. This might occur in communities which have experienced high unemployment or where there is a single dominant employer. In these situations, it must be hoped that the effective pursuit of organisational survival and quality will ultimately force those in power to adopt a less dominant position, and engage the willing co-operation of the workforce by recognising that quality cannot be achieved without it.

16.9.3   Critical review

Overall, Flood's adherence to the concept of a complementarist approach to organisation, and to problem solving, proposes a holistic avenue for the pursuit of the quality ideal. He precludes no ideas which are theoretically substantiated, requiring only that they be used in full understanding of the principles and world-views which underpin them.

The principal tenets of various strands of quality management are subsumed into his approach, thus ensuring participation, appropriate measurement, a wide range of tools and the coherence generated by a deeper level of understanding. The approach overall then offers a considerably enhanced perception of the 'quality problem'.

The generality of the approach would appear to render it directly relevant to both manufacturing and service industries, although it will suffer many of the same shortcomings as the dominant approaches when dealing with the very soft aspects of organisational behaviour. For example, it may be possible to specify what words should be used in any given transaction – and this is often done. What cannot be specified is the sincerity with which the words are spoken and most certainly not the response of the particular customer to each utterance. The sincerity conveyed is probably more important to the customer than the exact form of words. Sincerity can only be attained when the staff member truly believes in what he or she is saying. No methodology exists which can guarantee such belief, although approaches do exist which make it possible.

Flood's approach appears to have potential to enhance the implementation of quality programmes. This has yet to be proven.

Summary

This chapter has first provided a brief overview of the field of organisational cybernetics and its relationship with quality. Many writers (for example Beckford, 1993, 1995, 2016; Beckford & Dudley, 1998a, 1998b, 1999; Beer, 1959, 1979, 1981, 1985; Dudley, 2000; Espejo & Schwaninger, 1993) have worked with and sought to develop cybernetic ideas on effective organisation. The second part of the chapter introduced the concept of 'soft systems'. In this view organisations are not products of objective reality but products of the interpretations put on them by their members. The different approach to solving organisational problems necessitated by this view was introduced and the implications for the pursuit of quality discussed. Readers wishing to expand their knowledge of soft systems should consider the work of Checkland (1981), Mason & Mitroff (1981), Checkland & Scholes (1990).

In the final part of the chapter Flood's systemically based approach to TQM was outlined. This showed how Flood captured the essence of the reductionist approaches and embedded them in a systemic framework. Readers should see Flood (1993) for a fuller understanding.

KEY LEARNING POINTS

Organisational cybernetics

Key definition:
the science of effective organisation

Key beliefs:
quality is a product of effectiveness, organisations are extremely complex, exhibit self-regulation, are probabilistic

Tools of cybernetics:
the black box technique, feedback, variety engineering, recursion

Cybernetics and quality:
descriptive, diagnostic and prescriptive model, offers parallels to mainstream quality thinking, knowledge workers supports Quality Circles approach, distributed power demands management commitment, the cybernetic view supports and enables kaizen

Soft systems

Key definition:
the study of problems in human activity systems

Key beliefs:
objectives must be agreed through participation before the study of methods becomes meaningful

Tools of soft systems:
participation, debate, consensus building

Soft systems and quality:
participative approaches can reduce conflict, quality programmes must address hearts as well as minds

Question

When do YOU use 'soft' approaches to problem solving in your day-to-day life? Why do you use them?

Compare Ohno's Toyota Production System with the principles of cybernetic systems.

17 Business Process Re-Engineering

'... ideas are good for a limited time – not forever'

Robert Townsend, *Further Up the Organisation*, 1985

Introduction

This chapter discusses both Business Process Re-Engineering and the practices of Six Sigma. Business Process Re-Engineering (BPR) emerged as a formal business practice in America during the 1980s and early 90s although the term was used in the discipline of operations research (Wiener, 1947) as early as the 1940s. In its current incarnation, it is an essentially pragmatic approach that resulted from observation and evaluation of the efforts of several companies to re-invent themselves. It can perhaps be most usefully thought of as a form of business strategy focused on gaining competitive advantage through efficiency improvement and exploitation of information technology, rather than as a theoretically rooted approach to management problem solving. Michael Hammer & James Champy (1993) formalised and crystallised the approach, which is characterised as systemic and capitalises on many established problem solving methodologies and techniques.

Six Sigma will be considered in the second part of the chapter and, according to Pande & Holpp (2002), is 'not merely a *quality* initiative; it is a business initiative'. It is about re-engineering your business processes or products such that they perform with almost no defects.

17.1 What is BPR?

BPR challenges many of the assumptions that have underpinned the way organisations have been run for the last two centuries. First, and consistent with the emerging dominance of systems thinking in the area of quality, it rejects the idea of reductionism – the fragmentation and breaking down of organisations into the simplest tasks. BPR prefers the systemic recognition of flows of inter-connected activities with a common purpose. Second, it encourages organisations to capitalise on substantial developments made in information technology (IT). Although applying IT cannot be the driver for BPR, it is nonetheless a powerful enabler of radical redesign with both internets (data and things) having a role to play. Third, BPR enables organisations to take advantage of the more highly developed education, skills and capabilities of the staff they employ. People are treated within BPR as McGregor's (1960) capable 'theory Y' individuals rather than as lazy, incompetent 'theory X' machine parts.

BPR embraces many of the developments in management thinking arising in the recent past, particularly those concerned with the management of human resources. Ideas such as empowerment are fundamental to the BPR oriented company.

17.2   Discontinuity, chaos and complexity

Central to BPR process is the idea of 'discontinuous thinking', a notion raised by Hammer & Champy, but earlier given prominence by Handy (1990) in *The Age of Unreason*. Discontinuous thinking and the idea of 'discontinuity' demand some explanation.

The Western world relies on continuous thinking, largely derived from scientific thinking. Continuous thinking is incremental, an apparently seamless, flowing approach based on small, incremental changes. This has served extremely well and retains immense value in certain areas. It is reflected in the continuous improvement (kaizen) approach to quality adopted successfully by many companies throughout the world. However, this approach is inadequate to either solve the problems currently besetting organisations, or to realise the true potential of the dramatic advances in the ways that organisations can capture data about performance, manipulate it and generate information for decisions. Readers will recall Handy's view cited in chapter 3.

The call for discontinuous change may be seen as 'special pleading' by management gurus and consultants seeking for a 'new' product to sell – perhaps just another form of organisational snake-oil; a solution in search of a problem – after all it does represent the opportunity for major projects and large fees! This, though, would be an extremely cynical view and would ignore the substantial theoretical support which can now be drawn upon in this area from the 'hard' sciences, particularly biology and physics. That Hammer, Champy and other writers in this area have not drawn on these sources does not negate the value of their work; it merely reflects different backgrounds and knowledge bases. It is fair to say, though, that their work would be substantially enhanced by the explicit recognition and use of the insights contained in these sciences. As suggested by Flood & Jackson (1991), if there is no underpinning science to the work of management gurus, they have nothing to rely on but experience, and nothing to pass on to subsequent generations but stories.

The mathematically substantiated science of organisational cybernetics (discussed in chapter 16) is concerned with the control of dynamical systems, those which are changing or evolving. This science has, in its contemporary interpretation, been evolving since the 1940s. It embraces the potential for discontinuity as part of its structure and enables organisations to become discontinuous in the way they operate; embracing a whole new philosophy of management and decision making and distributing power in ways previously unheard of. Early development of this work involved mathematicians, biologists, physicists and engineers. This work was developed by Stafford Beer and has subsequently been adopted, developed and adapted by others including Beckford (1993, 2016) and Dudley (2000).

More recently, other developments of this work in the hands of physicists, biologists and others have demonstrated that discontinuities may be considered as natural phenomena. Catastrophe theory (a branch of mathematics) is cited as the original identifier of the 'butterfly effect' – in which a butterfly beating its wings in one part of the world may generate a thunderstorm in another – the potentially massive consequences of a relatively minor disturbance or perturbation in a dynamic system.

Complexity theory (Waldrop, 1992) has shown how in dynamical systems equilibrium (a stable state) emerges from apparently random or chaotic behaviour, and how indescribably complex systems can be studied and their behaviour understood. These systems again can be disturbed from their stable states by minor perturbations, and then, changing discontinuously for a period, settle into a new point of stability. Studies of complexity in systems identify that patterns are often present in what at first sight appear to be random oscillations (Taleb, 2010).

Chaos theory (Gleick, 1987), which some might argue is not significantly different to complexity theory, has shown how systems apparently evolve chaotically while, under further examination, pattern and order can be discerned in movements about a representative point in phase space. Often, system behaviour is almost repeated in a kind of spiral dynamics forming orbits around a fixed point. The orbit may never be quite the same twice, but the fulcrum (or turning point) of the orbit remains the same. Again, minor disturbances can cause major effects.

These developments reflect much of the earlier thinking in the systems and cybernetics paradigms and are given great credence by the contemporary facility to model such systems on computers which now allow us to represent the consequences graphically. Early studies, which did not have this advantage, relied upon the mathematical knowledge of the reader for their proof.

Grasping the concept that discontinuity is as natural (if not more so) as continuity, while discomfiting to many, must ultimately be seen as reassuring – since many discontinuities are met in life. The task of management is to drive and exploit the discontinuity, steering the organisation so that it leads to its survival. The ultimate alternative is the discontinuity that is called death, or in the case of organisations, liquidation and bankruptcy. Discontinuity is sure to arise within organisational systems, but its consequences are a function of management decisions and actions.

17.3   What drives BPR?

Hammer & Champy (1993: 1) suggest that the alternative to BPR is for 'corporate America to close its doors and go out of business'. The comment describes the behaviour of organisations for many years. When faced with increasing costs at home and competition from abroad, many have chosen, in effect, to export jobs rather than products. An argument already adequately explored in chapter 1 of this book and given new life in the continuing economic crisis which arose in 2008. The same imperatives which drive the quality movement should drive BPR.

Thus a key impetus for BPR is the imperative of economic survival for mature organisations and nations. Whilst the focus for Hammer & Champy is the US economy, the arguments apply equally well to the UK, Europe and to certain Asian economies. The message is to stop exporting jobs and start re-inventing the way we perform work, in order to match the lower costs of manufacturing elsewhere.

It must be recognised at this stage that the imperative does not simply apply to the manufacturing sector but also to service industries and the public sector. The exporting of 'information processing' based tasks, supported by the explosive developments in the capabilities and use of information technology, does send jobs to many other countries.

Resistance to BPR and inhibition of its application in both the public and commercial sectors of the economy arise from the same sources. The focus of both tends to be short-term; a product of government financial systems and commercial employment contracts. So long as there are profits (or an adequate budget) today, there is no need for action to be taken. Even where the need can be identified by those with the power of decision, they often lack the will or commitment to take action since the consequences of failure, or benefits of success, will not be felt during their own incumbency.

17.4   What does BPR mean?

Hammer & Champy define BPR as:

> the fundamental rethinking and radical redesign of business processes to achieve dramatic improvements in critical, contemporary measures of performance, such as cost, quality, service and speed.

This underlines that most established organisations have grown up with, and still adhere to, outmoded, traditional methods of work which are now relatively inefficient and often ineffective. These methods have often evolved into convoluted, complex ways of dealing with activities with many steps, checks and balances. They are, in many cases, rendered redundant by the development of both production and information technology, by the universal spread of education and by our current understanding concerning the needs and capabilities of people. Added to this should be the exponential growth in our understanding of the systemic nature of the world, and the sophisticated methodologies and tools which have been developed in order for us to manage our organisations more competently. The key words (Box 17.1) in the definition will now be examined.

Fundamental is a clear call for the organisation to examine itself at the most basic level. Hammer & Champy suggest the question 'Why do we do what we do?' Perhaps this should go further and ask the question 'What do we do?' This second question demands that the participants focus on the purpose that they perceive for the organisation – that is, a redefinition of the organisation's goal – without which any improvement, however radical, may actually become trivial or banal. It is important that the organisation focuses on doing the right thing to the best of its ability – not on doing the wrong thing better!

Radical means

> not making superficial changes or fiddling with what is already in place, but throwing away the old.

Within the rigorous process of Interactive Planning, Ackoff (1981) offered the process stage of 'idealised redesign'. Ackoff simply asks the question: 'If you were designing the organisation today what would it look like?' This implies NOT working from established processes and procedures, but designing the organisation from scratch on a clean sheet of paper.

Box 17.1   Business Process Re-Engineering: Key words

Hammer & Champy:
Key word 1)   Fundamental
Key word 2)   Radical
Key word 3)   Dramatic
Key word 4)   Processes
Key word 5)   Performance

In impact it is much the same as zero-based budgeting, since it forces a fundamental re-appraisal of every activity within the organisation.

Dramatic implies that BPR does not seek to achieve marginal or incremental improve-ment in performance, the normal 5–10%. For companies with that scale of problem (if they are sure of it), the process of BPR may be too powerful. The focus is on companies which want, or need, to achieve much more substantial performance improvements. Personal experience shows that through effective BPR practice improvements of 35–50% are achievable. Within certain processes up to 70% is claimed. It is suggested that every company should undertake a study of its processes to determine what level of improvement might be available. Simply being at or near best in class, which seems to satisfy Hammer & Champy, is not enough. If you are the best, but another organisation finds a way of being better, you will face the re-engineering challenge anyway. Far better to undertake this activity while ahead of the pack and profitable, than while running behind trying to catch up.

Processes are defined by Hammer & Champy as the 'value-chain' or 'cost-chain' running through the organisation and linking its inputs to its outputs. A process is the series of revenue generating or cost incurring steps involved in delivery of a product or service to a customer. Certain industries, for example chemical and oil producers, are inherently process focused at an operational level. Processes describe the enchained patterns of activity of the organisation. Many other organisations are broken down into functional departments with 'baronial' (Jay, 1987) responsibilities for parts or sub-set activities. Those involved often have limited awareness that they form part of the overall chain, and sometimes no idea what value or cost they generate for the organisation. They are narrowly focused on a particular task, with no knowledge or interest in how this contributes to fulfilling the purpose of the organisation or the needs of its customers. Readers will realise the relevance to quality when recalling Deming's contribution to the quality movement in his recognition of internal 'supplier-customer' relationships.

Performance, while not highlighted by Hammer & Champy, is a very significant word. Performance does not necessarily mean profit, although this is the common interpretation. Rather it should be taken to mean the fulfilment of the purposes of the organisation and the effective utilisation of resources.

BPR relies on several unconventional ideas. First, the orientation of the organisation towards its processes rather than its functional and often fragmented activities (an orientation becoming more common). Second, it requires the drive and ambition to make far reaching and 'dramatic' improvements, and that must arise from senior management. Third is what Hammer & Champy call 'rule-breaking', a willingness to challenge the conventions of the organisation. Finally is the creative use of information technology. This means using it to enable genuine improvements in performance, rather than to set in electronic tablets of stone the established ways of working.

Added to these should be the concepts of bravery and determination so often absent from corporate life – attentive readers will recall the quote from Machiavelli in this regard.

Prior to concluding this section it is worth noting what is NOT meant by BPR. For Hammer & Champy what it does not mean is downsizing, rightsizing, restructuring, automating or any other management activity which may or may not be necessary or desirable. These things should happen anyway, and of course may result from re-engin-eering, but that is not the purpose of the BPR process.

If that is how the organisation interprets re-engineering then two things are certain. First, that the process will fail (as do over 50% of so-called re-engineering projects), as the management commitment and understanding needed to really make it work will be absent.

Second, the organisation will grow back all of the parts reduced in size since no fundamental change in its basis of operation will have occurred. The problem will simply be deferred rather than solved, dissolved or resolved.

Business process challenge

I was recently invited by a large company to undertake on behalf of the Board a rapid high-level review of their processes, people and systems to provide an assessment of the scope for improvement and to assist them in deliberations over their five year strategy.

A service company with a lot of people, few significant assets and a very strong track record with a small number of highly loyal customers, they have in recent years invested substantially in first enhancing their core business processes and second in developing bespoke information systems to support those processes both internally and for their customers. These investments have delivered substantial gains in performance. The clients are receiving measurably better service than ever and the cost of delivery has fallen by about 20% while profit margins have been maintained. This is a substantial achievement in an organisation whose costs are mainly driven by the number of people it employs.

The challenge looking into the future is to establish how to continue to drive down costs and maintain margins when the limits to incremental process improvement are being reached or breached. Given that people can only work so hard for so long and that they can only operate equipment effectively and safely for reasonable periods of time, these limits are real.

The company processes are now in a rabbit hole; they can continue to refine and polish the processes but all improvement is incremental. They will reach a point where they can no longer 'do more for less' but will only be able to 'do less for less', an outcome which will not suit their clients.

It is time for them to step back from the operational focus, to lift their eyes to a more distant horizon, reimagine the best ways to fulfil their purpose and then redesign their processes to deliver it.

17.5   The BPR process

The process of undertaking BPR draws on a wide variety of tools, approaches and understanding. Many of these have been or will be elaborated within this book, for example statistical methods, communication issues, problem solving tools, process mapping tools and the use of information technology.

In this brief section the focus of attention will be on the overall process, called the 'Business System Diamond'. This is presented in Figure 17.1.

When adopting a process based approach to organisation, it is essential to identify the key processes. These in turn control the number, nature and content of jobs which lead towards the definition of structure. Arising from the new expectations concerning desirable outputs (the results of processes) and the activities of employees, it is possible to define the management and measurements systems necessary for performance (and it should always be remembered that the tendency is for those characteristics which are measured to be delivered). Finally, with the other linkages in place, the values and beliefs of the members of the organisation will be modified.

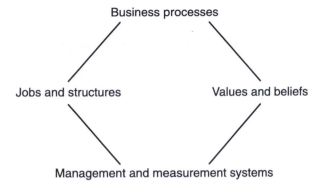

Figure 17.1 The Business System Diamond.

It can easily be seen how each stage in the diamond drives the next. The diamond also suggests an iterative process; having successfully re-engineered, the culture of the organisation should be supportive of aspirations to further development. This may be interpreted as a call back towards continuous improvement.

17.6   BPR and quality

There is some ongoing debate as to whether BPR replaces or subsumes the pursuit of quality, or quality subsumes BPR. This debate is sterile. The pursuit of quality is about 'rightness' in all the actions and interactions of an organisation both internally and externally. The greater part of the quality methods and tools are incremental in their impact and lead the organisation towards the 'kaizen' philosophy of continuous improvement. This implies linear, continuous change in the organisation. Quality embraces the hidden potential for change while recognising that incremental change only improves what is already done, while BPR may fundamentally change what is done. If a procedure or part of a process is redundant, in the sense that it adds no value to a product or service, improvement in its efficiency is a false gain. While efficiency improvement reduces the amount of waste, the procedure still remains as a cost in the system. The adoption of BPR techniques in process analysis can help to overcome this problem, eradicating procedures rather than improving them. BPR and quality are complementary not competitive.

Perhaps somewhat perversely and as with the strategic process outlined in chapter 2, it is vital that the BPR process itself exhibits appropriate quality characteristics. If the BPR process is flawed, then the outcome will also be flawed.

17.7   Six Sigma

Six Sigma has, arguably, been in course for many years. The roots of the modern quality movement in the 'Shewhart Cycle' (Deming, 1986) and the notion of statistical process control provide the base from which Eckes (2003) derives Six Sigma as '3.4 defects per million events'. Pande & Holpp (2002) suggest that 'to be a Six Sigma pizza shop, you would have to have on time pizza delivery 99.9997 percent of the time'.

Eckes (2003) suggests that:

> At its foundation, Six Sigma is teaching everyone in the organization to become more effective and efficient.

Eckes suggests that Six Sigma is rooted in three components:

- Business process management;
- Scientific method;
- Culture.

Pande & Holpp (2002) on the other hand suggest that the 'efforts target three main areas:

- Improving customer satisfaction;
- Reducing cycle time;
- Reducing defects.'

So, the first addresses the how of Six Sigma, the second addresses the why. Now, having considered the thinking of the quality gurus and the ideas of systems thinking it is tempting to suggest that there is nothing to see here, the ideas and the approaches have all been seen before AND we know that, by and large, they work. So, what is new?

Pande & Holpp, having first declared the death of TQM, claim three characteristics which separate Six Sigma from prior programmes:

- Customer focus;
- Return on investment;
- Changing how management operates.

So, nothing new there either, in particular the return on investment which is surely a function of how any particular system of management is applied and can be achieved through the application of the Juran, Deming and Ohno methods as it can be through a Six Sigma programme.

The focus on 'how management operates' is to be welcomed; it is in fairness an aspect of business improvement which has been underplayed in previous work, although all of the gurus place strong emphasis on the criticality of management to the process, with Deming (1986) estimating that '94% [of problems] belong to the system' (responsibility of management). Other gurus' estimates are not dissimilar. Similarly, Deming calls for 'constancy of purpose, for management assuming leadership for change, for continuous improvement' and all rooted in the use of statistical information to inform decisions.

The tools and techniques outlined in the Six Sigma literature are, similarly, direct uses or developments of those derived from the earlier work. Pande & Holpp talk about 'six themes':

- Focus on the customer;
- Data and fact driven management;
- Processes;
- Proactive management;
- Boundaryless collaboration;
- Drive for perfection.

The first of these perhaps reflects the work of Crosby and Ohno. The second and third appear rooted in Deming. The fourth and fifth will be found in Taguchi and Oakland, while the last again would reflect Crosby and Ohno in particular. Within the tool set of Six Sigma are such techniques as problem solving, brainstorming and DMAIC (Define, Measure, Analyse, Improve and Control), Affinity and Fishbone Diagrams, Flowcharts (Process maps), Statistical Measurement and Sampling techniques.

Nothing I have said should detract in absolute terms from the value of Six Sigma. However, what it appears to do is bring together in a new combination threads, tools and themes from across the management literature. If by doing so the process helps some organisations to improve their effectiveness and efficiency then that is a good thing. However, there is nothing within the tool set that will assist the organisation in addressing the far more fundamental challenges of large-scale and fundamental adaptation, challenges which will become ever more frequent and demanding in a changing world.

Summary

This chapter has discussed the concept of Business Process Re-Engineering and Six Sigma and placed them in the context of theoretical developments in recent years. The links to systemic approaches based on cybernetics, complexity science and chaos theory were explored. In the latter half of the chapter, BPR was defined and its key process explained. While this chapter draws heavily on the pioneers of BPR (Hammer & Champy, 1993), readers may wish to extend their knowledge by considering the work by Johansson et al (1993), and by moving beyond this narrow focus to consider the work of systems thinkers in depth. Meanwhile Six Sigma was shown to be a repackaging of well established tools and techniques under a new label.

KEY LEARNING POINTS

Business Process Re-Engineering

BPR definition:
radical reinvention of organisations on process lines

Key characteristics:
pragmatic and empirical, not theoretically based, systemic, exploits developments in technology

Central themes:
discontinuity, radical change, cybernetic understanding, complexity theory, chaos theory

Key drivers:
economic, social, environmental

Method:

The Business Systems Diamond, Process Analysis, Job and Structure review, Management and Measurement Systems, Values and Beliefs

BPR and quality are complementary

Six Sigma

Brings together a range of tools and techniques into a systemic method for reducing waste and improving performance

Question

What barriers would you expect to meet in designing and implementing a Business Process Re-Engineering programme? How could Six Sigma contribute to that work?

18 The learning organisation

'The ability to learn faster than your competitors may be the only sustainable competitive advantage'

Aries De Geus, cited by Senge, 1990

Introduction

This chapter introduces early ideas about adaptation and learning based on Ashby's 'Design for a Brain' (1956) before considering the specific work of Peter Senge (1990), the 'guru' of the learning organisation. Senge's 'Fifth Discipline' identifies five principles for learning and seven learning disabilities which inhibit the development of truly successful organisations. Flood (1999) revisited this theme to bring to the field a deeper and more robust appreciation of the breadth and power of systemic thinking applied to the notion of learning. There is an emerging literature in the field of learning, or adaptive, organisation, and readers should consider *Images of Organisation* (Morgan, 1986), *The Innovating Organization* (Pettigrew & Fenton, 2000) and *The Intelligent Organisation* (Beckford, 2016) to further develop their understanding.

Learning results from a cycle of planning, experimentation, reflection and consolidation which the PDCA or EPDCA cycles of Shewhart, Deming and Oakland reflect. A learning organisation employs these cycles systemically throughout its horizontal and vertical dimensions. This means learning has to become embedded in the organisation's processes, systems and structure and in the behaviour of its people.

18.1 Organisational learning

Organisational learning is often associated with issues of data mining and knowledge management (Hislop, 2013; Jashapara, 2010), frequently evidenced in physical retention of documented records in an organisation. The presumption is that in knowledge based economies such information constitutes an organisational asset, and that it should be managed in the same ways as other assets. This has given rise to growth in document management systems, data mining approaches and the creation of more substantial organisational archives. All of which rather misses the point!

Organisational learning is not about recording history, the storage and retrieval of data, it is about organisational processes and behaviours which co-adapt with changes in the internal and external environments. A learning organisation learns about its environment whilst simultaneously teaching it, influencing it to be more susceptible to the products and services offered.

The two typical examples of this are marketing activity and political propaganda. This learning and teaching must occur at least at the same rate as the environment is changing. Changes in behaviour of the people must also happen; they must actively support and encourage adaptation rather than inhibit it.

Lessons can be drawn from the work of evolutionists such as Darwin (2008), which help us to understand that in a persistently evolving environment those species which survive are those which best adapt to their environment over time. Those characteristics of a species which enable its survival in any one time period may ultimately lead to its failure when the environment changes. Thus there is a conflict. To maximise opportunities for survival in the present requires characteristics which meet the demands of the present. To maximise opportunities for survival in the long term necessitates characteristics which cannot even be known about, but which the species or entity must be capable of evolving if it is to survive. This capability must, to some extent, detract from the closeness of fit to the current environment! In effect, it makes it inefficient (by pure short-term measures) but effective in the long term. This conflict applies at least as much to organisations as it does to living species. It may be argued that the organisational case is stronger because the economic ecology changes faster and sometimes more drastically, than that of the world in general.

Drawing on Ashby (1952) to resolve this conflict for organisations, it is necessary to do three things simultaneously – and at various levels of organisation. It must:

> Pursue efficiency in its current interactions with the market-place; persistently pursuing faster, cleaner and cheaper means of delivering present products and services to present markets;

> Monitor (understanding as well as gathering data) the organisational environment searching for new opportunities; consider the closeness of fit to the market (and influencing that market) and reflecting on past performance to create future products and services for future markets;

> Conduct a meaningful dialogue internally which enables the organisational objectives, stimulated by considerations for the future, to be translated into the organisational reality of the future.

In essence, the organisation is attempting to move smoothly to ensure a continuous fit between its product and service offerings and the changing demands of the customers and is reflected in Dudley's Trialogue (2000) and Beckford's Intelligent Organisation (2016). Such an approach means that the organisation must structurally separate, either physically or in the behaviour and understanding of employees, those activities and roles necessary to enable evolutionary, adaptive behaviour to occur. Commonly, organisations are oriented around current products, services and markets. Often, little or no attention is paid to the future, and consequently the organisation confronts unexpected events for which it has carried out no preparation. The demands of operating today's business nearly always over-ride the necessity of creating tomorrow's and the organisation dies, very often by being absorbed by another.

Organisations do not exist (except in the sense of a legal entity) other than through the interactions of their constituents. They are socially constructed, assembled to achieve a common aim and ultimately cannot learn except through the interactions of their human members. The collective memory of an organisation is best described through its culture, the ways of thinking and behaving which are common to its members. Organisational learning is not then about the addition of data to a corporate memory, although such memories are capable of being created, but about change in the organisation through altered relationship structures and adaptation of the individual and collective behaviour of its members. Offered in figure 18.1 is my cybernetic interpretation of how such adaptation might take place.

Members of the company through their interactions with the environment come to question the way in which things are done (questioning), by comparing their real world experience with the organisation's model of 'self' (their model of the organisation and its environment). They conceive potential solutions to the defined problem (conceptualisation) and design an experiment to test their hypothesis (experimentation). The results of the experiment are fed back to them and the organisational model is modified according to their new experience (consolidation). They proceed to manage the organisation in accordance with the modified model. Learning fails to take place when the last of these steps, consolidation, does not occur.

Alert readers will have noticed the direct comparison which can be drawn here with the learning approaches established in the Deming Cycle (Plan, Do, Check, Action), Ishikawa's Quality Circles (which focus on problem solving) and Taguchi's prototyping methodology. Questioning, conceptualisation, experimentation and consolidation are drawn from Handy (1985).

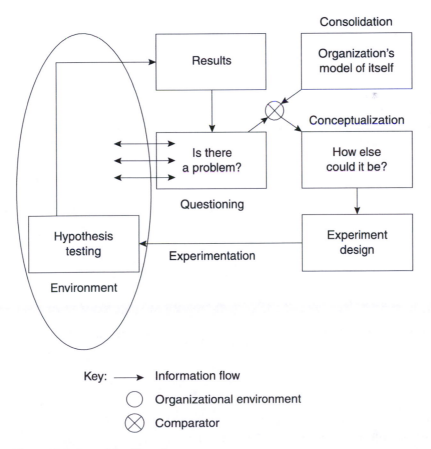

Key: ⟶ Information flow
⚪ Organizational environment
⊗ Comparator

Figure 18.1 A model of learning.

18.2   Senge's learning organisation

A 'learning organisation' is defined simply by Senge as one where:

> people continually expand their capacity to create the results they truly desire, where new and extensive patterns of thinking are nurtured, where collective aspiration is set free, and where people are continually learning how to learn together.

The idea is supported in other parts of the literature. Beer (1979, 1981, 1985) writes about adaptive, ultra stable systems – organisations which are capable of reacting to situations and conditions not envisaged when they were designed. Both Ackoff (1981) and Checkland (1981) call for participation, exploration and critical reflection; essential activities for learning. The critical systems work of Flood, Jackson and others can also be called upon to support this view with its calls for complementarism (requiring understanding of different theories and methodologies), sociological awareness (different cultures) and emancipation (the growth and development of human freedom). A key work in this area comes from Flood & Romm (1996) in which they elaborate an approach to 'triple-loop learning'. Senge also draws widely on the literature in organisation theory and business practice, although not systems dynamics (Forrester, 1961 [2013]; Wolstenholme, 1990) to support his work.

Looking at Senge's definition, there are a number of key words and phrases. First, his learning organisations are clearly focused on people. However, this is not in the sense of the mainstream human resource literature which aims to satisfy human needs and wants, but in an approach centred on developing human potential, which he suggests will in turn lead to those same satisfactions.

Second, 'continually' implies a commitment to an ongoing process, a further move away from the static thinking which dominated earlier management science.

Third, 'create the results' suggests that people's abilities enable them to control and create the future of organisations. This reflects the thinking of Ackoff and others. However, we cannot deny that limits exist to the potential control exerted by organisations; these limits being enforced by the actions of others in a competitive world.

Fourth, 'new patterns of thinking' reinforces the points previously made. While not necessarily rejecting all the old thinking, the new should be capitalised on where appropriate. Finally, there is 'collective aspiration and learning together'. Here Senge seems to object to much of the development of Western society which, arguably, has seen a move away from collective, shared values and hopes towards a rather more self-interested, individualistic world (Hofstede, 1980). This is perhaps reflected in life in such areas as divorce rates, executive compensation packages, the increasing trend towards litigation over

---

Box 18.1   The learning organisation: Key words and phrases

Peter Senge:

Key word 1)   People
Key word 2)   Continually
Key word 3)   Create the results
Key word 4)   New patterns of thinking
Key word 5)   Collective aspiration/Learning together

relatively minor matters and the drift away from religiously based societies towards a more secular approach.

The issue of learning is given real prominence when the leaders of large industrial organisations take it seriously. Senge quotes from Arie De Geus (see opening of chapter), while Peters (1992) makes the comment 'there is a surplus of everything', i.e. that there is more capacity in the world to create goods and services than to consume them. This can only generate further competitive pressure, driving down prices and margins and consequently profits. It is not simply about learning to work 'smarter' to do better, but simply to survive.

18.2.1   The learning disabilities

Senge suggests that even the 'excellent' companies may only be performing at a mediocre level. He proposes that the ways we design and manage our organisations, the narrow, convergent ways we are taught to think and to interact, create 'fundamental learning disabilities'.

'I am my position' argues that we become what we do for a job. The classic example of this is first meetings or parties when we introduce ourselves and are almost always asked 'What do you do?' Our response – 'I am a ...' defines us as being our work. Alternatively, we might argue that we do what we do because we are who we are.

'The enemy is out there' reflects our natural tendency to place blame or guilt elsewhere, rather than to acknowledge our own faults. This tendency has been recorded in literature since at least biblical times. Commenting on the illusion of taking charge, Senge suggests that when we think we are being 'proactive' very often we are just being differently reactive. He proposes that 'true pro–activeness comes from seeing how we contribute to our own problems' – perhaps something that requires insight from beyond the narrow confines of the management literature!

Our reductionist views of the world, the tendency to fragment and analyse, leads us to a 'causal chain' view of the world, hence the fixation on events rather than processes and interactions. This has already been challenged with the recognition of the systems based approach. Senge suggests in this area that our focus on events prevents us from seeing the patterns in continuing processes which tell us much about what is actually happening.

The parable of the boiling frog was fully rehearsed in chapter 3. It is the recognition of the need for discontinuous change and, perhaps, learning to be uncomfortable with continuity in a non-linear world. Chaos! Complexity!

Taken at the simple, individual level, if we reflect on our actions and their consequences then we learn. There are many people in the world who whilst claiming 30 plus years

---

Box 18.2   The learning disabilities

Learning disabilities:

Disability 1)   I am my position;

Disability 2)   The enemy is out there;

Disability 3)   The illusion of taking charge;

Disability 4)   The fixation on events;

Disability 5)   The parable of the boiling frog;

Disability 6)   The delusion of learning from experience;

Disability 7)   The myth of the management team.

experience actually have one year's experience 30 times – they do not reflect and do not learn. We do not always learn from experience as, particularly in organisations, consequences of our actions cannot be known in this way. They may well extend across organisational boundaries and have impacts for future time which we are not in a position to assess. Beer's Viable System Model (1985) addresses this point with its emphasis on information management. The VSM calls for an internal model of the organisation within the meta-management and for abandonment of the traditional functional silos or stovepipes of management. This is drawn on in Beckford (2016).

Suggesting that management teams are often little more than gentlemanly turf wars, Senge (following Beer and others) talks about the 'myth' of the management team. He recognises that appearances are often more important to people within organisations than reality. This means that often the management team is not a team at all, particularly when under pressure. In reality each member is fighting to defend his own credibility and position in adversity and, often, polite divisions are drawn between areas of responsibility which simply avoid the potential for conflict, rather than resolving tensions and developing mechanisms for working together as would be the case in a real team environment. By definition, members of a team can only win as a team, never as individuals – thus all of their efforts are directed to that end. We then end with what Argyris (cited by Senge, 1990) calls 'skilled incompetence'; 'teams full of people who are incredibly proficient at keeping themselves from learning'.

All readers will be familiar with these issues within their organisations. Senge requires that the familiarity is made within ourselves, a much more difficult task.

18.2.2   *The five disciplines*

Senge proposes that in order to overcome our difficulties with organisations and learning, we must adopt five disciplines, that is, become disciples of five beliefs.

Readers of this book will be familiar with the ideas of systems thinking. Senge's work draws heavily on the theories and practice of Systems Dynamics developed by Jay Forrester (1961). Flood & Jackson (1991) offer a full critique of that approach. Here it is sufficient to say that the work studies the behaviour of non-linear dynamic systems.

Personal mastery refers to the discipline of personal growth and personal learning. It demands of the individual an open-minded, inquiring approach leading to them creating their own future. Taking into account here the critical systems commitment to 'sociological awareness', the extent to which personal mastery is achievable will be a product of the capabilities and the cultural and educational background of the individual.

Mental models are formed because it is clearly impossible to know in finite detail all there is to know – our minds carry only abstractions from reality. These are necessarily more limited

---

Box 18.3   The five disciplines

Five disciplines:

Discipline 1)   Systems thinking;

Discipline 2)   Personal mastery;

Discipline 3)   Mental models;

Discipline 4)   Shared vision;

Discipline 5)   Team learning.

than the full richness of reality and while Beer (1985) suggests they are 'neither true nor false but more or less useful', Wilson (2002) questions the extent to which we can be truly conscious of our mental models. Problems arise when the models are significantly flawed, which is often the case, or when it is forgotten that they are simply models, and become perceived as reality itself. In these cases reliance on them is certain to be equally flawed. Senge suggests that learning to unfreeze and regenerate our mental models of the world is critical.

Shared vision is the call for all stakeholders in the organisation to have a common (or unitary) view of what the organisation is and what is to be achieved. Senge suggests that when there is shared vision then everyone desires the same things. To achieve this the vision cannot be 'handed down from the mountain' like the Ten Commandments as is so often the case, but must be built from the ground. This calls for the sort of participative approaches espoused by Checkland (SSM, 1981), Ackoff (IP, 1981), Beer (Syntegration, 1994) and Ulrich (CSH, 1983).

Team learning does not easily occur but is driven by a number of key characteristics. Senge suggests that the team members must have first embraced the other four disciplines already described. The first key characteristic is alignment (the shared vision); the team can accomplish little unless there is a commitment to the same outcomes. Second is the need to think and consider 'insightfully' [sic] about complex issues. Third is the need for co-ordinated action, here Senge refers to championship sports teams and jazz ensembles enjoined in 'operational trust'. Finally there is recognition of the need for the team's effectiveness to be spilled over into other connected (and usually) subordinate teams. This final point reflects the concept of recursion from the systems literature.

Holding all of these insights together is one, so far unstated, requirement. That is the need for effective communication, both vertically and horizontally throughout the organisation. Effective communication requires a subtlety of approach often absent from daily dialogues. It means effective listening as well as effective speaking. It sometimes requires discussion and at other times direction. It does not mean the generation of conflict or the adopting, as is so often the case, of rooted, entrenched positions, nor reliance on dogma or ideology. These ways of 'communicating' lead more often to breakdown and obfuscation or unsatisfactory compromise, which conflict with the other disciplines.

18.3   Quality and learning

This brief section seems now almost redundant. The whole basis of the pursuit of quality rests in the idea of learning, in finding ways of carrying out activities so that the outputs of an organisation more nearly match the requirements of its customers. If the same mistakes are repeated, then clearly no learning is occurring and no quality improvement is being attained. The kaizen philosophy demands improvement in all processes all of the time. Learning is implicit in this. It can then be argued that any organisation successfully pursuing quality is also learning, and any organisation pursuing learning is also improving quality. The two words imply each other in the organisational context; the organisation needs to be structured in a way which makes this possible.

Summary

This chapter has given a brief introduction to the idea of organisational learning and the 'learning organisation' according to Senge. Readers should refer to the works suggested in this chapter to further develop their understanding and knowledge.

KEY LEARNING POINTS

Organisational learning

The organisation must be structured to:

   Interact with the present more efficiently
   Monitor and anticipate the future
   Manage the interaction of the two

Organisational learning is NOT about data mining and knowledge management but about structural and behavioural adaptation

Senge's learning organisation

Key definition:

a learning organisation is one engaged in an iterative, circular process of evolution.

The seven disabilities:

   I am my position;
   The enemy is out there;
   The illusion of taking charge;
   The fixation on events;
   The parable of the boiling frog;
   The delusion of learning from experience;
   The myth of the management team.

The five disciplines:

Systems thinking, Personal mastery, Mental models, Shared vision, Team learning

Organisational learning means adaptation of individual and collective behaviour

Learning implies quality implies learning

Question

Compare and contrast the 'learning' models of the quality gurus with that of Senge's learning organisation.

19 Service quality management

'The idea of using skills to assure quality is not new
(consider the medieval craft guilds)'

Beckford & Dudley, 1998

Introduction

In previous editions the ideas of this chapter were presented as 'Skills Based Quality Management'. They have been further revised to deal more widely with the issue of service quality management as a whole and further connected to the notion of the Intelligent Organisation (Beckford, 2016). The original chapter, underpinned by an understanding of organisational cybernetics (Beckford, 1993), drew on an international series of seminars aimed at introducing a fundamentally different approach to quality management for the service and professional sectors. The ideas were subsequently developed into a paperless Quality Management System compliant with ISO 9000:2000.

Quality is an emergent property of a 'system' or organisation achievable through three dimensions of knowledge. Management of the whole system enables the delivery of quality products and services, however 'quality' may be defined. The three dimensions of knowledge considered are:

- Know Why: Purpose, Outcomes, Vision, Values;
- Know How: Behaviours, Attitudes, Skills and competences;
- Know What: Systems and processes.

Considering these dimensions this chapter seeks to reflect the idea that no problem of quality can be solved through a single approach or paradigm but only through an integrated, systemic approach that 'solves' the problem in multiple dimensions simultaneously. This is because in altering any one of the three dimensions we necessarily impart tension to the others, meaning that they too must change or else the tension will cause the organisation to revert to an approximation of its previous state. Quality must be considered as one amongst a number of performance parameters that any organisation, seeking its own survival, must achieve. As I have said elsewhere (Beckford, 2016):

> Performance, effectiveness, is measured by the extent to which an organisation fulfils its purpose. ... Sustainable performance is not then one-dimensional but multi-dimensional with dynamic interdependence between the dimensions

Typically, 'the quality project' becomes tired, superseded or subsumed into another, at which time the quality issues which had been suppressed re-emerge. The dominant approaches explored earlier in the book, despite the intent of their originators, largely address the issue of quality at the level of 'symptom' rather than disease. They tend, though not absolutely, to deal with quality in isolation from other factors. Like painting rotten wood, these solutions might 'solve' the problem of presentation but do not address the underlying lack of management understanding which leads to service and product quality issues. Is it the most effective way to sell a consultancy service related to quality though? It is much more comfortable for the manager to buy into something which locates the problem somewhere other than in his or her own decisions.

The critiques of the quality gurus identified that none fully addressed the question of how to properly engage senior management with the idea of pursuing a 'quality' strategy. While each talks about it as necessary, they say little or nothing of how to achieve it. 'Know why' lies at the heart of this. Many organisations pursue quality (and other) strategies as a response to environmental change either in the regulatory regime . . .

'you must have ISO 9000 in order to tender for this business'

or the market . . .

'everyone else in our market is pursuing quality, we had better do it too'.

In neither case is quality being pursued as a good thing in its own right. Knowing why is really asking about the purpose of the organisation, the reason it exists and the need it aims to fulfil and designing a strategy which ensures that the purpose is fulfilled in the most effective manner. Knowing why gives focus on organisational purpose in the context of which, quality methods, tools and techniques are useful. Without such clarity of purpose they are relatively sterile or limited in benefit.

Systems methods already outlined in the preceding chapters can be useful for this determination of purpose. Checkland's 'Soft Systems Methodology' (1981) is a seven step methodology designed to uncover the objectives and desires of the human actors in any situation and, through semi-structured discussion, allow the generation and alignment of individual and organisational purposes. The process of this methodology is laid out in figure 19.1.

Similarly, organisational cybernetics (chapter 16) enables the diagnosis of the current purposes of the organisation. It achieves this through a structured analysis that uses the 'Viable Systems Model' (Beer, 1979, 1981, 1985) as an idealised solution with which the perceived reality of the situation can be compared. This allows identification of what purposes the organisation is currently capable of fulfilling, comparing that with the desires and objectives of the 'owners' and defining a decision space within which management can make choices about the future and present of the organisation.

For any strategy to succeed it is vital that the actors in the organisation have defined their purposes, explored their values and beliefs (the things that bind them together) and, in the context of those definitions, have decided what success means. Success must be defined in a way that has shared meaning for both the customer and all members of the organisation, giving direction and purpose to all the decisions that they make. I am reminded of the tale of the three bricklayers. On being questioned, the first said 'I lay bricks', the second, with a broader view, said 'I build walls', the third, understanding the purpose and vision of the organisation, said 'I build cathedrals'. Once a determination on purpose has been made, senior managers must always act and speak consistently with it – this demonstrates their commitment to the purpose. It has the beneficial side effect of simplifying many management decisions since all that has to be asked is 'does this decision or action contribute to or detract from the fulfilment of our purpose?'

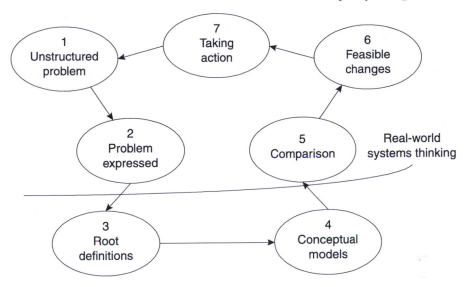

Figure 19.1 Soft Systems Methodology.

The second dimension of knowledge is 'know how' – the skills, competences, behaviours and attitudes that will enable the formation of effective working groups or teams, and the application of those skills and competences to the delivery of services and products. Again, 'know why' creates the context in which the right tools and methods can be chosen (the 'know how') to support any particular strategy. These tools are widely written about in the quality and human resources literature and need not be explored here. It is vital that all the actors in the organisation have, or acquire, the blend of skills and talents necessary to achieve the purpose – and where they do not exist, the primary task of management is to facilitate their learning. This learning must be set in the context of the strategy.

'Know what' (systems and processes), with the application of skills and competences, can be designed to support the achievement of the purpose. Again, there are many tools and methods for system and process design. Clarity of purpose enables clarity of criteria for determining whether or not a system or process is effective. If it is a 'core' activity it should directly act to fulfil the purpose of the organisation. If it is an 'enabling' activity it should support the core activities. If it is neither 'core' nor 'enabling', it is discretionary – and it is legitimate to ask whether it is truly required.

Each of these three dimensions of knowledge, which are largely about understanding the 'model of self' (Beckford, 2016) of the organisation and its capacity to be sustainable, is now objectively measurable. Through them we can evaluate the effectiveness of the organisation and the extent to which it incurs 'muda' or waste in its operation. Quality, whichever definition is chosen, emerges from the interactions of the three dimensions of knowledge; it is not isolated from them or a function of any one dimension.

If there is no clear definition of purpose or rationale for the existence of the organisation, no understanding of the need it exists to fulfil, then it is impossible to know whether quality is being achieved in its pursuit – because quality, along with other measurements of performance, can only be understood in the context of that purpose. Similarly, having the most highly skilled and competent workforce is only relevant when the requirements of the task (the 'know what') make effective and efficient use of those skills. Any skills across the

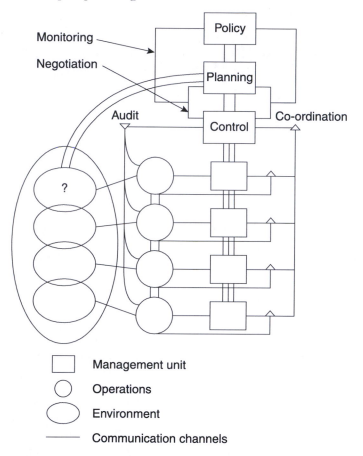

Figure 19.2 The viable system model.

organisation not required for the fulfilment of the task are wasted. Effective management would be seeking to exploit those skills, by redesigning processes, and thereby reducing the waste. Systems and processes must also be designed in the context of the purpose to be fulfilled. Any unutilised process, or system not focused on the achievement of the organisational purpose, is wasted.

The task of management is to recognise and embrace the tensions that will always exist between these three dimensions and manage them in such a way that, over time, the purpose is fulfilled and waste in each is minimised.

19.1   A service quality problem

The service sector has not yet fully come to grips with the quality challenge. While the drive in the manufacturing sector can be seen to have delivered substantial gains, this has not been the case in services.

There are for me two basic reasons for this. First, quality has been regarded widely, in both theory and practice, as conformance to specification or fitness for purpose or use. Quality is, for many, equated with standardisation, the inverse measure of deviation from a

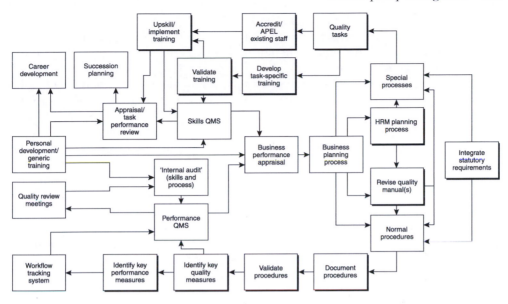

Figure 19.3 The skills based Quality Management System.

specification rather than the warm rosy glow of the experience of a good thing. Second, in service quality there is often no tangible product. Service, and therefore service quality, is an emergent property of the process of its provision.

The interaction of these points has driven the proliferation of paper based quality management systems which emulate those of manufacturing in that they are process oriented. For the achievement of service quality they are unusable. The attempt to capture the richness of service provision in process chart format makes them sufficiently large and complex as to be unintelligible. The fact is that no system which is internally consistent can completely capture all the complexity of the organisation. Hence these process charts are incapable of achieving the purpose for which they were designed. A quality management system that is incapable of delivering its intended outcome is, by its own definition, poor quality. What is still needed is a re-thinking of quality and quality management appropriate to the service sector. This re-thinking is laid out in figure 19.3.

This figure, with Business Performance Appraisal and Planning at its heart, shows the chain of relationships throughout the business that enable performance. This almost circular causal chain represents a form of organisational homeostat showing how each area impacts on each other and that ultimately all loops back to impact performance. The requirements of the lower half of the figure are well resolved in much of the quality literature; they are requirements concerned with tasks and procedures. The upper half of the figure is concerned with skills – the knowledge, talents and capabilities that individuals bring to bear on the fulfilment of their duties. Historically this has been neglected.

19.2   A Service Quality Management System (SQMS)

The essence of SQMS is simple. The professions in particular, and the service sector in general, rely for service quality on the professionalism and judgement of the individual employee or partner. Not everything can be proceduralised and, in the service sector, the customer often falls through the gap between alternative procedural outcomes. The only way to solve the problem of quality in the service sector is to employ appropriately trained, educated staff and grant them the freedom necessary to do the job.

SQMS is an approach to quality and to the construction of an effective and manageable Quality Management System (QMS) based on the development and recording of the skill base (including behaviours) of a service organisation and its systems and processes in the context of its purposes:

- Effective means that the QMS provides the information necessary for the maintenance and improvement of service quality;
- Manageable means, quite simply, small.

Reflecting the three dimensions of knowledge, is the fundamental belief that, in the service context, the complexities of service provision and the improvement of its quality cannot be modelled in a once and for all manner in the style of the industrial model of quality control. Such a model will be largely ineffective. The traditional, documented procedure based approach to quality management is guaranteed ultimately to fail.

In order to be effective, any system designed to maintain quality must explicitly recognise not only the nature of applied skill (which calls for judgement), but provide robustness in practice and embed it in a structure both sensitive to new data and intelligent enough to learn. Similarly, service quality must embrace the distinction between delivering process outputs, which is skill oriented, and achieving customer outcomes, which relies on a synthesis of process, skill and behaviour to stimulate a relationship.

Processes, whether in manufacturing or services, are designed to secure a particular output, i.e. the delivery of the product or service. However, other than at a purely transactional level or where there is no human involvement (ticket machines?), there is a service element which falls outside the process. This service element exists at two levels. The first level is the skill level of service – were the right words used and so on. The second level is about behaviour, the emotional interaction between the server and the customer. The emotional interaction is the one where the service outcome as opposed to the process output is achieved. Emotional engagement is what ensures that the customer comes back and is a key element that cannot be captured and documented in a traditional Quality Management System.

Service quality is about people and process

At 7am I walked from my hotel to the nearest supermarket to buy a newspaper. The self-service till demanded that I either buy a bag or place my own on the scales (who needs a bag for a newspaper); there wasn't a 'no bag required' option. I duly placed my lap top bag (5 kg with assorted chargers and cables!) on the scales at which point the till panicked (bag too heavy) and called for a member of staff. Now the point of self-service tills is that the supermarket can reduce the numbers of staff by outsourcing the work to the customers . . .

. . .

After a two minute wait a member of staff ambled round the corner and immediately paid attention to the person stood at the next till (who had just arrived), not bothering to find out who should be served first.

I placed the necessary money on the till, called to the member of staff that I had done so and left. In this instance not only did the mechanised process fail (the lack of a 'no bag' option) but the human interaction failed ('Good morning, now who was first?').

While the 'process' was complete (I successfully bought a newspaper) the 'service' was non-existent. The message the supermarket conveyed most effectively is that it does not care about its customers. The process it put in place to enable customer self-service failed at the first hurdle; the process to provide a member of staff when needed failed because the particular member of staff either did not care who should be served first, or more probably, had not been trained to find out.

And, as I walked away, I could only imagine staff member saying to the other customer, 'what a rude man'.

Will I use them again, probably not, on the next occasion when they are the choice I will read my newspaper on line.

The point?

The supermarket has attempted to improve quality, by which IT means consistency, reliability and reduced costs, by implementing an automated system, a manufacturing based service model in which each transaction is cheaper for them. I wonder how many such cheap transactions are no longer happening because they have forgotten that 'service' is the core of the supermarket experience and the customers think:

'well, if they can't be bothered then neither can I'

... and are either not shopping at all, are shopping elsewhere or are sourcing the service on line where they have no real expectation of 'service'.

The next morning I read the paper on my smartphone.

In addition, the SQMS must be small and unintrusive enough to be willingly used. To achieve this it must be transparent to those who use and manage it. Such a system necessarily involves the planning, intelligence gathering, human resources and operational levels of the organisation in an integrated whole. The alternative is to continue to create the systems which have, in so many service organisations, fallen into disrepute and disuse.

Given the capabilities of contemporary information technology, it is only sensible that the method outlined takes advantage of this. This choice of technological platform for the approach is a convenience rather than a necessity. The concepts are independent of the choice of information media.

19.3   The overall structure

SQMS is based in a wider model of organisation rooted in the Viable Systems Model (see chapter 16) and elaborated in the three dimensions of knowledge mentioned above. Figure 19.3 illustrated those parts of the organisation that relate directly to quality, while Beckford (2016) integrates the whole. The process of delivering quality is the result of the interactions of highly inter-connected sub-processes, and it is important to note that many of these continue to be susceptible to traditional performance monitoring and control methods. The model is made more robust by this and by their utilisation in an intelligent manner. This element of the model is represented by the flows in the lower half of the diagram.

When the links to the environment available through the business planning process are activated (why are we here? what are we going to do?), the whole model represented by the diagram provides the ability for the organisation to learn from its experience, changing its behaviours and even its values over time in relation to environmental (market) and internal changes. The diagram is a simplification of a highly complex process containing many circular and self-referential sub-processes. Unfortunately, managers all too often argue for the simple – 'give me simple propositions, simple charts and simple answers'. Unfortunately these do not work!

Section 6 of the ISO 9001:2000 standard was the first attempt to explicitly deal with the effective management of skills, although this was also possible under the 'special processes' clause of the 1994 standard, though the potential of this was usually ignored by quality experts and auditors. Now under section 7 of ISO 9001:2015, the standard has arguably gone backwards since 2000, reinforcing the process and compliance focus but not meaningfully addressing the behavioural or relationship dimensions of service quality.

The distinguishing factor of the SQMS approach is that it explicitly uses skills as the basis of process quality with the organisational processes themselves being captured at a higher, less detailed, level. This means that task and procedure descriptions are minimised or even eradicated in many situations.

The quality of the outputs in this approach is assured through the determination of the abilities and competence needed to deliver the service; a process known as 'qualification'. Once a process is 'qualified', formal quality assurance is achieved by ensuring that only those operators whose skills match those needed for the special process are permitted to work on it. This, though embryonic and static, is the beginning of a skills based QMS and is entirely consistent with the relevant ISO standard. Where we go further is embracing the outcome for the customer, which must include not just the service process but how he or she experiences the service process. How does it make them feel?

The traditional attraction of process control is based on the premise that the better you control the process the less error, and the less error the higher the quality. As service is a process, the less error in the process the higher the provision of service quality. How can this be achieved?

All services are 'special processes' in the language of ISO 9000:1994. Fundamental process control can be achieved by recognising and treating them as such. A further chapter – or even whole book – could be written on the interpretation of 'control' – it is not the purpose of this text to explore it. Readers should be aware that, in this instance, control refers to creating a situation where the individual can be self-controlled because he or she shares the objectives of the organisation, has the skills necessary to complete the task and the autonomy required to adapt service delivery to the needs of the individual customer.

Services are delivered by people. Therefore process control in the context of service provision is the control of the behaviour of the people providing the service. Appropriate behaviour, assuming the absence of malice, is behaviour which is likely to achieve the purpose of the service being provided. This is assured by ensuring that the provider of the service has the skills, knowledge, competences and adopts the values necessary to the provision of the service.

Services are also delivered to people. People (especially clients, patients, passengers, customers) vary, therefore no two service provision events are ever identical. Even assuming an impossible situation such that the education of the service provider ensures that they are consistent in approach, there will be as many variations on a single service as there are recipients. This is why the complexities of service provision arise and judgement is required which demands autonomy for the operators (Beckford, 2016). It is the potential variety of the situations that arise in service provision which, of necessity, defeat the traditional process engineering approach to quality management. It is not possible to model all possible situations in advance; therefore it is not possible to specify all activities and solutions in advance. It is not then possible to chart the process fully in advance – not even with charts a mile long – and it is the very attempt that creates bureaucracy.

In contrast to machines, people are extremely good at dealing with complexity. This ability to deal with complex situations and make sensible decisions in the absence of complete data (to exercise judgement) only becomes prominent when the people involved have become skilled, educated or trained for the task at hand, have a clear understanding of the purposes to be fulfilled and are imbued with the necessary values. They do the right thing right because it is the right thing, not because the process says so!

Utilising this human ability to deal with complexity has two distinct advantages over the traditional 'chart, measure and count' approach in the assurance of quality in service provision. The first is that it significantly reduces the amount of paper necessary to the operation of the system. Quality relevant procedures can be stated in a descriptive form, i.e.

The ideal situation in this model is:

- **Input:** Client with problem;
- **Process:** Negotiate solution to problem;
- **Output:** Client without problem.

And whilst it must be accepted that this ideal will be difficult to achieve in some cases, complicating the documentation of the process to be undertaken will not make it any less difficult. Indeed, the production of rigid procedure charts (which as has been argued cannot entirely capture any situation) may give a false impression of the operation of the process, and may very well remove the things that would allow a solution to be reached – negotiation, informed choice and compromise – creating a 'Jobsworth' mentality. The second advantage to be gained runs in parallel with the first. By ensuring that individual service providers have the skills necessary to carry out the tasks they have been set, it is possible to devolve responsibility and to increase autonomy. That, in general, reduces direct supervision costs, enhances the sense of responsibility of the individual affected and provides the opportunity for him or her to learn. They will also make mistakes; the measurement of success is in the rate at which mistakes are reduced!

Because professionals draw on a shared body of core knowledge (see figure 19.5) in their decision making processes, it is possible to predict the range of solutions professionally available to the front line providers with a degree of accuracy. This standardises the outcomes at the level of 'client perceived quality' without the necessity of standardising the potential solutions available to non-standard clients.

The professionalism implicit in this model allows the quality of the outputs of the organisation to be 'process controlled' rather than 'post delivery inspected' (see figure 19.6), a meaningless activity in the service context as it can only ever be complaint management. This is because the evaluation of the service provided using a mechanistic process is possible

Figure 19.4 A process.

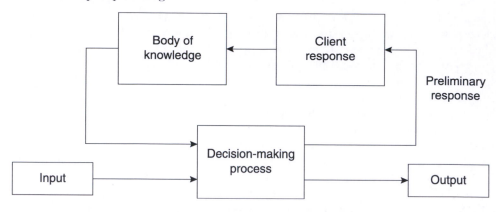

Figure 19.5 Applying skills.

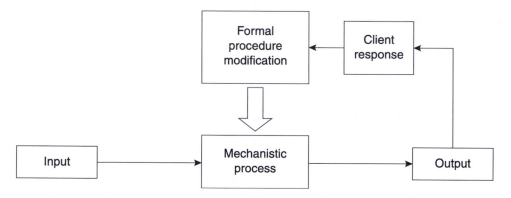

Figure 19.6 Applying procedures.

only after the event, rather than as an integral part of it. By defining the skills necessary to the fulfilment of the task:

- the complexity of the procedural system necessary for its control is reduced, process definition is transformed into a statement of professional competence (less paper);
- the level of managerial and supervisory intervention is reduced, tasks become owned by the front line provider (less overhead cost);
- the level of perceived autonomy at the individual level is increased and greater personal responsibility is taken for the delivery of quality (lower alienation from task);
- the process becomes more flexible, the potential for client perception of quality is increased (fewer complaints).

19.4   The model for a systemic QMS

In its purest form the creation of a systemic QMS is very simple:

- Identify the tasks to be undertaken;
- Identify the skills and behaviours necessary to undertake the tasks;
- Ensure that only those people that have these skills and exhibit those behaviours undertake the task.

In practice, however, each of the three stages will contain sub-tasks and require ongoing operational validation. Identification of the tasks to be undertaken is, effectively, a mapping of those processes that are vital to service provision. Outcomes of this stage of the approach should be:

- key tasks identified;
- relevant flow diagrams produced;
- statement of those tasks that cannot be reduced to flow diagrams;
- identification of tasks which are routine or frequently repeated and thus susceptible to standard performance measures.

The selection of key tasks tends to be a negotiation process between the QMS designers and the users. It is advantageous to keep an open mind regarding the perception of what is and is not a key process; decisions made at this stage can return to haunt the intervention later on. A useful guide is to recognise that key tasks are those which either (Beckford, 2016):

- Generate value for clients and customers;
- Enable the value generating processes.

Selection of the processes for inclusion on the skills based side of the design process is based on a heuristic relating to the complexity of the charting necessary to map the process. If it is possible to achieve significant complexity reduction through the acceptance of some minimal level of skill on the part of the operator, it can be assumed that there are also significant operational efficiency gains to be made by using a skills based approach to the quality assurance of the process (see figures 19.4 and 19.5).

The demands of the quality management model presented in figure 19.3 are satisfied by the outcomes of this stage of the approach through the production of:

- documentation of those processes that can be represented as linear flows, including control points and performance measures (figure 19.5);
- generic description of those processes that cannot be represented as linear flows but are 'routine', including control points and performance measures (figure 19.7);
- a statement of those processes that cannot be represented as linear flows and are 'non-routine'.

With the operational elements of the model defined (in the case of the linear processes) or described (in the case of non-linear processes) and performance measures stated, it is possible to move onto skills definition. It should be noted that the two assumptions in figures 19.7 and 19.8 are that the processes themselves are fixed. For the most part linear processes are input controlled and routine skills based processes are activity controlled.

The skills used in an organisation are categorised into three types:

- generic;
- role specific;
- professional.

Each of the skill types, and their level of development and importance to the operation of the organisation, have an impact on the type of QMS which is appropriate. This categorisation, shown in figure 19.9, indicates a model of the inter-relationships between the varying skills

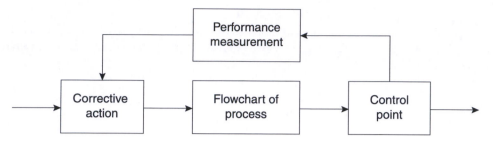

Figure 19.7 Performance management.

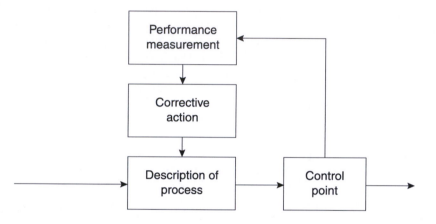

Figure 19.8 Performance improvement.

available in a service organisation. It also provides a basis for deciding the extent to which a planned education and development programme can be used to enhance performance and, therefore, the type of QMS appropriate to support it.

In practice, the effective service organisations will rely on a balanced utilisation of all three skill types. Each sharing the common characteristic that, as the operations of the organisation move toward a dependence on skills typical of the upper half of the diagram, it will become increasingly difficult to control quality using the more traditional charting approach. A quality management system which aims to support the improvement of the performance of the organisation will focus on role performance. Hence the skills baseline in any organisation is the ability necessary to follow the process flow charts.

However, as the organisation moves away from the baseline, to the 'non–linear but routine' tasks, the skill necessary to absorb the complexity generated moves onto the lower end, and to the left, of the scale. Such skill levels are consistent with the ability to operate competently within the established processes. This competence within processes is reflected throughout the left of the diagram. As the operator becomes more skilled, the imperative changes from the achievement of objectives to the setting of these objectives.

Tasks in this category might be typified by such roles as telesales or help–desk operation. They are susceptible to performance measures such as 'How many?', 'How often?', 'How long?' or 'How accurate?' The human operators are trained to deal with the procedural aspects of the task and have some limited discretion to deal with 'non–standard' occurrences.

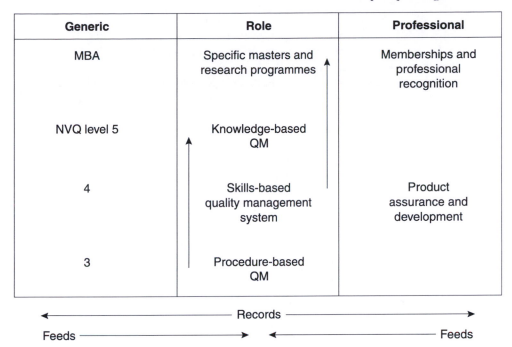

Figure 19.9 The hierarchy of skills.

As the individual moves up this scale s/he contributes to the organisation through their management or administrative skills.

To the right of the scale the emphasis is very different; it is on the consideration of what the processes can or should be. Professional knowledge brings with it the capacity for critical reasoning around the structures through which the service is provided, and forms the basis of the non-linear, non-routine skill set. At this end of the scale the imperative is not 'What are the objectives?' but 'What are suitable indicators to measure the objectives by?'

It is not possible to set commercial performance indicators for professional skills, as the focus of these skills is based on the integrity of the professional discipline. The professional contributes to performance through the appropriate application (and in some cases extension) of the body of professional knowledge to the furtherance of organisational objectives. To a large extent the only performance indicator applicable to the professional is the performance of the core product in the market.

Choice of skill type (i.e. generic, role specific, professional) should be based on the contribution to the process and will provide (in conjunction with the appraisal process and personal career ambitions) indicators as to the appropriate development strategy for individual role incumbents.

At this point it should be possible to assign 'qualifications' or skills lists to the roles identified. The lists should also identify those qualifications where possession is a legal requirement. Ensuring the skills-to-task link has two main elements:

- skills assessment;
- records management.

The skills possessed assessment section of the link comprises the appraisal process of the organisation. Operational service quality can then be assured through the creation of an auditable documentation system which demonstrates that the skill sets of operators at least meet the skill set necessary to carry out the specified task.

The idea is that organisations possess a body of skills held by their personnel and a set of skills needed which have been identified through role analysis. It is relatively simple to construct a relational database to carry out this task and to extend its utility to the creation of personal development plans, pre-selection for internal promotions and the generation of job specifications for recruitment purposes. At its most simple, the database need comprise no more than two tables, each containing a set of triples.

The adoption of this approach to quality management has a clear impact on the role of the HR department in a large organisation. It becomes very clearly the focus of a strategic operation whose role is to ensure that the individual and aggregate skill set of the employees is at least equivalent to the needs of the organisation all of the time. This approach has implications for training, recruitment, promotion and retention policies – but is the key to consistent service quality. Strategic human resource development, as a sub-set of the wider strategic function, forms the link between current and future performance by managing the skills base of the organisation.

In concert with all this, and beyond the scope of this book to properly explore, is the need for the values espoused by the organisation to be shared by all of its employees and demonstrated through their behaviour in interaction with each other and with customers. Where values are not shared the organisation is doomed to failure; similarly, if the values of the organisation are abusive, neglectful or dismissive of the customers then the system will fail.

19.5   SQM review

For an organisation to maximise its gain from investment in QMS certification it must have the lightest possible negative impact on the organisation whilst generating the maximum business value. It should not be cumbersome or bureaucratic and must generate more benefit than it generates cost. In particular it must directly act to enhance rather than inhibit the performance of the organisation in every respect. Experience shows that most fail to achieve this.

The SQM approach differs from traditional systems in a number of ways. First, it is rooted in the purposes of the organisation and based on a dynamic, learning organisation approach, driven by events within the process and linking directly to business planning, staff performance and staff development processes.

The SQMS, like the Intelligent Organisation (Beckford, 2016) learns at two levels. First, it promotes learning by individuals, the improvement in skills and competences which closes the 'know how' gap. Second, it stimulates learning at the organisational level, adapting itself on the basis of recorded experience and enabling informed, structured adaptation of the organisation. The second key difference is that the approach directly supports the business or organisational needs. It is driven by business performance appraisal and planning, operational processes and active skills management, and feeds the outputs directly back into them and links directly to the achievement of purpose.

The Systemic QMS represents a major challenge to the dominant methods of addressing the problem of quality. It has significant benefit in a service environment as well as providing new insights to manufacturing management quality programmes. The SQMS is best adopted in an organisation which is prepared to embrace the organisational and philo-sophical changes associated with the pursuit of true effectiveness.

Summary

This chapter has given insight to a wholly new approach to systemic quality management focused especially on the service sector. Readers should refer to the work of Beckford & Dudley (1998a, 1998b, 1999), Dudley (2000) and Beckford (2016) to extend and develop their knowledge.

KEY LEARNING POINTS

Services are different to manufacturing

Skills Based Quality Management recognises:
Management and development of professional skills is the key to service quality;
Procedures can never substitute for human interaction and judgement;
Skills are acceptable as the foundation of an ISO 9000:2000 quality management system.

SQM is:
Tested in a variety of sectors
In need of further development

Question

Compare the skills based approach to quality with that taken by your own organisation.

Part four

Quality in practice: A case study

User guide

In the first three parts of this book a substantial platform has been developed for thinking about quality theory and the dominant methods. Those parts have been built on a theoretical platform with practical insights provided through the vignettes; it has presented theory in practice.

In this edition, part four continues the approach of its predecessor and, through an extended case study, presents practice in theory – embedding descriptions and critique of methods, tools and techniques as they are called for in the telling of the story. The story is 'real' in as much as all of the issues described actually occurred – fortunately, they did not all happen to one business!

Methods, tools and techniques are introduced in context, their strengths, weaknesses and utility considered – but they will not be fully described or evaluated. Each has a supporting reference base through which it can be fully explored, and you are encouraged to examine the original sources for a detailed understanding of application.

As with parts one, two and three, part four can be used in two ways. It can provide a straightforward critical introduction to those tools for achieving quality, which are derived from the various theories already explained. For those with a practical focus this section provides a comprehensive tool kit, enabling the pursuit of a quality initiative in a way that is both practically informed and theoretically sound.

20 Western Paper: A problem of quality?

'Now do THIS!'

Stafford Beer, 1985

Introduction

This chapter sets out the background to Western Paper, an extended case study. It begins the process of discovery, which is the first stage in any consulting process. For the avoidance of doubt, Western Paper does exist, but not by that name, and it does not have all the problems and issues that will be ascribed to it. The actual situation has been extended with additions from other cases as necessary to ensure the presence of those characteristics necessary for completeness in the study. Names and places have been changed throughout and any remaining similarity to real people or places is entirely coincidental.

20.1 Background

The following information was discovered during an initial telephone conversation with the GM of Western Paper.

Western Paper is a small company within the UK Division of a global paper producer and distributor. It operates on two sites, one for production and another some seven miles away for storage and conversion (the breaking down of large reels of paper into customer specific products).

On the production site there is also a small enabling (Beckford, 2016) function with Accounting, HR, Health and Safety and Sales. Production planning forms part of the sales office. The paper mill is run by the Operations Director, and there is a General Manager responsible for both Western Paper and another mill, Coastal Paper, about 50 miles away. The GM splits his week between the two locations.

Western Paper has for some time been struggling to achieve its performance targets and its continued existence is under threat from the Group level. Discussions about whether to close or sell the business are active although there is a hold on any decision while the GM develops and applies a turnaround plan. The production and sales workforce are well established and stable while the conversion workforce are mainly new or casual labour, and the facility is very old. The Finance Director has been in post for a couple of years but does not have a background in manufacturing and has proved unable to establish a meaningful financial information platform on which to make decisions. Production volume is erratic, quality is very variable and the business has a very low 'on time, in full' (OTIF) figure for deliveries. Late deliveries cause complaints from customers who depend on the mill for their own production and sales. These complaints lead the Sales Director to insert additional, out of run order, colour and weight changes in the production flow which causes both delays to other planned work and reduction in overall volume due to the product changeovers.

The Operations Director is working the plant hard to produce as much volume as possible (something that could be achieved by reducing the number and range of products and increasing batch sizes) while the Sales Director, fighting in a challenging market against cheaper imported paper, is pushing in the opposite direction, pursuing low volume, highly specialized products. The single paper machine on which these have to be produced is both small and old. The company has been starved of capital investment for several years due partly to its own poor financial performance, partly because its much larger sister organisations, with which it competes for capital, are producing stronger business cases.

Western Paper is the largest local employer with several generations of some families employed. In fact some jobs have been passed from parent to child. The impact of failure on the local economy and on some families would be substantial, while the dominant thinking is that 'the mill has always provided work for our family and always will'.

The GM, an experienced paper maker, is seeking help to understand the challenges faced and to develop and implement a plan to save the business.

The outcome of the telephone call was an invitation to propose a scheme of work initially to investigate the situation, diagnose the problems and resolve the issues.

20.2   Initial reflections

This is clearly a dynamic and complex problem situation. It exhibits a number of characteristics reflective of complex systems, substantial variety, questions of purpose and intent, human issues, ongoing change, inadequate information. Working from the story heard so far, it is clear that a 'scheme of work' that properly addresses the range of issues identified will be quite extensive. Thinking about what is now known highlights that there are:

- *Cultural and relationship issues with the workforce*: partly historical and embedded and partly arising from the current threat of closure and management behaviour.
- *Structural concerns*: Western Paper is a relatively small organisation embedded as a subsidiary of a global organisation. It is inevitable that any work will need to consider the relationship between the two and respond to its demands and will need to take account of the Western Paper Head Office functions. The internal organisation structure of the whole is unclear at the outset, but it is likely that this too will need to be considered in resolving any performance and management problems.
- *Management concerns*: the General Manager, who is relatively newly appointed, will have inherited issues from his predecessors, is facing the need to secure his own position and has the additional challenge of managing Coastal Paper so only spending half (or thereabouts) of his time at Western.
- *Productivity concerns*: clearly the current sales and production strategies are inconsistent with each other and whilst perhaps not the cause of the issues, are a contributory factor. It may also be the case that the staffing of the business with mainly families drawn from a close local community may limit the available skill set and knowledge base. There may be some resistance to delivering improvement. Similarly the 'conversion' site is clearly a significant challenge. The impression gained from the conversation is that there are substantial productivity challenges at that location as well.

- *Viability issues*: the General Manager is concerned to secure the long-term viability of Western Paper while recognising that the business is under threat. It is apparent from the information provided that the business critical problems to be addressed are distributed amongst production, conversion and sales and that decision is needed about the initial focus of attention.

This is not then a simple problem of quality; indeed, quality has not been mentioned so far. There are undoubtedly aspects of the problem situation that lend themselves to a traditional, quality type approach – but given the range of issues, which one could be sensibly chosen?

The methods of Crosby, Deming, Feigenbaum and Oakland would all lend themselves to key aspects of the production issues and the workforce engagement process, while Ishikawa, Ohno, Shingo and Taguchi would all have much to say about the pure operational aspects – however, none of these could support an initial intervention.

The methodology of Total Systems Intervention (TSI) (Flood & Jackson, 1991) (figure 20.1) might be adopted. However, to be consistent with the TSI methodology the project would have to give primacy to one dimension of the problem situation, necessitating solving the identified problems in series. This situation demands a parallel approach – one in which several aspects of the problem situation can be resolved simultaneously.

The requested intervention (or scheme of work) will need to be designed around a whole systems, synthesized, approach. At this stage of the process the prime candidates for this are Soft Systems Methodology (Checkland, 1981) which will cater for, at least, the initial stage of engagement with the Directors. This can be deployed in parallel with Organisational Cybernetics (Beer, 1985) using Beer's Viable Systems Diagnosis (Beer, 1985; Beckford, 1993, 2016) which can focus on the organisational and informational issues and provide a base for exploring the process issues – for which another tool, Process Analysis, will be required.

To obtain the information necessary to understand the problem situation and to address all of the interconnected problems, it will be necessary to use, initially at least, the first stage of

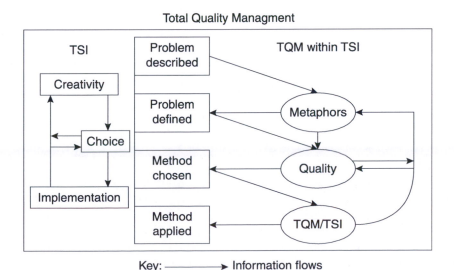

Figure 20.1 TQM within TSI within TQM.

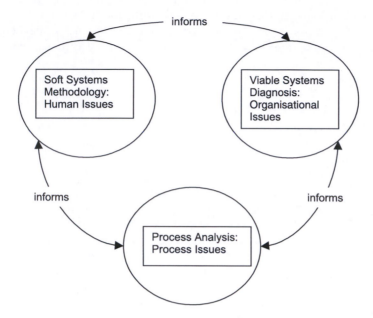

Figure 20.2 Tools for the first intervention.

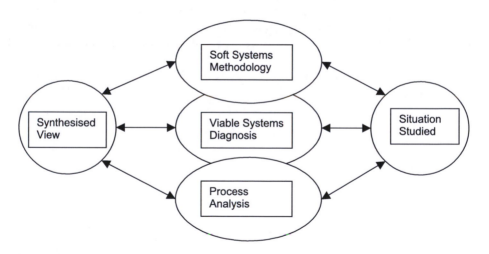

Figure 20.3 Synthesising the diagnosis.

Soft Systems Methodology, Organisational Cybernetics and Process Analysis concurrently (figure 20.2). The process of enquiry for each will inform the others.

These different approaches, based on different views and assumptions about the nature of the world, will provide at least three perspectives on the nature of the problems to be solved. These views and assumptions can then be synthesised, through dialogue and discussion, into a single, very rich understanding of the situation (figure 20.3).

Soft Systems Thinking and Organisational Cybernetics have already been introduced; brief methodologies for their use are included in chapter 23. Readers seeking a deeper understanding of Viable Systems Diagnosis should refer to the work of Beckford (1993, 1995) and Beer (1985) and for Soft Systems Methodology, Checkland (1981). Process Analysis and a method for its application are outlined in chapter 21. For a fuller source readers should consider Kanji & Asher (1996) or the Six Sigma work of Eckes (2003) or Pande & Holpp (2002). This chapter will concentrate on the integrating framework.

20.3   Iterative methodology

It must be clear that the problems of Western Paper will not be solved with a single programme, solution, action or intervention. It can be argued in fact that to do so would be to prejudice the overall outcome before the multiple pathologies identified have been properly understood. It is clear that there are problems with both product and service quality but at best, addressing either in isolation from the other and the context in which both are contained would be unhelpful. It seems rather more as if they need to go through a series of interventions, each of which moves them one stage closer to 'solving the problem'. This will need to be designed to diagnose and validate the inter-related problems, develop a framework for their resolution and an implementation pathway.

VSMethod, figure 20.4, provides a process map for the conversation between Western Paper and the consultant. The purpose of the method is to develop, at the centre of the process, a shared model of the problem to be addressed; that is a single picture of the situation which expresses the viewpoints of all the relevant participants and the findings of the different methodologies. Achievement of this unified view enables the development of possible solutions and agreement about the next steps to be taken.

The method is based on enabling the participants to articulate their views and compare them with what is understood about idealised organisations (theoretical models

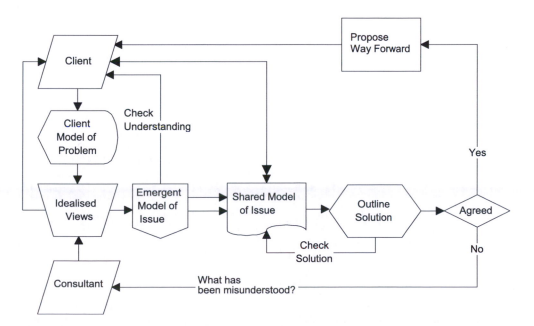

Figure 20.4 Developing a shared model.

of how organisations 'ought' to be if they are to be successful). These theoretical models can and should embrace all possible valid perspectives on the situation (a perspective is valid if it expresses the views of one or more participants) and appropriate levels of detail.

The initial outcome, the shared model of the problem, is the basis for action in the next stage – which might include further investigation and analysis, some direct improvement action, testing of possible solutions and so on. Figure 20.5 shows how the method cycles through a process of enquiry, testing/evaluating, reflecting (and re-affirming or modifying the chosen direction) and then taking further action. The figure shows four iterations – this is entirely arbitrary; the number of iterations is a function of the size and complexity of the problem situations being addressed.

Alert readers will have noticed that this method is in many ways reminiscent of the Shewart or Deming (PDCA) Cycle, Oakland's EPDCA Cycle and even ISO 9001:2015. However, there is a major difference. This method, unlike the others, explicitly includes a requirement on each cycle to re-engage with the relevant client and re-validate the shared model of the situation. This is vital; needs change and emerge, the organisation evolves, individuals change roles and perspectives and the external environment in which all of the activity is ultimately carried out is also dynamic. A reflective cycle which does not include refreshing the shared understanding will inevitably generate divergence between the optimum solution and that which, in the end, will be imposed rather than jointly developed.

The subsequent chapters of part four will follow the method outlined.

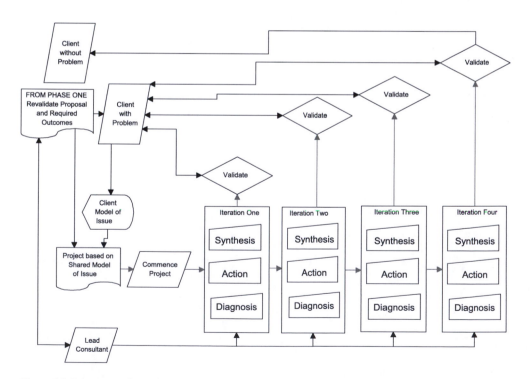

Figure 20.5 Iterative framework for action.

Summary

This chapter has introduced the problem situation at Western Paper and argued for an overarching, iterative methodology for addressing the issues raised. The next chapter will pursue the first iteration of the formal project.

KEY LEARNING POINTS

Client problems and issues do not come as neatly packaged as Academic and Consultants' methodologies

Selection of any one methodology to the exclusion of all others necessarily means that some aspects of the situation will not be considered or that others will obtain undue prominence.

A selection of methodologies, simultaneously applied, with their findings integrated through a rich dialogue will produce the broadest understanding.

An iterative methodology must include refreshing and re-affirming the shared model of the world developed in the initial investigation.

Question

Consider the Western Paper information from the perspective of either Crosby or Deming. What issues would their approach have highlighted, and which might have been played down or ignored?

21 First intervention

'the vital few, the useful many'

Joseph M. Juran

Introduction

This chapter considers the process and findings of the first intervention whilst introducing and reviewing the core methodologies. While the three chosen methodologies were applied concurrently and the finding synthesised into a whole systems view of the problem situation (figure 20.1), the findings of each part of the intervention are described here sequentially. The synthesised view is elaborated in the next section. The use of the selected methodologies will reveal those aspects of Western Paper which appear to be important based on the initial conversation. They will not reveal some other aspects, and one challenge for any consultant conducting a review is to separate those things which are important and must be acted upon from those which are interesting but unimportant.

21.1 Soft Systems perspective

This element of the intervention was primarily focused on engaging the senior management. It involved developing an understanding of the purpose, vision and values of the management; that is their objectives for the organisation, the constraints under which they saw themselves working and, importantly, the rationale for their choices. Soft Systems Methodology is outlined below.

21.1.1 Soft Systems Methodology

Principles and conception

Soft Systems Methodology (SSM) (Checkland, 1981) rests on the assumption that the resolution of complex problems (of which achieving quality may be considered one) relies on the subjective views of the participants in any situation. SSM has been developed for use in ill-structured situations where there is an absence of clarity in the definition of the problem and no agreement as to what action is required to solve it. SSM, commonly led by a facilitator familiar with the methodology, enables a variety of viewpoints to be elaborated and evaluated by a group of problem solvers allowing them to make informed choices about the future. It is considered that by exploring the various

Box 21.1   Seven stages of Soft Systems Methodology

Peter Checkland:

Stage 1)   Finding out;

Stage 2)   Rich picture;

Stage 3)   Root definitions;

Stage 4)   Re-design;

Stage 5)   Real world comparison;

Stage 6)   Debate and decision;

Stage 7)   Taking action.

viewpoints in an open forum and evaluating their strengths and limitations, an approach to improving the situation can be generated to which all participants will commit themselves. Solutions generated through the seven stage process of enquiry which is the methodology of SSM will normally lead to changes in three dimensions – attitudes, structure and procedures. It is considered that as many people as possible should be involved in the SSM process, and, although often facilitated, it does not have to be driven by 'experts'; it can be used by managers as part of everyday working practice.

SSM – Methodology

SSM consists of a seven stage process and should be used in an iterative manner. Although this description starts at stage 1, any other starting point would generate an equally valid result. The methodology is pursued by the members of the organisation although it may be facilitated by a 'problem solver' – often a consultant.

The first two stages take place in what is called the 'real world'; that is they are based on the experience and knowledge of the participants and of how things are perceived by them.

Stage 1 consists of exploring the problem situation and gathering information about it through observation, evaluating formal data (such as company records) and interviews.

Stage 2 is often an entertaining stage and is usually expressed in the form of a cartoon (called a 'rich picture'). This consists of creating a representation of the problem situation as it is experienced by the participants. Stages 1 and 2 taken together lead the participants to define a number of themes or systems which they need to examine. These can usefully be thought of as processes within the overall organisation studied.

Stages 3 and 4 are abstract processes designed to explore how things could (and arguably should) be as opposed to how they are, as perceived by the actors. They are concerned with what Ackoff (1981) calls 'idealised design'. Stage 3 develops concise statements about the purpose of the various systems or processes, called 'root definitions'. The 'root definition' presents an ideal view of what the relevant system 'ought' to achieve and is refined through the use of six principal elements (Box 21.2) and six key questions (Box 21.3).

Stage 4 uses the validated root definitions to re-design the activities (the transformation process) aiming to overcome the limitations of current transformations. The 'conceptual model' developed identifies the minimum set of activities necessary to ensure that the transformation achieves its purpose. The set of activities is ordered into a

Box 21.2   Six principal elements of a system

Six elements of a Soft System

Customers: those who gain by or suffer from the activity;
Actors: those who perform the activity;
Transformation: the action itself;
Weltanschauung: the world-view of the situation which validates the action;
Owners: those who can stop the activity (often the management);
Environment: external constraints upon the system behaviour.

Box 21.3   Six questions for refining 'root definitions'

'Root definitions'
Question 1)   What is required?
Question 2)   Why is it required?
Question 3)   Who will do it?
Question 4)   Who will benefit?
Question 5)   Who will be hurt or damaged?
Question 6)   What external factors constrain the activity?

process based on how the activities would occur in the 'real world' – this ensures that carts are not put before horses! It may be necessary to define sub-sets of activities which naturally group together, perhaps under the headings of operations, control, co-ordination and so on (rather like the VSM model seen in the next section).

The aim of stage 5 is to compare the models constructed with the real world understanding of the group members. This enables them to highlight possible changes in the actual situation to bring it closer to the systemic ideal now developed. Devices for this might include highlighting areas of difference, generating and ranking (for evaluation) options and generating projections of possible futures (in the style of the scenario planning technique used by Royal Dutch Shell).

At stage 6 the comparisons drawn in the previous stage provide the basis for discussion and debate amongst the participants. This should lead to the selection of culturally feasible changes in the actual situation – that is, changes which are systemically desirable and are considered achievable within the culture of the particular organisation.

There are few, if any, absolute rights or wrongs at this stage. The point of the exercise is more the process itself (for generating mutual understanding and appreciation) than for the outcomes – although unless these lead to practical and beneficial changes in the organisation it may be seen as somewhat sterile. The final outcome should be a set of changes to which all parties are willing to commit themselves.

The final stage of the process, stage 7, is taking action, that is implementing within the real-world situation the changes that have been proposed. These may affect any part of the totality of the organisation studied, that is its structure (organisation design, job design), attitudes (the culture and values) and procedures (the actual operations of the organisation). The total process is shown diagrammatically in Box 21.1.

Critical review

While SSM does not preclude the inclusion of large numbers of people in the process, the approach is often recognised as working best with relatively small numbers. The methodology offers no specific help in using SSM in a situation where there are large numbers and where some degree of 'order' needs to be brought into the enquiry process, say in a factory employing 2,000 workers, or in a total organisation which might employ hundreds of thousands of staff in a distributed network of offices and factories. A more apparently useful approach for such organisations is Ackoff's Interactive Planning (IP) (Ackoff, 1981) which will be discussed later. This approach adheres to the participative and subjective views recognised in SSM but provides a structured method for involving all of the people in the organisation in the process of creating its future.

SSM has great strength in its capacity to bring together groups with diverse opinions and offer them a structured process through which those opinions can be debated. However, it does not offer any form of desired, or ideal-type, outcome. It does not suggest any principles to which an ideal solution should adhere other than the forming of a consensus view. The solutions proposed therefore will ameliorate the concerns of those participating in the process but not necessarily others who, either willingly or not, are excluded from the process. Neither will it necessarily adhere to any specific organisational, cultural or procedural principles which might be thought desirable. Unless these things are already present within the 'weltanschauung' of the participants or introduced at the problem definition stage, there is no scope for them to be considered.

An interesting comparison can be made here between SSM, the Quality Circles of 'kaizen' and the Six Sigma Team DMAIC Problem Solving Process. The key difference is that SSM enables the participants to consider the whole of the organisation of interest whereas the others are constrained to the particular work process or organisational unit. They are therefore of limited value in addressing complex or higher order challenges.

The key findings arising from the application of the first stage of Soft Systems Methodology are now discussed.

It is quite clear, both from the initial telephone call and from the subsequent structured discussion using the first stage of SSM that the purpose imputed to the situation by the senior management is the sustainable viability of Western Paper – profit being recognised as a constraint upon their continued existence. Coastal Paper falls outside the scope of the study although it clearly has an impact on the availability and focus of the GM. In order to achieve profitability they recognised the need to establish a co-operative working situation in which production, conversion and sales were aligned in order to realise the potential of the business. A number of issues were discovered during this stage that will need further inquiry and possible action.

While the General Manager had a very approachable style, management meetings were unplanned and, when they happened, were lacking in structure and focus. Meanwhile the Operations Director, reflecting his background, was clearly operating a level or two below his title, being intimately involved in the day to day running of the paper machine and losing sight of the conversion and with no oversight of warehousing activities. Management was thoughtless, that is to say, the prevailing method of decision making was to do that which has always been done.

Morale was poor with workers well aware of the threat to the future of the business and consequently to their security and that of their families. Nothing being done by management was addressing or alleviating the concern, indeed, much of it was considered to be making things worse. The employees were neither engaged with the current operating model, nor were they being invited or encouraged to support the turnaround of the business.

Communication was poor throughout the organisation. In a noisy, widespread site with small numbers, significant physical distance between people and ineffective supervision; consistency of messaging was hard to achieve and, in the absence of clear instructions, individuals did what they believed was the right thing. It became clear that nobody had an adequate view of the whole process.

Health and Safety requirements were not always being met and the old machines were being operated in a manner that could have led to significant safety breaches. This was partly because 'no funds are available for that repair', partly through the familiarity with such equipment that often leads to carelessness.

The whole Personnel function was carried out by the Personnel Manager who had previously been in management posts in production, health and safety and quality; posts in which he had failed to achieve required performance.

The Sales Director who had been at Western Paper in the same role for some 26 years exhibited attitudes and behaviours that demonstrated first that he was making decisions in the absence of meaningful data, second that rather than being committed to satisfying customer requirements he was committed to appeasing customer demands. There is a significant difference between these two things. The first demands an understanding of what the customer needs in order to fulfil a specification, the second tends to sacrifice some other aspect of performance in order to achieve sales. This was damaging to the business as it was introducing needs for either very small batches or very light paper specifications, neither of which were commercially viable.

Meanwhile, driven by a demand for '100 good tonnes' each day, the Operations Director was making paper which ended up in the warehouse because there was no order for it. In answer to the question 'why did you make that?' he would answer 'because it was running well'.

Clearly there was a need to develop a sense of shared purpose amongst the management team, to build together a recovery plan for the whole business and to re-make meaningful relationships with customers. Underlying it all was evidence that the information being used throughout the business whether about prices, costs, volumes, weights or product specifications was, at best, out of control, at worst, non-existent and that there was no overall process for operating or managing the business.

SSM was not enough.

21.2   Viable Systems perspective

This element of the intervention was primarily focused on understanding how the organisation functioned and was controlled, why it worked that way and the issues that this gave rise to. The work involved developing an understanding of the structure, measurement and information systems and how these aligned with the desires and expectations determined in the soft systems intervention. Embedded work processes are dealt with in the next section. Viable Systems Diagnosis is outlined below.

21.2.1 Viable Systems Methodology

The Viable System Model in theory

The Viable System Model (VSM) was developed by Stafford Beer from the principles of Organisational Cybernetics – the science of effective organisation (chapter 16). Beer considered an organisation to be viable when it is capable of survival in a given environment and capable of learning and adaptation to changes in that environment. To achieve this ultrastable state, the process of its management must have five functions: Implementation, Co-ordination, Control, Planning and Policy, which taken together constitute the viable system.

The model enables multiple interpretations of any organisational situation to be developed, all according to the same principles, but focused on the different purposes imputed to the organisation by its various observers. Through this modelling process, dialogue and debate is generated, from which an agreed organisational purpose can be derived and a most useful approach developed.

The approach to organisational cybernetics espoused by Beer rests on five principles:

- Observer dependency
- Systemic thinking
- Black box method
- Self-regulation
- Ashby's Law of Requisite Variety
  (see Beckford, 1993)

VSM – Conception and construction

The VSM is a general model of any organisation. It is concerned with mechanisms of adaptation, communication and control. It consists of the stated five sub-systems each of which is of equal importance to the effectiveness of the organisation. These sub-systems are richly interconnected by a network of information loops in continuous operation. The whole system is capable of learning which in this context means co-adaptation between the system and its environment – perhaps a form of Lamarckian evolution.

Implementation creates the products or services. Co-ordination and control mechanisms ensure cohesion of the organisation and allow for the maximum appropriate autonomy to implementation. This maximises the self-regulating tendencies and enables the resolution of problems as near to source as possible. This generates two outcomes each of which has clear relevance to the pursuit of quality, while autonomy enables greater motivation at more junior levels in the organisation. Higher management is freed to concentrate on the issues of greatest relevance to them.

Planning enables the organisation to interact with its environment, influencing and being influenced. This function helps to ensure that changing customer requirements are known to the organisation – a vital part of the quality process. Policy is responsible for the whole organisation, creating and sustaining its identity and arbitrating between demands for change and stability. It is the policy function which determines whether or not the venture will be organised for quality.

The organisation is considered as embedded in an environment and consists of two parts – Operations and Management (see Figure 21.1). The boundaries between these three elements are thought of as permeable. This permits the continuous communication which is necessary between the elements. The diagrammatic conventions demand that these normally be shown as discrete information channels and this will be the case in subsequent diagrams.

Figure 21.2 demonstrates the next step in building the VSM by separating the three elements and showing the communication channels which are used to either amplify or attenuate variety. The variety of the environment is absorbed by the organisation, and its management and operational and managerial variety are amplified into the environment. The standard strategies by which this is achieved were reviewed in chapter 16.

Figure 21.2 provides an overview of an entire organisation interacting with its environment. Most organisations will consist of a set of implementation units embedded in a total organisation, for example the divisions of a multi-national company, the branches of a bank or the production lines within a factory. Each must have the capability to be viable, within the constraints imposed on it by its membership of the containing organisation. Equally, within each unit will be found further lower level units, each of which must again be viable. The lowest level unit for practical purposes is the individual worker. This 'nesting' effect is called recursion and constitutes a special form of hierarchy built on organisational logic rather than power.

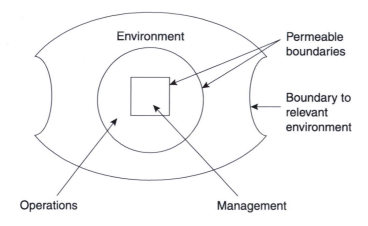

Figure 21.1 The organisation in its environment.

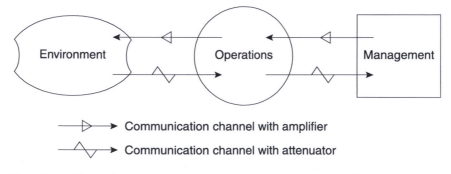

Figure 21.2 The environment, operations and management separated.

A chain of recursively embedded viable systems is presented in Figure 21.3. Each oblong box encapsulates a complete recursion.

Figure 21.4 shows all of the operational elements of an organisation at the same level of recursion, for example the divisions of a company. This set constitutes the implementation function of the organisation, the parts which fulfil its purpose(s). The communication channels are simplified in this presentation.

This shows that for each division there is some degree of overlap between the environments. This could represent shared customers, physical overlap between geographical marketing areas or competition for customers whose requirements could be satisfied by either of two or more product ranges from the same company. For example, for a computer manufacturer the overlap might represent customers whose requirements could be satisfied by either a large PC network or a mid-range system.

A co-ordinating mechanism deals with sources of oscillation or conflict between the parts. It would be possible to achieve this through a higher level edict – a set of rules or policies handed down by senior management – but an approach has two principal effects. Every exception to policy would need to be sanctioned at the highest level which would increase the volume of communication and potentially overload the senior management. The degree of freedom which the individual elements enjoy would also be severely constrained. This would reduce flexibility at the operating level, inhibit the development of 'kaizen' and fail to fully utilise the self-regulating properties of the organisation.

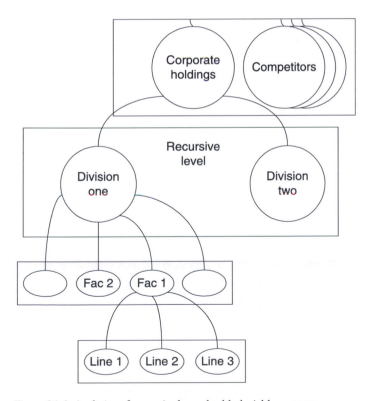

Figure 21.3 A chain of recursively embedded viable systems.

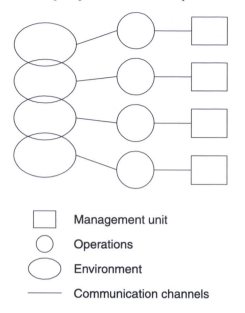

Management unit

Operations

Environment

Communication channels

Figure 21.4 A set of implementation elements.

Finally, the organisation would come to be seen as oppressive, since individuals would perceive themselves to have limited freedom of choice and action.

Prime examples of this co-ordination are progress chasers/production controllers in factories, the creation of a timetable in an educational institution, the allocation of service bays in a car dealership or telling windows in a bank. Figure 21.5 presents the organis-ation with the co-ordinating mechanism in place.

A second feature included in this diagram is the links between the operational elements. These represent the informal communication which always occurs between stages in a process, or divisions of an organisation.

The next stage in the process of management is the regulation of the ongoing activities of the organisation. Control is concerned with the allocation of resources to the operational elements, with accountability for those resources and with adherence to corporate and statutory regulations.

This is achieved through two principal processes, resource bargaining and auditing. Resource bargaining is the process of budgeting for resources which is carried out in all organisations. The VSM requires this to be carried out on a negotiated basis. The control functions and the operational elements should engage in meaningful discussions about what resources are required and what objectives are to be achieved with them. The resource bargaining process should encompass all of the resources utilised and objectives set: money, staff, equipment, profitability, quality standards and so on.

The control function is made up of the various departments involved in regulatory activity. This would include units such as administration, personnel, production management, perhaps the General or Divisional Manager's office and quality assurance.

Audit is a sporadic intervention by each of the control departments in the operational elements. This serves to increase their knowledge and understanding of how those

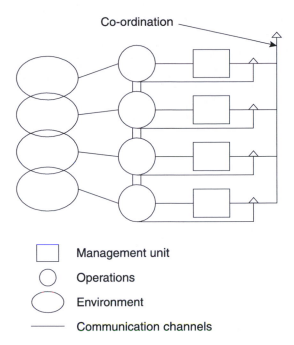

Co-ordination

Management unit

Operations

Environment

Communication channels

Figure 21.5 Operational elements with co–ordination and interaction.

functions are performing. It is essential that these audits be sporadic; if they are not then they will lose their effect.

The control function being in place, the organisation may now be considered to be self-regulating. It will be able to function effectively, carrying out its allotted tasks. Parallels may be drawn between this and devices such as heating/air conditioning systems which are self-regulating against a target temperature in the same way. Figure 21.6 presents the model at this stage.

An organisation which is simply self-regulating will not be viable in the longer term, since it cannot respond to environmental changes. Neither will it be capable of generating continuous improvement since it has no facility for development. This brings us to planning.

Planning covers all of the research and development activity of the organisation. It may be concerned with market research and marketing activity, product development, financial planning, staff training and development and most certainly is the root of quality planning. The planning functions interact with the emergent environment, considering possible courses of action for either adapting the organisation to the environment, or where appropriate, influencing the environment towards the organisation. The planning and control functions also interact with each other, continuously re-negotiating the resource allocations and objectives of the organisation.

This process of negotiation will almost inevitably lead at times to conflict and dispute, the control functions wishing to maintain the status quo, while the development functions wish to promote change. The conversation between them will be monitored by the last management function, policy, which arbitrates between them according to the ethos of the organisation.

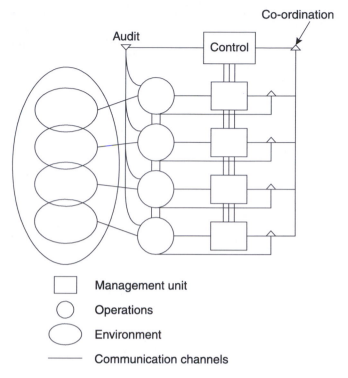

Figure 21.6 The self-regulating organisation.

The ethos is the set of values and beliefs that underpin the philosophy of the venture. Policy may be considered to be fulfilling an equivalent function to that of co-ordination at the implementation level. There is however one significant difference. The policy function represents the entire organisation to the outside world and is the formal link to the next higher level of organisation. The complete Viable System Model is represented in figure 19.2.

At this stage, the model can be linked back to the prior writings on quality with the consistent demands from all writers for top management commitment. It is clear that without this commitment the quality initiative will fail and such commitment demands changes in both the words and actions of the senior management. If organisations are as closely linked as is suggested by the Viable System Model (and from experience they seem to be so) then the actions and behaviour of the policy making group may affect the behaviour of those in the rest of the organisation. If they are serious about quality then this message will filter through very rapidly; if they are not the message will move just as fast. Through the cybernetic model, the justification for senior management commitment to quality is realised because they transmit vital messages throughout the organisation and to the environment – the customers and suppliers.

The model of an effective organisation is complete, and one constructed in accordance with this framework will be viable, but there remain three major points to be made at this stage. First, the communication channels must be in continuous operation, and second, they must be capable of carrying more information in a given time than the transmitting system is capable of generating. This ensures that information is not lost or distorted in the system (Silver, 2012). Similarly, it is important to remember that every time information crosses a boundary it must be translated into the 'language' of the receiving system. For example, a message concerning volumes or types of individual transistors or capacitors may have no meaning for a receiving department whose 'currency' is expressed in financial terms, or in units representing aggregations of components such as computers or keyboards.

An organisation designed in accordance with these design principles does not look like the conventional hierarchy, but more like Figure 21.7

In this, the operational parts of the organisation are focused on the present market. The management is considering the wider market – other present and potential future opportunities. Strategy joins the two together, representing the continual dialogue between the corporate and operational managers. In order to provide adequate information to all managers for effective management, the corporate managers continually review the interaction with the environment in terms of business performance appraisal. The operational managers use the performance monitoring system to consider current performance in relation to characteristics such as efficiency, productivity and speed. Information arising from that system is also provided to the corporate managers for inclusion in the business performance appraisal. The operational processes, management processes, skills and competences record provide the standing information necessary to support management decision making.

An organisation designed along these lines will be viable.

It is perfectly legitimate to use this approach to specifically examine only a single aspect of the organisation. It is possible, and often useful, to model purely the quality management function. Such an approach ensures that the effectiveness of the quality programme is understood at all levels in the organisation. It may be found that while the senior management have implemented a quality programme, this has purely been done at the operations level and no changes have been made in other parts of the organisation to support it. For example, control may be focusing purely on volume as an output

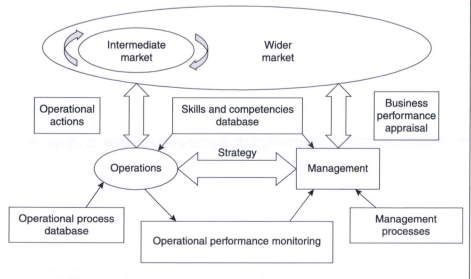

Figure 21.7 The ultrastable organisation.

measure and ignoring the quality issue. Development may be focused on the demand for new products and ignoring customer calls for better quality of existing products.

Critical review

The VSM can be, and has been, applied to organisations of all sizes and types from one-man businesses to entire nation states (Beckford, 2016). It has a general applicability and utility which exceeds that of other organisational models. The model fully embraces the interaction between the organisation and the environment in which it is embedded and caters for the definition of the organisation and its purposes by its stakeholders.

The model is criticised for being difficult to use in practice and although the methodology appears lengthy and complex, it can be very rapid in use. The standard modelling format generates great economy.

The model is also criticised for focusing on static rather than dynamic goals, although this criticism rather misses the point of the model. Similarly, it is argued that the model can lead to and support autocratic management behaviour. While this argument is easier to sustain, it must be noted that the principles of the model call for appropriate levels of autonomy, and if this is not granted the organisation will not be viable. The major barrier to its use is the necessity of devolving power within the organisation and this requirement frequently generates resistance from those already in power.

In the field of quality systems the model has been used by Flood (1993) to deal with the structural elements of the organisation whilst Beckford and Dudley (1998a, 1998b, 1999) and Dudley (2000) have used it as the basis of a complete approach to skills based quality management.

When Western Paper is diagnosed using the Viable Systems Model, what is actually happening is compared with the ideal as represented by the model. The following is discovered.

> *Western Paper has two sites some seven miles apart. The main site is home to the stock yard, paper machine and the enabling functions. The second site contains the warehouse, despatch and conversion facility. The Warehousing and Despatch unit has its own manager while the Conversion unit is managed by the Operations Director. Each day the Conversion Supervisor and Warehouse/Despatch Manager are expected to attend meetings during the course of the day at the primary site. All the buildings are very old and the paper machine itself dates from the 1950s. It has an annual capacity of 50,000 gross tonnes with a target net output of 35,000 tonnes, i.e. about 100 saleable tonnes of paper per day.*

> *The traditional organisation chart of Western Paper is shown as Figure 21.8. Examining this chart it is clear that the organisation is functionally arranged and that functional and hierarchical structure may inhibit cooperation and collaboration. This finding is confirmed when it is found that, to the extent that a performance management regime exists, each person who reports to the General Manager is expected to produce results independently of the others, i.e. there is no consistency of expectations across the organisation. While their performance expectations are not in conflict as they have been in other cases, they nonetheless are competing rather than collaborating.*

Thought of in process terms it is quite clear that the functional arrangements may impede overall performance. One example of this was the Operations Directors drive for '100 good

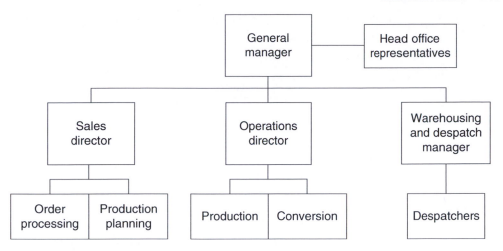

Figure 21.8 Western Paper organisation chart.

tonnes per day'. The definition of a 'good tonne' was that the paper should be saleable. So, when the machine was running well and the paper quality was good, the operators would keep running the product beyond the planned quantity in order to hit the volume target even though other products, for which there were outstanding orders, were falling behind. The Conversion unit, being operated by a Supervisor at a significant physical distance from the main plant, was failing to meet any and all productivity targets set for it. It was difficult for this Supervisor to be held to account when, as was often the case, the work in that area was waiting for output from the paper machine, output that would not arrive because the operators were focused on pure volume. The understanding that the organisation structure coupled to the behaviour of the senior staff and the inadequate performance regime led to a consideration of the information flows around the business – which should (Beckford, 2016) map to the organisational architecture. It was rapidly discovered that Western Paper had several computerised information systems, e.g. finance, sales, stock management, warehousing, SCADA, but these were not joined together in any meaningful way so that use of information relied upon human interaction. In addition, a number of systems, such as production planning and scheduling, were largely manual and run separately from the computerised systems. Looking at the systems themselves it was determined that much of the data held was inaccurate and that procedures for maintaining the systems, the data and the reporting were not being followed. One consequence of this was the absence of a product costing or pricing system. Sale prices were being set by the Sales Director on an arbitrary, best efforts, estimate basis and, after a brief analysis, were found to be falling well behind the costs being incurred by the business. Western Paper would have lost less money by paying customers £50 per tonne to take their business elsewhere.

21.3 Process analysis

This element of the intervention was focused on understanding and recording the production processes of Western Paper and the enabling processes through which they function – including information and behaviour. The work involved, in this case literally, exploring the sites from inbound stores to dispatch, capturing the flow of activities and understanding how the process worked; any changes of responsibility and how process performance was measured.

21.3.1 Process mapping

Process analysis

A core process is a sequence of activities linked across an organisation to deliver a product or service of value to an end-user customer. Enabling processes are internal sequences of activities which facilitate or support the operation of a core process.

Process recording in an established manufacturing environment is a straightforward activity as the process is largely defined by a construction or assembly flow (see Ohno, 1988: 48–50). In a service environment it is often more difficult since processes are often not recognised as such, their elements being linked across separate functional areas. For example, in a bank, processing a customer's cheque may involve the signature of an official for authorisation of payment, a cashier, a computer input operator and a filing clerk. Each of these individuals may work in a different department (functional silo) within the bank, and the process may be subject to a number of variations and sub-routines, dependent upon circumstances. For this reason, fragmentation of processes is common. For an organisation serious about achieving quality, it is vital to move beyond this fragmented approach to something more coherent. Process definition is vital in this regard.

A process chart provides an overall picture of a connected set of value-adding activities by recording, in sequence, each of the operations. These operations are recorded regardless of who does them or where they are performed. Functional boundaries within the organisation are ignored for mapping purposes.

Process charting can be carried out at a number of nested levels or recursions. At the first level, the 'Total Process' records the process from start to finish, with a minimum of detail and identifies where exceptions and sub-routines occur. The second level 'Process Operation' or 'Task' details the specific actions taken at each stage (including the exceptions and sub-routines), while a third level 'Process Detail' or 'Procedure' studies detail, potentially down to the level of individual hand movements (a work study level of analysis). For many purposes, especially where a skills based approach is used, capturing information at the Total and Operational levels is sufficient. Figure 21.9 shows how the three levels are linked.

The process charts are developed by identifying particular operations and linking them together along with any inspections, audits or delays. The process may be defined in either a vertical or horizontal flow – whichever is more convenient – and, for clarity and economy of effort, ASME symbols are typically used to indicate each stage. The ASME symbols, with some additions, are provided in Figure 21.10.

It is common practice to give each process a unique name or identifier and to number the sequence of actions. The completed process charts provide a record of the operation and provide the basis for process analysis and critical examination. They also provide a basis for evaluation and measurement at process handover points (the connections between steps) and allow the identification of problem areas. Such charts may also usefully be overlaid on a plan or topographical diagram of the building layout indicating paths of movement. This can prove helpful in eradicating delays and identifying why and where quality problems occur, for example storage of temperature sensitive materials in

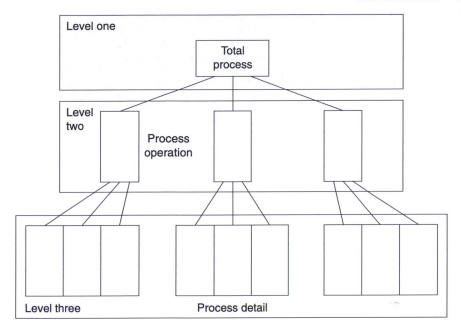

Figure 21.9 Nested or 'recursive' process levels.

○ Operations

□ Inspection/verification

◁ Movement

▽ File/end

D Delay

◇ Outside scope of inquiry

✕ Destroyed/thrown away

▣ Inspection more important than operation

⊡ Operation more important than inspection

Figure 21.10 ASME symbols.

an unprotected area. An example of a completed 'Total Process' chart overlaid on a building plan is provided in Figure 21.11.

This chart represents the receipt, preparation and despatch of a purchase order. The order is received by a storeman who prepares a request form, creates a folder and

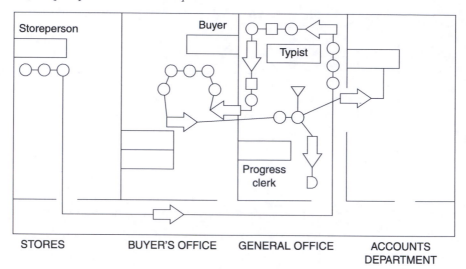

STORES   BUYER'S OFFICE   GENERAL OFFICE   ACCOUNTS
                                                         DEPARTMENT

Figure 21.11 A total process chart.

passes the folder to the typist (that is three operations). The typist types the order and passes it to the checker who checks the typed order against the request form and (assuming all to be correct) passes the order to a Progress Clerk. The progress clerk passes the forms to the relevant buyer for signature and return. The progress clerk then passes the order to the supplier, passes one copy of the order to the Accounts Department and holds the other in the buyer's file.

This process, which undoubtedly seems cumbersome to the reader, is a real example found in a UK factory and while obviously inefficient is not unusually bad compared with many other contemporary situations.

Most long-established organisations have not yet properly exploited the potential for process re-engineering enabled by innovative approaches to process management and contemporary information technology. One intervention provided an example of data being captured electronically in the first instance from a system outside the organisation being retyped at least five times within the organisation – a hugely inefficient process. Similar findings have been made as late as early 2009 in one global business – and the staff could see nothing wrong with it.

When Western Paper is examined using process mapping, the following matters are revealed – some directly concerned with the processes themselves, some relevant to the control of those processes and some simply discovered by walking through the two sites following a product.

While the organisation of Western Paper was shown in Figure 21.8, the process flow is shown in Figure 21.12. Whereas the functional division was managed in three separate silos, it is immediately obvious, when the overview process chart is considered, that there is a clear sequence of activities. They can join together into a coherent flow and there is a need to manage the flow as a whole in order to improve performance, reduce errors, minimise 'work-in-progress' and warehouse stocks and thereby meet customer requirements as expressed through Sales orders.

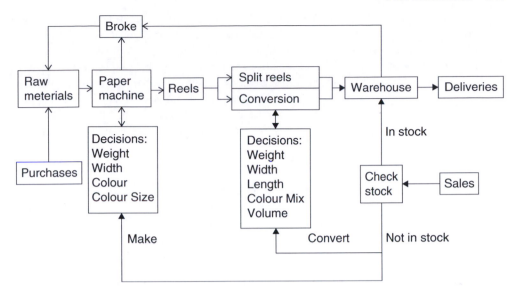

Figure 21.12 Western Paper process flow.

This was not possible in the established structure because of the disjointed and dysfunctional management, the absence of the 'process picture', the focus on local, functional optimisation and the varying definitions of success.

Initial and high-level analysis of the situation suggested that there was potential, through adopting a process management perspective, to:

- Reduce the product cycle time from twelve weeks to six;
- Immediately reduce 'aged stock' (i.e. that over 365 days old) by over 420 tonnes, generating a net cash inflow in excess of £200k;
- Over time to reduce stock by a further 3,000 tonnes, generating a further net cash inflow £1.8m;
- Redefine a 'good tonne' as one conforming to specification AND for which there was a customer order;
- Eradicate low volume and marginal product;
- Revise information flows to support key decisions.

21.4   Reflections and next steps

It is apparent that Western Paper factory is not as effective or efficient as is possible. The three methodologies used in parallel have each worked both to reveal particular issues on which they are focused and at the same time, each has provided confirmation of findings in other areas.

Overall, the studies show that Western Paper needed to address numerous cultural, organisational and process issues if the aspiration to viability was to be fulfilled. From a 'soft systems' perspective, it is evident that there is not an agreed view of the purposes of the organisation or the ways in which it should seek to fulfil them. Note, for example, the differing aspirations of the General Manager (viability) from the Operations Director (production at all costs). From the Viable Systems perspective there are evident weaknesses in communication and in clarity of responsibility for different areas. From a resource and performance management perspective Western Paper is 'out of control' – it is both over-producing and under-performing. When the examination comes from the process perspective it is easy to see why the other characteristics might apply. The processes have numerous handover points which are not well managed while the data and numbers used are inaccurate. Looking at managerial competence it appears that this is inadequate at all levels of the organisation. The lack of a meaningful measurement system means that managers and staff were often working hard to do the wrong thing in relation to the overall objectives.

Summary

This chapter has taken the first steps in simultaneously applying three methodologies to reveal different aspects of the situation under consideration. Through this it has provided three perspectives on Western Paper which have, briefly, been reported. In the next chapter, the study will progress to determine a way forward and to select tools and methodologies to help achieve success.

KEY LEARNING POINTS

No one methodology can address all aspects of a problem situation

Consider the use of multiple methodologies in parallel to reveal different perspectives and integrate them to a synthesised view.

The findings from one methodology will act to confirm or challenge the findings of the others.

Viable Systems

Key definitions:
a system is viable when it is capable of survival in a given environment and capable of learning and adaptation to changes in that environment

Principles:
observer defined systems, systems thinking, black boxes, self-regulation, requisite variety

Three modes:
descriptive, diagnostic, prescriptive

Critique:
general applicability, environmental interaction, observer definition, difficult to use, threatens established power bases, static not dynamic goals

Soft Systems Methodology

Key definition:
solving complex problems relies on the innate subjective views of the participants in a situation

---

Principle:
engage participants in the organisation in changing its operation, improve commitment to outcomes, purposes must be defined before means can be decided

Method:
seven stage process of enquiry – finding out, rich picture, root definitions, re-design, real world comparison, debate and decision, taking action

Critique:
best with small numbers, brings 'order' to a debate, caters for diverse opinions, no desired or ideal-type outcome other than consensus

Question

Use the methods and diagrammatic conventions of Soft Systems Methodology, Viable Systems Diagnosis and Process Analysis to create your own interpretation of Western Paper.

22 Second intervention

'Insanity: doing the same thing over and over and expecting different results'

Albert Einstein (attrib.)

Introduction

This chapter develops the Western Paper enquiry to the next stage both acquiring further detail as necessary and commencing action where appropriate. It continues with the Process Analysis and introduces the ideas of Interactive Planning, Process Measurement, Statistical Process Control, Quality Circles and Job Design.

22.1 Recap

The basic situation at Western Paper having been diagnosed using the methods introduced in the previous chapter, it is now possible to use other problem solving methods, again in parallel and in the context of the initial findings, to address the issues raised and establish a way forward. Summarising, it has been determined that there was:

- a lack of alignment or shared purpose, between the objectives and intent of the senior management, the middle management and the workforce;
- poor engagement of the staff generally;
- a weak management structure and ineffective process control;
- poor processes with numerous changes of poorly articulated responsibilities;
- a lack of meaningful measurement and evaluation of process and people performance;
- poor information and communication.

If the problems of Western Paper were to be properly addressed, it was necessary to achieve several outcomes. The first was to generate alignment between the objectives of the various, internal, stakeholders. Second was to analyse process performance, bring processes under proper control and design a management structure and measurement system which would enable effective performance. Third was to engage the production staff in designing and delivering further improvement.

   Interactive planning enabled the engagement of the whole workforce in the development of the future of Western Paper and re-established effective communication up and down the hierarchy. Process Measurement and Statistical Process Control provided an understanding of how well (or not) the processes were performing and a rational basis for evaluating improvement. Quality Circles, applied as complementary to Interactive Planning, began to engage the production staff in delivering locally developed process improvement. Kobayashi's 20 Keys methodology might also have been used to improve working patterns in specific locations. Job Design provided some useful insights into how roles could be revised to align skills and responsibilities more closely with the needs of the organisation.

The mapping of methodologies originated in figure 20.2 can now be extended to incorporate the additional approaches employed. This is represented in figure 22.1.

22.2 Engaging the internal stakeholders

The soft, ends oriented, issues at Western Paper were at this stage not resolved. Although Checkland's Soft Systems Methodology worked well for the small numbers of senior managers, it is not designed or intended to work with larger groups. To generate the potential for alignment of the entire workforce a different approach was required. Consideration was given to using Stafford Beer's Syntegration Methodology (Beer, 1994) however, its structure effectively limits it to groups of about 30 people and it is, like Soft Systems Methodology, a 'single-use' approach. What was needed in this situation was to generate an approach to alignment and communication both horizontally and vertically in the business, which would be of continuing use. The issues of communication and alignment would not be resolved through a single event; it was therefore necessary to adopt an approach which Western Paper could continue to use long after completion of this particular project. This led to the adoption of Ackoff's Interactive Planning.

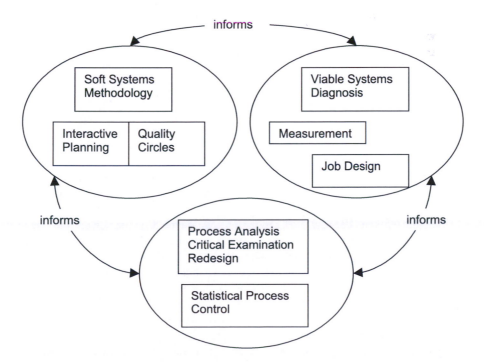

Figure 22.1 Tools for the second intervention.

22.2.1   Interactive Planning

Principles and conception

Ackoff holds the view that a planning methodology is required which enables people to plan for themselves, rather than be planned for by others. He sees this as enabling the participants to make their own values and ideals paramount in the planning process. This lets participants express their own perceptions of 'reality' rather than having the reality of others forced upon them and it necessitates wide participation in the creation of the future of organisations. Reflecting ideas already met in other approaches, IP recognises three sets of interests in the organisation. Those of the organisation itself as a purposeful, viable entity, the interests of the wider community (environment) in which it exists and the interests of the individuals who work within it.

Interactivist planners take into account the past, present and predictions about the future as inputs to a planning process aimed at creating their future and the mechanisms by which it can be achieved. They work with their conception of the ideal future for the organisation.

Interactive Planning rests on the three principles of participation, continuity and holism. The participative principle is that all stakeholders should participate in the stages of the planning process. Ackoff, like Checkland, suggests that the process of planning is more important than the plan which is produced, since it is the process which enables individual contributions to be made and which enhances understanding of the whole organisation by those involved with it.

The principle of continuity recognises that values and ideals of the stakeholders change over time and that further problems and new possibilities emerge during the implementation of any plans. For Ackoff this means that the plans must be adapted to meet these changes such that they continually reflect the current circumstances; perhaps they should be considered as forever in final draft form! This idea reflects the notions of learning and adaptation examined in earlier chapters and the organisational ideas discussed under Viable Systems Diagnosis in chapter 21.

The last principle is that of holism; that is systemic thinking. This suggests that planning should be simultaneously and interdependently carried out for the entire organisation (or at least as many parts and levels as is possible). The notion of holistic or systemic thinking was explored in chapter 15.

To enable the participative principle of Interactive Planning to be practised, Ackoff proposes a particular form of planning organisation. This form is seen as embedding the planning process as an integral part of the organisation. In this design the organisation is divided into planning boards. The heads of units within the organisation are members of boards at three levels, their own, the one above and the ones below. In this respect they act similarly to and may be characterised as like Likert's 'linking pins', or perhaps as the 'Policy' function in the Viable System Model which links recursive levels. At the highest level, external stakeholders are represented on the board, while at the lowest level all the workers are members of their unit board. This organisation could usefully be used as a design for linking the activities of Quality Circles within an organisation. These planning boards could also be seen as mechanisms for integrating processes.

While apparently time consuming, with some managers belonging to as many as ten boards, the organisation is considered to derive major benefit through improved

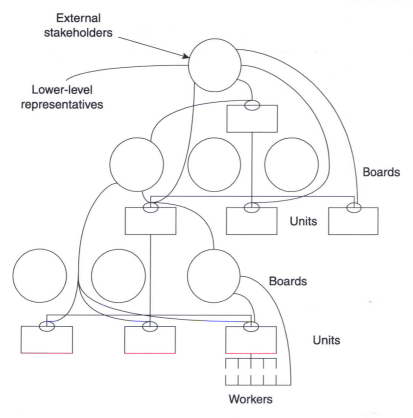

Figure 22.2 Organisational design for Interactive Planning (adapted from Ackoff, 1981).

communication, co-ordination and integration of ideas. Morale is also improved. The organisation of Interactive Planning is represented diagrammatically in figure 22.2.

It can clearly be seen that this structure does not replace the existing hierarchy, but interleaves with it. It is a hierarchy of planning rather than control. This generates possibilities of communication and debate which the hierarchy of power and position tends to inhibit. It is particularly noteworthy that the approach explicitly incorporates the views of external stakeholders who might, for example, include local government representatives, community leaders, suppliers and perhaps customers or consumers of the product or service or, in this case, the Western Paper owning group. This has evident implications for organisations pursuing quality programmes. For example, where a supplier development strategy is being pursued, suppliers can be linked into the planning process of the organisation. Similarly, customer feedback becomes truly meaningful when the customers form a part of the organisation.

Methodology

The methodology for IP includes five steps (Box 22.1). Holding to the systemic requirements of the approach, the process may be run in any order and the whole should be regarded as an iterative process with plans, as already suggested, being always in the latest 'draft' form.

Box 22.1   Five steps of Interactive Planning

Russell Ackoff:

Step 1)   Formulating the mess;

Step 2)   Ends planning;

Step 3)   Means planning;

Step 4)   Resource planning;

Step 5)   Design of implementation and control.

Box 22.2   Three methods of formulating the mess

Three types of study

Systems Analysis: which will detail the organisation, how it works and its environment;

Obstruction Analysis: which will unearth the obstacles to corporate development;

Reference Projections: which predict future performance by extrapolating current performance in the given environment.

Formulating the mess (step 1) consists of a SWOT type analysis intended to highlight the strengths, weaknesses, opportunities and threats faced by the organisation. Ackoff proposes that a useful device is to work out the 'future the organisation is currently in'. This is a scenario representing the future of the organisation if nothing is done about its internal situation and the environment continues to develop along the lines anticipated. Ackoff suggests that this requires three types of study (Box 22.2). A synthesis of the three sets of results is considered as a reference scenario of the current 'mess'.

Ends planning (step 2) seeks to specify the future the organisation wants. It begins with idealised redesign – a vision of the sort of organisation the stakeholders would create if they were free to do so. This involves selecting a mission, specifying the attributes of the design and designing the organisation. Normally, two versions of this are created – one constrained by the existing wider system, one unconstrained. The difference between these two idealised organisations indicates to what extent the organisation must address its efforts towards modifying its environment during the planning process.

Idealised re-design is a creative process and as such permits only two constraints. First, the design must be technologically feasible, that is it must not rely on a potential future invention or breakthrough. Second, it must be operationally viable, that is it must be capable of functioning if created.

Flood & Jackson (1991: 151) suggest that the design should answer to the criteria of the best 'ideal seeking system' that the stakeholders can imagine. From this point it is clear that the organisation designed must be capable of learning and adaptation. Ackoff's outline design for such a system requires it to be capable of:

- observation – to recognise opportunities and threats;
- decision making – enabling a response to those opportunities and threats;

- implementation – actually doing something;
- control – performance monitoring and self-correction;
- communication – the acquisition, generation and dissemination of information.

The alert reader will by now have identified some similarities in ideas between IP and other approaches already discussed such as the VSM with its requirement for implementation, co-ordination, control, development and policy – the five functions of management. Six Sigma might also spring to mind for some. It must be stated though that there are some fundamental differences in the theories underpinning the approaches.

Means planning (step 3) is the term used for the process of generating the 'hows' to support the 'whats' of the first two steps. It is concerned with making operational the changes considered necessary by those involved. Alternative 'hows' should be generated, perhaps using some of the techniques outlined in earlier chapters of this book and comparisons made to find the most effective.

Resource planning (step 4) looks at the requirements for materials, supplies, energy and services – all of the inputs to the organisation – as well as at facilities and equipment, personnel and money. For every aspect it is necessary to determine what changes need to be made in order to support the idealised redesign. This stage is very similar to the 'Internal Business Audit' in a strategic review process, as it attempts to assess the capabilities of the organisation and its personnel.

Implementation and control (step 5) is concerned with ensuring that the decisions made are carried out. This involves the allocation of tasks and the monitoring of their completion. The outcomes of implementation should be fed back into the planning process such that necessary modifications and further changes can be made.

Critical review

IP shares with SSM the criticism that its outcomes are bounded by the knowledge and expectations of the participants in the process. For quality to be addressed as an issue, it must be highlighted at the outset as part of the formulation of the mess. Similarly, at the implementation phase, the need for knowledge of quality theory and practice must be recognised.

While IP and Quality Circles appear to have much in common, they are differentiated in two ways. First, Quality Circles operate only at a single level within the organisation whereas IP links all levels. Second, Quality Circles are focused on purely localised operational problems whereas IP, used properly, has the scope to capture strategic perspectives from the lowest levels of the organisation. Quality Circles may be thought of as a problem solving technique, IP may be thought of as a way of managing the organisation.

Like SSM, IP is oriented towards defining the problem. It is focused on providing a methodology for generating solutions. It does not offer any guidance as to what those solutions should be demanding, only that they are derived in an emancipatory manner.

The key outcomes of the use of Interactive Planning can now be discussed. Purists might argue that the benefits of this approach were unduly limited by the prior use of other methodologies, which constrained what it was possible to do, and the approach is thereby rendered sterile. However, if it is accepted that Western Paper is not free to be whatever it wants to be, but has a degree of autonomy which is determined by its membership of the Group company, that argument is neutralised. Whatever the philosophical ambitions, Western Paper had limited freedom and any methodology applied to resolving its problems is subject to the same limits.

The previous chapter reported a number of the tensions that existed in Western Paper caused by poor communication, inadequate cooperation between the managers, foremen and workforce, poor information and utilisation. In an attempt to make the changes acceptable it was decided to formalise the daily operations meeting and use it as the initial planning board for Western Paper. Rather than launching a whole additional set of activities we determined that it would be more effective to modify the purpose and agenda of an established, if poorly utilised, event.

It was inevitable that the first events would require the senior management to begin building trust between themselves and the workforce. The process developed for each of the early events was designed to build some shared ground between the apparently 'opposing sides', to expose concerns and worries and to develop the basis of trust. To this end, participants at each event:

- proposed and adopted some 'rules of engagement';
- clarified the purpose of the events;
- ran an open discussion in which concerns could be discussed;
- exposed the limitations under which they could be run;
- focused attention on the issue of performance and developed very rapidly a daily 'dashboard' which they collectively designed, completed and used to inform their discussions.

This approach enabled the discussion to focus on the dashboard as an object with the discussion focused on how to improve the performance of the whole. This objectification lifted the argument away from the personal focus on individual performance and encouraged open discussion.

Western Paper belongs to a group and its freedom is thereby constrained – it cannot make choices which take it outside the boundaries imposed by that ownership. Equally, the individual processes are constrained in their freedoms by belonging to Western Paper. There were then legitimate and necessary constraints upon the discussions. Those things which were not for debate were exposed as limitations, these were:

> If the business was to survive and thrive it must improve production performance;
> They must be profitable – losses were not acceptable;
> The technologies in place – and the capital cost thereof – meant that survival was as a paper maker – and not anything else.

Those limitations understood, all other aspects were for free discussion within the methodology. The principal agreement to emerge from these first meetings was the joint desire to see the business thrive and to work towards that end. It was also recognised that, with the accepted limitations, the Interactive Planning boards would not be able to address all of the operational issues rapidly or frequently enough to deliver some of the benefits. They would, however, provide a useful integration device and enable the newly opened dialogue to be continued. They proposed therefore to introduce the idea of Quality Circles at the operational level to drive short-term and more focused productivity improvement and error reduction.

Interactive Planning therefore became accepted as a device for communicating vertically and horizontally throughout the business rather than just a planning and reinvention tool.

This breakthrough being achieved, which included greater integration of people, the second series of events focused on Obstruction Analysis (see Box 22.2) which identified the following as barriers to development:

- lack of clarity of responsibilities;
- managerial skills – at all levels;
- poor job design;
- lack of meaningful measurement;
- poor co-ordination of processes;
- inadequate performance management or reporting.

While Interactive Planning works well at the 'total system' level, it is not so useful at the level of individual work processes and tasks. These require a different mindset and a real depth of understanding of the production processes. It was with this in mind that a Quality Circles approach was taken for addressing operational challenges.

22.2.2 Quality Circles

Quality Circles are usually considered to be the brainchild of Dr. Kaoru Ishikawa (chapter 8) but have been adopted in a variety of forms by many companies throughout the world. The circles exist (Box 22.3) to identify and solve quality problems associated with a particular activity or interest group within the organisation.

The aims of using Quality Circles are to improve and develop the organisation, show respect for people and enhance their satisfaction in the job and to stretch them to their potential. Each circle is made up of between four and twelve workers led by a supervisor or manager. The focus of attention is on problems within their own area, although problems imported from a prior process should also be recognised. These become the responsibility of the supervisor or manager to address.

The effectiveness of Quality Circles depends upon a number of key factors. Prime amongst these is support from senior and operational management. If these levels obstruct, or inhibit the effort, even passively, then the initiative will fail. Similarly, participation by the workers must be voluntary, and both they and the leaders must be trained in appropriate techniques.

It is usually suggested that circle members have a common work background. This may be seen as inhibiting the development of solutions to problems that cross process or functional boundaries. It is certainly the case that a problem within a particular area may be solved by a circle drawing its membership from within that area. This approach, though, will not necessarily help with problems which cross internal boundaries and

Box 22.3 Aims for Quality Circles

- improve and develop the enterprise;
- respect human relations and build job satisfaction;
- stretch human potential and capabilities.

denies the use of inter-disciplinary teams. Inter-disciplinary working has been found to be extremely helpful in the discipline of operational research and is continuing to gain popularity in many other fields. The principal benefit of a 'common background' circle is that the membership will not feel that a solution has been imposed by an outside, disinterested body. A sense of 'ownership' in solutions is generally recognised as a powerful means of overcoming resistance to change.

The orientation of the Quality Circle is towards solutions. It is very easy for them to become enmeshed in complaints about the organisation and its management. This may be made manifest in moaning about other parts of the process, or fruitless comparisons of working conditions, pay rates and other issues which are not central to the purpose of the circle.

Organisation of the circle should be a matter of normal good practice for meetings; that is, a specific (but limited) time set aside, circulation of an agenda and invitations to attend to all members, together with managers and supervisors at least as a matter of courtesy. It is recommended that the leadership of the circle be rotated on a regular basis and that hierarchy in the circle be avoided. Apart from its benefit to active participation in the circle, this provides the opportunity for every member to try the role of manager, even if in a very limited sense. It may also be regarded as good training practice and an opportunity for a manager to see how individual workers might cope with more responsible and supervisory positions.

It is generally considered important that the efforts of the participants should be recognised, although debate continues about this aspect. One school of thought suggests that a participant in a Quality Circle is only fulfilling his or her responsibility to an employer by showing how improvement can be achieved. If satisfaction and increased job security are achieved through this then the effort brings its own reward. The other school of thought believes that an employee is paid to carry out a specific task and that extra responsibility should carry extra reward.

Any recognition or reward aspect needs to be related to the culture of the organisation and its geographical location. Decisions need to be made on the basis of the socio-cultural context of the particular organisation. This means that what may be appropriate in Hong Kong or Singapore may be wholly inappropriate in Tokyo or London.

Quality Circles do not stand on their own as an approach to TQM; they must be supported by other initiatives. One important weakness in this respect is the lack of a Quality Circle hierarchy for working across organisational boundaries and at higher levels in the organisation. This means that interactions cannot be recognised and appropriately addressed within this conventional approach.

At Western Paper, having introduced the concept of Quality Circles and facilitated the training and initial events, it became clear that there was much scope for improvement. Some of this fell within the remit of the local circles – and they followed a systematic approach (based on that offered by Kobayashi) to deliver those improvements. However, many of the issues fell across organisational boundaries, and had impact on the way that Western Paper was structured. For example, the circles determined that:

Poor process control and multiple handovers of responsibility were exemplified by high work in progress stocks, frequent delays, excess and aged stock of unsold product in the warehouse and very low 'on time in full' deliveries;

The approach of 'production at all costs' driven by the absence of meaningful measurement meant that 'production push' rather than 'demand pull' drove volumes. So, whilst the paper machine was fully utilised it was not achieving the net 100 good tonnes per day needed to meet customer requirements because much of what was produced had not been ordered.

Three of these issues demanded further analysis of the production process whilst the fourth, the competence issue, drove a desire to examine job designs within the business to determine whether better options might be available.

22.3   Improving processes

The core processes of Western Paper having been captured and a number of issues raised to do with control, changes of responsibility, performance measurement and so on, it is appropriate to continue this part of the project by analysing and critically reviewing them.

22.3.1   Process analysis

Process analysis and critical examination

Once a process has been defined it can be analysed. Of particular concern in the quality management context is the recognition of where error or failure does or may occur in the process. This enables focus to be maintained on those aspects most in need of improvement or re-development. It also provides cues for key measurement points at which statistical process control techniques may be most usefully employed.

The purpose of analysing the process at the outset is to eliminate unnecessary activities and to identify 'triggers' which start other processes and sub-routines. The critical examination should reveal the reasons for each activity and enable the compilation of a systematic and prioritised list of potential enhancements.

The benefit gained from critical examination is influenced by the attitude of mind of the analyst. The final result will depend upon the skill with which the process is recorded. Attention must be paid to the following points:

- Actions should be recorded factually and verified;
- Pre-conceived ideas must be abandoned;
- All aspects should be challenged and verified;
- Hasty judgements must be avoided;
- Small details must be recorded at the appropriate level (these may be more important than the major items);
- Hunches and 'bright ideas' should be set aside;
- Problematic attributes of the existing process must be exposed;
- New methods must wait for analysis to be completed.

This reflects the 'Six Sigma' basis of analysis.

There is debate as to whether the productive or non-productive parts of the process should be examined first – the former tending to lead to more rapid productivity improvements. In the quality context, and following the work of Ohno, the concern is with identifying where error and failure occur, as these are the causes of reducible waste. It is best if a systematic approach is taken; following the process from the start through to the end. This is because errors made in early parts of the process may be driving failure at later stages and it is important to eliminate these prior causes. I recently studied a production process in which the only way the manager of the second stage of the process could succeed was by ensuring that the first stage was seen to fail. Measurement of performance and error at key points of the process may be desirable as a means of identifying where failure occurs and in what proportions. The information so derived can be used to help in prioritising work.

The examination of the identified process can be carried out through a two stage sequence of questions which adopt the pattern shown in Box 22.4.

In contemporary organisations it is useful to ask similar 'means' questions about the machines and technology used to support the process. That is: what machines are used, are they suitable for the task, are they reliable, do their outputs match or exceed the task requirements and so on. These questions enable the analyst to determine precisely what the existing process is, to question it and to identify its flaws. The movement towards quality is begun by proposing alternatives and highlighting failures. Properly supported by valid statistical techniques this 'is-ought' approach is useful.

A final issue to address in this context is process naming. What the process is called may have a significant influence on how it is treated by both management and staff.

For example, whilst building a skills based ISO 9001 Quality Management System for a Hong Kong organisation a process called 'Customer Complaints' was identified. The volume of complaints was very high relative to the total number of customers and each was responded to effectively. However they were regarded as an interruption or intrusion in the 'real work' of the business. The volume being high, it was anticipated that some difficulties might arise with the quality certification process. It was decided therefore to examine this area in greater detail. The examination revealed that what the organisation called 'Customer Complaints' were actually requests for maintenance and repair work on the various premises managed by the organisation and were, in reality, 'Requests for Service'; that is, they were, for the most part, reports of minor building defects in need of attention – blown light bulbs, dripping taps, failed door locks. All matters which the organisation could not know about without advice from the customer.

It was therefore decided to rename the 'Customer Complaints' process as the 'Requests for Service' process. A complaint was deemed to arise where the same

---

Box 22.4   Critical examination procedure

Primary Questions:		Secondary Questions
PURPOSE:	What is done?	What else might be done?
	Why is it done?	What should be done?
PLACE:	Where is it done?	Where else might it be done?
	Why is it done there?	Where should it be done?
SEQUENCE:	When is it done?	When might it be done?
	Why is it done then?	When should it be done?
PERSON:	Who does it?	Who else might do it?
	Why do they do it?	Who should do it?
MEANS:	How is it done?	How else might it be done?
	Why is it done like that?	How should it be done?

fault was reported more than once – that is the organisation had failed to respond. The impact was to change the attitude of the tenants – because they perceived that the organisation had created a better communication facility for them – and to change the attitude of the staff to dealing with 'Requests for Service'. The number of genuine complaints fell substantially.

Method development

Method development covers a range of techniques which can be used to identify alternatives to the established process and ways of overcoming quality problems. It relies on creative thinking about the situation and in turn requires an open and inquiring mind. A lateral approach is useful, as it attempts to find fresh angles from which to view the process. Determination to succeed is important as is an acceptance that all ideas can be treated as equally valid at the outset even though they may appear remote from the problem. Creative thinking is supported by a variety of techniques. Readers might wish to refer to the works of Edward De Bono for further inspiration.

Brainstorming is a method of enabling groups of individuals, normally between four and twelve in number (as for Quality Circles!), to generate ideas for problem solving. The process is relatively simple. The group leader outlines the problem and answers any questions submitted by the members. Thereafter the group generate ideas which are recorded without comment or judgement on flip charts, white boards or sometimes on 'post-it' stickers. After about half an hour (or when the ideas dry up) the ideas are evaluated by the group. Those offering most apparent value being subject to further evaluation and, where appropriate, experimentation and development.

It is vital that the leader of a brainstorming session is experienced in problem solving and is able to create and maintain enthusiasm amongst the group members.

Analogies are also useful. An analogy is an agreement or commonality in certain characteristics between things which are otherwise different. To use analogies is to apply alternative knowledge and experience to a problem. The problem solvers consider items which are different but possess similar attributes to the problem under consideration. This approach encourages cross-fertilisation of ideas from different professional backgrounds and disciplines. There are three types of analogy which are particularly useful.

Functional: What else does what this process does?
Simple: What does this process look like?
Natural: How is this done in nature?

This last is a particularly helpful approach since natural systems tend towards self-organisation, effectiveness (if not always apparent short-term efficiency) and evolution.

Morphological analysis is a systematic method of creating possible lists of logical combinations of variables already known to solve a problem. It enables the range of possible solution spaces to be matched and a 'most reliable' method to be chosen. One example of this could be solving a delivery problem as follows:

Method: Post, Courier, In-House Delivery System
Speed: JIT, Same Day, Overnight, Non-Critical
Packaging: Crushproof, Airtight, Palletised, Unimportant

The possible number of logical combinations of variables is $3 \times 4 \times 4$ – there are 48 possible solutions to the delivery problem (given that each combination of variables is possible, some, such as Post and Same Day, are 'illegal' solutions, that is to say they will not work). Once the range of possible solutions has been defined, quality and other criteria can be applied to identify those which meet expectations and requirements.

Listing and combining attributes is another way of highlighting potential for improvement in a process. This technique requires the creation of a list of the attributes that the process must possess in order to fulfil the requirements – such as Zero Defects. Changes to the process are then proposed which enable these attributes to be attained.

Heuristic analysis fits within the context of kaizen quality thinking. The heuristic method is to generate changes to the process, apply them and review the results. The results are then used as the platform for testing further changes, and so on in an iterative cycle. This is similar to the 'PDCA' cycle proposed by Deming (chapter 6) and to the ideas of organisational learning outlined in chapter 20. Heuristic improvement should never stop but, to be effective, must be used in a systematic rather than random manner. The principal disadvantage of the heuristic method lies in its inherently incremental nature. A heuristic approach may never generate the sort of radical, discontinuous (or step) change in a process that may be provoked by the use of other methods.

Convergent and divergent thinking are also useful approaches. Convergent thinking occurs when the analyst(s) attempts to separate the essential items of the process from the incidental. In this way the aim is to focus on the most important issues, reminiscent of Juran's 'vital few and useful many'. Divergent thinking is the opposite and occurs when the analyst(s) expands the problem to take account of other information that is not central to the defined process.

The Process Analysis and examination showed that the core process of paper production was essentially fixed; the paper machine only works one way. However the way in which that process was managed, the way it connected to prior and subsequent processes and the lack of information driving the processes were significant problems.

It seemed that the first issue to resolve was that of the management of the processes. Figure 22.3 shows how, when the whole business is considered, it forms three connected processes.

The first process is the one of receiving customer orders which should first go through a stock check (necessitating accurate and up to date stock figures). That should stimulate one of two things, either a despatch notice to the warehouse and fulfilment of the order or a 'make' notice to the operations team. The 'make' notice would stimulate an amendment to the production plan and be scheduled onto the machine, stimulating a 'pull' on the fibre stock and further down the supply chain to suppliers of fibre and other necessities. All product would at this point, be made to order, no product could be made for which there was not an established customer order. Some paper is sold as reels, some is converted; the split of volume across these would be determined by customer order. The warehouse operation becomes essentially a marshalling point where orders can be assembled ready for despatch rather than stock held awaiting an order.

Achieving this was not an overnight change, the change was channelled through the daily operations meeting with the evidence of improving performance (made clear in the

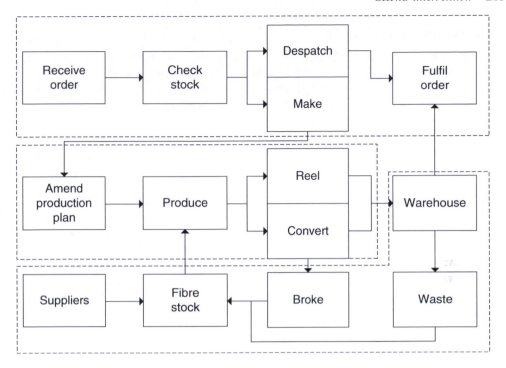

Figure 22.3 Connected processes.

daily dashboard) providing the stimulus to the management team to persist with the changes and, in particular, to sustain and develop the conversation across the process break points.

This was reinforced by several other actions at this stage:

- The development of a costing and pricing model;
- A stock audit and de-stocking project;
- Data cleansing across multiple systems.

Establishment of new Service Level Agreements (SLAs) with customers coupled to a reduction in the product range to remove unpopular or unprofitable products.

22.3.2   Statistical methods

This is not a textbook on statistics – that is something best left to a true expert in the field and Logothetis (1992) has already been suggested as providing a useful text.

However, it is usually necessary within any consulting intervention to undertake some level of quantitative analysis – and that involves statistical calculations of some sort, because you are necessarily working with a sample of activities and it is important to understand how well that sample represents the whole situation being considered. This section then provides an introduction to some of the limitations of statistics and how they are often (mis)used.

Statistical methods

Statistical methods offer techniques for measuring and evaluating performance and performance improvement on a sampling basis. However, they also offer the greatest scope for fooling both others and yourselves. They must be used properly, intelligently and with full understanding of their accuracy and implications.

Statistics are frequently used to support decision making – and support is their proper role. They should not become the only factor used to make a decision. There are a number of reasons for this. First, they may not be accurate. Even where machine counted, measures of volume, throughput and so on can often generate misleading numbers. When people are involved in the counting process a degree of error is almost inevitable – try counting sheep in a field or fish in a pond – the difficulty of counting is similar to counting finished products on a production line or service events in a retail outlet. Similarly, however accurate the actual numbers, if some critical process event has been overlooked the measurements, and the statistics derived from them, will be wrong.

Second, statistics represent probabilities, not actualities – remember the number of 'averages' used in the calculation of standard deviation – particularly where batch or sample sizes vary. The answers given for these calculations are 'more or less' accurate – never precise. Third, since the calculations are, to some degree 'wrong', pure reliance on them is bound to generate some degree of mismatch to reality, often leading to complaints and witch hunts.

Fourth, understanding how the numbers are driven is much more important than the numbers themselves. Pure reliance on the statistics leads to a focus on improving the statistics rather than improving the process which supports them. It is frequently observed that in a failing or struggling company the focus is on reducing costs. Company wide cuts are imposed, for example 10% of head count or 10% of wage costs. While in the short term this might address the specific problem of immediate cash flow it usually does nothing for the medium- to long-term future of the company.

As it is with money so it is with quality. A short-term hard-nosed push for quality is a recurring feature of organisations. However, unless changes are developed for the production processes, the common causes of failure are simply overridden. Once the pressure is released the system will revert to its previous behaviour. A further phenomenon is called squeezing the snake. In this case a quality problem is identified at a particular stage of a process through a Statistical Process Control mechanism. Managerial pressure is applied to that point and performance improvement is generated, the quality problem reduces. What is not realised until much later is that the problem has not disappeared, it has simply been moved, either back up the process by constricting the inputs to the problem area or further down the process by widening the exit point (usually by varying the criteria for quality).

Common statistical errors

A headline in the UK press proclaimed that 'Women are safer drivers than men!' This headline generated much debate in the press, on radio and TV with many men incensed by the claim (their manliness insulted) and many women and men responding to the headline by citing examples of poor driving by the other sex.

The whole debate was highly entertaining but built on an entirely false premise. The headline created for the original newspaper article had one intention – to sell more newspapers. In the newspaper tradition of 'never let the truth get in the way of a good story' the journalist involved had distilled a useful headline, with strong emotional impact, from a probably rather dull report. The research had been undertaken by the insurance industry in relation to claims experience amongst British insurers. What the research actually established was quite simple – women, on average, make less frequent insurance claims than men, and, again on average, the size of their claims is smaller.

The research findings themselves can be accepted – they are probably pretty accurate, they do not though establish the superiority of either female or male drivers. So what is established?

> The average claim by women drivers, on policies held in their own names, is smaller than the average claim by male drivers;
>   The average frequency of claims in respect of those policies is lower for women drivers than for men.

These statements have everything to do with the claims experience of the companies participating in the research relative to female and male policy holders. They say nothing of substance concerning the safety or otherwise of either sex behind the wheel of a car and, because claims are made by the policy holder, they cannot differentiate between a wide number of aspects of the claims experience. For example:

1   The number of claims made by female policy holders whose cars were, at the time of the damage, being driven by men;
2   The number of claims made by male policy holders whose cars, at the time of the damage, were being driven by women;
3   The number of vehicle repairs carried out for which no claim is made;
4   The number of accidents for which no repair is carried out;
5   The difference in claims between high-mileage drivers and low-mileage drivers – i.e. the average miles driven per claim made – a measure perhaps of relative safety;
6   The relative value and cost of repair of vehicles driven by either sex;
7   The context in which accidents take place, i.e. urban, rural, motorway;
8   The speed of vehicles when accidents occur;
9   The meaning, in context, of *average*.

One other key factor underpins this headline – what did the journalist mean by 'better'? It can be seen that the headline has been used for the purposes of the journalist, while the research on which it was based was almost certainly for an entirely different purpose. The headline, though probably not the research itself, was meaningless in statistical terms.

It is vital when developing and applying statistical techniques that the claims made as a result of quantitative analysis are not subverted to other ends. Some common errors are:

Data-collection: a common error is to rely on statistics for which the raw data has been collected in an unreliable manner. A good example of this is the measurement of footfall on the pathway outside a shop or fast food outlet. Footfall (the number of people passing by) is generally regarded as a good guide to the likely number of customers for an outlet in the location. Even with the best of intentions and concerted effort, the count of passers by will have some degree of inaccuracy, simply because the method of measurement is unreliable. Often such numbers are compiled from the 'best estimates of those who know' – in other words an entirely subjective measurement. When these subjective measurements are summed, aggregated, averaged and otherwise manipulated, they give results with a degree of accuracy which is entirely spurious. If the base data is no better than subjective estimate – then neither is the end result – however well it has been manipulated!

Sampling error: on every occasion where a sample (as opposed to an entire population) is used, the opportunity exists for either accidental or deliberate bias to be introduced to the survey. The sample must be sufficiently large and properly selected for any meaningful data to be derived from it.

Missing numbers: tying in with sampling error is failure to provide (either deliberately or accidentally) the key figures which validate (or otherwise) the statistic. If the population is one million and the sample size is ten then a statistic which claims '100% of respondents agreed with our findings' is meaningless unless the sample size and confidence factor are also quoted. In this case the confidence in the accuracy of the answer would be low!

The wrong average: there are three different types of average – the mean, the median and the mode. These are in turn the arithmetic average (total divided by number), the middle one and the most frequently occurring! It is important to know which average is being used in each context and what it really tells you. That is, for what purpose the statistic is being quoted.

Spurious correlations: it is often found that there is some apparent correlation between the incidence of two events or happenings and somebody, somewhere states that because they appear to correlate then one must be the cause of the other. This causal chain view of the world has already been challenged in part three of this book. When a correlation is proposed it is vital to understand why the proposer suggests it and to examine the evidence for and against the proposal – particularly to consider what other factors might explain the co-incidence of the events. For example, creative people such as musicians, artists, writers are also often seen as heavy drinkers or users of narcotic drugs. There is a positive correlation between artistry and substance abuse. Does one cause the other? Could I be a great artist if I were to drink more? Could I drink more if I were a great artist? A third factor must be allowed to intrude. The third factor is personality. Perhaps an individual who challenges convention in one area of his/her life will also challenge convention in others – the causal link is not artistry and substance abuse but arises through personality. It is necessary to challenge the assumptions which underpin the causal link view of events.

Misleading presentation: many statistics are reported graphically. Pictures of a situation are often easier for people to understand than the raw numbers derived from surveys and samples – they also make it easier to misrepresent either deliberately or inadvertently the real situation. For example 'an increase in the rate of decline' can be represented as an upward path – if it is the rate of decline which is being reported! The words tell the truth – things are getting worse, the picture with its upward sloping line suggests the opposite! Similarly a slow rate of growth in something can be presented as fast by the simple device of shortening the horizontal axis relative to the vertical axis on a graph.

It is always important to know:

Where did the statistics come from?
How big was the sample size?

How representative of the total population was the sample?

What average(s) have been used – and for what purpose?

What point was the presenter of the statistics trying to prove?

What counter-evidence was found – and perhaps not presented?

What assumptions underpin the points being made?

Summary

Good, accurate statistics are vital for performance measurement, but they cannot replace competent, informed management. Good, that is accurate, well founded and reliable statistics can tell the manager much about what is happening within the processes of a organisation. That is the limit of their usefulness. The statistics say nothing about why the reported events occur – which is much more important. Statistics are simply a statement of the characteristics and events the managers have chosen to record. Demanding an improvement in the statistics – as managers often do – will ensure they get just that! The processes, products or services of the organisation will not change at all. Managers need to look behind the reported numbers and consider the deeper aspects of the organisation. Aspects to consider might include the quality and amount of supervision, the reliability and accuracy of equipment, the feelings and attitudes of the staff, the expectations of the customers (many complaints are after all the result of a mismatch of the customers' expectations – created through marketing – and the reality of the product or service – as produced by the organisation).

Readers are reminded to develop their understanding further through the use of a good text on statistical quality methods such as Logothetis (1992) or operations management such as Slack et al (1995).

The statistics for Western Paper were, in the end, quite simple. A single paper machine with a design capacity of 1,000 tonnes production per week. The machine had controllable in process variability, adjusting the weight per square metre and the paper width. At the beginning of the process recycled fibre in four tonne lots was mixed with colourants which combined with the weight and width mix gave a range of about 270 products at the reeler, the end of the paper machine itself. Of these reels (which could vary in width and weight and would be split into working widths) some would be despatched directly to customers, others were sent to the conversion process.

Process control up to this point was relatively simple and was a function of the expertise of the machine operators. Production losses were driven first of all by the product changeovers where an hour of production (four tonnes) was lost with each significant change of weight or colour, secondly by paper breaks (where the tension in the paper machine causes the paper flow to split and the machine has to be stopped and the paper refed through). Paper breaks were more frequent as the product reached the outer variations of weight, particularly with the lighter products. These were difficult to eliminate on a very old machine in which little capital had been invested.

However, this level of variability could be managed within the process plan. Far greater, and less predictable, variation arose in the sales cycle (which precedes production), the conversion process which succeeds it and the 'call off' process whereby customers demanded product which was being warehoused for them.

Initial process variability was of such amplitude and frequency that statistical analysis would have been redundant. It was necessary initially to damp these gross oscillations with rather less finesse. The variability primarily arose from a number of sources:

- Sales process and customer orders;
- Production failures (breaks, volume overruns, machine failures, product remakes);
- Conversion failure (poor management of an essentially manual process);
- Insertion of additional orders to the production plan (usually arising from previous failure);
- Poor information availability (meaning for example that product was being made when it was already in stock – but 'the system' didn't know that);
- Poor 'work–in–process' stock control.

The daily dashboard and IP meeting was used as the primary operational planning device and, through coaching and mentoring, operations staff in all areas were encouraged to communicate more effectively with their colleagues. The revisiting of the sales process, coupled to revised customer contracts and stricter adherence to SLAs, began to reduce the gross variations at the 'pull' end of the process and the whole system began to respond to the regularisation of the customer drumbeat. A great example of how, even at a very high level of consideration, lean thinking can be introduced to a situation and begin to deliver the necessary disciplines to decisions and behaviour.

Whilst the first of the production problems was addressed by the use of more effective information, the second required the business to look at both job design and the skills mix necessary to perform the required tasks which required considerable dexterity.

22.3.3   Job design

Job design covers a range of issues associated with obtaining improvement in quality through enhanced job performance. It involves recognising that, to a large extent, jobs have historically not been designed but more often have been initially described and subsequently allowed to evolve. Re-design may have been undertaken in the pursuit of greater efficiency and error reduction, including the application of work study and Organisation and Methods techniques, but this will have often served to fragment tasks into smaller parts. Frequently managers do not know how any given employee actually uses the working day. Decisions about particular tasks have often been made without understanding of the whole process or the purpose to be served.

This section proposes a variety of approaches which help to address the problems caused including dissatisfaction, fragmentation and ineffectiveness.

Often, organisations are not systematically developed and work is allocated on the basis of current workload and/or past experience. In this way work appears to move randomly around the organisation. Consequently little sense of ownership or responsibility for particular aspects of the work is engendered amongst the workforce. On that basis of allocation the work has little or no meaning or value to them.

Creating natural work units (Box 22.5) means adopting a different approach whereby logical (or natural) groupings of work are created and allocated to individuals or teams, each accepting total responsibility for the work allocated. If the employees can identify with the work, there is a greater opportunity for them to take ownership and pride in accomplishment. A sense of ownership of the task and pride in its completion will often lead to improved quality through the sense of responsibility of the individual.

Natural or logical groupings of tasks may be developed along a number of dimensions, dependent on what is to be achieved.

It is of course necessary to maintain an equal work-loading in the creation of these work units This may mean either allocating more staff to a particularly heavy workload area, or creating vertical or horizontal sub-divisions of the work. This can be achieved by cross matching categories, for example matching a geographical area with an industrial sector or by delimiting authority for taking action. An example of this is the use of lending authorities in banks which are often split both horizontally and vertically; for example, a lending officer may be able to authorise loans up to £220,000 in a particular market segment while another lending officer can authorise loans from £220,001–1,000,000 in the same sector.

Jobs have often been broken down into tasks (and even sub-tasks) so that in order to create a complete product or service a team of five or six people is needed. In the service industries in particular, these people may be in separate areas or departments.

This is apparently highly efficient (in the sense of Adam Smith's Pin Factory) since the individuals become highly adept at the particular task. However, simple, repetitive tasks often provide little or no challenge and hence provoke little interest from the employee. This lack of interest leads to dissatisfaction, falling productivity, increased error rates and absenteeism and often increased labour turnover – this last item leading to increased recruitment and training costs. This approach rests heavily on the work of Frederick Taylor (1911), and may be considered at least partly responsible for some of the problems of industrial relations seen in Western countries throughout this century.

Box 22.5   Natural work units

Geographical:	each worker is assigned work arising from a particular location, for example a Country, County or District;
Organisational:	each worker may be allocated work according to its divisional or departmental source;
Alphabetical:	customer processing work may be divided according to alphabetical groupings, for example A–D, E–K, L–R, S–Z;
Numerical:	Work in a supply depot may be allocated to clerks according to bin locations or part numbers;
Customer:	Work may be allocated according to customer size or type. For example some Banks have divided customers into four principal sectors – large corporate, small business, high net-worth individuals, mass-market – and these divisions are reflected in their allocation of work;
Industry Sector:	each employee specialises in servicing customers, or making products in particular market segments, for example engineering, property, education, medical and so on.

Re-combining tasks into complete jobs can help to counter this source of dissatisfaction, allowing the employee a sense of pride and achievement in what is created. Using task combination, the employee is given the chance to manage his or her work, rather than being simply required to repeat the same simple task again and again.

To implement this approach it is necessary to have a comprehensive understanding of the work process. This can be obtained through the use of the process charting techniques discussed in chapter 23 of this book. Analysis will need to be undertaken at the Process Operation or Process Detail level. An alternative is to involve the affected staff in the redesign. They already know the process and, from experience, they normally have a good understanding of how changes and improvements can be achieved.

In most organisations, the worker works, while the supervisor or manager, at least notionally, carries out the tasks of planning, organising, controlling and co-ordinating. Conventionally, tasks, performance standards, time frames and objectives are set by the management for their subordinates with little or no consultation. This can mean that the worker feels no obligation to achieve those targets which they consider as belonging to the management rather than themselves.

Vertical loading (Box 22.6) consists of allowing responsibility to descend through the organisation so that workers are allowed a degree of freedom in setting their own standards, thereby accepting a degree of responsibility for their achievements. Equally, degrees of latitude in decision making can be increased, empowering the employee to solve problems and take appropriate action.

Using the vertical loading approach can enable the reduction or removal of some control and checking activity; the assignment of more demanding tasks and increased levels of authority amongst the workforce. This, if properly handled, should lead to a virtuous circle of improvement at the lower levels and should enable managers to concentrate more effectively on the issues which really matter about their own work. Successful use of vertical loading depends upon three key characteristics amongst the workforce. They must be willing to accept the additional responsibility, they must have the appropriate ability and the level of training and competence must be commensurate with the need of the task.

It is the responsibility of management to ensure that these conditions are met and to provide appropriate training where necessary. Management must also ensure that scope is provided for the empowered staff to become accustomed to their freedoms and to learn to use them wisely. It is almost inevitable that at the outset mistakes and errors will occur whilst staff learn to apply skills of decision and judgement, which were previously the exclusive preserve of the management. Mistakes must be accepted at the initial stage as part of the learning process and management must avoid the temptation to withdraw the freedoms and re-take direct control whilst the employees learn to work with the new found freedoms.

Box 22.6   Key requirements for vertical loading

A willingness to accept responsibility;
Ability which matches the increased requirements;
A level of training commensurate with the new responsibilities.

Decision making is based on information. Very often employees exist in what might also be considered an information vacuum. They are unaware of performance standards (or even if they exist), receive a performance appraisal once a year (or once every two years in many public sector organisations) and gain no specific current information on how well, or badly, they are performing their particular task. Frequently where appraisal systems do exist they are used as instruments of blame and punishment rather than enablers of improvement.

In these circumstances, the employees will set their own standards, either explicitly in conjunction with each other, or more commonly on an individual basis – doing what they think is best for them. Nature abhors a vacuum, and in the absence of information from management, the workforce will create their own. This may or may not be in line with management expectations. To correct this, task feedback information (Box 22.7) must be provided and to be effective must be driven by the process itself, must be as near 'real-time' as possible, must be continuously provided and must be meaningful to the recipient. Failure to meet any of these conditions will render the information useless.

The word feedback is one of the most commonly abused in the English language. In this book it means information drawn from the output side of a process which is compared with a target with the comparison being used as the basis for adjusting the input to the process.

Using the insights provided by Ohno and the power of contemporary information technology, none of these requirements is difficult to achieve. However, the most frequent difficulties arise with the last requirement. What constitutes meaningful information for a manager may be very different to that for the worker affected. For instance, a manager may wish to work with reports expressed in terms of profit and loss, i.e. with monetary measurements of performance. For the worker in the service department of a car dealership monetary measures may be meaningless. They may measure performance in terms of the number of vehicles serviced or the level of utilisation of servicing bays. It is useless then to provide information to these individuals on profit or loss, since that data cannot be used by them for control and self-management purposes. It is more useful and more effective to use information technology to provide information to each recipient which is meaningful in their own terms.

The idea of the self-managed work team is essentially an extension of vertical loading. While an overall task is set, the team are free to organise themselves towards its achievement, having either no supervisor, or appointing their own from within the team, often on a rotational basis. In extreme cases, the self-managed work team will take responsibility for organising holiday schedules and other activities which have traditionally been regarded as the exclusive province of management. The team will have the freedom and responsibility to devise improvements and changes within

---

Box 22.7 Task feedback information

Driven by the process itself;
Real time (or as near as possible);
Continuous;
Meaningful (it must be in the recipient's language).

a process, and will often have ways of communicating successes and failures to other teams.

The quality function

The role and position of the quality function are of great importance in relation to both the Job Design and the position within the organisation.

A normal position for the Quality Inspectors, Quality Control or Assurance Manager in many organisations is as a direct reportee of the Production Manager. This serves to institutionalise the potential conflict between them and allows the Production Manager the final decision.

Such an approach enables the Production Manager to override quality decisions in the pursuit of some other interest, for example shipping a full order, regardless of quality, to satisfy the customer in the short term. It also enables the manipulation of other data such as productivity, labour utilisation and even reject/rework levels.

It is vital that the Quality Assurance function enjoy complete independence from the Production function in order that effective inspection and audit become possible. In a company which has fully adopted the quality ethic, this becomes a much less significant issue, since quality ideas will be embedded in the workforce and quality standards will be clearly defined and recognised. In these circumstances the quality decisions, to a large extent, may make themselves. There will be limited scope for arbitrary decisions.

A key factor in creating an organisation for quality is the recognition of processes and the consequent realisation that each part of a process has customers, either internal or external. A company which uses these processes as the cornerstone of the way in which it is organised, and sets its quality criteria in recognition of the needs of customers, will become an organisation for quality.

The change mechanisms established at Western Paper encouraged and supported the engagement of all the staff in contributing to the changes necessary. Through the mechanisms of Interactive Planning and Quality Circles in particular, they were able to substantially participate in the re-design of their jobs. The re-design changed the reach and scope of many positions, reducing the number of 'handovers' in the production process whilst giving purpose and focus to the role of Operations Director who was made responsible for the whole of the process, from stock yard to warehouse, his customer being the customer order. In concert with the re-designed jobs, staff became concerned with defining the information needed to carry out their tasks effectively and efficiently.

22.4   Reflections and next steps

This second intervention in Western Paper demonstrated significant progress. Starting from the diagnosis provided in the previous chapter, the project focused at a whole process level and began to develop new approaches to staff engagement, interaction and communication. A shared, aligned view of the future was generated together with an understanding of what was required to achieve it and processes were redefined and understood. Control was made more effective. The beginnings of effective measurement were put in place and performance improvements were delivered. Jobs have been redesigned with the active involvement of the affected staff who felt a greater sense of ownership and responsibility.

Summary

This chapter has extended the case study and introduced a number of additional tools and techniques to help address the situation. The intention has been to show what can be done and the logical flow of choices. The assumptions and world-views underpinning the multiple methodologies in use have been respected but given new meaning by being applied in the context of a systemic intervention. Limitations to autonomy have been understood and accommodated. A potentially sustainable improvement has been generated.

In the final chapter tools will be introduced to help ensure that potential is realised.

KEY LEARNING POINTS

A variety of tools and methods can be used in context and in conjunction with each other to address complex problems;

Any one tool will necessarily focus on part of the problem to be addressed;

Statistical techniques are essential to aid real understanding – but must be used with intelligence and wisdom;

Interactive Planning and Quality Circles can be used together to engage the whole workforce;

Process Examination and Review can highlight the potential for real improvement;

Job Design can be used as a device for both engaging staff and solving the problems;

Meaningful measurement is essential to success.

Question

Consider Western Paper production process through the Toyota Production System approach and develop an information solution to support it.

23 Final intervention

'And now, the end is near'

Paul Anka, 1967

Introduction

This chapter completes the Western Paper case study by considering external factors. It introduces the ideas of supplier development which is embraced very strongly by Japanese businesses and benchmarking which is now widely used both internally and externally. Chapter 14 introduced ISO 9001:2015 as the basis of a quality management system standard and chapter 19 introduced a contemporary approach to the QMS; this chapter will reflect a more conventional approach.

23.1 Recap

Western Paper has progressed from the initial disordered state to one where it is becoming internally consistent and coherent, is developing sound processes and damping variability through well designed jobs with clear performance criteria and accountability. This is all good progress, but it is not enough. To do the best possible job internally is one thing, but sustainability demands that any organisation fully engage with the world outside itself. That means comparing its performance with that of its neighbours and competitors, working with its suppliers to bring their performance up to that needed – and critically, exposing its performance to some form of audit through pursuit of recognition of its quality performance.

This chapter will examine benchmarking and supplier development. Figure 23.1 shows how these inform the information flows between the core elements of the process.

23.2 Benchmarking

It is inadequate to define improvement relative only to internal measurements. Organisations must define quality and improvement in terms of customers' requirements and relative to the 'best' of the competition. The foundation for quality improvement is to know how good or bad a set of products and services are when compared to others in the same market-place, particularly as they are perceived by customers. The 'fact' that one product or service is technically better than another (as might be argued for the Macintosh and Sun computer operating systems when compared with that from Microsoft) is not enough.

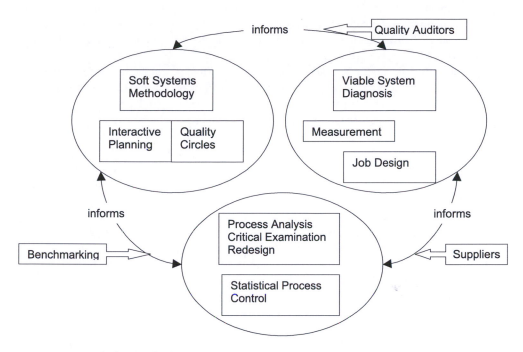

Figure 23.1 Tools for the final intervention.

Microsoft, through more effective interaction with the customers, has achieved and sustained a dominant market position, a position sustained even in 2015 with respect to personal computers, although Apple and Android operating systems have established dominant positions in the mobile computing market.

It is creating the foundation for quality improvement – across all aspects of the product or service – which benchmarking helps to establish.

23.2.1 *What is benchmarking?*

Benchmarking, also now often called 'best practice' – and reinterpreted and broadened for the UK public sector as 'best value' – is used by large and small organisations throughout the world to help them understand their own performance against the best that they can measure. This enables them to more profitably develop and grow their businesses.

> Benchmarking is a process of comparison between the performance characteristics of separate, often competing, organisations intended to enable each participant to improve its own performance in the market-place.
>
> Benchmarking first allows us to obtain a clearer understanding of competitors' success factors and of customers' requirements. This understanding will lead to reduced complaints, a sharper focus on customer needs and higher levels of customer satisfaction. Discovering process improvements will assist in reducing the costs associated with rework, rectification, waste and other quality problems.

Benchmarking will also enable innovations (either of process or product) to spread more rapidly through an industry and across industries where appropriate – for example in supply or distribution logistics where many problems are similar regardless of the industry.

Benchmarking involves a number of simple steps. The first establishes what, from the customers' perspective, makes the difference between one supplier of a product or service and another. It is important to remember that the customers' perception – not the actual, technical quality of the product or service is what matters. The second step is setting standards according to the best practice found, that is regarding best practice as the 'benchmark' for the organisation's performance. The third step is to determine by what means the benchmark organisation achieves those standards. The final step is utilising the capabilities of the staff to meet and, if possible, exceed the standards observed.

It is important to understand that what is important in benchmarking is not the industry, but the core characteristics of the product, service or activity. While it may be ideal to benchmark one airline against another, this may be difficult for reasons of competition, politics or law (for example, where such behaviour may be regarded as anti-competitive or likely to lead to cartel pricing). On the other hand, it is perfectly reasonable to compare an airline's marketing or logistics function with those of a newspaper or a bread bakery since the products share a significant characteristic – nobody buys yesterday's bread or newspaper – no one can occupy an airline seat once the flight has left! A similarly useful comparison can be drawn between customer and enquiry handling in a bank and that at an airline counter or in a department store. The core process may be the same even though the particular questions may be very different.

Benchmarking provides a rigorous framework through which the benefits outlined above can be obtained. It enables a disciplined, demanding assessment of performance in areas which are crucial to the particular organisation. It also enables avoidance of the errors and mistakes already made by others, thus preventing further re-invention of the wheel.

Two major limitations on performance improvement can be usefully addressed through benchmarking. First is the limitation to knowledge which so often affects organisational performance. Experience and knowledge are often bounded by the particular environment in which they are gained. Unless individuals have the opportunity of wider exposure, they are largely closed off from developments which could improve their process. Thus they become content with the way things are – because they know of nothing different or better.

Second the syndrome known as NIH – Not Invented Here – can be overcome through benchmarking. NIH is a typical response by many organisations and employees to proposed changes to improve performance. It is often accompanied by remarks such as 'that may work alright in xxxx but it just wouldn't apply here', frequently supported by 'because we're unique', 'our circumstances are different' or 'our customers don't expect' or some similar excuse. The truth is that NIH is a defensive ploy intended to inhibit the disruption to established patterns and habits of work and the effort that is often associated with a change programme. If the employees who will be affected by a change are involved in its design through the benchmarking programme, then they will be much less likely to resist the change and more likely to develop unique aspects which will 'make it work here'.

Overall, benchmarking requires senior management commitment, particularly to supporting actions arising from the exploration. It also requires staff to be trained and guided in the process to ensure that maximum benefit is obtained. Finally, it requires allocation of part of the relevant employee's time to enable it to be carried out.

How is benchmarking done?

There are only five steps (Box 23.1) to a benchmarking process regardless of the size of companies involved. However, larger companies may indulge in greater amounts of data gathering than smaller ones and may have to be conscious of issues surrounding anti-competitive or monopolistic behaviour.

Step one, appraising and identifying which characteristics to benchmark, can be achieved through 'Pareto Analysis'. While it is possible to benchmark every characteristic of a process, the return to the company from doing so will vary substantially. Remembering Juran's comment on 'the vital few, the useful many', it is worth trying to determine at the outset in which activities the company needs to excel to succeed in its particular business. A substantial improvement in a process which delivers no benefit to customers will not necessarily or directly improve the competitive position, although it may generate improvement in profit performance which may be of great importance. Quality benchmarks might include aspects such as reliability, longevity, consistency, accuracy, levels of in-process rework or rectification, service intervals, after-sales response and so on. Factors which affect profitability – and which may enable more effective competition through reductions in prices – include reductions in rework, working stocks, inventory levels and relationships between factors such as sales dollars (or other currency) per employee, enquiry to sale conversion rates, space utilisation and increasingly the effectiveness in use of management information systems.

The selection criteria for projects should be based on delivery of maximum benefit to the customer rather than on matters which might be considered as exciting or interesting to a particular professional group. Approaches based on the latter view often lead to major disappointment. Characteristics to be benchmarked should be:

> those which are of genuine concern to the customer;
> those which are of material importance to the organisation;
> those where a problem is recognised.

The second step is deciding which other organisations to benchmark with. In the case of a very large, perhaps divisionalised operation, it may be perfectly reasonable to start by internal benchmarking, for example comparing the distribution logistics processes of

---

Box 23.1   Five steps in benchmarking

Step 1)   Identifying what characteristics to benchmark;
Step 2)   Identifying benchmarking partners;
Step 3)   Designing the data gathering methodology;
Step 4)   Selecting analytical tools;
Step 5)   Implementing changes.

two factories. If this is not possible then it is necessary to look outside the organisation for benchmarking partners. A starting point is to ask the customers who they regard as the best in your particular business; after all it is the customers that you are trying to satisfy. This will also help to identify those characteristics of performance which the customers regard as important.

Other sources include the press, trade and industry associations, industry expert consultants or academics. Looking overseas the various trade commissions, embassies and state departments should be able to provide useful leads. For example in Hong Kong the Productivity Council could help, while in the UK there are a number of organisations focused on benchmarking practice and co-operation.

There are four key issues to address in selecting benchmarking partners:

> Do the companies have some knowledge of each other?
> Is there a customer–supplier relationship already?
> Is the partners' experience directly relevant to our needs?
> Are they as good as their reputation suggests?

It is quite normal for a company's reputation to outlast the quality of its goods or services; equally some companies with established 'bad' reputations may have made substantial performance improvements. For example, in the 1970s the FIAT Company developed a reputation for building cars which rusted very quickly and very badly. This has not been the case for many years, yet the reputation still surrounds their products despite the evidence on the roads that the reputation is unfair.

Finally, and as mentioned before, is the exchange of information with this partner permissible? Apart from any legislative issues, organisations need to be aware of limitations on the transfer of technology to and from certain countries and for certain purposes. These general cautions need to be supported by appropriate legal advice and of course the application of common sense.

Step three, designing the data gathering methodology moves beyond the basics of ensuring that any statistical methods are rigorously applied and the results meaningful, to the real issue of how to physically obtain the information. The first and most readily available sources are in the public domain, for example company annual reports, press articles, trade association journals and libraries, academic studies (where these have been undertaken and published) and from the various bodies and consultancies which specialise in enabling benchmarking. While normally direct competitors will only exchange data through a third party, such as a trade association, some may be amenable to a direct contact – particularly if the company approaching them is able to offer comparable assistance to them on another issue. For example, you may swap information on staff retention and development programmes for information on distribution logistics. As long as each party perceives there to be a fair exchange (in terms of problems solved) the volume of data will probably not be an obstruction. What is vital at this stage is that the data necessary to enable the benchmarking to be carried out is identified right at the outset – nothing is worse than having to return to the partner for more information, nothing is more unhelpful than designing improvements based on incomplete or inaccurate information.

The fourth step reflects the similar stage in process review. The key difference is that rather than seeking general improvement, the search in the benchmarking exercise is for specific differences between processes which give one a significant performance margin over the other. This recognition of the performance gap is the basis for improvement, recognising always that what works for one company in one set of circumstances will not necessarily work for another in a different set.

The fifth and final step is implementing changes. Technically this is quite straightforward. New performance standards need to be set based on the improvement scope identified. The lowest level of management with an overview of the whole process affected, appropriately supported, needs to take direct responsibility for implementing the changes. Additional resources must be provided to support the changes if required. For example, overtime working may be necessary to create a window enabling the absorption of disruption associated with a particular change. This might occur in a despatch unit where a redesign of the storage layout could demand that a significant amount of space be created in the short term. Finally, a performance monitoring programme must be implemented to make progress visible.

Benchmarking, like quality improvement, is never complete. It is a continuing process and although the incremental gains from the first exercise are likely to be the largest, the process should be continued to ensure that the organisation always reflects best practice in the particular area.

Critical review

Benchmarking is essentially an exercise in organisational humility. It demands that rather than being complacent about how good an organisation is, it respects the idea that there may be others in the industry who carry out a particular process more effectively. Effective means cheaper, quicker and more closely meeting customer expectations. The organisation then has to set out to learn from those higher performers.

Technically, as has been shown, benchmarking is not a difficult process. Each of the five steps is relatively straightforward and, overall, it amounts to emulating the best and trying to improve on their performance. As any author will tell you, it is far harder to write an original book than to prepare a review or critique of another's.

The risk with benchmarking is that the organisation only aspires to be as good as the rest and sets its sights accordingly. This means it simply copies others' practices without adapting them to the particular and unique set of circumstances in which it operates. Relying on such a model (a model is simply a representation of reality), the organisation will never achieve the levels of performance of the organisation copied. This is because the model does not reveal everything about the organisation or its circumstances, only those characteristics which the modeller thought important.

The second problem with straight copying is of course that no competitive advantage is gained. The process simply levels the playing field further, reducing diversity in the market and thereby reducing effective consumer choice. If there is no measurable difference between products or services then purchasers will make their choices on other criteria such as convenience, accessibility or taste (fashion), the last of which is extremely fickle.

Benchmarking is a potentially valuable technique for quickly lifting the performance of an organisation. However, establishing benchmarks must be used as the platform for significant improvement over the best, if it is genuinely to improve the competitive position of the organisation rather than simply keep it in the game.

The global paper industry is characterised by strong competition between a relatively small number of major suppliers to a large number of customers. Formal benchmarking externally was too difficult for Western Paper; the only real benchmark target within the industry was a direct competitor. In this instance, Western Paper undertook some informal benchmarking with other group companies and with friendly rivals. The principal benefits derived from the approach were:

> Some useful comparisons of process performance could be made which demonstrated progress;
> Engagement of the staff and management with each other brought benefits of communication;
> The use of the costing and pricing model in customer negotiations began to generate much more substantial knowledge of competitor behaviour and capabilities, simply using the cost data as a benchmark itself.

Combined working on product quality by bringing together staff from across the business to create a more effective production management and performance reporting regime.

Within the time limitations of the project, benchmarking did not extend to other businesses.

23.3   Supplier development

Suppliers of both materials and services are critical to the achievement of quality. The quality of material inputs to a manufacturing process are strong determinants of the quality of output. The quality of bought in services, such as distribution and logistics, accounting, information technology support and building or machine maintenance, affect either the production process or the interface with the customer, for example through deliveries or invoicing. Clearly, a part of being a quality organisation is ensuring that the external factors affecting the input and output ends of the internal processes meet the requisite quality standard.

What is supplier development?

Supplier development is best thought of as a business policy espoused by a company which is serious about achieving quality. It involves a commitment by that company to set and attain internal quality standards, which meet the requirements of its customers, and to support its suppliers in enabling them to meet those same requirements.

Traditionally, companies wishing to exercise a degree of control of the upstream or downstream elements of the value chain have followed the route of vertical integration, either through development of their own services, or through acquisition. However, these traditional routes have usually proven less than fully successful. The company loses the focus on its core business, often operating the other parts of the business less successfully and at greater cost than specialists, so that instead of excelling at one task it becomes mediocre at many. Equally, it is frequently the case that overall profitability is adversely affected. Supplier development moves away from this strategy, recognising its inherent difficulties and limitations, and respecting the expertise and knowledge specific to the fulfilment of a particular need.

Supplier development requires that the company changes its posture in relation to its suppliers. Traditionally, the buyer–supplier relationship is adversarial, each party seeking to maximise its own benefit from the relationship. Supplier development requires that this relationship become co-operative or collaborative such that buyer and supplier work together to maximise mutual interests. This demands a change in buying processes. The placing of orders based on lowest price and sealed tenders has to cease, with a change to open exchange of information and negotiations based on a willingness to achieve an equitable outcome for both parties. For example, the need for each party to generate an adequate return on its efforts must be respected.

A move towards using a single supplier is also advocated by some writers (for example Deming, 1986: 35–40). This policy has both advantages and drawbacks. Positively, utilising a single source of supply should ensure greater reliability of inputs in terms of consistency, lack of variability (that is closer adherence to standards) and the potential for continually improving standards and reduced paperwork. From the supplier's perspective, they are perhaps assured of a particular level of order, potentially higher order values, greater certainty in their business planning and longer production runs with bigger batch sizes (reducing down-time and set-up time which both in turn may increase productivity), more reliable payment and availability of additional expertise (from their customer).

Looking at the drawbacks, the buying organisation may close itself off to other options, reducing the opportunity for speculative or spot purchases of materials (which meet requirements) and may reduce its leverage in price negotiations with the supplier, particularly when supplier power is high (Porter, 1980). The organisation becomes vulnerable to changes in strategy, tactics or performance by its supplier. This is particularly important when the product or service purchased is critical to the process. An example of this would be when distribution is contracted out to a dedicated haulage firm which then, for reasons unrelated to the particular contract, experiences financial or other difficulties such as a strike or limitation on the availability of vehicles. From the supplier's perspective, becoming the sole source of supply to a particular organisation may involve the dedication of a significant proportion of its resources to fulfilling that order. In this case, it in turn may become vulnerable to any difficulties experienced by its customer or any change of product or strategy on their part. For example, if the buyer ceases to produce a particular product, or suffers from extensive competition leading to falling volumes, the fortunes of the supplier are similarly affected. This is a particular issue for small businesses acting as specialist suppliers to large organisations. The maintenance of the relationship and the volume of resources required to maintain the supply can swamp the small company.

The foregoing comments are general considerations which must be addressed before any sole supplier relationship is agreed. It may be that both parties feel that the advantages outweigh the disadvantages and associated risks in the particular case, and choose to proceed. On the other hand, one or the other may find that the relationship would make them especially vulnerable in which case they should instead seek alternative arrangements.

Clearly, there is a significant degree of risk to a supplier if the agreement with a buyer constitutes a significant proportion of the total business and for whatever reason limits the ability to undertake business with other parties. That being said, there is also significant potential advantage to the buying organisation in successfully pursuing the strategy of supplier development, particularly in the creation of a long-term and stable relationship.

How is supplier development undertaken?

The decision to pursue a policy of supplier development can only reasonably be undertaken by an organisation already fully committed to quality and which recognises that improved input quality is necessary to support its implementation programme. To pursue this policy when the organisation is not already achieving high standards may well be seen by the supplier as an attempt to shift the blame for quality failure. Such an approach is unlikely to be well received.

Supplier development takes place in seven stages (Box 23.2). The first stage is crucial. If the senior management are not committed to the process and its outcomes (including the need to provide short-term financial support and to commit workforce resources to the strategy), it will fail.

The second stage is to audit and evaluate the processes in which the suppliers' inputs are used to ensure that these meet the current internal expectations. Similarly, the inputs themselves must be formally evaluated. If a process is failing because of internal factors then no amount of supplier development will cure it. Similarly, if suppliers are to be approached to improve their performance, it is vital that the buyer can precisely demonstrate the need by showing the impact on their own output.

Stage three is for the buying organisation to determine what standards it expects its suppliers to achieve and, consequently, what changes are necessary and which desirable. It is important to discriminate between those aspects which are essential to acceptable performance (that is meeting requirements) and those which would be beneficial in the longer term, but are not currently essential. This stage, taken together with stage two, defines the gap between the current performance of the supplier and the necessary performance. This defines the initial scope for the supplier development strategy and provides a basis for measuring subsequent performance improvement.

The first three stages simply prepare the ground for approaching suppliers. The buying organisation is now equipped with the information necessary to engage in meaningful discussions. Stage four is the development of agreement with the identified suppliers. Clearly, if the suppliers are not willing to join in with the programme then nothing is lost, since the organisation is fully prepared to approach alternative sources with a clear idea of its expectations. The supplying organisation must be prepared to make the same commitment to improving performance as the buying organisation.

Box 23.2   Seven stages of supplier development

Stage 1)   Senior Management commitment to supplier development;
Stage 2)   Audit and evaluation of internal standards;
Stage 3)   Define and quantify the desirable or necessary changes;
Stage 4)   Develop agreement with identified suppliers;
Stage 5)   Form joint teams and develop training programme (if necessary);
Stage 6)   Teams define precise objectives, deliverables and timescale;
Stage 7)   Implement changes and monitor impacts.

The basis of moving forward should be a written agreement setting out the aims and objectives of the programme and the benefits to be delivered.

Stage five is the formation of joint problem solving teams tasked with pursuing the various benefits. These should take the form of Quality Circles and may require training or development input in order to function effectively. Ideally, these teams should include representatives of all relevant functions in the two organisations. For example, a team made up exclusively of product buyers and sales staff would not be effective since they are likely to have only limited knowledge of the problems of the particular product or service when in use. Operational staff must be regarded as fundamental to such a team which should have the authority to draw on other resources when appropriate, for example accounting staff (for costings), statisticians (for the development of process control measurement) and so on.

Stage six is the implementation phase when the designated teams should initially define precise objectives, tasks and timescales in the light of the current performance gap. Implementation itself should more or less follow the pattern of Quality Circle operation using the same quality tools and techniques.

Finally, stage seven is concerned with implementing any changes arising and monitoring the impacts against the expected benefits. It may be that for very large organisations a supervisory or steering board is required to oversee the implementation programme (particularly if a part of the strategy is to transfer the learning which takes place to other parts of the respective operations). For smaller organisations this should not be necessary.

Like most other aspects of a quality programme, supplier development can never be considered as complete. It is an ongoing, iterative process which aims to continually improve performance for the benefit of both parties.

Critique of supplier development

There is clearly significant benefit to be gained by organisations working together to improve performance. They can streamline processes, reduce costs, enhance productivity and more adequately satisfy their customers' expectations. The drawbacks to this strategy principally surround the issue of vulnerability of either the supplier or buyer through dependence on a single source. This vulnerability relates to financial leverage and to the risks of failure to supply.

To be successful, a supplier development strategy relies upon absolute commitment by both parties to making the arrangement work and willingness and intent to act in the utmost good faith at all times. It probably also relies on the buyer having sufficient power relative to the supplier so as to expect compliance to the process. It may well rely on the exercise of power.

The principal suppliers to Western Paper were the recycling company (a member of the same group with which it had no negotiating power over either price or specification of inbound fibre stock), the energy supplier and the water company (where again it had no significant negotiating strength). These suppliers were substantially able to dictate to Western Paper the conditions and cost of supply. The ability of Western Paper to work with such suppliers to deliver improvement was very limited. Their leverage was very low, and they could provide no meaningful incentive to them to improve the product or service. The simple truth for Western Paper was that its salvation could only lie in self–improvement coupled to negotiating better supply deals as and when the opportunity arose.

Western Paper themselves were of course suppliers to both converters and retailers of their paper products. These had the advantage of being a speciality in terms of weight and colour ranges but against this was the ready availability of supply from other countries. If Western Paper did not solve its own problems its future was far from secure. At the conclusion of the project Western Paper was in course of being sold to an overseas competitor.

The intention has been to show how adopting a systemic mindset from the commencement of an enquiry and designing that enquiry in an iterative manner can enable a wide selection of quality thinking and tools to be brought into use in an appropriate context.

None is necessarily right or wrong; each is appropriate to a user, a time and a situation – the trick is knowing which ones to pick and when.

Summary

This chapter has completed the Western Paper case study by introducing external relationships and a selection of tools for dealing with them. The tools have been applied in the context of the original 'why, what and how' questions raised in earlier chapters ensuring their fit to the problem situation.

Much more could be said about Western Paper, the tools chosen – and those not chosen – and about the contexts for their use. The curious reader is encouraged to explore those parts of the quality literature that seem interesting; students are encouraged to read everything!

KEY LEARNING POINTS

Supplier Development

Key definition:
buyers working co-operatively with suppliers to improve quality throughout the value chain

Key technique:
commitment, audit and evaluation, define changes, develop agreement, form teams, define precise objectives, implementation

Critique:
benefits through streamlining, cost reductions, enhanced productivity, drawbacks from vulnerability of suppliers, unbalanced power within the value chain, potential to reduce choice and variety

Benchmarking

Key definition:
the practice of formal comparison of processes and systems with other organisations as the basis for improvement

---

Key technique:
identify key characteristics, identify partners, design data collection methodology, select tools, implement changes

Critique:
demands humility, willingness to learn

Risk:
only match, not exceed competitor performance, hence danger of levelling not competing

Question

Which is important, producing quality goods and services or gaining external accreditation?

Glossary of terms and abbreviations

AGIL:	Adaptation, Goal, Integration, Latency
Aphorism:	a short, clever saying expressing a general truth
Benchmarking:	formal comparison of one organisation against another with the aim of performance improvement
Black box:	a technique for studying the behaviour of complex systems
BS 5750:	British Standard quality management system (now subsumed in ISO 9000)
Business Process Reengineering (BPR):	a process oriented organisational performance discipline
Business Systems Diamond:	a meta-methodology for BPR
Call-centre:	a centralised telephone enquiry service
Comfort zone:	an accustomed way of behaving and working
Complementarism:	an approach to problem solving in which choice and use of methodology is guided by the characteristics of the situation and understanding of the theory underpinning the method
Cowpaths:	naturally developed processes in organisations
CSH:	Critical Systems Heuristics
CSR:	Corporate Social Responsibility
CST:	Critical Systems Thinking
Culture:	the set of values and beliefs which guide behaviour in an organisation or nation
Deterministic/ determinism:	entirely predictable system behaviour
Direct costs of quality:	the visible costs of quality failure
Emergent properties:	behaviour which is exhibited by a whole system but by none of its parts
Empirical:	derived from practice or observation, not theory
EN 29000:	European Standard quality management system (now subsumed in ISO 9000)
Feedback:	self-regulation of a system by using output to manage input

GDP per capita:	the amount of income generated by a nation divided by its population
Guru:	originally a Hindu spiritual teacher, now used to refer to leaders in a discipline
HACCP:	Hazard Analysis Critical Control Points – a food production management system
Heuristic:	a process of trial and error
Holism/Holistic:	the attempt to deal with whole organisations rather than parts
HR:	Human Resources
Invisible costs of quality:	consequential and hidden costs of quality failure
IP:	Interactive Planning
ISO 9001:	2015 International Standards Organisation guidelines for a Quality Management System
ISO 14001:	2015 International Standards Organisation guidelines for an Environmental Management System
Just-in-time (JIT):	a system of supply which delivers parts to a production process when they are required, obviating the need to hold stocks
Kaizen:	a Japanese belief system oriented towards continuous improvement in ALL aspects of life
Kanban:	the operating system to support JIT
Lean manufacturing:	a manufacturing methodology developed to eliminate waste, usually thought to be based on the Toyota Production System
Mechanistic:	a view of organisations which suggests that they and their staff can be organised to behave like machines
Meta:	of a higher logical order
Methodology:	a systematic set of methods for studying issues and problems
Muda:	waste
NIH:	Not Invented Here – a barrier to change
Normative:	concerned with defining ethics and social standards
Organismic/ organic:	a view of organisations as being like organisms
Organisational Cybernetics:	the science of effective organisation
Paradigm:	a personal framework of thought or system of beliefs
PDCA Cycle:	a systematic continuous improvement cycle
Poka-Yoke:	defect = zero
Probabilism/ probabilistic:	behaviour which is partly random or unpredictable
Process:	all the operations required to complete a task
QA:	Quality Assurance
QC:	Quality Control
QFD:	Quality Function Deployment
QMS:	Quality Management System
Quality Circle (QC/QCC):	a problem solving team for quality issues
Recursion:	structural invariance at different levels of an organisation

Reductionist/ Reductionism:	a way of studying organisations through fragmentation and analysis
Replacement cycle:	the time period between repeated purchases of a good or service
Rework:	fixing or repairing finished goods before despatch
Self-regulation:	the ability of a system to manage itself
Slipping Clutch Syndrome:	an effect on productivity and quality when a production system is placed under pressure
SMED:	Single Minute Exchange of Die – a fast change process for machine tools
Soft systems:	the study of human activity systems
SOSM:	System of Systems Methodologies
SSM:	Soft Systems Methodology
Stakeholder:	any person or organisation affected by or involved with an organisation
Statistical Process Control (SPC):	a quantitative system for monitoring process performance
Statistical Quality Control (SQC):	a quantitative system for monitoring quality performance
Supplier development:	a business strategy of co-operation between buyer and supplier to jointly improve quality
Systemic:	an approach which deals with whole systems and the interactions of their elements and the environment
Total cost:	the lifetime cost of purchasing and maintaining a product
Total Quality Control:	Feigenbaum's approach to quality and management
TQM:	Total Quality Management
TSI:	Total Systems Intervention
Variety engineering:	techniques for managing probabilism
VSD:	Viable System Diagnosis
VSM:	Viable System Model
Zero defects:	a quality target focusing on error free production

Further reading

Throughout this book reference has been made to a wide selection of sources which have been found informative and interesting in the attempt to understand the role of quality in the wider context of management thinking, organisation theory and emergent social issues. Following is a list of texts which will help the reader to explore further the themes and issues raised in this book.

Beer, S. (1959) *Cybernetics and Management*, Wiley, New York. Beer exposes in detail how an approach to organisations rooted in cybernetics can be applied to revolutionise management thinking.

Beer, S. (1974) *Designing Freedom*, Wiley, Chichester. Beer discusses the impact of conventional management thinking on the development of society and suggests ways in which the apparent threats to freedom can be overcome. This book is Beer's most lucid attempt to elaborate his philosophy.

Crane, A., Matten, D. & Spence, L. (2008) *Corporate Social Responsibility*, Routledge, Abingdon. A good selection of readings and cases which act as a positive support to understanding the key issues and arguments in this field.

Crosby, P. (1979) *Quality Is Free*, Mentor, New York. Crosby introduces his quality approach in a highly readable, accessible text.

Deming, W. E. (1986) *Out of the Crisis*, The Press Syndicate, Cambridge. Deming elaborates his fears for the future of American industry and proposes solutions based on his quality thinking and practice.

Feigenbaum, A. V. (1986) *Total Quality Control*, McGraw-Hill, New York. This text provides a full explanation of Feigenbaum's approach to managing for quality.

Feld, W. M. (2001) *Lean Manufacturing*, CRC Press, Florida. This text provides a sound introduction to methods, tools and techniques for applying lean thinking.

Flood, R. L. (1993) *Beyond TQM*, Wiley, Chichester. Flood develops his holistic approach to Total Quality Management drawing on his background in systems science. The book is readily accessible to non-specialists in systems and quality.

Galbraith, J. (1974) *The New Industrial State*, Penguin, London. Galbraith develops an argument about the power of big corporations in the future economy of the world.

Hannagan, T. J. (1986) *Mastering Statistics*, 2nd Edition, Macmillan Education Ltd., Basingstoke. Hannagan provides an introduction to the development and use of a wide variety of statistical techniques.

Hoff, B. (1994) *The Tao of Pooh and the Te of Piglet*, Methuen, London. Hoff provides an insight to Western systems thinking through a re-interpretation of elements of Chinese philosophy.

Hoyle, D. (1994) *ISO 9000 Quality Systems Handbook*, Butterworth-Heinemann Ltd., Oxford. Hoyle provides an easy to follow guide to developing and installing a quality management system.

Huczynski, A. & Buchanan, D. (1991) *Organisational Behaviour*, 2nd Edition, Prentice-Hall International (UK) Ltd., Hemel Hempstead. This text provides a substantial and reader friendly guide to the principal strands of management thinking which dominate contemporary organisations.

Huff, D. (1973) *How to Lie with Statistics*, Pelican, London. Huff explores in an entertaining but ruthlessly critical manner the ways in which poor understanding of statistics are used to manipulate decision making.

Ishikawa, K. (1986) *Guide to Quality Control*, 2nd Edition, Asian Productivity Organisation. This book, based upon Ishikawa's practical work, was originally developed as a guide for the work of Quality Circle members.

Juran, J. M. (1988) *Juran on Planning for Quality*, Free Press, New York. This substantial and detailed text provides the most useful guide to Juran's thinking and his approach to achieving quality.

Kanji, G. P. & Asher, M. (1996) *100 Methods for Total Quality Management*, Sage, London. The authors provide an easy to follow, simple 'how to' guide covering the major activities in a TQM programme.

Kotler, P. & Lee, N. (2005) *Corporate Social Responsibility*, Wiley, New Jersey. An introductory text covering the breadth of thinking in this area.

Logothetis, N. (1992) *Managing for Total Quality*, Prentice Hall International, London. Logothetis provides a guide to the statistically based methods for achieving quality.

Lovelock, J. (1979) *Gaia: A New Look at Life on Earth*. Lovelock explains the development of his theory of the environment. Appreciation of this perspective helps in understanding the environmental imperative for the pursuit of quality.

Oakland, J. S. (1993) *Total Quality Management*, 2nd Edition, Butterworth-Heinemann Ltd., Oxford. Readable and well structured, Oakland elaborates in detail his programme for attaining quality.

Ormerod, P. (1994) *The Death of Economics*, Faber and Faber, London. Ormerod explores the assumptions which underpin much of currently dominant economic theory, highlighting the weaknesses and flaws which he perceives.

Pirsig, R. M. (1974) *Zen and the Art of Motorcycle Maintenance (An Inquiry into Values)*, Black Swan Edition, Arrow Books, London. Presented as an account of a man's journey with his son, the book reflects a process of enquiry into two strands of quality thinking, the technical and aesthetic.

Shingo, S. (1987) *The Sayings of Shigeo Shingo*, Trans. A. P. Dillon, 1987, Productivity Press. Shingo's message is expressed through his many mottos for achieving quality.

Stickland, F. (1998) *The Dynamics of Change*, Routledge. Based on his doctoral research, fascinating insights into the processes of organisational change through analogies with the natural world.

Taguchi, G. (1987) *Systems of Experimental Design*, Vols. 1, 2, Unipub/Kraus, International Publications, New York. Taguchi's own guide to his process for developing quality within the product and the production process.

Waldrop, S. (1992) *Complexity*, Simon & Schuster, New York. Waldrop reports the development of complexity theory giving insight to thinking about organisations as non-linear dynamical systems.

Warboys et al (1999) *Business Information Systems, A Process Approach*, McGraw Hill. Very useful for understanding how to build information systems to support and reflect process orientation in organisations.

References

Ackoff, R. L. (1981) *Creating the Corporate Future,* Wiley, New York

Anka, P. (1967) *My Way*

Ashby, W. R. (1952) *An Introduction to Cybernetics,* Chapman and Hall, London

Ashby, W. R. (1956) *Design For A Brain,* Chapman and Hall, London

Bank, J. (1992) *The Essence of Total Quality Management,* Prentice Hall International, London

Barnard, C. (1938) *The Functions of the Executive,* Harvard Press, USA

Beckford, J. (1993) *The Viable System Model, A More Adequate Tool for Practising Management?,* PhD Thesis, The University of Hull

Beckford, J. (1995) Towards a Participative Methodology for the Viable Systems Model, *Systemist,* UK Systems Society

Beckford, J. (1998) BPR: Ten Steps to Failure, *Institute of Business Process Reengineering, Winchester,* available at http://beckfordconsulting.com/Papers/BPR%20Ten%20Steps%20to%20Failure.pdf 30th May 2016

Beckford, J. (2002) *Quality,* 2nd Edition, Routledge, UK

Beckford, J. (2010) *Quality: A Critical Introduction,* 3rd Edition, Routledge, Oxford

Beckford, J. (2016) *The Intelligent Organisation,* Routledge, Oxford

Beckford, J. & Dudley, P. (1998a) Size Isn't Everything, *Management Issues in Social Care,* Vol 6, 1

Beckford, J. & Dudley, P. (1998b) That's Not Very Big, Is It?, *Management Issues in Social Care,* Vol 5, 4

Beckford, J. & Dudley, P. (1999) It's What You Do with It That Counts, *Management Issues in Social Care,* Vol 6, 3

Beer, S. (1959) *Cybernetics and Management,* Wiley, New York

Beer, S. (1966) *Decision and Control,* Wiley, Chichester

Beer, S. (1979) *The Heart of Enterprise,* Wiley, Chichester

Beer, S. (1981) *Brain of the Firm,* 2nd Edition, Wiley, Chichester

Beer, S. (1985) *Diagnosing the System for Organisations,* Wiley, Chichester

Beer, S. (1994) *Beyond Dispute: The Invention of Team Syntegrity,* Wiley, Chichester

Bendell, T. (1989) *The Quality Gurus: What Can They Do for Your Company?,* Department of Trade and Industry, London, and, Services Ltd., Nottingham

Brynjolfsson, E. & McAfee, A. (2014) *The Second Machine Age,* Norton & Company, New York

BS OHSAS: 18001:2007 (2007) *Occupational Health and Safety Management Systems,* British Standards Institution, London

Burns, T. & Stalker, G. M. (1961) *The Management of Innovation,* Tavistock, London

Burrell, G. & Morgan, G. (1979) *Sociological Paradigms and Organisational Analysis,* Heinemann, London

Carroll, L. (1866) *Alice's Adventures in Wonderland,* Macmillan and Co., London

Checkland, P. B. (1978) The Origins and Nature of 'Hard' Systems Thinking, *Journal of Applied Systems Analysis,* 5(2):99

Checkland, P. B. (1981) *Systems Thinking, Systems Practice,* Wiley, Chichester

Checkland, P. & Scholes, J. (1990) *Soft Systems Methodology in Action,* Wiley, Chichester

Clemson, B. (1984) *Cybernetics: A New Management Tool,* Abacus, Tunbridge Wells

Clutterbuck, D. & Crainer, S. (1990) *Makers of Management,* Macmillan

Crane, A., Matten, D. & Spence, L. (2008) *Corporate Social Responsibility,* Routledge, Abingdon

Crosby, P. (1979) *Quality Is Free,* Mentor, New York

Dale, B.G., van der Wiele, T. & van Iwaarden, J. (2007) *Managing Quality,* 5th Edition, Blackwell, Oxford

Darwin, C. (2008) *On the Origin of Species,* World Classics Edition, Oxford University Press, UK

De Bono, E. (1970) *Lateral Thinking: A Text-book of Creativity,* Spain Press, London

Deming, W. E. (1982) *Quality, Productivity and Competitive Position,* Massachusetts Institute of Technology, Massachusetts

Deming, W. E. (1986) *Out of the Crisis,* The Press Syndicate, Cambridge

Dennis, P. (2007) *Lean Production Simplified,* Productivity Press, New York

Drucker, P. (1969) *The Age of Discontinuity,* Heinemann, London

Dudley, P. (2000) *Quality Management or Management Quality?: An Adaptive Model of Organisation as the Basis of Organisational Learning and Quality Provision,* PhD Thesis, The University of Hull

Eckes, G. (2003) *Six Sigma for Everyone,* Wiley, New Jersey

EFQM Excellence Model 2013, EFQM Publications, 2012

Eliot, G. (1859) *Adam Bede,* Wordsworth Classics (2003), London

Espejo, R. & Schwaninger, M. (1993) *Organisational Fitness, Corporate Effectiveness through Management Cybernetics,* Campus Verlag, Frankfurt and New York

Fayol, H. (1916) *General and Industrial Management,* SRL Dunod, Paris (Trans. Constance Storrs, 1949, Pitman, London)

Feigenbaum, A. V. (1986) *Total Quality Control,* McGraw-Hill, New York

Feigenbaum, A. (2014) http://www.industryweek.com/quality/dr-armand-feigenbaum-managing--quality-part-1, 20 April 2016

Feld, W. (2001) *Lean Manufacturing,* CRC Press, Florida

Fiedler, F. E. (1967) *A Theory of Leadership Effectiveness,* McGraw-Hill, New York

Financial Times, 26th November 1986

Flood, R. L. (1993) *Beyond TQM,* Wiley, Chichester

Flood, R. L. (1999) *Rethinking the Fifth Discipline,* Routledge, London

Flood, R. L. & Carson, E. R. (1988) *Dealing with Complexity,* Plenum, New York

Flood, R. L. & Jackson, M. C. (1991) *Creative Problem Solving,* Wiley, Chichester

Flood, R. L. & Romm, N. R. A. (1996) *Diversity Management: Triple Loop Learning,* Wiley, Chichester

Follett, M. P. *Definition of Management,* http://mpfollett.ning.com, 16 April 2016

Forrester, J. (1961) *Industrial Dynamics,* Martino (2013), USA

Galbraith, J. (1974) *The New Industrial State,* Penguin, London

Gilbert, J. (1992) *How to Eat an Elephant: A Slice-by Slice Guide to Total Quality Management,* Tudor, UK

Gleick, J. (1987) *Chaos,* Heinemann, London

Goetsch, D. & Davis, S. (2014) *Quality Management for Organizational Excellence,* Pearson Education, UK

Greengard, S. (2015) *The Internet of Things,* MIT Press, Cambridge

Hammer, M. & Champy, J. (1993) *Business Process Reengineering,* Nicholas Brealey, London

Handy, C. (1985) *Understanding Organisations,* 3rd Edition, Penguin, London

Handy, C. (1990) *The Age of Unreason,* Arrow, London

Heller, R. (1989) *The Making of Managers,* Penguin, London

Herzberg, M., Mauser, B. & Synderman, B. B. (1959) *The Motivation to Work,* 2nd Edition, Wiley, New York

Hislop, D. (2013) *Knowledge Management in Organisations: A Critical Introduction,* OUP, Oxford

Hofstede, G. (1980) Motivation, Leadership and Organization: Do American Theories Apply Abroad?, *Organizational Dynamics,* Summer 1980, 42–63

Hortensius, D. (2013) http://www.iso.org/iso/home/news_index/news_archive/news.htm?refid=Ref1709

Huczynski, A. & Buchanan, D. (2013) *Organizational Behaviour,* 8th Edition, Pearson Education, Harlow, UK

Hume, D. (1777) *Essays Moral, Political and Literary*

IPCC (2014) *Climate Change 2014: Synthesis Report,* Contribution of Working Groups I, II and III to the Fifth Assessment Report of the Intergovernmental Panel on Climate Change [Core Writing Team, R.K. Pachauri and L.A. Meyer (eds.)]. IPCC, Geneva, Switzerland, 151

Ishikawa, K. (1980) *QC Circle Koryo,* QC Circle Headquarters, Japan

Ishikawa, K. (1985) *What Is Total Quality Control? The Japanese Way,* Prentice Hall, London

Ishikawa, K. (1986) *Guide to Quality Control,* 2nd Edition, Asian Productivity Organisation

ISO 9001:2015 (2015) *Quality Management Systems Requirements,* BSI Standards Publication, London

ISO 14001:2015 (2015) *Environmental Management Systems,* ISO Switzerland

Jackson, M. C. (1990) *Organisation Design & Behaviour, An MBA Manual,* The University of Hull, UK

Jackson, M. C. (1991) *Systems Methodology for the Management Sciences,* Wiley, Chichester

Jashapara, A. (2010) *Knowledge Management: An Integrated Approach,* Pearson, Harlow, UK

Jay, A. (1987) *Management and Machiavelli,* Hutchinson Business, London

Johansson, H. J. et al (1993) *Business Process Reengineering,* Wiley, Chichester

Johnson, G. & Scholes, K. (1993) *Exploring Corporate Strategy,* 3rd Edition, Prentice Hall, Hemel Hempstead

Junewick, M. (2002) *LeanSpeak,* Productivity Press, New York

Juran, J. (1988) *Juran on Planning for Quality,* Free Press, New York

Juran, J. (1989) *Juran's Quality Control Handbook,* McGraw-Hill, US

Juran, J. M. & De Feo, J. A. (2010) *Juran's Quality Handbook,* 6th Edition, McGraw-Hill, New York

Kanji, G. K. & Asher, M. (1996) *100 Methods for Total Quality Management,* Sage, London

Levinson, W. (2002) *Henry Ford's Lean Vision,* Productivity Press, New York

Logothetis, N. (1992) *Managing for Total Quality,* Prentice Hall International, London

Lovelock, J. (1979) *Gaia: A New Look at Life on Earth,* Oxford University Press, Oxford

Lovelock, J. (1988) *The Ages of Gaia,* Oxford University Press, Oxford

Lovelock, J. (1991) *Gaia: The Practical Science of Planetary Medicine,* Gaia Books Ltd., London

Lovelock, J. (2001) *Homage to Gaia,* Oxford University Press, Oxford

Lovelock, J. (2006) *The Revenge of Gaia,* Allen Lane, Penguin Books, London

Lovelock, J. (2009) *The Vanishing Face of Gaia,* Allen Lane, Penguin Books, London

Lynn, J. & Jay, A. (1982) *Yes Minister,* BBC, London

Machiavelli, N. (1513) *The Prince* (Trans. G. Bull, 1961, Penguin, London)

Maslow, A. (1970) *Motivation and Personality,* 2nd Edition, Harper & Row, New York

Mason, R. O. & Mitroff, I. I. (1981) *Challenging Strategic Planning Assumptions,* Wiley, New York

Mayo, E. (1949) *The Social Problems of an Industrial Civilisation,* Routledge & Kegan Paul Ltd., London

McGregor, D. (1960) *The Human Side of Enterprise,* McGraw-Hill, New York

Morgan, G. (1986) *Images of Organisation,* Sage, London

Oakland, J. (1993) *Total Quality Management,* 2nd Edition, Butterworth-Heinemann Ltd., Oxford

Oakland, J. (1999) *Total Organizational Excellence,* Butterworth Heinemann, London

Oakland, J. & Morris, P. (2011) *TQM: A Pictorial Guide for Managers,* Routledge, London

Ohno, T. (1988) *Toyota Production System,* Trans., Productivity Press, New York

Pande, P. & Holpp, L. (2002) *What Is Six Sigma?,* McGraw-Hill, USA

Parsons, T. & Smelser, N. J. (1956) *Economy and Society,* Routledge & Kegan-Paul, London

Peters, T. (1992) *Liberation Management,* Macmillan, London

Peters, T. (2016) http://tompeters.com/columns/what-gets-measured-gets-done/, 15 April 2016

Peters, T. J. & Waterman, R. H. (1982) *In Search of Excellence,* Harper Collins, New York

Pettigrew, A. & Fenton, E. M. (Eds.) (2000) *The Innovating Organization,* Sage, UK

Pine, B. J. (1993) *Mass Customization,* Harvard Press, Cambridge, MA

Porter, M. (1980) *Competitive Strategy: Techniques for Analysing Industries and Competitors,* The Free Press, Macmillan, New York

Porter, M. (1996) What Is Strategy?, *Harvard Business Review,* Nov.–Dec. '96, 61–78

Pugh, D. & Hinings, C. R. (Eds.) (1976) *Organizational Structure – Extensions and Replications: The Aston Programme II,* Gower Publishing, London

Pugh, D. S. (1990) *Organisation Theory,* 3rd Edition, Penguin, London

Pugh, D. S. & Hickson, D. J. (1976) *Organisation Structure in Its Context: The Aston Programme 1,* Saxon House, Aldershot

Pugh, D. S. & Hickson, D. J. (1989) *Writers on Organizations,* 4th Edition, Penguin, London

Pyzdek, T. & Keller, P. (2013) *The Handbook for Quality Management,* McGraw-Hill, USA

Saunders, A. (1957) Steven Roper Comic Strip, Publishers Syndicate, in Quotable Quotes, *Readers Digest,* http://quoteinvestigator.com/2012/05/06/other-plans/

Schein, E. (1988) *Organizational Psychology,* Prentice Hall, New Jersey

Schmied, H. (1995) *R&D – Management in Europe,* Gabler Verlag, Wiesbaden, Germany

Schmied, H. & Brown, K. (2009) *The Five Dimensions of Project Planning,* Ermite, Strasbourg

Schoderbek, P. P., Schoderbek, C. G. & Kefalas, A. G. (1990) *Management Systems: Conceptual Considerations,* 4th Edition, Business Publications, Dallas

Seddon, J. (2008) *Systems Thinking in the Public Sector,* Triarchy Press, Axminster, UK

Senge, P. M. (1990) *The Fifth Discipline,* Century Business, London

Shingo, S. (1987) *The Sayings of Shigeo Shingo,* Trans. A. P. Dillon, 1987, Productivity Press, New York

Shingo, S. (2016) http://www.process-improvement-japan.com/shigeo-shingo.html, 21 April 2016

Silver, N. (2012) *The Signal and The Noise,* Penguin, London

Singleton, W. T. (1974) *Man-Machine Systems,* Penguin, London

Slack, N. et al (1995) *Operations Management,* Pitman, London

Stewart, M. (2009) *The Management Myth,* Norton, New York

Summers, D. C. S. (2009) *Quality Management,* Pearson, New Jersey

Taguchi, G. (1986) *Introduction to Quality Engineering: Designing Quality into Products and Processes,* Quality Resources, White Plains, New York

Taguchi, G. (1987) *Systems of Experimental Design,* Vols. 1, 2, Unipub/Kraus International Publications, New York

Taleb, N. (2010) *The Black Swan,* Penguin, London

Taylor, F. (1911) *The Principles of Scientific Management,* The Plimpton Press, Norwood

Torrington, D., Hall, L. & Taylor, S. (2008) *Human Resource Management,* 7th edition, Pearson, Harlow, UK

Townsend, R. (1970, 1985) *Further Up the Organisation,* Michael Joseph, London

Trist, E. A. & Bamforth, K. W. (1966) Some Social and Psychological Consequences of the Long-wall Method of Coal-getting [sic], *Organisation Theory, Selected Readings,* 3rd Edition, Ed. D. S. Pugh, 1990, Penguin, London

Ulrich, W. (1983) *Critical Heuristics of Social Planning,* Haupt, Berne

United Nations Framework Convention on Climate Change, Paris, 2016

Waldrop, S. (1992) *Complexity,* Simon & Schuster, New York

Weber, M. (1924) Legitimate Authority and Bureaucracy, *Organisation Theory, Selected Readings,* 3rd Edition, Ed. D. S. Pugh, 1990, Penguin, London

Wiener, N. (1947) *Cybernetics or Control and Communication in the Animal and the Machine,* The Massachusetts Institute of Technology, Massachusetts

Wilde, O. (1890) *The Picture of Dorian Gray,* Lippincott's Monthly Magazine

Wilson, T.D. (2002) *Strangers to Ourselves: Discovering the Adaptive Unconscious,* Harvard University Press, Cambridge

Wolstenholme, E. (1990) *Systems Enquiry: A Systems Dynamics Approach,* Wiley, Chichester, UK

Woodward, J. (1965) *Industrial Organization: Theory and Practice,* Oxford University Press, London

Index